The
Private
Pilot's
Licence
Course

JEREMY M PRATT

ISBN 1 874783 50 0

Flying
Training

This book is intended to be a guide to the flying training element of the PPL course. It **does not** in any way replace or overrule the instruction you will receive from a flying instructor at a flying training organisation (FTO). No part of this book overrules or supersedes the Air Navigation Order (ANO), Air Information Publication (AIP), Aeronautical Information Circulars (AICs) and other documents published by a competent authority; the flight manual/pilot's operating handbook for the aircraft being flown; the pilot order book/flying school syllabus; and the general provisions of good airmanship and safe flying practice.

First Edition 1994

Copyright © 1994 Airplan Flight Equipment Ltd & Jeremy M Pratt

The Private Pilot's Licence Course Flying Training

ISBN 1 874783 50 0

for Maggie and Tony

Airplan Flight Equipment, Southside, Manchester International Airport, Wilmslow, Cheshire SK9 4LL UK   Tel: 061-499 0023   F ax: 061-499 0298

contents

contents

editorial

AUTHOR: JEREMY M PRATT

Jeremy Pratt took his first flying lesson aged 14, paid for by weekend and holiday jobs at his local airfield cleaning aircraft and working in the hanger. Later he also worked in the air/ground station of the airfield and in the operations department of an air taxi company. He completed his PPL after being awarded an Esso/Air League scholarship and became a flying instructor at the age of 19. Since then he has taught students for the Private Pilots Licence, the associated ratings and applicants for professional flying licences. He also flies as a commercial pilot in a variety of roles including pleasure flights, aerial photography/survey and traffic reporting.

He has been Managing Director of Airplan Flight Equipment since 1985, is author of the 'Pilot's Guide' series, the 'Flight Computer Instruction Manual'; and has also co-authored, compiled and contributed to, a number of aviation books and publications.

TECHNICAL ADVISORS:

Jim McBride - a B757 captain with a major UK airline, Jim is a former Royal Navy pilot with the rare distinction of having gained both fixed and rotary 'wings'. He has also flown as a civilian flying instructor and an air-taxi pilot. Jim is an authorised display pilot flying Beech 18 and Harvard aircraft and is a serving officer in the RAF Volunteer Reserve, flying Chipmunks with an Air Experience Flight.

Bill Stitt - Chief Flying Instructor of Horizon Flying Club, Bill has been a flying instructor for over 20 years and is a delegated flight examiner. He has been training instructors for ten years and is a member of the AOPA Instructor Committee. He is married to a flying instructor and their teenage daughter also flies!

Phillip G Mathews - Chief Flying Instructor of Cotswold Aero Club , Phil has over 7000 hours experience of flying light aircraft. He gained his PPL at the age of 17 and went on to achieve an ATPL through the 'self-improver' route. Phil also runs his own business teaching applicants for the PPL and IMC rating technical exams.

Martin Rushbrooke - Senior Flying and Standards Instructor at Barton (Manchester) airfield, Martin qualified as an Air Cadet glider pilot in 1964 and gained his PPL in 1966 through an ATC flying scholarship. Martin is a PPL examiner, Commanding Officer of 162 (Stockport) ATC squadron and has flown over 50 types of aircraft.

Piers Smerdon - Chief Flying Instructor of the Commercial Aviation Academy, Piers has over 14,000 instructional hours. He has instructed at Bodmin, Guernsey, Denham and Leicester and currently teaches applicants for instructor ratings, professional licences and Instrument Ratings. He is also Training Captain for a Midlands based air taxi company.

Acknowledgments

This book would also not have been possible without the assistance of the following people and organisations:

Aviation Picture Library
Beaufort Air Sea Equipment
Civil Aviation Authority
Derby Aero Club
Steve Dickinson
Peggy Follis
Stuart Green
Ian McConochie CFI
  Woodvale Aviation
Chris Mathews
Wendy Mellor
John Nelson
Ravenair
Ian Sixsmith CFI
  MSF Aviation
Rob Taylor GDi studio
Visual Eyes

V

No person is born with the instinctive ability to fly an aeroplane. It is worth remembering that the best and most experienced pilots in the world (even your flying instructor!) started out not knowing an aileron from an elevator or an ASI from a VSI.

The aim of the PPL course is to take you from a point that assumes no pre-knowledge of aviation to the position of qualifying as the holder of a Private Pilot's Licence. There is nothing unduly complicated or difficult about learning to fly and there are no formal educational requirements. Indeed the best qualities of a student pilot are an enthusiasm for flying, a willingness to learn and the patience and resolve to complete the course.

This book is intended as an aid to the flying training element of the PPL course. It DOES NOT in any way replace or overrule the instruction you will receive from a qualified flying instructor at a Flying Training Organisation (FTO). No textbook can cover every possible option and variation involved in flying all the different aircraft types, from all locations, under all possible circumstances. It is the job of your flying instructor to adopt the rules and mechanics of flying an aircraft to suit the particular circumstances. This book is designed to be used in conjunction with those which cover the technical part of the PPL course. Within this book important concepts and rules tend to be introduced in basic form at first, then expanded upon as the course progresses. Thus an important concept such as lift is at first explained in very basic terms early in the course, with a more detailed description coming later when your knowledge and experience will have developed sufficiently to give you a better appreciation of the principles of flight. This 'step-by-step' approach is central to the PPL course and is the underlying philosophy of this book.

Throughout this book the pilot, instructor etc. is referred to using the pronoun 'he'. This has been done purely to avoid the cumbersome and repetitive use of 'he or she'. I ask for the understanding of all female readers.

I have also used the convention of qualifying airspeed as 'fast' or 'slow' rather than 'high' or 'low'. Whilst this may slightly irritate the grammatically pure, it is my personal preference when referring to airspeed.

In an age where the extraordinary quickly becomes the mundane, the ability to fly an aeroplane is still special and a significant personal achievement. Few writers, (and certainly not this one !) can adequately express in words the aura of flying - it's one of those things in life you just have to experience for yourself to understand.

Good luck; Be safe; Happy landings

Jeremy M Pratt

July 1994

Aircraft Familiarisation

This first exercise is to introduce you to the basics of the aircraft's design and construction, its controls and systems. Your instructor will show you how to use the aircraft checklist, and you will learn certain emergency drills. At this very early stage of your training you will not be expected to cover all of the exercise in one session. However, it must be fully completed before you fly solo.

BACKGROUND BRIEFING

▶ **Aircraft Construction**

▶ **Cockpit Layout**

▶ **Main Aircraft Systems**

▶ **Use of Checklist and Pilots. Operating Handbook/Flight Manual**

▶ **Airfield Sense**

BACKGROUND BRIEFING

▶ Aircraft Construction

Although the design of basic training aircraft can vary greatly, the main components of an aircraft are common throughout.

The wing provides the *lift* force that enables an aircraft to fly. Aircraft can be high-wing, low-wing or occasionally mid-wing.

The main components of the wing

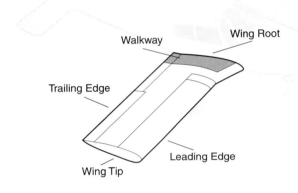

Walkway Wing Root Trailing Edge Leading Edge Wing Tip

LEFT> A high-wing, single-engine Cessna 152

MIDDLE> A low-wing, single-engine Piper PA-38 Tomahawk

RIGHT> A mid-wing, twin-engine Piper Aerostar

The lift provided by the wing is independent of the engine power.

The fuselage incorporates the engine, the cockpit and the tail section.

The main components of the fuselage

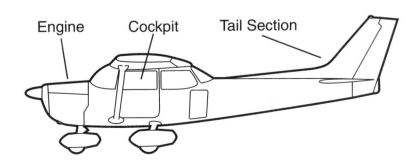

Engine Cockpit Tail Section

Aircraft Familiarisation

The engine is located under the cowlings ahead of the cockpit, and it drives the propeller at the front of the aircraft. ALWAYS take great care around the propeller; if in ANY doubt, keep well away from it. The tail unit is located some way behind the cockpit and its components provide an aerodynamic balancing force to give the aircraft stability and control. The tailplane can be in a low, medium or high position on the fin. A high tailplane (as on the PA-38 Tomahawk) is usually known as a 'T-Tail'.

① Fin

② Tailplane

Rear Fuselage

The main components of the tail section

① Also known as the *'vertical stabiliser'*

② Also known as the *'horizontal stabiliser'*

High Tailplane

Low Tailplane

LEFT> A high-tailplane aircraft (Piper PA-38 Tomahawk)

RIGHT> A low-tailplane aircraft (Cessna 152)

The undercarriage on modern aircraft consists of main wheels under the wing or fuselage and a nosewheel under the engine. However, some aircraft have a tail-wheel instead of a nosewheel.

LEFT> A nosewheel aircraft (Piper PA-28 Warrior Cadet)

RIGHT> A tail-wheel aircraft (de Havilland Chipmunk)

Background Briefing

There are three main flight controls. The *ailerons* are at the outboard trailing edge of the wings, and are interconnected so that as one aileron moves up the other moves down. The *rudder* is fitted to the fin. The *elevators* are attached to the rear of the tailplane.

The primary flying controls

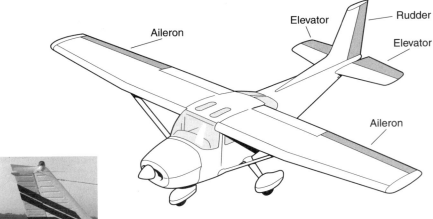

The all-moving tailplane, or stabilator, of the Piper PA-28 Cherokee

Some aircraft (e.g. PA-28 Cherokee/Warrior) have a combined tailplane and elevator, known as an *all-moving tailplane* or *stabilator*.

Most training aircraft are fitted with *flaps*, which are located at the inboard trailing edge of the wing.

The fully lowered flaps of a Piper PA-38 Tomahawk

▶ Cockpit Layout

Most training aircraft have side-by-side seating. The left-hand seat is for the pilot-in-command and this is the seat used by the student. The instructor sits in the right-hand seat. Your instructor will show you how to enter and leave the cockpit and how to open and close the doors or canopy. Once seated, you can adjust your seat to give a good view over the instrument panel and enable you to reach the controls and switches. With the seat in position you should fasten and adjust your seat belt. Your instructor will show you how to adjust your seat and how to fasten, adjust and release your seat belt.

The pilot's feet must comfortably reach the rudder pedals ahead of the seat. The rudder pedals are linked through cables and pulleys to the rudder and, on most aircraft, to a steerable nosewheel. Through the rudder pedals the pilot controls the rudder and also, when on the ground, steering. The rudder pedals may also be fitted with 'toe brakes'.

Aircraft Familiarisation

Directly in front of the pilot will be either a *control column* (sometimes called the *stick*) or a control wheel. Both types work in the same sense and are normally called the control column. The control column is linked to the ailerons and the elevators/stabilator by cables and pulleys. Moving it forward and back controls the elevators; moving it to the left or right controls the ailerons. The rudder pedals and control column are duplicated on the instructor's (right hand) side.

LEFT> The control wheel of a Cessna 152

RIGHT> The control sticks of a Robin 200

The *throttle* controls the engine power and it can be either a 'plunger' type or a 'quadrant' type. In either case moving the throttle FORWARD INCREASES engine power, while moving the throttle BACK DECREASES engine power.

LEFT> The 'plunger'-type throttle control, fitted here to a Cessna 152. Pushing the throttle FORWARD, INCREASES power. Pulling the throttle BACK, DECREASES power.

RIGHT> The 'quadrant'-type throttle control, fitted here to a PA-28 Cherokee Pushing the throttle FORWARD, INCREASES power. Pulling the throttle BACK, DECREASES power.

The instrument panel contains various instruments, switches, circuit breakers etc.. Directly in front of the pilot are the basic flight instruments.

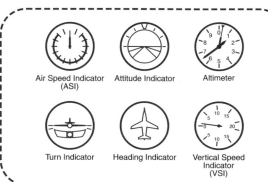

The six basic 'flight instruments' are most often arranged in this standard box

The instructor will show you where to put any baggage and items you may need in flight. You will also be shown the location of the fire extinguisher and the first aid kit.

▶Main Aircraft Systems

As part of your technical course you will learn about the various aircraft systems. For now there are a few main systems to know about.

Layout of the brake system of a Piper PA-28 Cherokee

The brake system controls the brakes on the main wheels, it is operated by toe brakes fitted to the rudder pedals or a hand-operated brake lever. There is also a parking brake; the method of operating this varies between aircraft types.

The electrical system is controlled by the pilot through the *master switch*. The electrical system supplies power to the lights, radios and some instruments. On some aircraft types (mostly high-wing) the flaps may be electrically operated. The engine DOES NOT require electrical power from the aircraft's electrical system once it is running, it incorporates magnetos which derive electrical power from the rotation of the engine.

The standard electrical master switch in a C-152

The fuel system supplies aviation fuel to the engine from fuel tanks which are most often located in the wings. There is a fuel selector in the cockpit to control the flow of fuel from the fuel tanks to the engine.

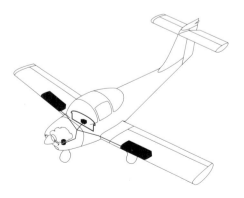

Layout of the fuel system of a Piper PA38 Tomahawk

▶ Use of Checklist and Pilots. Operating Handbook/Flight Manual

Your Flight Training Organisation (FTO) will provide you with a checklist for the aircraft you are learning on.

It is important to do all checks in accordance with this checklist. As a general rule, checks done on the ground are read from the checklist and checks in flight are done from memory. All should be completed carefully and methodically. Each checklist item is there for a reason, and it is easy to miss an item if you rush or are distracted. Each aircraft has its own individual Pilot's Operating Handbook/Flight Manual (POH/FM) which contains information about the aircraft, its systems, operating procedures and performance. The limitations and requirements described in the flight manual must be complied with at all times.

An example of a popular aircraft checklist

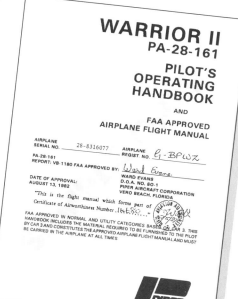

The title page of an aircraft's Pilot's Operating Handbook/Flight Manual (POH/FM). Each individual aircraft has its own individual POH/FM which contains detailed information on the subject aircraft. It is a legal document and the procedures and limitations it contains must be complied with.

▶Airfield Sense

The manoeuvring area and apron of an active airfield—even a small one—is an unfamiliar environment to most non-pilots. For your own safety, and the safety of other airfield users, you should follow a few simple guidelines:

- Stay well away from any aircraft with an engine running or an aircraft about to start its engine. Do not walk in front of moving aircraft.

- Do not drop litter and collect any you come across. Foreign Object Damage (FOD) is potentially very dangerous to aircraft.

- Smoking is not permitted on the manoeuvring area, on the apron, or in the hangars. Smoking is usually banned inside the aircraft as well.

- Do not leave chocks, tie-down weights or any other such objects where they might be hit by an aircraft.

- If you come across any obstructions, pot holes, debris etc that you think might be dangerous - tell someone!

Exercise

1e

Emergencies

Emergencies are rare in modern training aircraft. However, if an emergency should occur, the ability to act correctly and promptly is essential. This is most likely to happen when the pilot has been properly trained in emergency procedures and regularly practises them. Here are listed three emergency drills, which should be committed to memory and practised regularly. The emergency procedures listed in this book can act as a guideline only. Refer to the aircraft checklist and POH/FM for emergency drills and procedures specific to the aircraft you are flying.

FLIGHT EXERCISE

▷ **Fire on the Ground**

▷ **Cabin Fire in the Air**

▷ **Engine Fire in the Air**

Flight Exercise

▷ FIRE ON THE GROUND

If taxying, stop clear of other aircraft, buildings, fuelling areas etc..

THROTTLE - CLOSED

MIXTURE - FULLY LEAN (IDLE CUT OFF or ICO)

FUEL - OFF

MAGNETOS - OFF

MASTER SWITCH - OFF

BRAKES - PARKING BRAKE ON

Evacuate the aircraft, taking the fire extinguisher with you if circumstances permit. Stay upwind of the aircraft.

▷ CABIN FIRE IN THE AIR

Most likely to be an electrical fire, characterised by the acrid burning smell.

MASTER SWITCH - OFF if electrical fire suspected

ELECTRICAL CIRCUITS - OFF to isolate fault

CABIN HEATER/DEFROST - OFF

FIRE EXTINGUISHER - Use only if absolutely necessary, then ventilate cabin immediately.

▷ ENGINE FIRE IN THE AIR

THROTTLE - CLOSED

MIXTURE - FULLY LEAN (IDLE CUT OFF or ICO)

FUEL - OFF

MAGNETOS - OFF

CABIN HEATER/DEFROST - OFF

Refer to the aircraft checklist and POH/FM for the specific emergency drills and procedures relevant to the aircraft type you are flying.

Your instructor will show you how to leave the aircraft in an emergency on the ground and where to find emergency equipment i.e. fire extinguisher and first-aid kit. If the aircraft you are flying has any emergency exits, you also need to know how to use these.

Preparation for Flight and Action After Flight

A safe, professional flight starts with proper pre-flight preparation. Your instructor will show you how to prepare for flight, and you should aim to develop good habits now, rather than trying to change habits or re-learn at a later date. The after-flight actions are just as vital, whether the aircraft will be flying again in a few minutes or a few days. You should leave the aircraft and its documentation the way you would want to find it, with no nasty surprises.

BACKGROUND BRIEFING

▶ **Personal Preparation**

▶ **Flight Authorisation**

▶ **Flying Equipment Required**

▶ **Booking-Out Procedure**

▶ **External Checks**

▶ **Internal Checks**

▶ **Starting**

▶ **Starting Problems**

▶ **Power and Pre-Take-Off Checks**

▶ **Closing Down**

▶ **Moving, Security and Tie-Down**

▶ **Post-Flight Documentation**

BACKGROUND BRIEFING

▶ Personal Preparation

Being sure that you are properly prepared to fly is just as important as the preparation of the aircraft. Indeed, more accidents are caused by pilot error than by aircraft failure. As a pilot you will learn several checklists and mnemonics so here is one to use before every flight :

'I'm safe'

I   Illness - am I ill or do I have any symptoms ?

M   Medication - am I taking any medication that has side-effects ?

S   Stress - am I under undue stress - family, financial, work, health ?

A   Alcohol - have I drunk any alcohol in the last eight hours, or a significant amount within 24 hours ?

F   Fatigue - am I well rested ?

E   Eating - have I had adequate nourishment ?

If in any doubt - do not fly.

Remember the 'I'm safe' checklist before every flight

▶ Flight Authorisation

Before flying, the pilot must record some basic details of the intended flight. In the case of a training exercise the flight is then authorised by an instructor. The authorisation sheet also contains details of previous flights. On this sheet, or an attached document, any aircraft defects or unserviceability are recorded and any rectification action noted. It is the pilot's decision whether or not to accept the aircraft. A minor fault that will not cause great concern to an experienced pilot may be far more important to a student pilot.

The flight authorisation sheet must be filled out before flight

FLIGHT RECORD SHEET

1 Serial No	2 Date	3 Aircraft Type	Registration	4 Pilot/Instructor	5 Pupil/Passenger(S)	6 Exercise or Nature of Flight	7 Authorised By	Duration	
	16-11	PA-38	G-BGKY	SMITH	TAYLOR	EXERCISE 4	JMS	1.20	

▶ Flying Equipment Required

Generally, you will not require any special clothing when flying. One item of equipment you must always carry, however, is a current aeronautical chart of the area in which you will be flying. You will be issued with a chart when you begin your training. Practise using the chart and relating the local landmarks you see when flying to their appearance on the chart. The chart also shows controlled airspace, restricted airspace and other aeronautical information.

VALIDITY OF AERONAUTICAL INFORMATION
Aeronautical information on this chart includes
relevant changes notified by UK AIP AMENDMENTS
published up to 17 Feb 1994 with an implementation
date of 31 March 1994.
Users should consult the UK AIP for changes after
31 March 1994.

THIS CHART WILL BECOME OBSOLETE
AFTER APPROXIMATELY 12 MONTHS.
INFORMATION CIRCULARS SHOULD BE CHECKED
FOR THE PUBLICATION OF THE NEXT EDITION

USERS ARE REQUESTED TO REFER CORRECTIONS
AND ANY COMMENTS ON THE PORTRAYAL OF
TOPOGRAPHICAL AND AERONAUTICAL
INFORMATION TO:-
NATIONAL AIR TRAFFIC SERVICES.
AERONAUTICAL CHART SECTION.
AP7, ROOM T1120,
CAA HOUSE, KINGSWAY,

You should carry a current aeronautical chart every time you fly

▶ Booking-Out Procedure

Before taking off you must give details of your intended flight to the Air Traffic Service Unit (ATSU) on the airfield. Depending on the nature of your flight the booking-out could be a simple phone call, completing an airfield movements record or filing a full flight plan. At some airfields the booking-out can be done by radio, but check first!

▶ External Checks

The aircraft checklist details the external 'pre-flight' checks. The exact details vary between different aircraft types, so always refer to the checklist or POH/FM when flying a new type of aircraft. Some elements of the external checks will be common to all types.

- aircraft security: remove all tie-downs, tow bars, control locks, chocks and pitot covers. This sounds obvious, but pilots try to fly with one or more of these attached every year - check to be sure.

- general appearance: check that the aircraft sits level and 'looks' right. Also check that there are no obvious leaks, pools of fuel under the aircraft etc.. Most aircraft are of stressed-skin construction, meaning that the skin of the aircraft helps to carry the loads and stresses that affect the aircraft. Any dents, punctures or wrinkles of the skin may indicate more serious damage to the aircraft. Aircraft of Glass-Reinforced Plastic (GRP) construction may show cracks in the skin if the aircraft structure has been damaged.

Don't forget to check for the obvious when carrying out the pre-flight checks (tow-bar still attached to nose wheel leg).

- flying controls: move the flying control surfaces gently to check that they are operating properly. Be careful not to use force on the control surfaces or bang them against the control stops.

- fuel: the fuel contents must always be checked visually before flight. You will learn to judge the fuel level in the tanks (using a dipstick if available) to estimate total fuel

contents. The fuel also needs to be checked for purity. A sample is taken into a fuel sampler and checked for colour (e.g. 100LL AVGAS is blue), sediment or globules of water. Globules or a sharp division of colour in the sample indicates the presence of water in the fuel - which is not acceptable. If in doubt, take more samples and ask the advice of an instructor or engineer.

LEFT> ALWAYS visually check tne fuel tank contents. Your instructor will show you how to do this on the aircraft you are flying

RIGHT> A fuel tester is used to check a fuel sample for purity

- undercarriage: on training aircraft particularly, the undercarriage can have a hard life. The undercarriage leg is of an oleo or leaf-spring type. On the oleo type, check that the correct amount of the shiny oleo is visible and that there is no oil leaking

from around the seals. The hydraulic lines to the brake units should be secure, with no leakage of hydraulic fluid (coloured red). The tyre should have at least 2mm of visible tread. There should be no bald patches or cuts. Look for signs of under-inflation or over-inflation of the tyres. Also the creep marks painted on the tyre and wheel rim should be aligned.

LEFT> The spring leaf-type undercarriage leg (Piper PA38 Tomahawk)

RIGHT> The oleo-type undercarriage. About 4 inches (10 centimetres) of shiny oleo isvisible on this Piper PA28 Cherokee

- oil: the engine oil is checked using a dipstick which is located under the cowling. The oil level cannot be checked accurately until at least ten minutes after the engine has stopped. The dipstick is taken out, and wiped, then the level is re-checked. Whilst checking the oil level look over the engine for evidence of loose wires, frayed leads, oil leaks etc.

- windscreens and windows: all windows and windscreens should be clean. A particular problem is insects on the windscreen. They should be removed using a soft cloth or sponge and warm, soapy water. This is essential to help the pilot maintain a good lookout. An approaching aircraft and a squashed insect on the window can look very similar at first glance.

If you are in any doubt about anything you come across during the external check, do not hesitate to ask an instructor or engineer for help or advice. With experience the external checks are carried out without direct reference to a checklist. To keep in practice, use the checklist occasionally to do them. You may find that your memory is not as infallible as you thought!

Always take care around an aircraft propeller. The propeller of this Piper PA28 Cherokee has been marked to be more conspicuous when rotating

▶Internal Checks

The internal checks are detailed in the checklist. Follow them through carefully - do not try to rush through them from memory. When you are carrying passengers it is necessary to brief them, especially on the operation of the doors and seat belts and the location of safety equipment.

Loose articles in the cockpit represent a serious safety hazard. Check for loose articles when you first enter the cockpit and remove or stow any you find. Be careful that the equipment you are carrying e.g. pens, rulers, etc does not 'go missing' during the flight - you never know where they might end up. Even a single pen or pencil could foul a control cable or linkage.

▶Starting

As part of the external checks you will have ensured that the aircraft is in a safe location to start up. Loose gravel or stones under the propeller, or a blocked exit on the taxiway, represent obvious points to avoid. Be aware also of the propeller slipstream generated once the engine has started - is the aircraft parked outside an open hangar door, or too close to another aircraft? Immediately before starting it is vital to check visually that the propeller area is clear. Also look all round for anybody who is—or is about to be—in the propeller area. A rotating propeller is surprisingly easy to miss on a noisy, busy apron area. As a final check it is common practice to open a window/door, call "CLEAR PROP" and wait briefly before starting.

Further checks are carried out, after starting, two of which are common to most light aircraft. These are to check that the starter warning light has gone out and that the oil pressure registers within 30 seconds of start. These two checks in particular should become instinctive, although they are listed in the checklist.

▶ Starting Problems

Two possible problems during engine starting are:

A flooded engine - the engine has been 'flooded' with too much fuel and so will not start. If flooding is suspected, the following procedure may apply - refer to your checklist or the aircraft's POH/FM which may override this general advice.

Magnetos - off

Throttle - fully open

Mixture - fully lean (ICO)

Operate the starter through a few turns, then repeat the starting checklist without priming.

Engine fire on start - very rare occurrence.

Assuming the starter is still engaged - continue operating and:

Mixture - fully lean (ICO)

Fuel - off

Throttle - fully open

The fire should go out when the fuel stops. Then stop cranking the engine and proceed with the 'engine fire on ground' procedure. The aircraft checklist, or POH/FM may give a procedure which overrides this general advice.

▶ Power and Pre-Take-Off checks

The power and pre-take-off checks are usually carried out after the aircraft has taxied to the holding position for the runway in use. Stop the aircraft facing into wind. Then check visually that the propeller slipstream will not cause any damage or inconvenience behind the aircraft.

Carry out the checks methodically from the checklist and do not hesitate to cancel the flight if you find something wrong. At this stage there maybe a strong psychological pressure to disregard a problem and fly - after all, you are right next to the runway. Do resist any such feelings: each checklist item is there for a reason, and unlike driving a car you obviously cannot stop an aircraft in flight to sort out a problem. There is an aviation maxim:

Never get airborne unless you are completely happy with the aircraft and its serviceability

"Better to be down here, wishing you were up there;

than up there wishing you were down here."

- and it's quite true !

▶ Closing Down

Usually light aircraft 'park' after flight without outside assistance. If you are being given marshalling signals, however, remember that these are for guidance only; the pilot remains legally responsible for the safety of the aircraft. After closing down, leave the cockpit tidy, with no loose articles. As a final safety check before you close the door, confirm that the master switch is off, the magnetos are off with the key out and the fuel is off. As you get out of the aircraft, glance over it for any change in its external condition since you did the pre-flight external check.

▶ Moving, Security, Tie-Down

The aircraft may have to be moved after it has been shut down, e.g. into a hangar. Whenever possible, light aircraft are best moved with a towbar that fits on to the nosewheel. If a towbar is not available, your instructor will point out the parts of the aircraft that can be pushed or pulled. Do not try to move an aircraft unaided. Apart from being heavy and awkward machines to manhandle, it is very easy to hit something with those long wings and distant tail - ask anyone who has done it! Note that when an aircraft is parked inside a hanger the parking brake is left off so that the aircraft can be moved if necessary.

Securing an aircraft which is not inside a hanger is done in accordance with the weather conditions and the Flying Training Organisation (FTO) procedures. The parking brake must be set and possibly wheel chocks will be put in place as well. A pitot cover to protect the pitot head and internal/external control locks may also be used. The aircraft has a number of 'tie-down' points from which a rope or cable is secured to a ground tie-down anchor. Your instructor will show you how to secure the aircraft properly, advice may also be found in the POH/FM.

Aircraft that are not hangared need securing well and protection from the weather

▶Post-Flight Documentation

At some airfields it may be necessary to 'book in' with the Air Traffic Service Unit. If you have been on a local training flight from your home-base airfield, booking in is unlikely to be required. The authorisation sheet must be completed with details of your flight and any defect must be recorded. Your personal flying logbook should also be completed at this stage.

Remember to complete your log book after each flight. Take great care of your log book. It will become the only complete record of your flying experience

Air Experience

This exercise takes the form of a short local flight with an instructor, to give you a taste of being airborne and flying in a light aircraft. Although no formal instruction is given, you will have the opportunity to fly the aircraft and to get used to using the aircraft's intercom.

FLIGHT EXERCISE

▷ **The Air Experience Flight**

Flight Exercise

▷ The Air Experience Flight

Where at all possible, the flight will take place in good visibility conditions that will allow the instructor to point out some of the main landmarks around the airfield. During the flight you will soon learn if your seating position and seat-belt adjustments are comfortable. If they are not, ask your instructor to help you change them, since discomfort will distract you from the learning process (and the fun of flying). When you handle the controls, you may be surprised at how little control movement is needed and how readily the aircraft responds. You may also be impressed by the natural stability of the aircraft - it does not suddenly pitch or roll if you let go of the controls. If at any time you feel at all unwell, tell your instructor right away. It is not uncommon to feel a little queasy on a first flight, so don't worry - you will soon become used to the sensation of flying. The air experience flight is an introduction to the pleasures of flying a light aircraft, before you begin the instruction of learning to fly. Above all enjoy this flight! It is your first step towards becoming a pilot.

Effects of Controls

Exercise

4

The purpose of this exercise is to learn the effects of the controls when operated independently in flight. This exercise is the foundation of learning to control the aircraft. Lessons you learn here will prove invaluable at later stages of your training.

In the background briefing you will find reference to aerodynamic principles such as lift, drag, thrust etc. These terms and principles are described only in basic detail in this exercise, but are expanded upon in the following exercises as your knowledge and awareness develop to give you a better understanding of the principles of flight.

The exercise may be split into more than one flight, and elements of it will recur and may be revised in later flight exercises. As at all other times, tell your instructor right away if you do not understand a certain point, or would like to see another demonstration. Your instructor is there to help you learn and will be glad to explain a point again or repeat a manoeuvre.

BACKGROUND BRIEFING

▶ **Flying Lesson Format**

▶ **The Planes and Axes of Movement**

▶ **The Function and Initial Effect of the Three Primary Flying Controls**

▶ **The Further Effects of the Three Primary Flying Controls**

▶ **The Effect of Differing Airspeeds**

▶ **The Effect of Propeller Slipstream**

▶ **The Effect of Differing Power Settings**

▶ **The Trimming Controls**

▶ **The Flaps**

▶ **Carburettor Heat**

▶ **Mixture**

▶ **Cockpit Heating and Ventilation**

▶ **Other Controls**

Exercise

4

Effects of
Controls

FLIGHT EXERCISE

▷ **Purpose**

▷ **Airmanship**

▷ **The initial effect of ELEVATOR**

▷ **The initial effect of AILERON**

▷ **The initial effect of RUDDER**

▷ **The further effect of AILERON**

▷ **The further effect of RUDDER**

▷ **The effect of differing airspeed**

▷ **The effect of propeller slipstream**

▷ **The effect of differing power settings**

▷ **The effect of elevator trim**

▷ **The effect of flaps**

CONCLUSION

BACKGROUND BRIEFING

▶Flying Lesson Format

Typically a lesson covers one, or more, flight exercises and will take the following form:

Background briefing - this is often carried out by the student 'self-studying' from a text book or course notes. Some Flying Training Organisations (FTOs) may give briefings and lectures in addition.

Pre-flight briefing - at the FTO immediately before the flight your instructor will brief you on the air exercise and answer any questions you have.

In flight - your instructor will fly each manoeuvre, as it was described in the pre-flight briefing. Then you fly the manoeuvre under the guidance of your instructor.

After flight debrief - this normally takes the form of a short discussion when your instructor reviews the flight, the progress you have made, and any particular points to concentrate on. The instructor will then tell you the next exercise to be flown so that you can cover the background briefing for that exercise in advance.

Before moving on to the next exercise, re-read the material for the exercise you have just flown. You will find that it seems simpler now that you have flown it, and you will retain the important points if you refresh your memory within 24 hours of flying the exercise.

▶The Planes and Axes of Movement

	PLANE OF MOVEMENT	CONTROL SURFACE	COCKPIT CONTROL MOVEMENT
	PITCH	Elevators/ Stabilator	Control Column Forward and Back
	ROLL	Ailerons	Control Column Left and Right
	YAW	Rudder	Rudder Pedals Left and Right

An aircraft operates in three dimensions and, as you might expect, each of the three primary flying controls moves the aircraft in one of the planes of movement. The axes are fixed in relation to the aircraft, not the horizon - for example whatever the aircraft attitude, elevators control pitch as the pilot sees it.

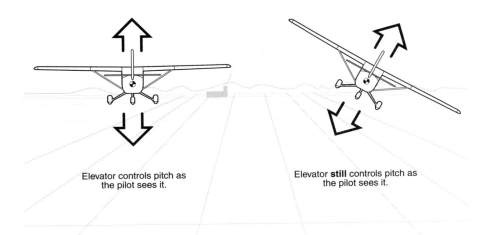

The planes of movement are fixed relative to the aircraft, NOT the horizon.

Elevator controls pitch as the pilot sees it.

Elevator **still** controls pitch as the pilot sees it.

▶ The Function and Initial Effect of the Three Primary Flying Controls

Each control surface functions by altering the airflow around it. The movement of the aircraft around an axis is governed by how quickly and how far the control column is moved. Each control surface is located some distance from the centre of gravity (CG) - for practical purposes assume the CG is about where the pilot is sitting. The distance between the control surface and the centre of gravity gives the control leverage and enhances its effect.

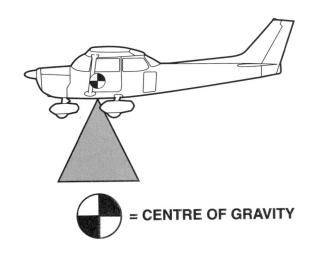

The centre of gravity (CG) is the point at which the aircraft will balance. There is equal weight ahead of and behind the CG.

◐ = **CENTRE OF GRAVITY**

Effects of Controls

The elevator (or stabilator) controls the aircraft in pitch. As the control column is moved back, the elevator (or stabilator) moves up. The change of the angle of the elevator or stabilator, relative to the airflow, creates a force acting downwards. This downforce at the tail pivots the aircraft around the centre of gravity and the aircraft pitches nose-up. The aircraft continues to pitch nose-up until the control column is moved back to the neutral position. As the control column is moved forward, the elevator (or stabilator) moves down and lift is created acting upwards. This up force at the tail pivots the aircraft around the centre of gravity and the aircraft pitches nose down. Once again, the aircraft continues pitching nose-down until the control column is returned to the neutral position.

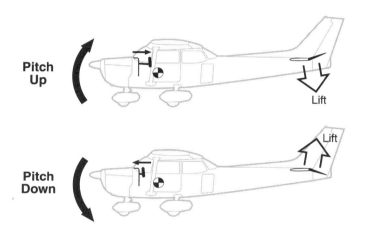

When the control column is moved back, the elevator (or stabilator) moves up,creating a downforce at the tail. The aircraft pivots around the CG and PITCHES nose-up.

When the control column is moved forward, the elevator (or stabilator) moves down, creating lift upwards at the tail. The aircraft pivots around the CG and PITCHES nose-down.

The ailerons control the aircraft in roll. As the control column is moved to the left, the left aileron moves up and the right aileron moves down. These control deflections alter the amount of lift produced by each wing - the left wing is now producing less lift than the right wing. This 'imbalance' of lift causes the aircraft to roll to the left. The aircraft continues to roll until the control column is centralised. When the control column is moved to the right, the aileron movements are reversed, the lift 'imbalance' of the wings is reversed and the aircraft rolls to the right, until the control column is centralised.

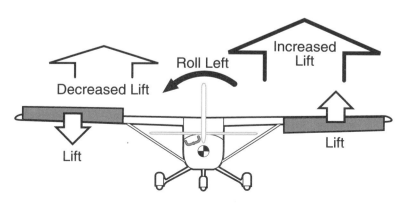

Viewed from behind

When the control column is moved to the left, the deflection of the ailerons changes the amount of lift produced at each wing. The aircraft ROLLS to the left.

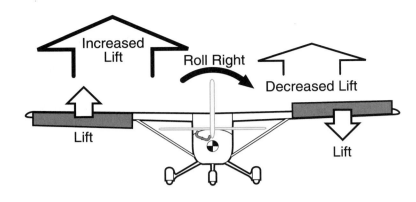

When the control column is moved to the right, the deflection of the ailerons changes the amount of lift produced at each wing. The aircraft ROLLS to the right.

Viewed from behind

The rudder controls the aircraft in yaw. As the left rudder pedal is depressed, the rudder moves to the left. This rudder deflection creates a lift force at the fin and rudder, acting to the right. The aircraft pivots around the centre of gravity (CG) and the aircraft yaws to the left. When the rudder controls are centralised, the aircraft stops yawing. As the right rudder is depressed the rudder moves to the right. Lift is created acting to the left at the fin and rudder, and the aircraft yaws to the right as long as the right rudder is depressed.

LEFT>When the left rudder pedal is pressed, the change of lift at the fin/rudder pivots the aircraft around the CG, and the aircraft yaws to the left.

RIGHT> When the right rudder pedal is pressed, the change of lift at the fin/rudder pivots the aircraft around the CG, and the aircraft yaws to the right.

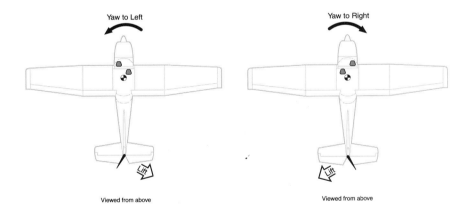

Even a light aircraft has some inertia, so the movement of the aircraft about an axis is not instant when a control is moved. When flying larger, heavier aircraft the effect of inertia can be quite pronounced and the pilot has to allow time for a control movement to take effect.

▶The Further Effects of the Three Primary Flying Controls

In the flight exercise it is only the further effects of the aileron and rudder that are demonstrated. Arguably the elevators have a further effect, in that when the aircraft is pitched nose up, the airspeed will decrease and when it is pitched nose down, the airspeed will increase. However, it is a matter of opinion whether or not this is a true further effect.

As you have already seen, the initial effect of the ailerons is to control the aircraft in roll. To demonstrate the further effect of aileron, the aircraft will be rolled to a banked attitude using the ailerons. The ailerons are then centralised to stop the roll and leave the aircraft in a banked attitude. In this condition the aircraft will tend to slip 'downhill' towards the lower wing. As the aircraft slips, the airflow striking the fin from one side creates a lift force. The aircraft pivots around its CG and 'weathercocks' into the airflow - the aircraft yaws towards the lower wing, although no rudder has been applied.

So, the initial effect of aileron is roll, the further effect is yaw.

If the roll and yaw are left unchecked the aircraft will begin to descend in a gradually steepening spiral known as a *spiral descent*, with increasing roll, increasing airspeed and loss of height. However, this spiral descent is easy to correct, as you will find during the flight exercise.

Roll Left

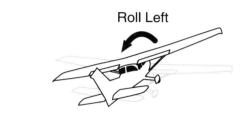

Slip

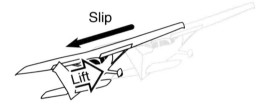

Yaw

The further effect of roll. After the aircraft has rolled, it slips towards the lower wing. The airflow is now striking the fin/rudder from one side. Lift is created at the fin/rudder, and this yaws the aircraft towards the lower wing.

Incidentally, there is another yawing effect present whilst the aircraft is actually rolling, known as adverse yaw. This effect is considered during the turning and slow flight exercises.

Yaw

Looking now at the rudder, you will have seen that the initial effect of the rudder is yaw, whilst the aircraft is yaws it is, in effect, skidding through the air. Whilst yawing, the wing on the outside of the 'skid' (ie the right wing in a left yaw) has a faster airflow around it than the inner wing. This faster airflow increases the amount of lift this wing produces. Conversely, the slower airflow around the inner wing reduces the lift it produces. The result of this imbalance of lift is that the aircraft rolls in the same direction as it is yawing - even though no aileron has been applied. Again if this condition is left to develop a spiral descent will gradually develop. So the initial effect of the rudder is yaw, the further effect is roll.

The further effect of yaw. When the aircraft is yawing, the wing on the 'outside' of the turn is moving faster. The faster airflow creates more lift at this wing than at the slower moving, 'inner' wing. This lift imbalance causes the aircraft to roll in the same direction as it is yawing.

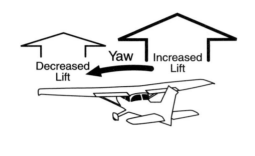

The point to appreciate is that stability in yaw and stability in roll are interrelated. A movement in yaw will affect roll and vice-versa.

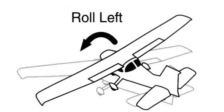

Roll Left

▶ The Effect of Differing Airspeeds

The flying controls function by altering the airflow at their location. It follows that at different airflow speeds, the effectiveness and feel of the controls is altered. At a fast airspeed the controls are very effective, and only small control movements are needed to achieve the desired result. At a slow airspeed the controls are much less effective, and larger control movements are needed.

The 'feel' of the flying controls becomes an important cue to the pilot. Once familiar with the feel and effectiveness of the controls at the normal cruising airspeed, the pilot should be able to sense from the controls if the aircraft is flying at a significantly faster or slower airspeed.

▶The Effect of Propeller Slipstream

The slipstream generated by the propeller increases the speed of the airflow within a 'tube' surrounding the fuselage behind the propeller. Most training aircraft are fitted with a fixed-pitch propeller rotating at the same speed as the engine. At high power settings there is increased slipstream and increased airflow speed within the slipstream. At low power settings there is decreased slipstream and decreased airflow speed inside the tube. Any flying controls inside the slipstream will be affected by differing slipstream speeds, just as they are affected by differing airspeeds. Usually the elevator\stabilator and rudder are affected by the slipstream effect. However if the aircraft has a high tailplane ('T-tail') the elevator may be outside the slipstream effect. The ailerons, out at the end of the wings, are outside the slipstream.

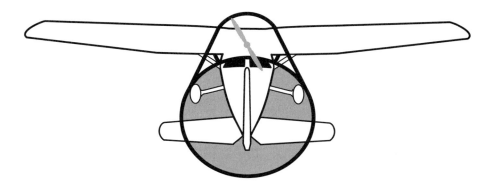

The propeller slipstream increases the speed of the airflow behind the propeller

It is important to note is that in a high power/slow airspeed situation the rudder and elevators of a low-tailplane aircraft will still feel effective due to the slipstream effect, despite the slow airspeed.

▶The Effect of Differing Power Settings

The aircraft is designed to be stable at its normal cruise airspeed and power setting, so that at 'normal cruise' the pilot has the least work to do to maintain this condition. If any other power setting is used, there is an associated pitch and yaw force.

The aircraft's stability in pitch is governed in part by a balance between the thrust force provided by the engine and the drag force caused by the movement of the aircraft through the air. On most light aircraft, the thrust line is lower than the drag line.

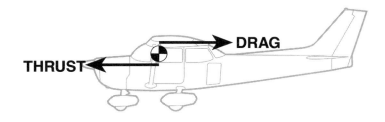

DRAG

THRUST

On a light aircraft, the thrust line is usually below the drag line.

If power is increased, both the thrust and drag increase. The result of this change in the thrust/drag coupling is that the aircraft pitches nose up. If power is reduced, thrust and drag decrease and the aircraft pitches nose down. The pitching movement is aided by the change in airflow over the tailplane, which alters the lift force produced there.

When power is increased, the stronger thrust/drag couple pitches the aircraft nose up. The increased propeller slipstream also affects the airflow over the tailplane

Increased Power Pitch Up

When power is reduced, the weaker thrust/drag couple pitches the aircraft nose down. The decreased propeller slipstream also affects the airflow over the tailplane

Decreased Power Pitch Down

The aircraft's stability in yaw is largely achieved through the tail fin, and the airflow around the tail fin is affected by the helix of the propeller slipstream. On most modern light aircraft the propeller rotates to the right (clockwise) as seen from the cockpit. The helix of the propeller slipstream curves around the fuselage and meets the fin on its left side. The lift force created at the fin causes the aircraft to yaw to the left.

Where an aircraft has a clockwise rotating propeller (as viewed from the cockpit),the slipstream helix strikes the fin/rudder on its left hand side, creating a lift force that would tend to yaw the aircraft to the left.

To counteract this yaw force, some aircraft are built with the fin or the engine offset a few degrees from dead-ahead. However, it follows that this counter-force is fixed, and is designed to balance forces created when the aircraft is at the cruise power setting and airspeed. At a different power setting a movement in yaw will result.

To summarise, when power is increased beyond the normal setting, the 'counteracting force' designed into the aircraft is overcome and the aircraft yaws to the left. When power is reduced below the normal setting the 'counteracting force' overcompensates and the aircraft yaws to the right.

Increased Power

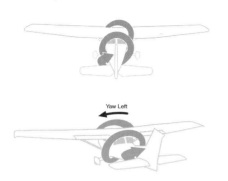

Decreased Power

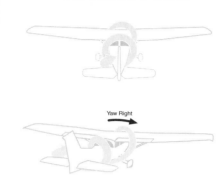

Where an aircraft has a propeller rotating to the left (anti-clockwise) the counteracting forces and yaw movements are reversed–i.e. when power is increased the aircraft yaws to the right.

There are other aerodynamic forces at work when the power setting is changed, but for now those described here are the main ones to consider.

▶ The Trimming Controls

In different flying conditions there are varying loads on the flying controls, particularly the elevator/stabilator and rudder. To relieve the physical work of flying the aeroplane accurately the elevator (or stabilator) is fitted with a *'trimmer'*. On some aircraft the rudder also has a trimmer.

The elevator trimmer usually takes the form of a small control surface *(trim tab)* on the trailing edge of the elevator. In a situation where, for instance, the pilot is having to exert a constant pull on the control column to hold the elevator in the up position, the control forces could be quite high and the pilot would soon become tired - no matter how good his arm muscles! The cockpit trimmer control is used to move the trim tab and so maintain the elevator in the desired position aerodynamically.

The aim is to trim so that no pressure at all is required to maintain the desired

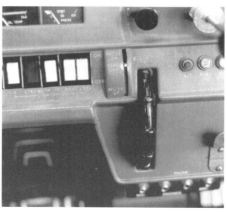

LEFT> A floor-mounted elevator/stabilator trimmer

RIGHT> A control panel-mounted elevator/stabilator trimmer

control position. Some aircraft achieve trimming through a spring in the elevator control-cable circuit instead of a trim tab. However, the trimmer works in the same sense and the pilot will notice no practical difference.

The trimmer is used to relieve control loads on the pilot, not to control the aeroplane. Always select the desired attitude and performance first, then trim to maintain it.

▶ The Flaps

The flaps are fitted to the trailing edge of the wings and are operated manually or electrically from a switch or lever in the cockpit.

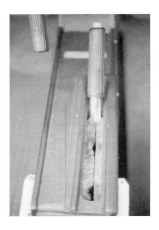

LEFT> A manually operated flap lever

RIGHT> A flap switch operating electrically powered flaps. The slot to the left of the control is the flap position indicator

When the flaps are lowered, the shape of the wing and hence the airflow around the wing are altered. The first stages or degrees of lowered flap (initial flap) cause a large increase in lift and a small increase in drag. As more flap is lowered (intermediate to full flap), there is a much smaller further increase in lift and a much larger increase in drag.

When flaps are lowered the first 10°- 20° creates greater lift and a little extra drag. As more flap is lowered, 20°- 40°, a little extra lift is created but much there is much more drag.

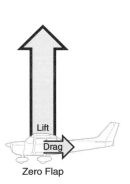

Zero Flap

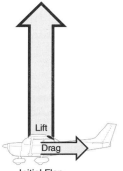

Initial Flap
10°- 20°
Flap Down

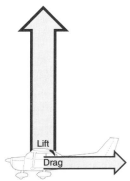

Intermediate-Full Flap
20°+
Flap Down

Effects of Controls

When the flaps are lowered, the aircraft will pitch nose up or nose down, depending on the aircraft type. In either case airspeed reduces due to the increased drag.

The use of flaps is limited by a speed known as 'VFE' - the flaps must not be operated when flying faster than this speed, nor should this speed be exceeded when flaps are lowered. On the airspeed indicator the VFE speed is the 'top' (faster speed) end of the white arc. Always check that the airspeed is within the white arc before operating the flaps, to prevent damage to the flaps and their operating mechanism.

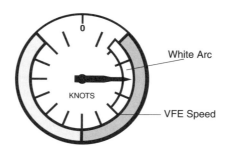

Flaps must only be operated when the airspeed is within the white arc range. The fast speed end of the white arc is VFE, the flap limiting speed.

▶ Carburettor Heat

In the majority of engines used for training aircraft, a carburettor supplies the engine with its fuel/air mixture. Should ice form inside the carburettor (which can happen over a very wide range of temperatures and conditions) the power from the engine will be reduced. The carburettor heat control routes hot air through the carburettor, melting any ice that may be present. When the pilot operates the carburettor heat control, there is a small reduction in power and possibly a little unevenness if any ice has melted.

The carburettor heat control is left in the fully cold position (usually with the lever up or the knob fully in) most of the time. It is used periodically (approximately every 10 minutes) by moving the control to the fully hot position (lever down or knob fully out) for no less than 5-10 seconds and then returning it to the cold position.

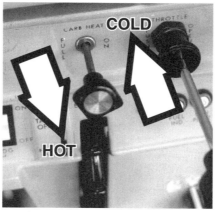

LEFT> The carburettor heat lever shown here is moved DOWN for HOT air, UP for COLD air

RIGHT> The carburettor heat knob shown here is moved out for HOT air, IN for COLD air

Usually the engine speed, measured in revolutions per minute (RPM), will return to the same setting as before the carburettor heat was used. If the RPM comes back to a higher setting then carburettor ice has been present and you will need to recheck regularly. The subject of carburettor icing and the use of the carburettor heat control is of great importance to the pilot and is covered in greater detail later in this book.

▶ Mixture

The fuel-air mixture in the carburettor is controlled from a red lever or knob next to the throttle - the *mixture* control. When flying at lower altitudes, the engine is normally operated with the mixture in the fully rich position - that is with the mixture control fully forward or in. At high altitudes the reduced air density means that less fuel is required to maintain the correct fuel-air ratio - the mixture needs to be 'leaned'. This is done by moving the mixture control back or out. An aircraft fitted with a fixed-pitch propeller (as are most training aircraft), will show an initial RPM increase as the mixture is leaned. The RPM will peak, then reduce as the mixture is leaned further. The mixture should now be enriched again until the RPM is on the 'rich' side of the peak. The mixture will need to be reset for any change in power or altitude. Different engines have different leaning techniques and limitations. For specific advice on mixture leaning refer to the aircraft's POH/FM.

The engine is stopped by moving the mixture control to the fully lean position—or *Idle Cut Off* (ICO). This completely shuts off the fuel supply to the carburettor.

LEFT> The quadrant-type mixture control shown here is moved FORWARD for RICH mixture and fully BACK for fully LEAN mixture, or Idle Cut Off (ICO)

RIGHT> The plunger-type mixture control shown here is moved FORWARD for RICH mixture and fully BACK for fully LEAN mixture, or Idle Cut Off (ICO)

▶ Cockpit Heating and Ventilation

Your instructor will show you the location and use of the heating and fresh air ventilation controls. Use them to maintain a comfortable temperature in the cockpit, if you are not comfortable, your concentration will be affected and flying will become harder work than it needs to be.

A CO (carbon monoxide) detector, as often found in the aircraft cockpit. A dark spot warns of the presence of CO.

The heating system usually takes its hot air from a shroud around part of the engine exhaust system. The significance of this is that if there is a crack or split in the exhaust system, fumes may enter the cockpit. These engine fumes contain carbon monoxide—a colourless, odourless gas which is potentially lethal. To guard against danger from carbon monoxide, always utilise the fresh air ventilation when using cockpit heat. If you suspect that exhaust fumes are entering the cockpit, do not hesitate to shut off the heating and open up the fresh air ventilation and even the windows.

▶ Other Controls

Your instructor will explain any other ancillary controls that may be important to the particular aircraft you are flying.

Flight Exercise

▷ PURPOSE

To learn the effects of the controls when operated independently in flight.

▷ AIRMANSHIP

What is airmanship ? Airmanship is the commonsense element of flying, but also the quality that differentiates a pilot from an aeroplane driver. More than anything else airmanship is about awareness - being aware of what is happening inside and outside the aircraft. Airmanship is best learnt by example. Watch your instructor and you will learn more about airmanship than any textbook can teach.

Handing over/taking over control

During your early flying lessons, control of the aircraft will be transfered between yourself and the instructor many times; it is obviously essential to avoid confusion over who is actually flying the aircraft at any given time. To ensure that this is so, you and your instructor will follow a set routine when you are handing over or taking over control.

When the instructor wishes you to fly the aircraft:

Instructor says "you have control"

Student takes the control column in one hand, other hand on the throttle, feet placed on rudder pedals.

Student says "I have control"

When the instructor wishes to take control again:

Instructor says "I have control"

Student removes hands and feet from controls.

Student says "You have control"

This simple routine should quickly become second nature. It is used at all levels of aviation, even in the cockpit of the biggest and fastest aircraft you will hear:

"You have control", "I have control"

Following through

When your instructor is demonstrating an exercise, he may ask you to 'follow through'. This means that you should place your hands and feet lightly on the controls, so that you can feel the control movements made by your instructor, without moving the controls yourself.

Flight Exercise

Lookout

Look out as much as you can. Point out to your instructor any aircraft you spot

Try to develop the habit now of looking outside the aircraft as much as possible at all times. This will enable you to look out for other aircraft and maintain an awareness of your location, changing weather etc. It will also make your flying smoother and easier! If you do see another aircraft, point it out to your instructor right away.

Attitude

You may notice how often your instructor refers to *attitude*, i.e. the aircraft attitude, the nose attitude etc. In this instance, attitude means the angle of the aircraft in relation to the natural horizon. Most often the attitude referred to is the attitude of the aircraft in pitch - a nose-high attitude, a nose-low attitude etc. There is also a 'normal' straight and level attitude. While you are learning the early flight exercises, each exercise will start and finish at the normal attitude.

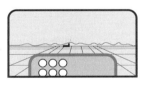

Normal
Attitude

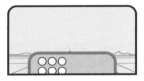

Nose-High
Attitude

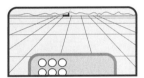

Nose-Low
Attitude

VFE

When using flap during this exercise, ensure the airspeed is below the flap limiting speed (i.e. VFE), that is, the airspeed is within the white arc marked on the airspeed indicator. Do not lower or raise flap if the airspeed is faster than VFE, or allow the airspeed to exceed VFE whilst flap is lowered.

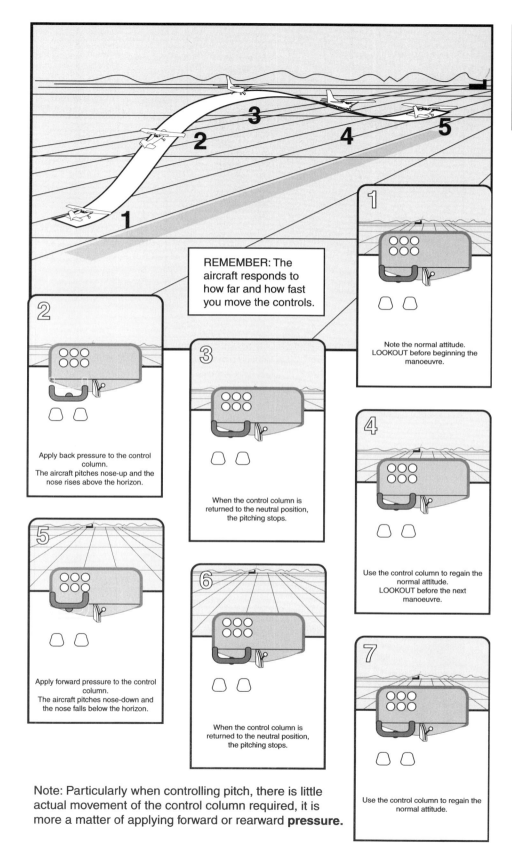

The initial effect of ELEVATOR

1

2

3

4

5

REMEMBER: The
aircraft responds to
how far and how fast
you move the controls.

1
Note the normal attitude.
LOOKOUT before beginning the
manoeuvre.

2
Apply back pressure to the control
column.
The aircraft pitches nose-up and the
nose rises above the horizon.

3
When the control column is
returned to the neutral position,
the pitching stops.

4
Use the control column to regain the
normal attitude.
LOOKOUT before the next
manoeuvre.

5
Apply forward pressure to the control
column.
The aircraft pitches nose-down and
the nose falls below the horizon.

6
When the control column is
returned to the neutral position,
the pitching stops.

7
Use the control column to regain the
normal attitude.

Note: Particularly when controlling pitch, there is little
actual movement of the control column required, it is
more a matter of applying forward or rearward **pressure.**

Effects of Controls

4.17

The initial effect of AILERON

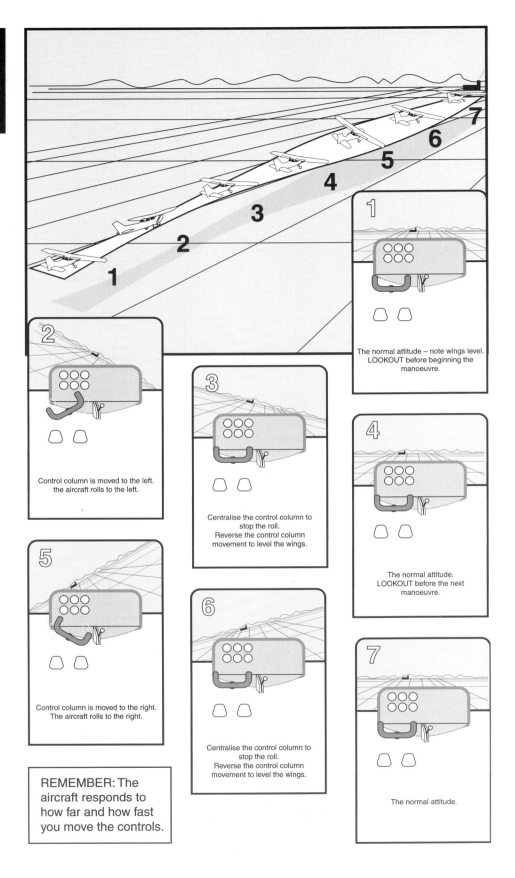

1 The normal attitude – note wings level. LOOKOUT before beginning the manoeuvre.

2 Control column is moved to the left. the aircraft rolls to the left.

3 Centralise the control column to stop the roll. Reverse the control column movement to level the wings.

4 The normal attitude. LOOKOUT before the next manoeuvre.

5 Control column is moved to the right. The aircraft rolls to the right.

6 Centralise the control column to stop the roll. Reverse the control column movement to level the wings.

7 The normal attitude.

REMEMBER: The aircraft responds to how far and how fast you move the controls.

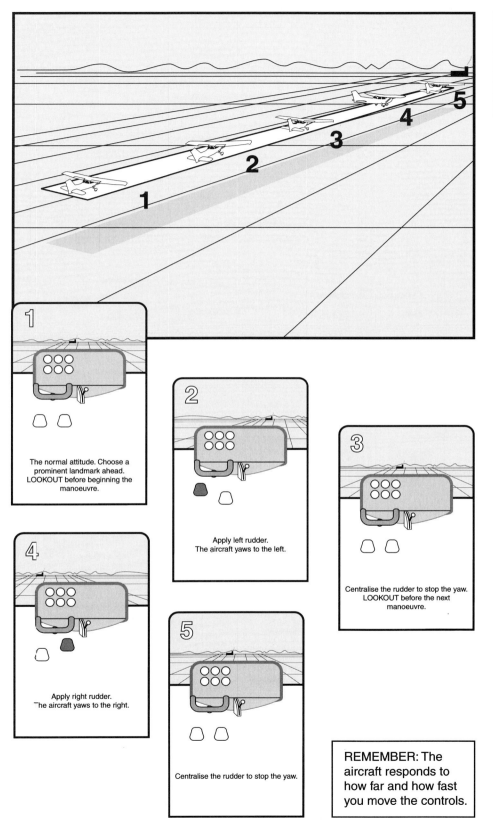

1
The normal attitude. Choose a prominent landmark ahead. LOOKOUT before beginning the manoeuvre.

2
Apply left rudder.
The aircraft yaws to the left.

3
Centralise the rudder to stop the yaw.
LOOKOUT before the next manoeuvre.

4
Apply right rudder.
The aircraft yaws to the right.

5
Centralise the rudder to stop the yaw.

REMEMBER: The aircraft responds to how far and how fast you move the controls.

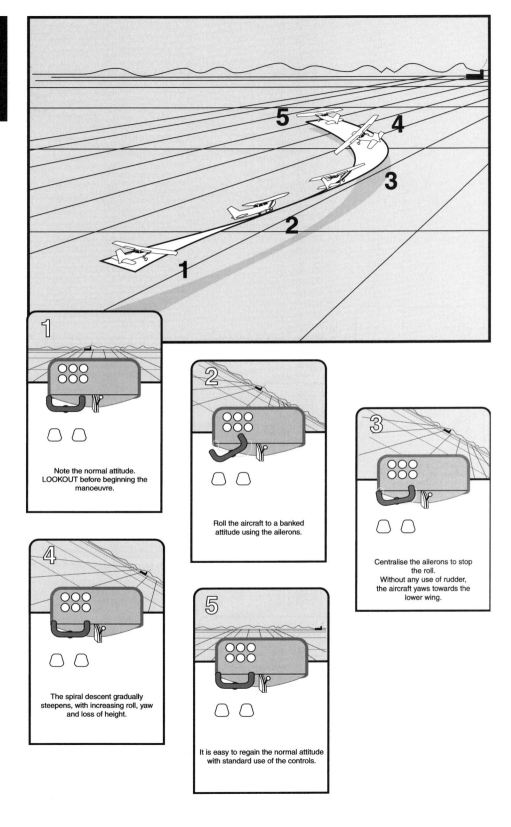

The further effect of AILERON

Effects of Controls

1
Note the normal attitude. LOOKOUT before beginning the manoeuvre.

2
Roll the aircraft to a banked attitude using the ailerons.

3
Centralise the ailerons to stop the roll.
Without any use of rudder, the aircraft yaws towards the lower wing.

4
The spiral descent gradually steepens, with increasing roll, yaw and loss of height.

5
It is easy to regain the normal attitude with standard use of the controls.

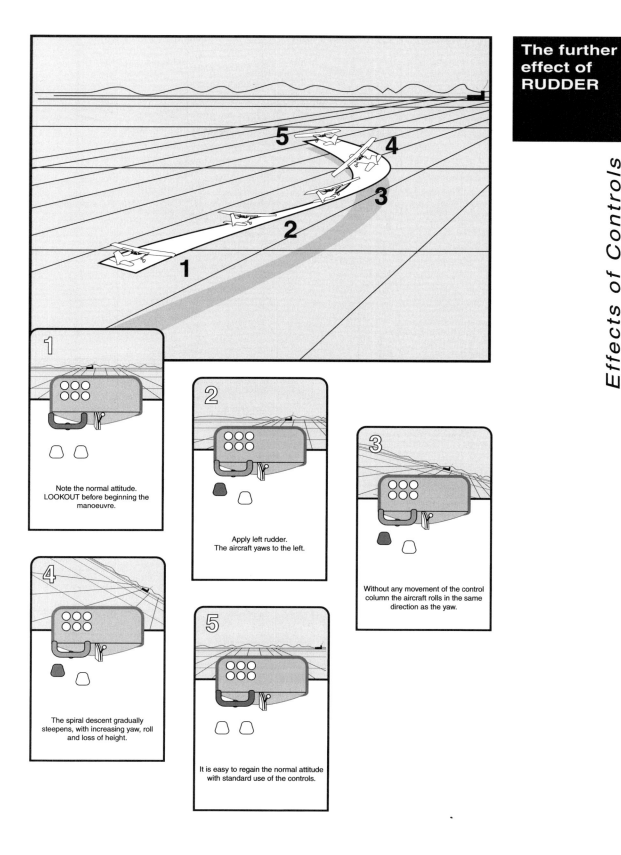

Effects of Controls

1
Note the normal attitude. LOOKOUT before beginning the manoeuvre.

2
Apply left rudder. The aircraft yaws to the left.

3
Without any movement of the control column the aircraft rolls in the same direction as the yaw.

4
The spiral descent gradually steepens, with increasing yaw, roll and loss of height.

5
It is easy to regain the normal attitude with standard use of the controls.

The effect of differing airspeed

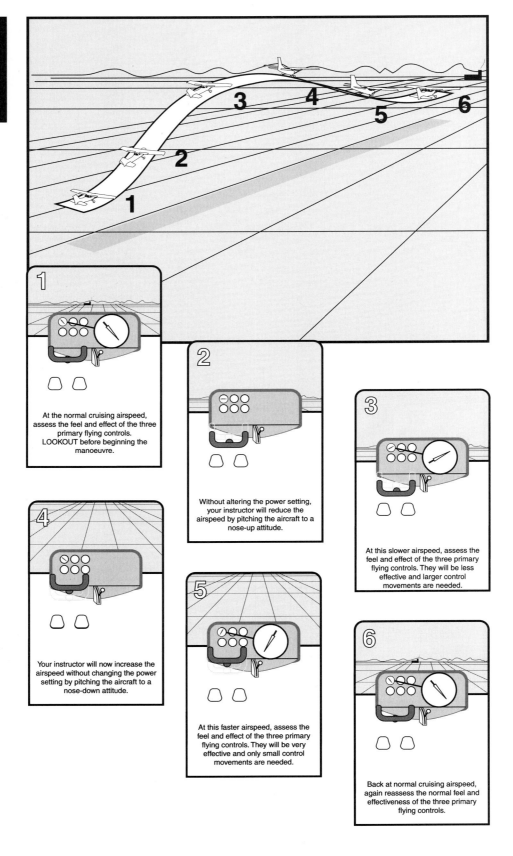

1 At the normal cruising airspeed, assess the feel and effect of the three primary flying controls. LOOKOUT before beginning the manoeuvre.

2 Without altering the power setting, your instructor will reduce the airspeed by pitching the aircraft to a nose-up attitude.

3 At this slower airspeed, assess the feel and effect of the three primary flying controls. They will be less effective and larger control movements are needed.

4 Your instructor will now increase the airspeed without changing the power setting by pitching the aircraft to a nose-down attitude.

5 At this faster airspeed, assess the feel and effect of the three primary flying controls. They will be very effective and only small control movements are needed.

6 Back at normal cruising airspeed, again reassess the normal feel and effectiveness of the three primary flying controls.

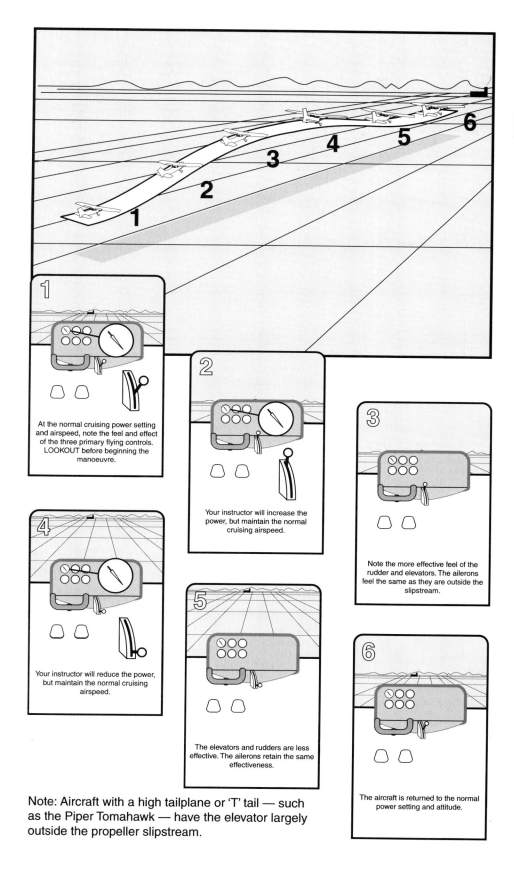

1 At the normal cruising power setting and airspeed, note the feel and effect of the three primary flying controls. LOOKOUT before beginning the manoeuvre.

2 Your instructor will increase the power, but maintain the normal cruising airspeed.

3 Note the more effective feel of the rudder and elevators. The ailerons feel the same as they are outside the slipstream.

4 Your instructor will reduce the power, but maintain the normal cruising airspeed.

5 The elevators and rudders are less effective. The ailerons retain the same effectiveness.

6 The aircraft is returned to the normal power setting and attitude.

Note: Aircraft with a high tailplane or 'T' tail — such as the Piper Tomahawk — have the elevator largely outside the propeller slipstream.

The effect of differing power settings

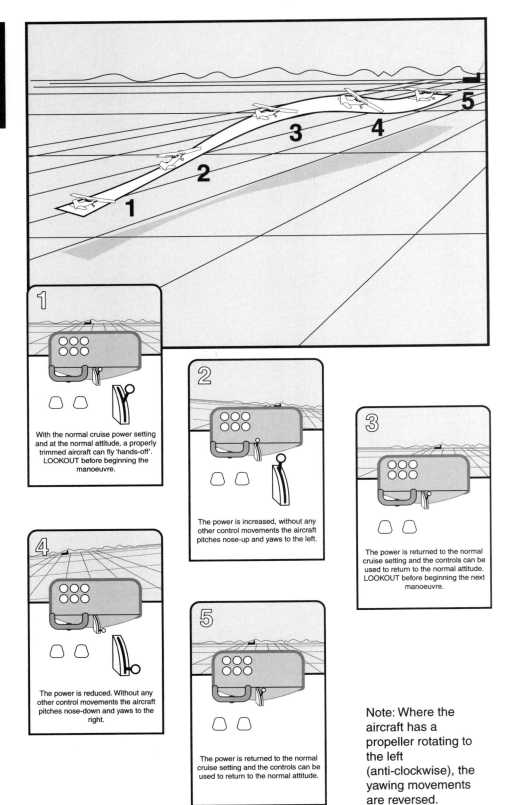

1
With the normal cruise power setting and at the normal attitude, a properly trimmed aircraft can fly 'hands-off'. LOOKOUT before beginning the manoeuvre.

2
The power is increased, without any other control movements the aircraft pitches nose-up and yaws to the left.

3
The power is returned to the normal cruise setting and the controls can be used to return to the normal attitude. LOOKOUT before beginning the next manoeuvre.

4
The power is reduced. Without any other control movements the aircraft pitches nose-down and yaws to the right.

5
The power is returned to the normal cruise setting and the controls can be used to return to the normal attitude.

Note: Where the aircraft has a propeller rotating to the left (anti-clockwise), the yawing movements are reversed.

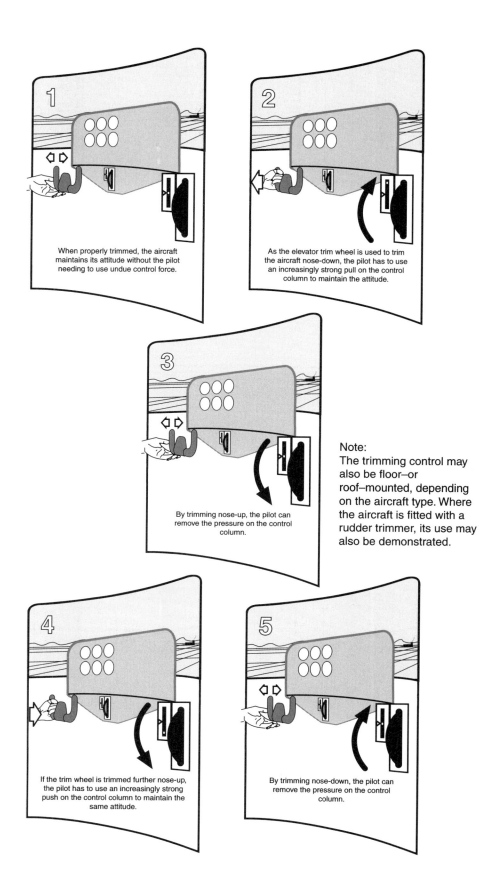

1 When properly trimmed, the aircraft maintains its attitude without the pilot needing to use undue control force.

2 As the elevator trim wheel is used to trim the aircraft nose-down, the pilot has to use an increasingly strong pull on the control column to maintain the attitude.

3 By trimming nose-up, the pilot can remove the pressure on the control column.

Note:
The trimming control may also be floor–or roof–mounted, depending on the aircraft type. Where the aircraft is fitted with a rudder trimmer, its use may also be demonstrated.

4 If the trim wheel is trimmed further nose-up, the pilot has to use an increasingly strong push on the control column to maintain the same attitude.

5 By trimming nose-down, the pilot can remove the pressure on the control column.

Effects of Controls

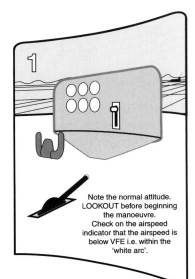

1

Note the normal attitude.
LOOKOUT before beginning
the manoeuvre.
Check on the airspeed
indicator that the airspeed is
below VFE i.e. within the
'white arc'.

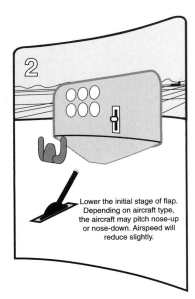

2

Lower the initial stage of flap.
Depending on aircraft type,
the aircraft may pitch nose-up
or nose-down. Airspeed will
reduce slightly.

3

As more flap is lowered,
most aircraft will pitch
nose-down, and airspeed
will reduce further.

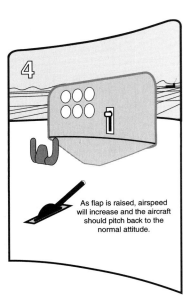

4

As flap is raised, airspeed
will increase and the aircraft
should pitch back to the
normal attitude.

Note: Flaps are normally operated in stages,
not in a continuous movement.
The cockpit illustrated has both manual and
electrically operated flap levers represented.

Conclusion

By the end of this exercise you should:

Understand the effect of each flying control when operated independently in flight.

Appreciate how the use of each of the flying controls will affect the attitude of the aircraft.

Understand the operation of the ancillary controls.

Appreciate some fundamental points of good airmanship.

There is a lot to learn in this first proper flight exercise, so do not hesitate to ask your instructor to clarify or repeat anything that you do not fully understand. The elements of this exercise appear in all the later flight exercises. Even in advanced flying, you will find points from it cropping up.

Exercise

4

Effects of
Controls

Taxying

In this exercise you will be taught how to manoeuvre the aircraft safely on the ground. You will also learn the checks and procedures carried out while taxying and some of the basic rights of way, Air Traffic Control (ATC) procedures and signals. You should also understand the emergency procedures to be used in the event of steering or brake failure. This exercise is taught in conjunction with the flight exercises at the beginning and end of each flight.

BACKGROUND BRIEFING

▶ **Pre-Taxying Checks**

▶ **Effects of Inertia**

▶ **Engine Handling**

▶ **Control of Direction**

▶ **Parking Area Procedures and Taxying in Confined Spaces**

▶ **Effect of Wind and Use of the Flying Controls**

▶ **Effects of Ground Surface**

▶ **Apron & Manoeuvring Area Markings**

▶ **Marshalling Signals**

▶ **ATC Light Signals**

▶ **Rights of Way on the Ground**

▶ **Rudder Check**

▶ **Instrument Checks**

FLIGHT EXERCISE

FLIGHT EXERCISE

▷ **Purpose**

▷ **Airmanship**

▷ **Moving Off**

▷ **Control of Direction on the Ground**

▷ **Use of Differential Braking**

▷ **Stopping**

CONCLUSION

Background Briefing

▶ Pre-Taxying Checks

The pre-taxying checks are normally done with reference to the aircraft's check list. Depending on procedures at the airfield from which you are flying, it may be necessary to obtain ATC clearance by radio before starting to taxy. You must take a good look around BEFORE starting to taxy, in case your exit path has become obstructed since you did your pre-flight check. If in any doubt do not taxy, but close down the engine and check for yourself.

▶ Effects of Inertia

You will probably notice that an increase in power is required to get the aircraft moving, particularly on a grass surface. Much less power will be needed once the aircraft is moving and your instructor will demonstrate the safe taxying speed, which varies according to the ground surface and prevailing wind. When taxying, be aware that a change in speed or direction will have to be anticipated because it is necessary to overcome the inertia of the aircraft, which wants to continue in the original direction at the original speed.

 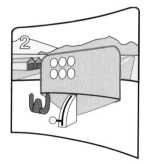

LEFT> A high power setting may be needed to overcome the inertia of a stationary aircraft and get it moving.

RIGHT> Once on the move, power is reduced to prevent the aircraft accelerating to an unsafe taxying speed

▶ Engine Handling

The engine power setting, adjusted by the throttle, is the primary means of controlling speed whilst taxying. To help the pilot make smooth throttle movements, the throttle friction control is set loose when taxying. When slowing or stopping the aircraft, the throttle should always be closed first and the brakes applied after.

The carburettor heat is normally kept at 'cold' when taxying. The reason for this is that the air inlet used when hot air is selected is unfiltered and so any debris, grass cuttings, dust etc. can enter the engine, increasing engine wear.

The pilot must monitor the engine temperatures carefully, especially in hot weather. Most light-aircraft engines are air-cooled and so rely on a good measure of airflow to remain at the correct operating temperature.

The aircraft checklist will specify an RPM setting to be used when the aircraft is stationary with the engine running. The engine is not left to idle on a closed throttle because this causes the spark plugs to 'foul up'.

▶ Control of Direction

Most light aircraft are fitted with a nosewheel, direction on the ground is controlled through the rudder pedals, which are linked to it directly or via springs. A nosewheel aircraft has the centre of gravity ahead of the main wheels (otherwise it would tip on its tail) which makes the aircraft directionally stable when taxying. To turn a force must be applied and maintained to keep the aircraft turning. This turning force is supplied by the rudder pedals which are applied in the direction of the turn and the pressure maintained during the turn, otherwise the aircraft straightens out again.

Where an aircraft is fitted with *differential braking* (most are), it is possible to assist the turn by applying the brakes to the left or right wheel only. This will give a tighter turn than using nosewheel steering alone.

LEFT> Where the rudder pedals are fitted with toe-brakes, the lower half of the pedals control the rudder (and nose wheel steering on most aircraft types).

RIGHT> The upper half of the pedals - the toe brakes - control braking

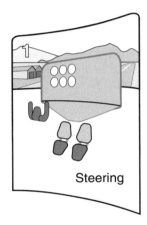

Steering

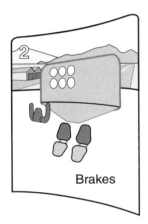

Brakes

Some nosewheel aircraft have no linkage between the rudder pedals and the nosewheel,and the nosewheel is completely free-castoring. These aircraft are still controlled through the effect of the rudder, but much more differential braking is required to control direction, especially when taxying with a crosswind.

▶ Parking Area Procedures and Taxying in Confined Spaces

Great care must be taken when taxying around other aircraft with an engine(s) running. The propeller slipstream of even a light aircraft can damage the controls of another aircraft behind; and the jet blast from an airliner starting to taxy can reach 80mph up to 120ft behind it.

When taxying in a confined space, consider the size of the aircraft in terms of wingspan and the length of aircraft behind you. A small change in direction can cause a large movement of the wing tips and tail unit.

When using differential braking to turn, extra power may be needed to keep the aircraft moving. Be aware of the effect the extra propeller slipstream may have behind your aircraft. Taxy slowly but avoid riding the brakes continually, since this will make them overheat and fade. Never use the power against the brakes while taxying. Avoid turning around a locked wheel because this will cause serious damage to the tyre. If you have any doubt about the clearance between your aircraft and an obstruction, do not hesitate to ask for assistance or shut down the engine and check for yourself.

▶ Effect of Wind and Use of the Flying Controls

Light winds generally have little effect on an aircraft taxying. If the wind is stronger however, control of the aircraft's speed and direction may become more difficult. A wind blowing from one side (a crosswind) will encourage the aircraft to 'weathercock' into wind, as the wind striking the side of the fin causes the aircraft to pivot around its centre of gravity.

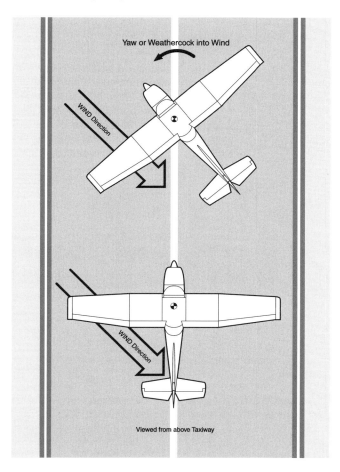

When taxying in a strong crosswind, an aircraft is prone to 'weather cocking' into wind.

The pilot will need to use the rudder pedals and possibly differential braking to prevent the aircraft weathercocking into wind and away from the desired taxying direction. Control of the aircraft will be greatly aided by the correct use of the flying controls with respect to the wind direction relative to the aircraft.

Used properly, the correct control positions will prevent the wind lifting the 'up-wind' wing. This possibility is a particular danger when the aircraft is experiencing a quartering tailwind. In strong winds reduce taxying speed and make all turns slowly.

The correct control column position, relative to the wind, will aid safe taxying.

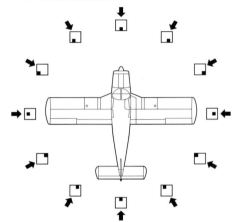

[■] Position of control column in cockpit

➡ Wind direction

Turning away from a crosswind–i.e. turning left when there is a crosswind from the right–may be difficult as the aircraft will be trying to weathercock back into wind. Exercise extreme caution if the wind speed exceeds half the aircraft's stalling speed. Better still, avoid taxying until the wind speed has reduced.

It is good practice to use the recommended control positions even when the winds are light. This will help you appreciate the wind direction, which is important during take-off. It also helps you to develop good habits which will be useful if you do taxy in stronger winds.

When making turns with a tailwind, taxy slowly and use the correct control column position. A 'quartering tailwind' will try to lift a wing, especially when turning.

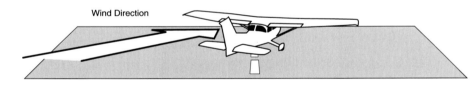

Wind Direction

▶ Effects of Ground Surface

The slope and type of ground surface will have a marked effect on the control of the aircraft whilst taxying.

A downslope increases taxying speed so less power is required, while taxying up a slope requires more power. Anticipate these effects to maintain a consistent taxying speed.

Taxying on hard surfaces requires less power than taxying on a grass surface. Avoid long grass, which may hide obstructions or holes. Try to avoid gravel or loose stones which can cause damage to the propeller and airframe, especially at high power settings.

Taxying

When crossing from one surface type to another (e.g. concrete to grass), the aircraft should be positioned to cross at an angle of about 45°, moving as slowly as possible and using the minimum power required to keep moving. These actions will minimise stress on the undercarriage and avoid the nose pitching up and down with the consequent risk of the propeller striking the ground.

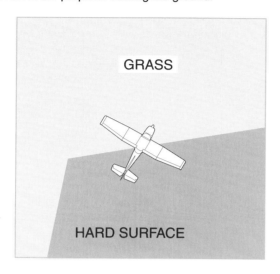

When crossing from one surface type to another, cross at a 45° angle, as slowly as possible, using the minimum power necessary

▶ Apron and Manoeuvring Area Markings

Some of the more common markings as illustrated below:

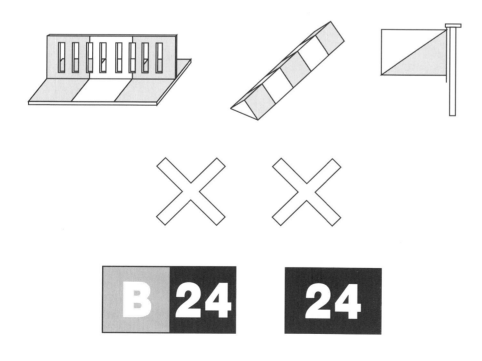

Orange/white marker boards or flags are placed at the boundary of an area where it is unsafe to taxy

Two or more white crosses mark a disused taxiway or runway.

A marker board with two digits identifies a runway (in this case runway 24).Taxiways and holding points are identified with a letter at larger airfields. On the left holding point B (Bravo) for runway 24 is illustrated.

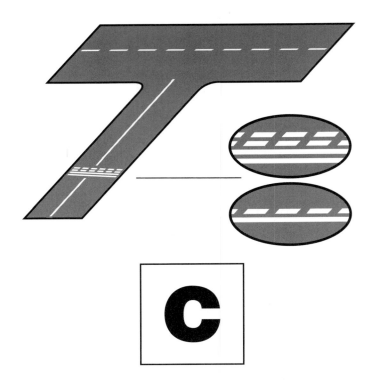

The holding point for a runway may have these taxiway markings. The lines can be single or double.

A black C on a yellow square indicates the point to which visiting pilots should report on arrival.

▶ Marshalling Signals

You may find yourself being given marshalling signals, usually to a parking bay at the end of a flight. A few of the common signals are illustrated below:

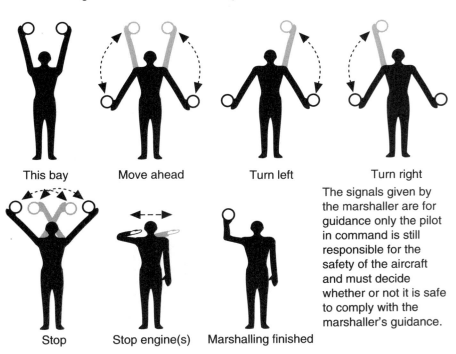

This bay   Move ahead   Turn left   Turn right

Stop   Stop engine(s)   Marshalling finished

The signals given by the marshaller are for guidance only the pilot in command is still responsible for the safety of the aircraft and must decide whether or not it is safe to comply with the marshaller's guidance.

▶ATC Light Signals

It is unlikely that you will see light signals being used, except in the event of a radio failure. The principal light signals to an aircraft on the ground are:

Light Signal	Meaning to Aircraft on Ground
STEADY RED	Stop.
GREEN FLASHES	Authorised to taxi at pilot's discretion.
WHITE FLASHES	Return to starting point on aerodrome.

▶Rights of Way on the Ground

There are certain rules concerning rights of way and priority of traffic on the ground. Notwithstanding these rules and any ATC instructions, it is ultimately the responsibility of the pilot to avoid collisions. The pilot in command is responsible for the safety of the aircraft and for not allowing it to endanger others.

Order of Priorities on the Ground:

1. Aircraft landing and taking off

2. Aircraft being towed

3. Aircraft taxying

4. Vehicles and pedestrians.

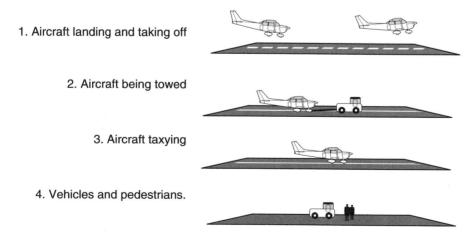

So, an aircraft taxying has
priority over vehicles and pedestrians, but gives way to an aircraft being towed and to aircraft taking off and landing.

When aircraft with the same priority are near each other, they shall avoid collision thus:

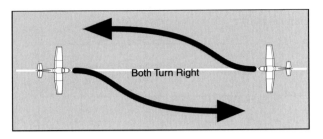

Where two aircraft are approaching head-on, each aircraft shall alter course to the right.

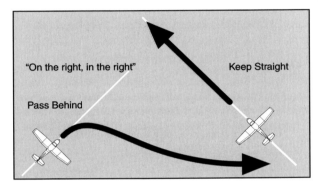

Where two aircraft are converging, the aircraft on the right has right of way "on the right, in the right".

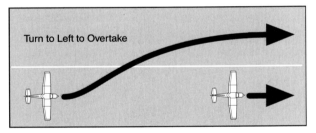

An aircraft overtaking another on the ground shall alter course to the left.

▶ Rudder Check

On aircraft which have rudder pedals linked directly to the nosewheel, it is not possible to check freedom of rudder movement when the aircraft is stationary. A rudder check can be carried out when taxying. The aircraft must be clear of other aircraft and obstructions and have an area wide enough to allow full rudder deflection to be applied. The aircraft should only be moving slowly when this check is being carried out. Differential braking should not be used during the rudder check.

▶Instrument Checks

When turning during taxying, four of the flight instruments can be checked. Your instructor will demonstrate how to check:

The turn indicator (or turn coordinator) including the balance ball

The attitude indicator (or artificial horizon)

The heading indicator (or direction indicator)

The compass

The instrument checks are usually carried out in the normal turns of the taxyway, each of the four instruments is checked in a left-hand and right-hand turn.

Flight Exercise

▷ PURPOSE

During this exercise you will learn to manoeuvre the aircraft safely on the ground.

▷ AIRMANSHIP

Lookout

Before moving off, always check that the aircraft will be able to manoeuvre safely. Maintain a good lookout whilst taxying - especially when near runways, active or not. Always visually check before crossing or entering a runway even after you have received ATC clearance. Always lookout before changing direction.

ATC Liaison

At an airfield with an Air Traffic Service Unit (ATSU), obtain taxying instructions before beginning to taxy. Have an airfield chart to hand for orientation and do not hesitate to ask for help if you are unsure of a instruction or clearance (or if you get lost!).

Brake Check

Check the brakes in the first few feet of taxying and give your instructor the opportunity to check the operation of his toe brakes. The brakes should also be checked before entering a parking area or confined space.

Exercise

5

Taxying

Moving Off

Taxying

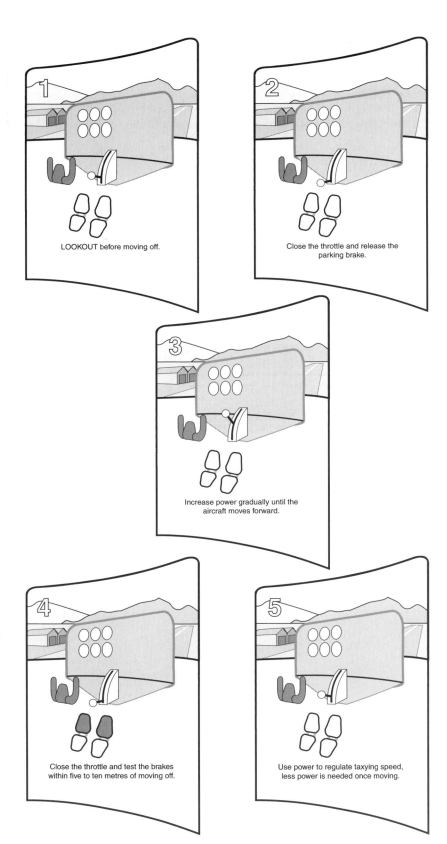

1. LOOKOUT before moving off.

2. Close the throttle and release the parking brake.

3. Increase power gradually until the aircraft moves forward.

4. Close the throttle and test the brakes within five to ten metres of moving off.

5. Use power to regulate taxying speed, less power is needed once moving.

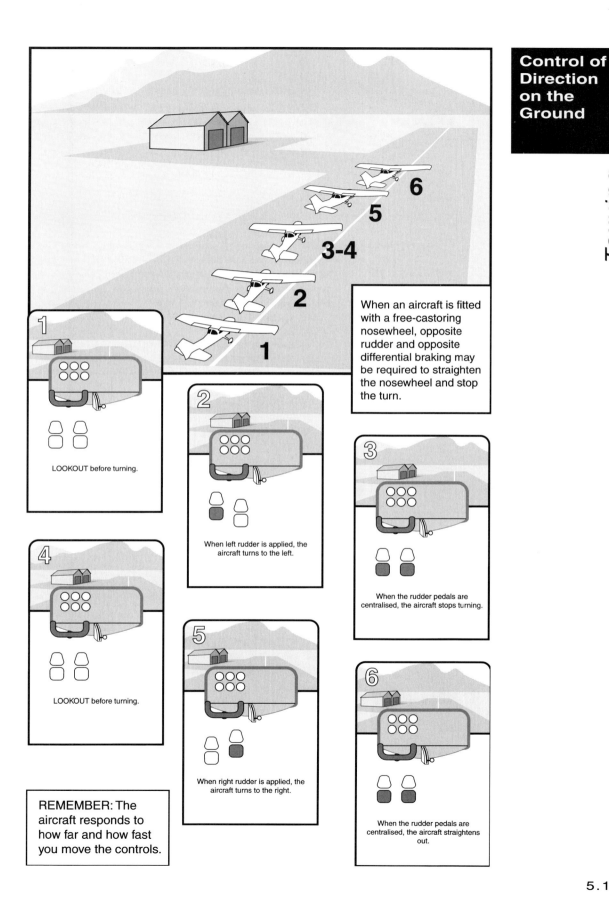

6

5

3-4

2

1

When an aircraft is fitted with a free-castoring nosewheel, opposite rudder and opposite differential braking may be required to straighten the nosewheel and stop the turn.

1

LOOKOUT before turning.

2

When left rudder is applied, the aircraft turns to the left.

3

When the rudder pedals are centralised, the aircraft stops turning.

4

LOOKOUT before turning.

5

When right rudder is applied, the aircraft turns to the right.

6

When the rudder pedals are centralised, the aircraft straightens out.

REMEMBER: The aircraft responds to how far and how fast you move the controls.

Use of Differential Braking

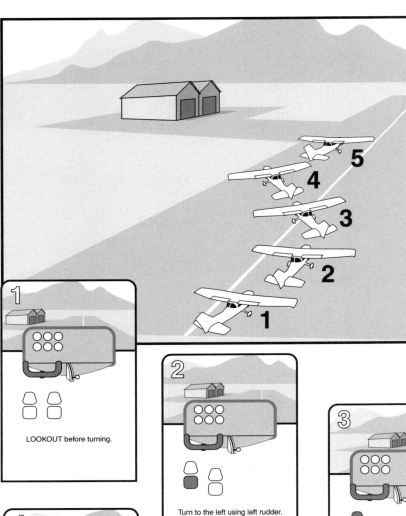

1
LOOKOUT before turning.

2
Turn to the left using left rudder.

3
Use the left brake to tighten the turn and reduce the turning circle.

4
Centralise the rudder pedals and release the brake to stop the turn.

5
Use right rudder and brake to return to the original heading.

When an aircraft is fitted with a free-castoring nosewheel, opposite rudder and opposite differential braking may be required to straighten out of a turn.

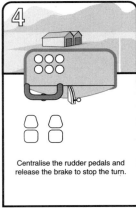

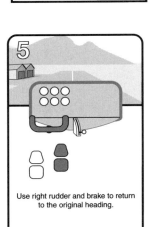

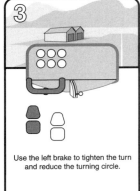

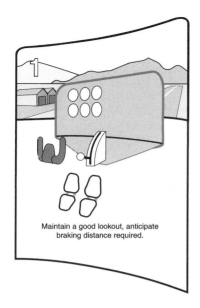

Maintain a good lookout, anticipate braking distance required.

To stop, close the throttle, then apply the brakes evenly.

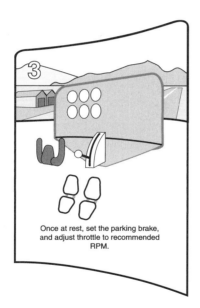

Once at rest, set the parking brake, and adjust throttle to recommended RPM.

Note: the aircraft should always be stopped with the nose wheel straight.

Conclusion

When this exercise has been completed, which will take several flight exercises, you should:

- be able to manoeuvre the aircraft safely on a variety of surfaces and in a variety of wind conditions.

- appreciate some of the essential precautions and checks required when taxying.

- understand some basic signals and right of way rules.

Taxying Emergencies

Although emergencies during taxying are very rare, there are three types of emergencies the pilot should be ready to cope with:

▶ **Steering Failure**

▶ **Brake Failure**

▶ **Emergency Stop.**

Background Briefing

▶ Steering Failure

In the event of a steering failure, the pilot should still have a degree of directional control through the use of the rudder and differential braking (where available). Stop the aircraft and request assistance.

▶ Brake Failure

Brake failure is an unlikely event. If brake failure does occur there will usually have been some warning signs or indications of an impending problem. If the brakes do fail the first priority should be to steer clear of any obstructions, close the throttle, and look for an open space in which the aircraft can come to a halt. If it is not possible to avoid obstructions, the fuel, engine and electrical systems should be shut down immediately and the aircraft steered to lessen the force of the impact - avoid a head-on collision with a solid obstruction.

▶ Emergency Stop

If an emergency stop is necessary, close the throttle and apply the brakes evenly, hard enough to stop the aircraft without locking the main wheels. Taxying fast, with a strong tailwind, on a slippery surface (i.e. wet grass, slush, ice), down a slope or through standing water will all increase the braking distance and increase the possibility of one or both main wheels locking under heavy braking.

Conclusion
You will practice emergencies throughout your flying training and should always remain alert to the possibility of a problem while taxying.

Straight and Level Flight

Thanks to the natural stability of the aircraft, straight and level flight is not difficult, especially once the aircraft has been correctly trimmed. That said, to fly straight and level accurately does take practice and the ability to fly properly straight and level consistently will take time to achieve.

This exercise is often divided into two flights. The first practises straight and level flight at the normal cruising speed, the second practises straight and level flight at differing airspeeds.

BACKGROUND BRIEFING

▶ **The Four Forces Acting on an Aircraft in Flight**

▶ **Equilibrium**

▶ **Lift and Factors Affecting Lift**

▶ **Drag and Factors Affecting Drag**

▶ **Stability in Pitch**

▶ **Stability in Roll**

▶ **Stability in Yaw**

▶ **Power + Attitude = Performance**

▶ **Slow Safe Cruise**

▶ **Maximum-Range Airspeed**

▶ **Maximum-Endurance Airspeed**

FLIGHT EXERCISE

Exercise

6

Straight and Level Flight

FLIGHT EXERCISE

▷ **Purpose**

▷ **Airmanship**

▷ **To Maintain Constant Altitude**

▷ **To Maintain Constant Direction**

▷ **To Maintain Balanced Flight**

▷ **At an Increased Airspeed**

▷ **At a Decreased Airspeed**

▷ **Slow Safe Cruise**

CONCLUSION

BACKGROUND BRIEFING

▶ The Four Forces Acting on an Aircraft in Flight

The principal four forces acting on an aircraft in flight are:

Weight The weight of the aircraft always acts vertically down.

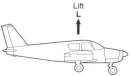

Weight

W

Lift Most of the lift is created by the airflow around the wings.

Lift
L

The four principal forces acting on an aircraft in flight

Thrust Thrust is provided by the engine through the propeller.

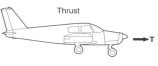

Thrust

→T

Drag Drag is the resistance to the passage of the aircraft through the air.

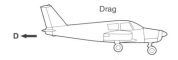

Drag

D ←

▶ Equilibrium

When an aircraft is in straight and level unaccelerated flight,

> Lift is equal and opposite to Weight

> Thrust is equal and opposite to Drag.

If the forces are not in equilibrium, the aircraft will not fly truly straight and level at a constant speed.

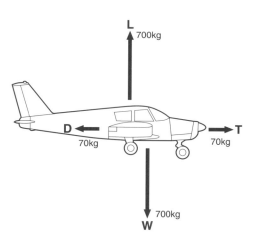

L 700kg

D ← 70kg

T → 70kg

700kg
W

The four forces when an aircraft is in straight and level, unaccelerated flight

▶ Lift and Factors Affecting Lift

Lift is created by the airflow around the wings.

The airflow meeting the wing is often referred to as the *relative airflow*. For practical purposes lift acts at about 90° to the relative airflow.

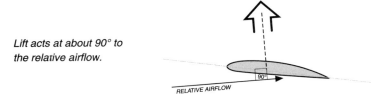

Lift acts at about 90° to the relative airflow.

The angle at which the relative airflow meets the wing is called the *angle of attack*.

There are several factors affecting the amount of lift produced by the wings. The main two factors controlled by the pilot are the airspeed and the angle of attack.

The airspeed is literally the speed of the aircraft through the air. A faster airspeed implies a faster airflow around the wings, and more lift is produced if all other factors remain the same. A slower airspeed implies that less lift is produced.

The amount of lift produced by the wing is also determined by the angle of attack. The wing of an average light aircraft produces lift over an angle of attack range

The angle of attack is the angle at which the airflow meets the wing.

from about -2° to +14°. The greater the angle of attack, the greater the lift produced until the critical angle (about 14°) is exceeded. Typically, in cruising flight the angle of attack will be about 4°.

So if an aircraft is flying at a fast airspeed, only a small angle of attack is needed to produce the lift necessary to maintain level flight. At a slower airspeed, a much greater angle of attack is needed to produce the required lift.

As the airspeed is changed, so the angle of attack must be changed to produce the same amount of lift.

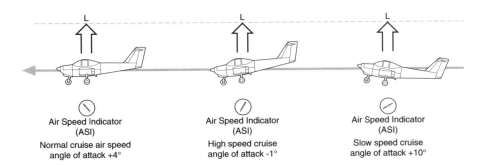

The concept of angle of attack is an important one to grasp. There is no instrument in a light aircraft to measure the angle of attack, and it is not necessarily the same angle as the aircraft's pitch attitude. However, changing the aircraft's attitude does alter the angle of attack in the same sense, i.e. pitching the aircraft nose down reduces the angle of attack.

►Drag and Factors Affecting Drag

Drag is the resistance to the passage of the aircraft through the air. There are two elements of drag; *parasite* drag and *induced* drag.

Parasite drag affects any moving object (i.e. a car). The faster the aircraft moves through the air, the greater the parasite drag - and vice versa.

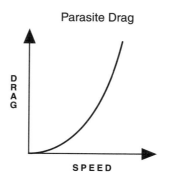

Parasite Drag

Parasite drag increases as airspeed increases.

Induced drag is related to the angle of attack. As an aircraft flies more slowly, and so has to fly at a greater angle of attack to maintain level flight, the amount of induced drag increases.

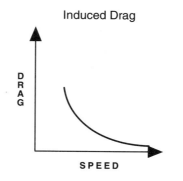

Induced Drag

Induced drag decreases as airspeed increases.

Drag acts parallel to the flight path, through a point that varies with the aircraft's attitude and configuration.

Total Drag =
Parasite Drag +
Induced Drag

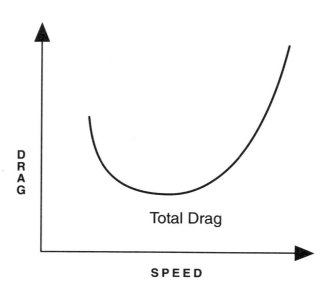

Total Drag

Change of total drag with airspeed.

▶ Stability in Pitch

The stability of the aircraft in pitch is largely determined by the arrangement of the lift and weight forces.

Most aircraft are designed to be stable in pitch. This is done by arranging the forces in such a way that weight acts through a point (the centre of gravity) that is ahead of the centre of the lift force. The couple between the lift and weight forces exerts a pitch down force, which is instrumental in making the aircraft stable in pitch.

The result of the couple between the lift and weight is a pitch-down force.

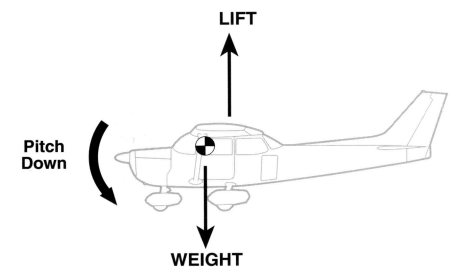

You will recall from exercise 4 that there is also a couple between the thrust and drag forces, which exerts a pitch-up force.

The result of the couple between thrust and drag is a pitch-up force.

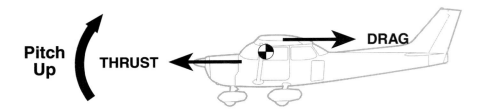

In practice, the thrust/drag couple is not strong enough to counterbalance the lift/weight couple and the aircraft is left with a residual pitch down force.

This pitch-down force is balanced by the tailplane or stabilator. The tailplane or stabilator can produce lift either up or down. Where there is a pitch-down effect, the tailplane will produce a downforce to balance the strong lift/weight couple.

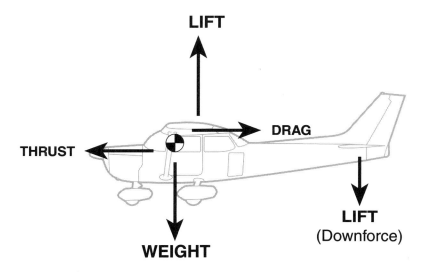

LIFT

DRAG

THRUST

LIFT
(Downforce)

WEIGHT

The 'balance' needed to make the aircraft stable in pitch is provided by the tailplane/stabilator.

The tailplane also aids stability in pitch if the aircraft meets a wind gust or some turbulence. If a gust causes the nose to rise, for example, the tailplane (or stabilator) will meet the airflow at a greater angle. Therefore it will produce less down-force (or more lift up) and cause the aircraft to pitch-down, back to its original attitude.

The position of the centre of gravity is a key factor in ensuring stability in pitch. The CG position varies with aircraft loading (i.e. passengers, fuel, baggage etc) and can be calculated by the pilot from the information provided in the aircraft's POH/FM. The POH/FM will state the forward and rear limits for the Centre of Gravity (CG) position.

THE AIRCRAFT MUST NEVER BE FLOWN WITH A CG POSITION OUTSIDE THE STATED LIMITS.

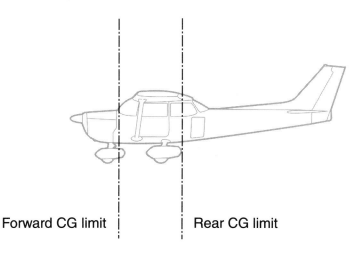

Forward CG limit | Rear CG limit

Every aircraft has a permitted forward and rear CG limit.

When the CG is close to the forward edge of its permitted limit there will be a long lever arm between the CG and the tailplane. This will make the aircraft very stable as a result of the increased leverage the tailplane force exerts.

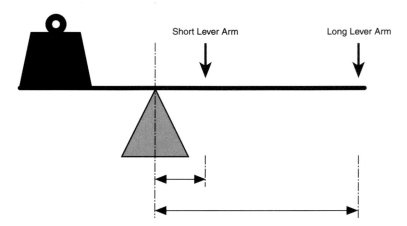

The longer the lever arm, the greater the leverage applied.

If, however, the CG is forward (fore) of its permitted limit the aircraft will become overstable and the pilot will have difficulty in manoeuvring. In an extreme case the aircraft may become uncontrollably nose heavy, especially at slow airspeeds when the tailplane is less effective, and the pilot may be unable to prevent it pitching nose down.

A forward CG gives the tailplane a long lever arm, so it has a strong leverage.

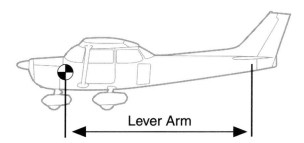

When the CG is close to the permitted rear (aft) limit there is a shorter lever arm between the CG and the tailplane. This will make the aircraft less stable and easier to manoeuvre.

If the CG is behind (aft of) the rear limit the aircraft will become unstable and difficult to control. It will seem tail-heavy and the pilot may be unable to prevent the aircraft pitching nose-up.

A rearward CG gives the tailplane a short lever arm, so it has a reduced leverage.

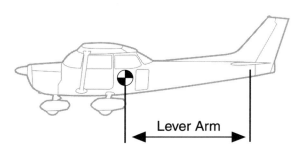

It is obviously important to ensure that the CG will be within its permitted limits throughout the flight. Not surprisingly, flying an aircraft when its CG is outside the permitted limits is illegal as well as highly dangerous. You will come to appreciate that in most light aircraft it is simply not possible to fill the aircraft with full fuel, full passenger load and full baggage load, and remain within the permitted CG range.

▶Stability in Roll

Stability in roll is largely provided by the angle of the wings to the horizontal - the *dihedral* angle.

Dihedral

The angle of the wings to the horizontal is the dihedral angle.

When an aircraft is in straight flight, but not wings-level, the sideways components of lift and weight cause the aircraft to slip towards the lower wing.

The airflow now meets the lower wing at a greater angle of attack than the higher wing. Therefore increased lift is produced from the lower wing, returning the aircraft to wings level flight.

Higher Wing
Reduced Angle of Attack
and Reduced Lift

Lower Wing
Greater Angle of Attack
and Increased Lift

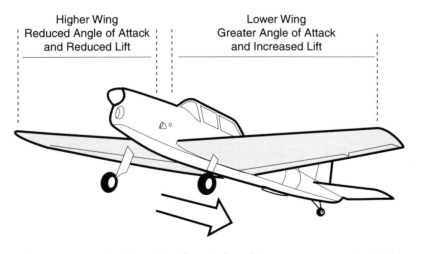

As the aircraft slips toward the lower wing, the lower wing has a higher angle of attack than the higher wing and produces greater lift - rolling the aircraft level

As you become more familiar with different aircraft types you may notice that low-wing aircraft tend to have more dihedral than high-wing aircraft. The CG position in a high-wing aircraft (below the wing) gives it greater natural stability in roll, and so it needs less dihedral. However, the reason for the greater roll stability of high-wing aircraft is subject to endless debate and countless opinions and theories, that are best left unexplored for now.

▶ Stability in Yaw

Stability in yaw is provided by the fin. When an aircraft skids (yaws) through the air, the airflow meets the fin at an angle (i.e. an angle of attack), which causes the fin to produce lift sideways. This pivots the aircraft around the CG to yaw the aircraft into the airflow and out of the skid.

The fin gives the aircraft stability in yaw

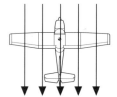

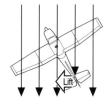

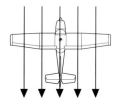

▶ Power + Attitude = Performance

Performance can be measured in terms of airspeed and rate of climb (or rate of descent). Airspeed is controlled through the control column (controlling the attitude). The rate of climb or rate of descent is controlled through the throttle (setting the power). This is an important point so it is worth repeating:

power controls altitude (or height)

attitude controls airspeed

To maintain level flight, the pilot sets the power required for level flight and adjusts the attitude to attain the correct airspeed. If the airspeed is correct but the aircraft is descending, more power is required. Conversely if the airspeed is correct but the aircraft is climbing, less power is required.

For each manoeuvre there is a power setting and attitude that should result in the desired performance

 POWER

+

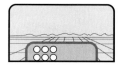 **ATTITUDE**

=

 PERFORMANCE

During the flight exercise you will come to recognise the correct attitude and normal cruise power setting to maintain level flight at the normal cruise airspeed. You will also come to appreciate the need to adjust both the pitch attitude and power setting to maintain level flight at different airspeeds.

It is also worth noting that if the aircraft is fitted with a fixed-pitch propeller (which most training aircraft are) a change in airspeed will induce a small change to the engine RPM. Think of the fixed-pitch propeller as a car engine with only one fixed gear, the car moves faster the engine RPM increases, even without any movement of the throttle. Conversely as the car (or aircraft) moves more slowly, the engine RPM decreases. The significance of this is that if increasing or decreasing airspeed significantly, it will often be necessary to make further minor corrections with the throttle to maintain the target RPM.

▶ Slow Safe Cruise

During the flight exercise you will practice cruise at a slower than normal airspeed, - usually with one stage of flap selected down (initial flap). This speed is known as *slow safe cruise.* The use of flap allows a lower nose attitude (improving the view ahead) and by reducing the stall speed, use of flap ensures that safe margin of airspeed remains between the slower cruising speed and the stall airspeed.

Slow safe cruise has several applications, apart from occasions when the pilot just wishes to fly more slowly than normal cruise. In a situation where a pilot is uncertain of position, for instance, flying at slow safe cruise would make sense - giving more time to locate the position while using less fuel. Likewise, if bad weather (i.e. poor visibility and/or low cloud base) has made navigation more difficult, slow safe cruise will make map reading easier.

It is preferable, of course, to avoid getting lost or flying into bad weather in the first place - prevention being better than cure.

▶ Maximum-Range Airspeed

At the maximum-range airspeed, the aircraft will fly the maximum distance for a given fuel load. There are many factors affecting best-range airspeed such as aerodynamic efficiency, engine power, propeller design, air density etc., we are not going to delve deeply into the subject here.

Theoretically the maximum-range airspeed is the airspeed at which there is the minimum drag. In practice the maximum-range airspeed is a compromise between airframe (aerodynamic) considerations and engine (power) considerations. The aircraft's POH/FM will have a section detailing techniques and figures for maximum-range flying and the pilot should refer to this.

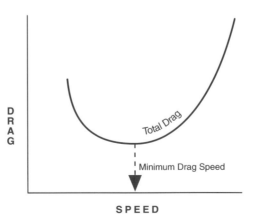

Theoretical maximum range airspeed is the minimum drag airspeed.

Maximum range = Maximum distance for the fuel load.

▶ Maximum-Endurance Airspeed

At the maximum-endurance airspeed the aircraft will be able to stay airborne for the maximum time with a given fuel load. However, as the maximum-endurance airspeed will be slower than the best-range airspeed, the aircraft cannot travel as far with its given fuel load, even though it is in the air for longer.

It is therefore important not to confuse endurance with range.

There are many factors which affect the best-endurance airspeed. Theoretically the best-endurance airspeed is the airspeed at which the minimum power is required to maintain level flight. Again, in practice, the pilot should refer to the aircraft's POH/FM.

Maximum endurance = Maximum airborne time for the fuel load.

Theoretical maximum endurance airspeed is the minimum power required airspeed.

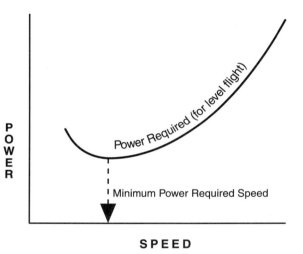

Power Required = Airspeed x Drag

Flight Exercise

▷ PURPOSE

To learn to fly the aircraft at a constant altitude, in a constant direction, at a specified airspeed, with the aircraft in balance.

▷ AIRMANSHIP

VFE

When using flap during this exercise, ensure the airspeed is below the flap limiting speed (i.e. VFE), that is, the airspeed is within the white arc marked on the airspeed indicator. Do not lower or raise flap if the airspeed is faster than VFE, or allow the airspeed to exceed VFE whilst flap is lowered.

Location

By the end of this flight exercise you should be finding it easier to spot the local-area landmarks pointed out by your instructor. Begin now to develop the habit of keeping a mental picture of your position in relation to the airfield. You should soon be able to find your own way back to it and have a good idea of your location within the local training area at all times.

Lookout

Lookout is covered in detail in the supplement to this exercise. Having successfully spotted traffic that may conflict with your aircraft, you should be aware of the proper rules of the air to avoid collisions. When aircraft are converging and are of different classes, the following priorities apply:

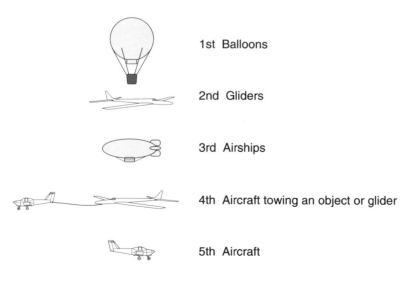

1st Balloons

2nd Gliders

3rd Airships

4th Aircraft towing an object or glider

5th Aircraft

Flight Exercise

It is the duty of the aircraft commander to take all possible measures to avoid a collision. In particular an aircraft must not fly so close to another aircraft as to create the danger of a collision and aircraft will not fly in formation unless the commanders have agreed to do so. Indeed you should never attempt to fly in formation with another aircraft until you have received proper instruction in formation flying. The aircraft that is obliged to give way shall avoid passing below or above the other aircraft or ahead of it unless well clear. Specifically, to avoid collisions:

Rights of Way in the Air and Collision Avoidance

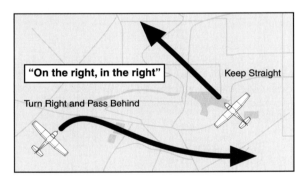

Both Turn Right

Where two aircraft are approaching head on - each aircraft shall alter course to the right.

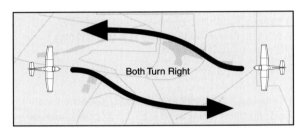

"On the right, in the right"

Keep Straight

Turn Right and Pass Behind

Where two aircraft are converging, the aircraft on the right has right of way (on the right, in the right).

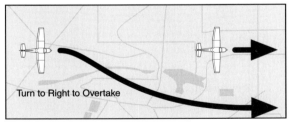

Turn to Right to Overtake

An aircraft overtaking another in the air shall alter course to the right.

Straight and Level

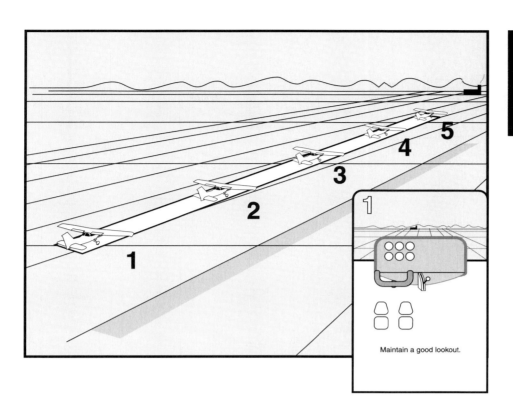

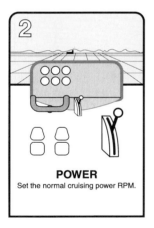

Maintain a good lookout.

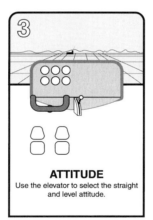

POWER
Set the normal cruising power RPM.

ATTITUDE
Use the elevator to select the straight
and level attitude.

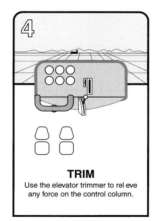

TRIM
Use the elevator trimmer to rel eve
any force on the control column.

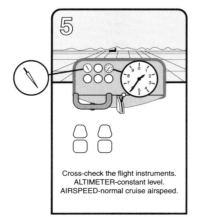

Cross-check the flight instruments.
ALTIMETER-constant level.
AIRSPEED-normal cruise airspeed.

To summarise:
POWER
ATTITUDE
TRIM
-Cross-check altimeter
and airspeed indicator.
-Make minor corrections
as necessary.
LOOKOUT

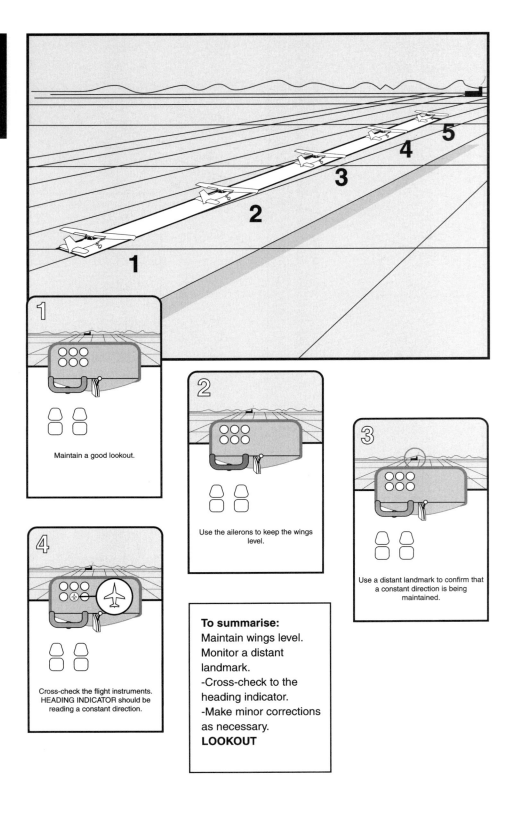

1 Maintain a good lookout.

2 Use the ailerons to keep the wings level.

3 Use a distant landmark to confirm that a constant direction is being maintained.

4 Cross-check the flight instruments. HEADING INDICATOR should be reading a constant direction.

To summarise:
Maintain wings level.
Monitor a distant landmark.
-Cross-check to the heading indicator.
-Make minor corrections as necessary.
LOOKOUT

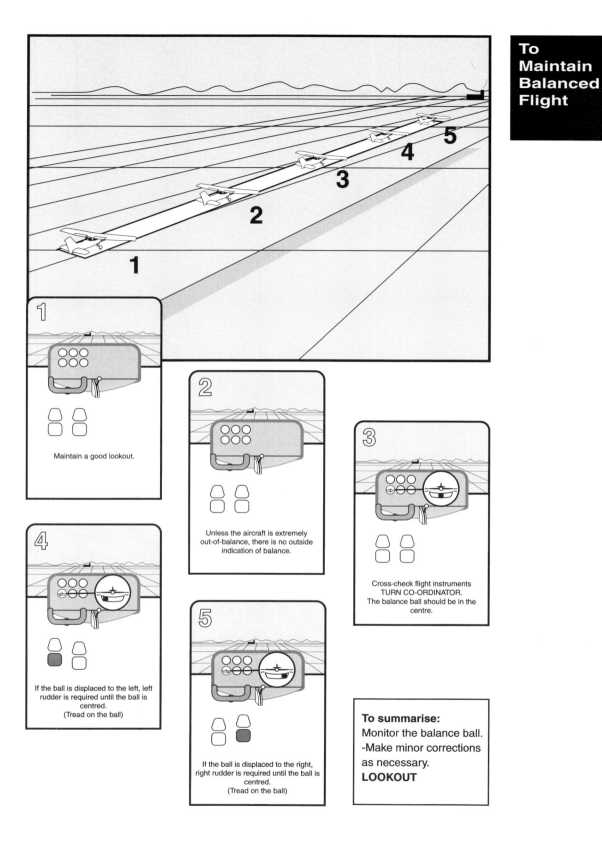

1 Maintain a good lookout.

2 Unless the aircraft is extremely out-of-balance, there is no outside indication of balance.

3 Cross-check flight instruments TURN CO-ORDINATOR. The balance ball should be in the centre.

4 If the ball is displaced to the left, left rudder is required until the ball is centred. (Tread on the ball)

5 If the ball is displaced to the right, right rudder is required until the ball is centred. (Tread on the ball)

To summarise:
Monitor the balance ball.
-Make minor corrections as necessary.
LOOKOUT

Straight and Level

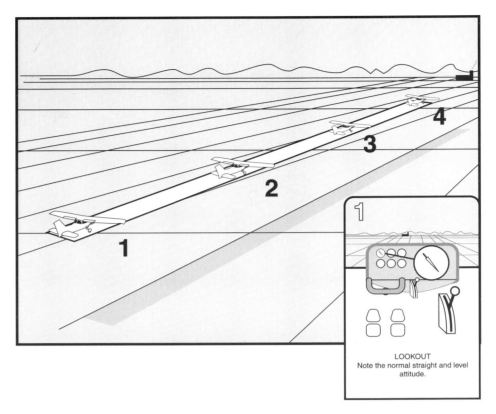

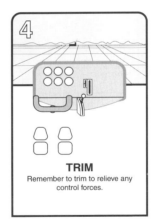

LOOKOUT
Note the normal straight and level attitude.

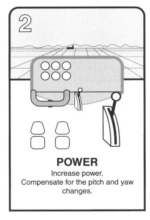

POWER
Increase power.
Compensate for the pitch and yaw changes.

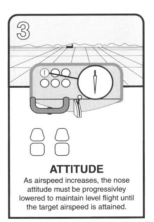

ATTITUDE
As airspeed increases, the nose attitude must be progressivley lowered to maintain level flight until the target airspeed is attained.

TRIM
Remember to trim to relieve any control forces.

To summarise:
POWER
ATTITUDE
TRIM
-Cross-check altimeter
and airspeed indicator.
-Make minor corrections
as necessary.
LOOKOUT

Straight and Level

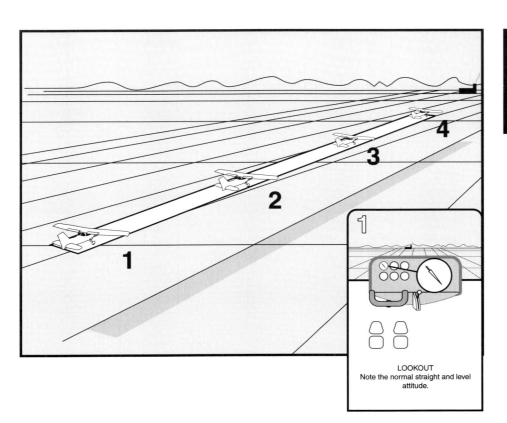

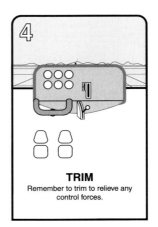

1

LOOKOUT
Note the normal straight and level
attitude.

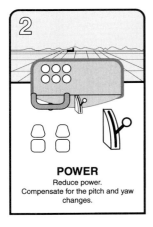

POWER
Reduce power.
Compensate for the pitch and yaw
changes.

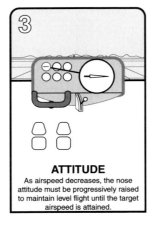

ATTITUDE
As airspeed decreases, the nose
attitude must be progressively raised
to maintain level flight until the target
airspeed is attained.

TRIM
Remember to trim to relieve any
control forces.

To summarise:
POWER
ATTITUDE
TRIM
-Cross-check altimeter
and airspeed indicator.
-Make minor corrections
as necessary.
LOOKOUT

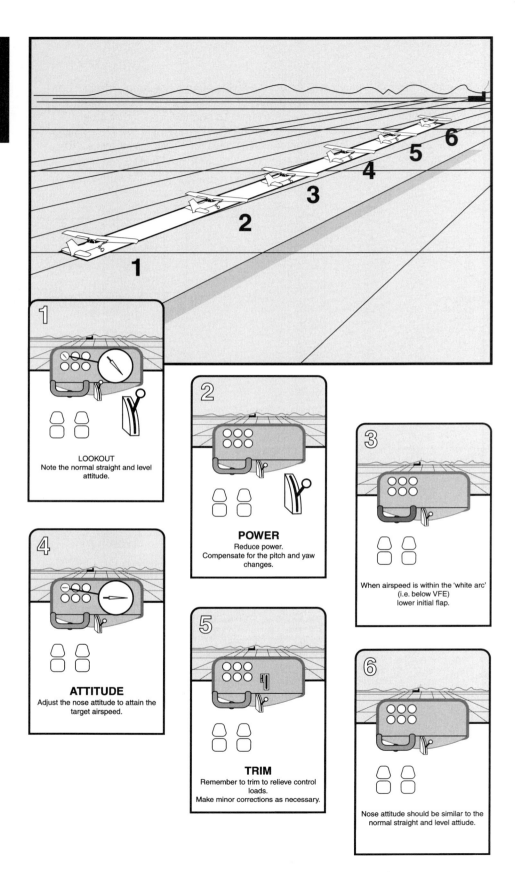

1

LOOKOUT
Note the normal straight and level attitude.

2

POWER
Reduce power.
Compensate for the pitch and yaw changes.

3

When airspeed is within the 'white arc' (i.e. below VFE) lower initial flap.

4

ATTITUDE
Adjust the nose attitude to attain the target airspeed.

5

TRIM
Remember to trim to relieve control loads.
Make minor corrections as necessary.

6

Nose attitude should be similar to the normal straight and level attitude.

Conclusion

By the end of this exercise you will be able to fly the aircraft accurately straight and level at a variety of airspeeds and in a variety of configurations. You will appreciate the design features which contribute to the aircraft's stability. You will also be developing your personal preferred lookout scan method, learning the landmarks of your local area and beginning to know the basic rules for collision avoidance. You will be able to practise straight and level flight every time you fly from now on.

Lookout Supplement 1

Even at this early stage you will have noticed how often lookout has been referred to as a point of good airmanship. Lookout is a very good example of what is meant by airmanship. It is quite possible to fly the aircraft on a clear day barely looking outside at all - but it's hardly safe!

Like any other flying skill, lookout has to be taught and constantly practised to stay proficient, and like other flying skills it may come into its own when you least expect it.

Whilst you are concentrating on mastering the basic flying manoeuvres, you may feel you have more than enough workload; however, you will find that your flying becomes easier and more enjoyable if you lookout first and scan the instruments second. For now a few basic pointers and techniques to help you develop your lookout scan.

1 Concentrate your scan in certain areas.

Concentrate your scan in an area between 10° above and below the horizon, 60° either side of straight-ahead.

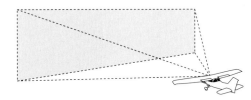

Obviously you need to lookout all around the aircraft, but the greatest threat is in an area between 10° up and 10° down and 60° either side of straight ahead. Look UP before beginning a climb, DOWN before beginning a descent and OVER YOUR SHOULDER before turning.

2 Focus on distant objects.

When the eyes are not specifically focused on an object, they naturally focus a few metres ahead - not the best place to spot an approaching aircraft! Be sure to focus on something distant such as the horizon, or a cloud, when scanning.

3 Develop a scanning technique.

Simply staring straight ahead, or just occasionally glancing around, is no substitute for a proper lookout scan. Your instructor may have a preferred scan method–there is no one way to scan, just find a method that suits you. Remember the eyes will only be able to detect a target when they are still, so trying to move your eyes smoothly around the sky will not aid look out. Here are two possible scanning methods:

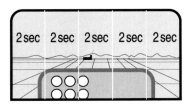

Block method

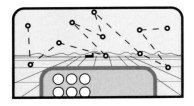

Wandering method

4 Constant bearing = constant danger.

When an aircraft is on a collision course with yours, it is most likely to appear as a stationary dot on the windscreen, not moving across the field of vision - a constant relative bearing. The problem is obvious. A stationary dot does not attract attention, and can be difficult to detect until it suddenly becomes very large and very frightening! If you spot an aircraft and it appears to be moving relative to you, the chances are you are not on a collision course, although you will want to monitor it. Where the aircraft is not moving across the windscreen, there is a very real risk:

constant bearing = constant danger.

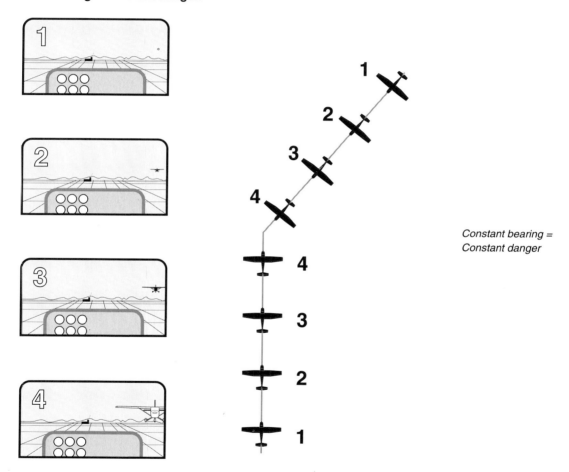

Constant bearing = Constant danger

constant bearing = constant danger.

5 Use the clock code.

When reporting traffic to someone else, or when traffic is reported to you, the *clock code* is used.

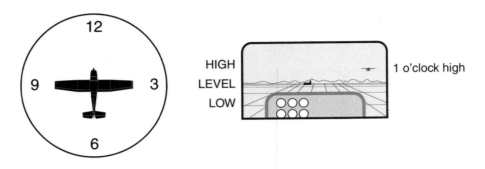

Straight ahead is 12 o'clock, behind is 6 o'clock, directly to the right is 3 o'clock etc. Traffic may also be qualified as being high, low or at the same level.

6 Keep the windscreen clean.

Do not fly with a windscreen that is covered with dead flies or smears. Ensure the windscreen is clean as part of your pre-flight check list.

7 Look after your eyes.

The military are not short of sophisticated equipment to detect and track other aircraft. Despite this, a study by the U.S. Navy Fighter Weapons School–Top Gun–no less, concluded that a pilot's eyes are the most important target-detection sensor.

Tiredness, smoking or illness will all reduce your eyes' performance. If you need glasses or contact lenses for far-field vision–use them. Sunglasses do not specifically help, unless glare is strong enough to hurt your eyes and make you squint.

Climbing

Having covered one basic flight manoeuvre—straight and level flight—we now move on to climbing. Initially you will practise climbing at the best rate of climb airspeed. Later (usually during a second flight exercise) you will climb at different airspeeds and in different configurations (i.e. using flap) and practise climbing at the best angle of climb airspeed. During the flight exercise the importance of good airspeed control becomes apparent and some of the lessons you learnt in exercise 4 will re-surface, e.g. effects of controls at slower airspeed, effects of increased power, effect of slipstream, etc. Logically enough, the flight exercise for climbing is combined with the flight exercise for descending.

BACKGROUND BRIEFING

▶ Forces in the Climb

▶ The Best Rate-of-Climb Airspeed

▶ Effect of Flap

▶ Effect of Altitude

▶ Effect of Weight

▶ The Best Angle-of-Climb Airspeed

▶ The Cruise-Climb

▶ Effect of Wind

▶ Engine Considerations

FLIGHT EXERCISE

Exercise

7

Climbing

FLIGHT EXERCISE

▷ **Purpose**

▷ **Airmanship**

▷ **Entering the Climb**

▷ **Maintaining the Climb**

▷ **Levelling Off**

▷ **The Effect of Flap**

▷ **Best Angle of Climb**

▷ **Cruise-Climb**

CONCLUSION

BACKGROUND BRIEFING

▶ Forces in the Climb

During a climb, the four forces described in Exercise 6 (straight and level flight) are of course still acting on the aircraft. However, the relationship is changed. Thrust and drag still act parallel to the flight path of the aircraft, and lift still acts at around 90° to the relative airflow. However, weight continues to act vertically towards the centre of the earth and so is no longer completely balanced by lift.

In fact a component of weight is now acting in the same direction as drag, so that in the climb thrust has to balance drag and a component of weight. The steeper the climb, the greater the component of weight acting with drag and the greater the thrust needed for the aircraft to climb.

It follows that climbing performance is essentially dictated by the power of the engine. Although in a climb the aircraft is still producing lift, this is not the major factor in climb performance. In fact, in a climb lift may be less than weight, i.e. less than the lift produced during level flight.

In a sustained climb, thrust has to balance drag and a component of weight.

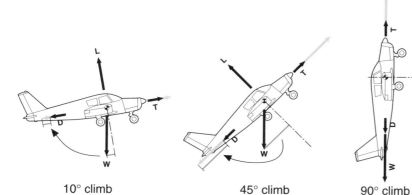

10° climb	45° climb	90° climb
T = D + 17% of weight	T = D + 71% of weight	T = D + W

The steeper the climb, the greater the component of weight acting with drag and so the greater the amount of thrust required to sustain the climb.

▶The Best rate of climb Airspeed

The best rate of climb airspeed will give the maximum increase in height in a given time. As you have seen, the climb performance of the aircraft is dictated by the engine power. The best rate of climb airspeed is the airspeed at which there is the maximum excess of power aviailable over power required.

The best rate of climb airspeed is the airspeed at which there is the greatest excess of power available over power required.

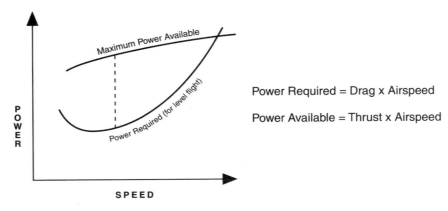

Power Required = Drag x Airspeed

Power Available = Thrust x Airspeed

The climbing performance of the aircraft and recommended climbing speeds will be found in the aircraft's POH/FM. The airspeed for the best rate of climb is referred to as Vy.

LEFT> Best rate-of-climb airspeed gives the maximum height gain in a given time.

RIGHT> The VSI reads rate-of-climb or rate-of-descent .

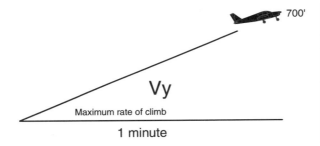

700'

Vy

Maximum rate of climb

1 minute

▶Effect of Flap

The effect of flap will depend on the aircraft type to a certain extent (i.e. the type of flap and certain aspects of the aircraft design the aircraft design).

During the flight exercise, flap is lowered during the climb and the original climb airspeed maintained. The extra drag created by the flaps lead to a decrease in the rate of climb. As more flap is lowered (intermediate to full flap) the further increase in drag further reduces the rate of climb. In fact, if the original climb airspeed is maintained some light aircraft may display little or no rate of climb once full flap is lowered.

Flap can be beneficial, however, when considering the best angle of climb. The use of initial flap allows a slower airspeed to be used in the climb, which may improve the climb gradient.

Climbing

Where flap can be beneficial in this way, details are found in the aircraft's POH/FM.

▶ Effect of Altitude

As altitude increases, the reduction in air density means that the power required increases but the power available decreases. This decrease in power available is true of a normally aspirated piston engine - which is the type of engine usually fitted to a light training aircraft. Where the engine is fitted with a turbocharger or supercharger, the engine will be able to maintain its maximum power output to a greater altitude.

With increasing altitude, the excess of power available over power required is reduced and occurs at a faster speed. Eventually the aircraft will reach an altitude where, even at full power, power available is equal to power required. In other words the aircraft can maintain level flight but cannot climb. This altitude is known as the aircraft's *absolute ceiling* and may be noted in the POH/FM. Another ceiling, the *performance* or *service ceiling*, may also be noted. This is the altitude at which rate of climb will become unacceptably low - less than 100fpm. For a training aircraft the service ceiling is generally a couple of thousand feet lower than the absolute ceiling.

For example, from a PA-38 Tomahawk POH/FM:

Service Ceiling - 12 000 ft

Absolute Ceiling - 14 000 ft

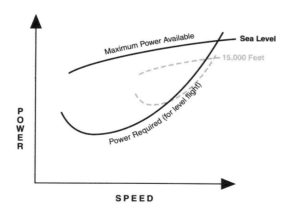

As altitude increases, air density reduces. Therefore engine power reduces, but the power required increases.

When the maximum power available = minimum power required, the aircraft cannot climb any higher and has reached its absolute ceiling.

▶ Effect of Weight

The effect of an increase in weight is much the same as the effect of an increase in altitude. Climb performance is reduced, a faster airspeed is required to maintain climb performance and eventually, if the aircraft is overloaded, it may not climb at all. The aircraft will have a certified maximum weight, and climb performance will be calculated using this weight. If the aircraft is overweight it will not be able to match the expected climb performance. As you would expect, overloading an aircraft so that its weight exceeds the permitted maximum is both highly dangerous and illegal.

▶The Best Angle of climb Airspeed

So far we have considered climbing performance in terms of rate of climb. The best angle of climb airspeed gives the maximum height gain over the shortest distance and in practice is used to clear obstacles. Best angle of climb occurs when there is the maximum excess of thrust over drag, which will be at a slower airspeed than the best rate of climb airspeed.

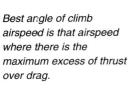

Best angle of climb airspeed is that airspeed where there is the maximum excess of thrust over drag.

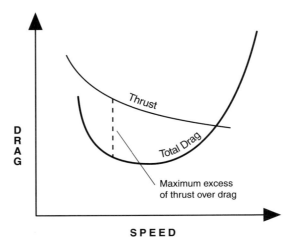

Where there is a practical difference between best angle of climb airspeed and best rate of climb airspeed, it will be detailed in the POH/FM. Best angle of climb (sometimes also referred to as best gradient of climb) airspeed is referred to as Vx.

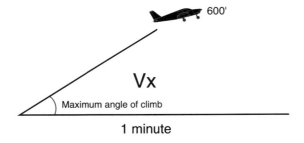

Best angle-of-climb airspeed gives the maximum height gain in a given distance.

Quite often the best angle of climb is achieved with initial flap extended–which allows the slower climb airspeed. This depends on aircraft type so check the aircraft's POH/FM for details. You will appreciate that obstacle clearance (for which the best angle of climb airspeed is used) is most vital immediately after take-off, so the POH/FM will often recommend the flap setting and airspeeds to be used to obtain the shortest take-off distance and the best angle of climb in the initial climb. Once the obstacles are safely cleared, the aircraft is accelerated to the best rate of climb airspeed and the flap is retracted.

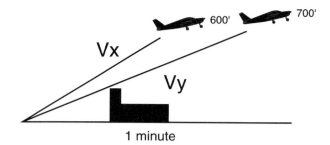

Airspeed Vx gives the best ANGLE of climb. Airspeed Vy gives the best RATE of climb.

▶ The Cruise Climb

Your instructor may demonstrate the cruise climb, which is flown at a higher airspeed than Vy or Vx, probably the normal cruise airspeed. Cruise climb can be useful when there is no pressing need to gain altitude quickly and the reduced climb performance is acceptable.

Because the airspeed is faster than the normal climb airspeed, the groundspeed is faster, the view ahead is improved (due to the lower nose attitude) and the increased airflow helps keep the engine cool.

▶ Effect of Wind

When flying into wind, the aircraft will attain a better climb angle or gradient than when flying in zero wind or with a tail wind.

The rate of climb is not affected by the wind.

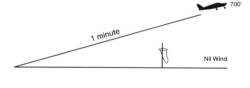

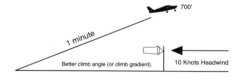

The prevailing wind direction and wind speed will have a marked effect on the climb gradient (angle of climb).

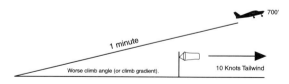

▶ Engine Considerations

During a climb the engine is working very hard, but due to the slower airspeed there is less airflow cooling the engine. It is important to monitor the engine's gauges carefully. Should the engine temperatures approach their permitted limits, it may be necessary to reduce power or increase airspeed to reduce the temperatures.

Exercise

7

Climbing

Flight Exercise

▷ Purpose

To learn to climb the aircraft at a specified airspeed, in a variety of configurations, and level off at a specified level.

▷ AIRMANSHIP

Lookout

As well as the standard lookout scan, visually clear the area the aircraft will be flying into before starting the climb. During the climb the nose-high attitude may cause a blind spot ahead; weave the aircraft regularly (every 500 feet or so) to check visually the area ahead. Alternatively 'dip' the nose to check ahead. Visually clear the area you are flying into as you level off.

During the climb, the higher nose attitude reduces the forward visibility.

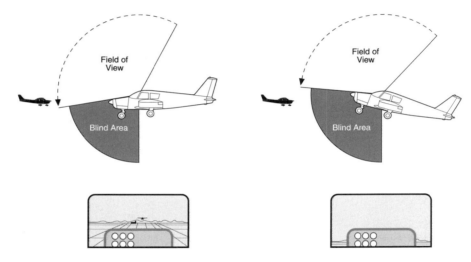

Engine Considerations

Monitor the engine instruments carefully during the climb (every 500 feet or so) and do not allow the maximum permitted temperatures to be exceeded.

VFE

When using flaps, remember to check the airspeed in relation to the VFE - airspeed must be within the white arc.

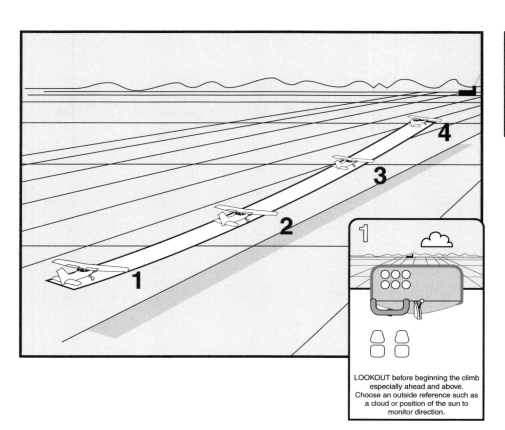

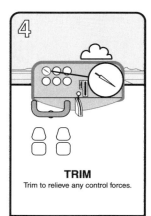

LOOKOUT before beginning the climb especially ahead and above. Choose an outside reference such as a cloud or position of the sun to monitor direction.

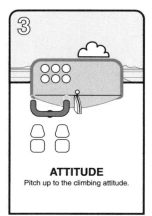

POWER
Set full power, anticipate the effect of yaw and use the rudder to stay in balance.

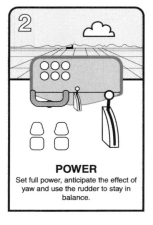

ATTITUDE
Pitch up to the climbing attitude.

TRIM
Trim to relieve any control forces.

To summarise:
POWER
ATTITUDE
TRIM

NOTE: Do not 'chase' the airspeed. After selecting a pitch attitude allow the airspeed 5/10 seconds to settle before making a further adjustment.
LOOKOUT

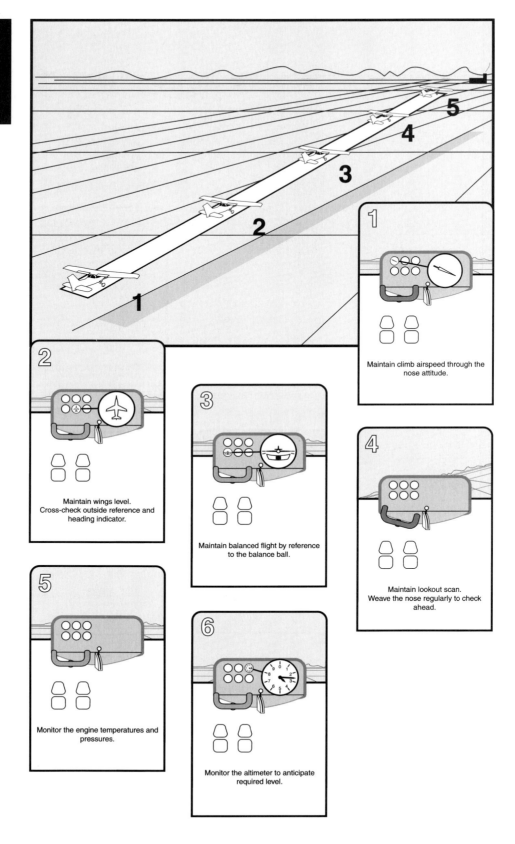

Maintaining the Climb

Climbing

1
Maintain climb airspeed through the nose attitude.

2
Maintain wings level. Cross-check outside reference and heading indicator.

3
Maintain balanced flight by reference to the balance ball.

4
Maintain lookout scan. Weave the nose regularly to check ahead.

5
Monitor the engine temperatures and pressures.

6
Monitor the altimeter to anticipate required level.

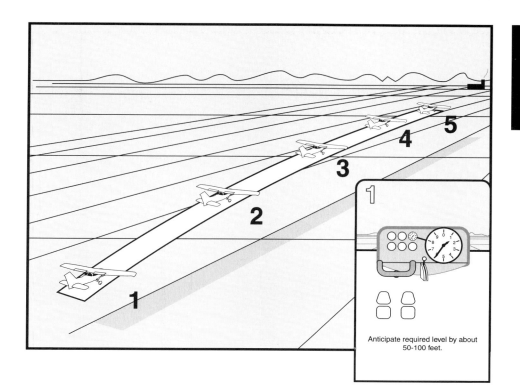

1

Anticipate required level by about 50-100 feet.

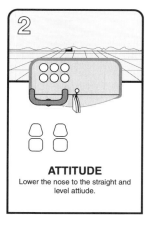

ATTITUDE

Lower the nose to the straight and level attiude.

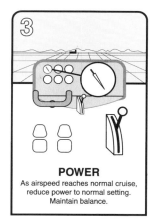

POWER

As airspeed reaches normal cruise, reduce power to normal setting. Maintain balance.

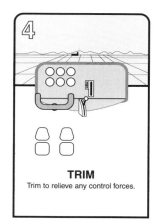

TRIM

Trim to relieve any control forces.

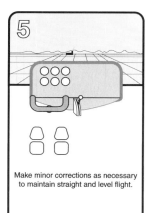

Make minor corrections as necessary to maintain straight and level flight.

To summarise:
ATTITUDE
POWER
TRIM
-Cross-check altimeter
and airspeed indicator.
-Make minor corrections
as necessary.
LOOKOUT

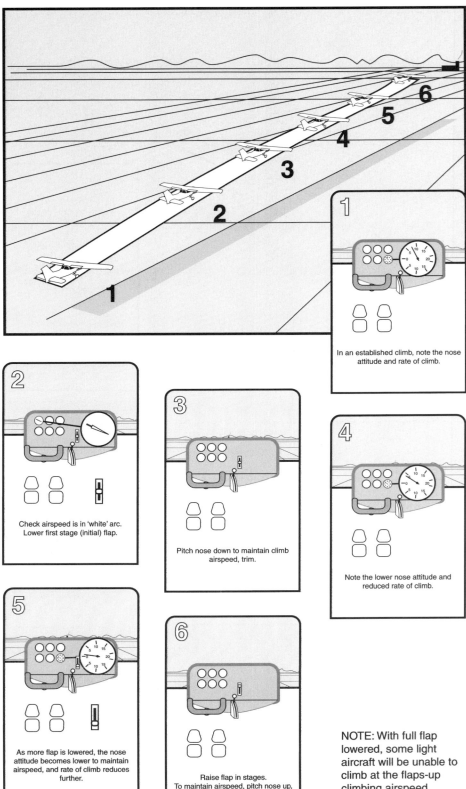

1
In an established climb, note the nose attitude and rate of climb.

2
Check airspeed is in 'white' arc. Lower first stage (initial) flap.

3
Pitch nose down to maintain climb airspeed, trim.

4
Note the lower nose attitude and reduced rate of climb.

5
As more flap is lowered, the nose attitude becomes lower to maintain airspeed, and rate of climb reduces further.

6
Raise flap in stages. To maintain airspeed, pitch nose up, rate of climb improves.

NOTE: With full flap lowered, some light aircraft will be unable to climb at the flaps-up climbing airspeed.

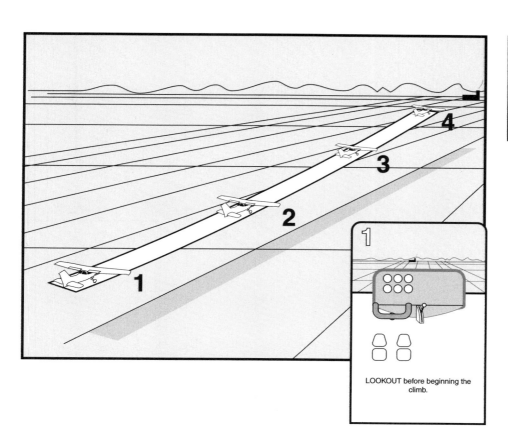

1

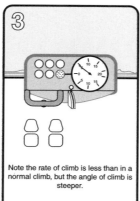

LOOKOUT before beginning the climb.

2

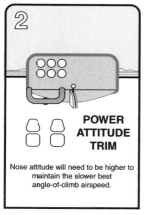

**POWER
ATTITUDE
TRIM**

Nose attitude will need to be higher to maintain the slower best angle-of-climb airspeed.

3

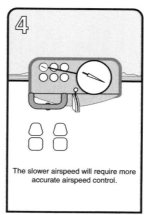

Note the rate of climb is less than in a normal climb, but the angle of climb is steeper.

4

The slower airspeed will require more accurate airspeed control.

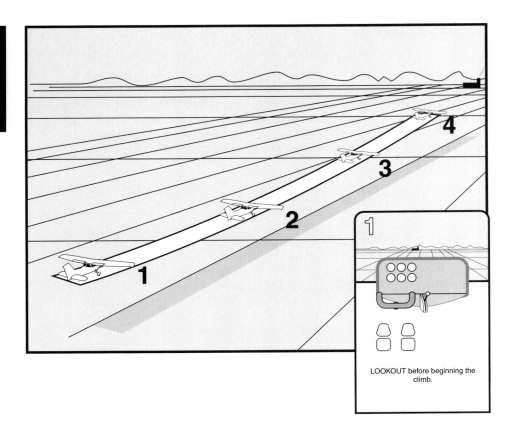

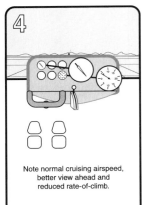

LOOKOUT before beginning the climb.

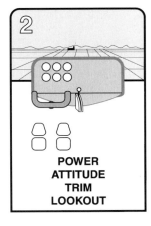

**POWER
ATTITUDE
TRIM
LOOKOUT**

Nose attitude is only slightly higher than for straight and level flight.

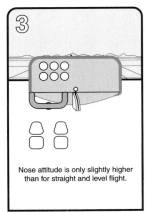

Note normal cruising airspeed, better view ahead and reduced rate-of-climb.

Conclusion

At the end of this exercise you will be able to safely and accurately climb the aircraft at a given airspeed and level off at a pre-determined level. You will find that your airspeed control and flying control co-ordination is improving, and you will have learnt that accurate trimming can greatly reduce your workload. You should appreciate the factors that will affect the climbing performance of the aircraft, and which climb airspeeds are appropriate in different circumstances.

Descending

What goes up must come down - preferably in a controlled manner! Whilst practising this basic flight manoeuvre you will first learn how to control the aircraft in what is referred to as a *glide descent*. In fact, for the purposes of the flight exercise the engine is still running in the 'glide' descent, but is throttled back to idle power.

Once you are proficient at the glide descent, the effects of power and flap will be explored and you will be able to fly the aircraft down the final approach to land.

You will come to appreciate how efficiently the aircraft does fly even with little engine power and you should become fully aware of the dangers of carburettor icing at low power settings.

This flight exercise is usually flown in two parts and is combined with the previous exercise (climbing).

BACKGROUND BRIEFING

▶ **The Forces in the Descent**

▶ **Gliding For Best Range**

▶ **Effect of Wind**

▶ **Effect of Weight**

▶ **Gliding For Best Endurance**

▶ **Effect of Flap**

▶ **Effect of Power**

▶ **Sideslipping**

▶ **The Cruise Descent**

FLIGHT EXERCISE

Exercise

8

Descending

FLIGHT EXERCISE

▷ **Purpose**

▷ **Airmanship**

▷ **Entering the Glide Descent**

▷ **Maintaining the Descent**

▷ **Levelling Off**

▷ **Effect of Flap**

▷ **Effect of Power**

▷ **Descending With Flap and Power**

▷ **Sideslipping**

▷ **The Cruise Descent**

CONCLUSION

▶ The Forces in the Descent

In the previous exercise - climbing - we saw that an excess of power over that needed for level flight allows the aircraft to climb. Not surprisingly the reverse is also true. If power is below that needed for level flight, the aircraft will descend.

In a descent one of the four forces - thrust - has been reduced or removed altogether. In a glide the nose-down attitude of the aircraft allows a component of weight to act in the same direction as thrust would normally (i.e. ahead of the aircraft) so balancing drag and maintaining a safe airspeed. Weight is balanced by the resultant of the lift and drag forces.

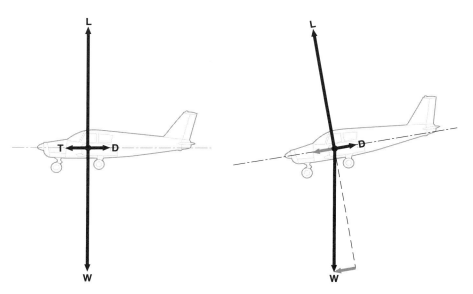

In the descent, a component of weight replaces thrust to balance drag.

The gliding range of the aircraft is governed by its aerodynamic efficiency - specifically its lift-to-drag ratio. When gliding the ideal is for the airframe to produce the maximum amount of lift for the minimum amount of drag, this is known as a good lift/drag (L/D) ratio.

▶ Gliding For Best Range

In a glide descent, the pilot would normally want to travel the maximum distance over the ground with the minimum height loss -i.e. the best (most shallow) glide angle. The glide angle is dictated by the L/D ratio.

The gliding angle of the aircraft is the same as the angle between the lift vector and the resultant.

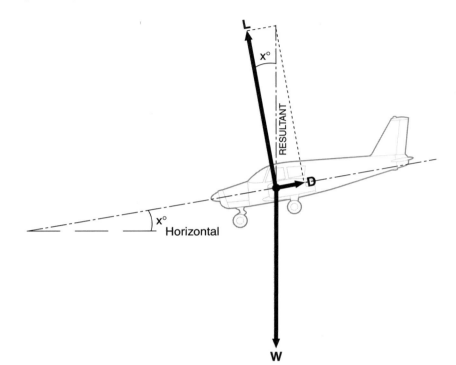

Descending

An aircraft that has a good L/D ratio (i.e. the maximum lift produced for the minimum drag penalty), will have a narrow angle between the lift vector and the resultant. The gliding angle is flat and gliding range is good. An aircraft with a poor L/D ratio has a steeper gliding angle and gliding range is less.

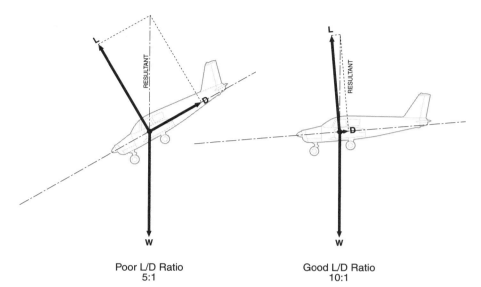

Poor L/D Ratio
5:1

Good L/D Ratio
10:1

The greater the lift generated and the less the drag produced, the smaller the angle between the lift vector and the resultant. This eqates to a more shallow gliding angle and therefore a greater gliding range.

A typical training aircraft will have a best L/D ratio of around 10:1, meaning that it is producing 10 units of lift for every 1 unit of drag. This ratio can also be interpreted as the aircraft travelling 10 feet forward for every 1 foot lost in height; or 10000 feet horizontally (about 1.6 nautical miles) for each 1000 feet lost in height. So the gliding angle and the gliding range are determined by the aerodynamic efficiency of the aircraft, providing it is flown at the recommended gliding speed at which the best L/D ratio occurs.

It is important to appreciate that the best L/D ratio will only occur at one specific airspeed. If the aircraft is flown at an airspeed faster or slower than this best gliding speed, the best possible L/D ratio will not occur and gliding range will be reduced.

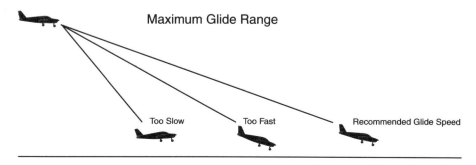

Maximum Glide Range

Too Slow   Too Fast   Recommended Glide Speed

Only at the recommended glide airspeed can the maximum glide range be attained.

▶ Effect of Wind

In looking at gliding angle and range, we have not yet considered one of the prime factors that will affect the gliding range - the prevailing wind. Gliding with a tailwind increases glide range, whereas gliding into a headwind reduces glide range.

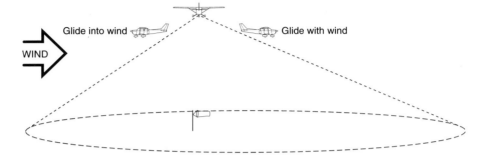

The prevailing wind will have a marked effect on glide angle (and therefore glide range). Gliding with a tailwind INCREASES glide range. Gliding into a headwind DECREASES glide range.

When encountering strong head or tail winds, the glide range may be increased by altering airspeed, i.e. reducing airspeed by about 5 knots when gliding with a strong tailwind, or increasing airspeed by about 5 knots when gliding into a strong headwind. Although this practice does have some benefits, it is not often taught in the early flight exercises because maintaining a stable airspeed is more important at this stage of your training.

The rate of descent is not affected by the prevailing wind. In other words, whether gliding into a headwind or with a tailwind, the aircraft will still reach the ground in the same time. What will alter is the distance it covers in the glide.

▶ Effect of Weight

At first thought the effect of weight is obvious; the greater the weight the less the glide range, right? WRONG. In fact, weight does not affect the gliding angle. Remember that the glide angle is governed by the L/D ratio.

Returning to the forces in a descent, you will see that an increased weight merely alters the length of the lift and drag vectors and the resultant; the gliding angle is not changed.

What has changed is the gliding speed. A heavier aircraft will have a faster best gliding speed than a lighter aircraft.

A training aircraft, with a small range of take-off weights, will not benefit significantly from being flown at different glide airspeeds for different weights. Normally just one gliding speed (that for maximum weight) will be noted in the aircraft's POH/FM.

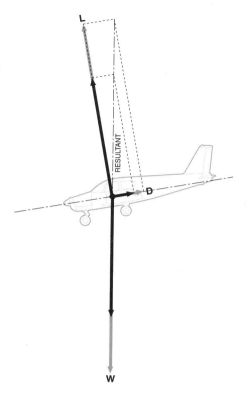

Weight does not alter the glide angle, only the glide airspeed. At a higher weight the length of the weight vector is longer. Therefore the length of the lift vector is longer, and because of the faster airspeed the drag vector is longer. The L/D ratio is unchanged and so the glide angle is unchanged.

▶ Gliding For Best Endurance

It is possible that on occasion a pilot might want to glide with a view to staying airborne as long as possible (i.e. with the minimum rate of descent) even though the gliding range will be reduced. The best glide endurance (minimum height lost in a certain time) occurs at a slower airspeed than the best gliding range airspeed–in fact at the minimum power required airspeed.

Gliding for best endurance is not common in powered aircraft, and a specific speed is rarely quoted in the POH/FM.

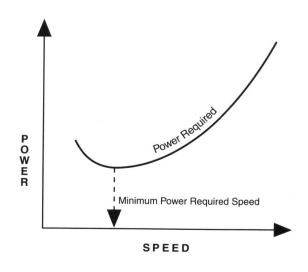

The best glide endurance (the greatest time airborne) is achieved at the minimum-power-required airspeed.

▶ Effect of Flap

The use of flap will increase drag and so worsen the L/D ratio, leading to a steeper descent. Although this may seem an undesirable effect, it does have a major advantage. Using flap in the descent will allow the aircraft to descend more steeply without increasing airspeed, which is a major consideration when approaching to land.

Flaps increase drag and so can be used to steepen the descent without increasing airspeed.

Effect of Flap at a Constant Airspeed

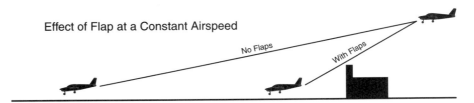

No Flaps

With Flaps

▶ Effect of Power

When power is used during the descent, the increased thrust means that a reduced component of weight is required to balance drag. The aircraft can be pitched nose-up to maintain a constant airspeed and the descent angle is reduced (and descent range increased).

As power is increased, the rate of descent and angle of descent decrease (if a constant airspeed is maintained).

At a Constant Airspeed

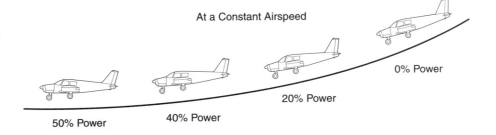

0% Power

20% Power

40% Power

50% Power

In practical terms, power is used to control the rate of descent, whilst the elevators control the attitude and therefore the airspeed. As this is an important point, it is worth repeating:

power controls altitude (in this case rate of descent)

attitude controls airspeed

▶Sideslipping

Flaps can be used in the descent to increase drag and steepen the descent. There is also a manoeuvre known as *sideslipping* which will give a similar effect.

To sideslip, the aircraft is banked and rudder applied in the opposite direction to the bank, so that the aircraft does not turn towards the lower wing. The result is that the aircraft slips sideways through the air. This causes a marked increase in drag and so leads to a steeper gliding angle and an increased rate of descent, without the airspeed increasing.

In a sideslip, the increased drag gives a steeper descent without increasing airspeed (until the aircraft is flown in balance again).

Before aircraft were fitted with flaps, sideslipping was a standard manoeuvre—especially during the final approach to land. Sideslipping does have several disadvantages, however. Flying the aircraft in such an out-of-balance condition can be uncomfortable for passengers and requires some skill on the part of the pilot to keep the aircraft descending in a straight line whilst maintaining the correct airspeed. Airspeed control can also be more difficult because the airspeed indicator may give incorrect readings in this out-of-balance situation. Rates of descent can become very high in a sideslip, and when the sideslip is corrected (and so the drag reduced) the airspeed can increase rapidly.

Not all aircraft are cleared to sideslip, especially with flaps down. The aircraft's POH/FM will advise if sideslipping is restricted or prohibited and there may be a warning placard in the cockpit.

▶The Cruise Descent

Although the flight exercise concentrates on the glide descent and controlling the approach to land with power and flap, often you may wish to lose height in a more gradual descent. In a *cruise descent*, the engine power is reduced (typically by 200 - 300 RPM), but the airspeed is maintained at the cruising speed by pitching the nose down to a shallow descent attitude. The result is a gradual descent (typically 500 feet per minute) whilst maintaining the cruise airspeed which gives a faster groundspeed. It is also kinder to the engine. In this type of descent you can use a simple rule of thumb to gauge at what point to start the descent toward an airfield. Read the height above the ground in thousands of feet, multiply by 3, and the result is the distance required (in nautical miles) to descend to ground level, i.e. at height 5000', start the descent 15 nautical miles from the destination.

Be careful - all sorts of factors such as groundspeed, aircraft type, prevailing wind etc. will affect this rule of thumb, but it will give you an appreciation of where to start your descent.

Flight Exercise

▷ Purpose

To learn to descend the aircraft at a specified airspeed, using a variety of power settings and configurations and to level off at a specified level. Also to practise controlling the final descent to land.

▷ Airmanship

Lookout

Visually check the area you will descend into before you start the descent. Maintain a good scan whilst descending - this should be aided by the low nose attitude, but it will help to 'weave' the nose regularly the check the area ahead. Be especially vigilant as you level off at your new altitude.

It will be difficult to spot an aircraft below you, because it may merge with the ground features from time to time.

The Altimeter

During the early flight exercises you will usually be using an altimeter pressure setting called 'QNH'. When QNH is set on the altimeter, the altimeter will read Altitude, that is vertical distance *Above Mean Sea Level* (AMSL). You will appreciate that the altitude read on the altimeter is not necessarily your height Above Ground Level (AGL). Mostly the ground you are flying over will be higher than sea level and so your height above ground level (AGL) may be considerably less than your altitude above mean sea level (AMSL). Your instructor will point out

When set to QNH the altimeter reads ALTITUDE Above Mean Sea Level (AMSL), NOT the height above the ground.

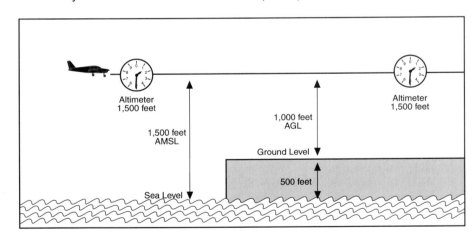

Altimeter 1,500 feet

1,500 feet AMSL

1,000 feet AGL

Ground Level

500 feet

Sea Level

Altimeter 1,500 feet

the terrain markings on your map and give you an appreciation of the average ground level in the training area above sea level.

If you are descending towards an airfield, you can check its altitude (in feet AMSL) which will be shown on the chart.

Flight Exercise

VFE

When using flap, be sure that the airspeed is slower than VFE (i.e. within the white arc on the airspeed indicator).

Engine considerations

In a glide descent, or with a low power setting, the engine will cool and becomes susceptible to spark-plug fouling - oily deposits build up on the spark plugs and reduce engine efficiency. The engine will also be particularly vulnerable to carburettor icing. The subject of carburettor icing is covered in the supplement to this exercise.

It will be standard practice to 'warm' the engine every 1000 feet or so in the descent by gently increasing the power for a few seconds and then reducing power again. When increasing power to level off, remember again to operate the throttle smoothly - be kind to the engine!

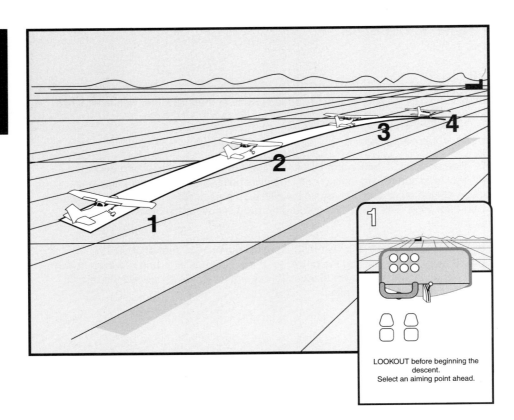

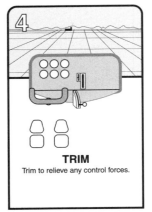

LOOKOUT before beginning the descent.
Select an aiming point ahead.

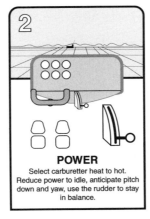

POWER

Select carburetter heat to hot. Reduce power to idle, anticipate pitch down and yaw, use the rudder to stay in balance.

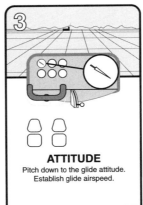

ATTITUDE

Pitch down to the glide attitude. Establish glide airspeed.

TRIM

Trim to relieve any control forces.

To summarise:
POWER
ATTITUDE
TRIM
Minor corrections.
NOTE: Do not 'chase' the airspeed. After selecting a pitch attitude allow the airspeed 5/10 seconds to settle before making a further adjustment.
LOOKOUT

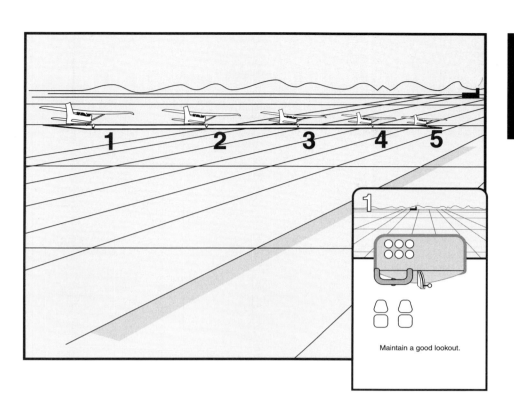

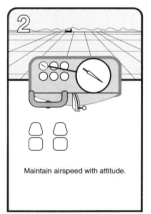

Maintain a good lookout.

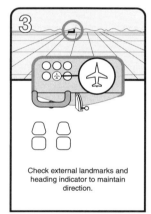

Maintain airspeed with attitude.

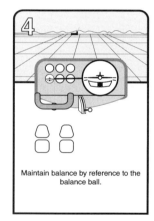

Check external landmarks and heading indicator to maintain direction.

Maintain balance by reference to the balance ball.

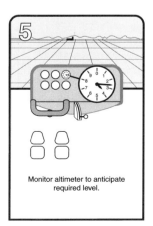

Monitor altimeter to anticipate required level.

NOTE: Remember to 'warm' the engine at regular intervals.

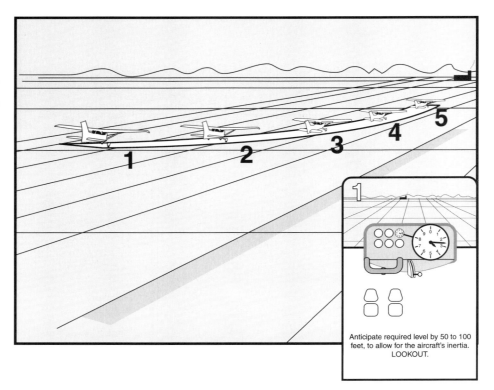

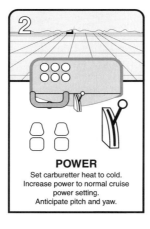

Anticipate required level by 50 to 100 feet, to allow for the aircraft's inertia.
LOOKOUT.

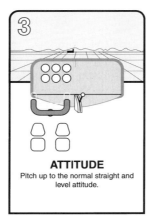

POWER

Set carburetter heat to cold.
Increase power to normal cruise power setting.
Anticipate pitch and yaw.

ATTITUDE

Pitch up to the normal straight and level attitude.

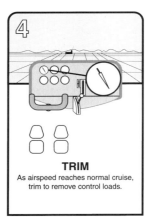

TRIM

As airspeed reaches normal cruise, trim to remove control loads.

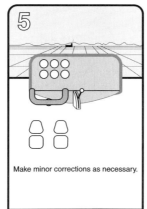

Make minor corrections as necessary.

To summarise:
POWER
ATTITUDE
TRIM
Minor corrections.
LOOKOUT

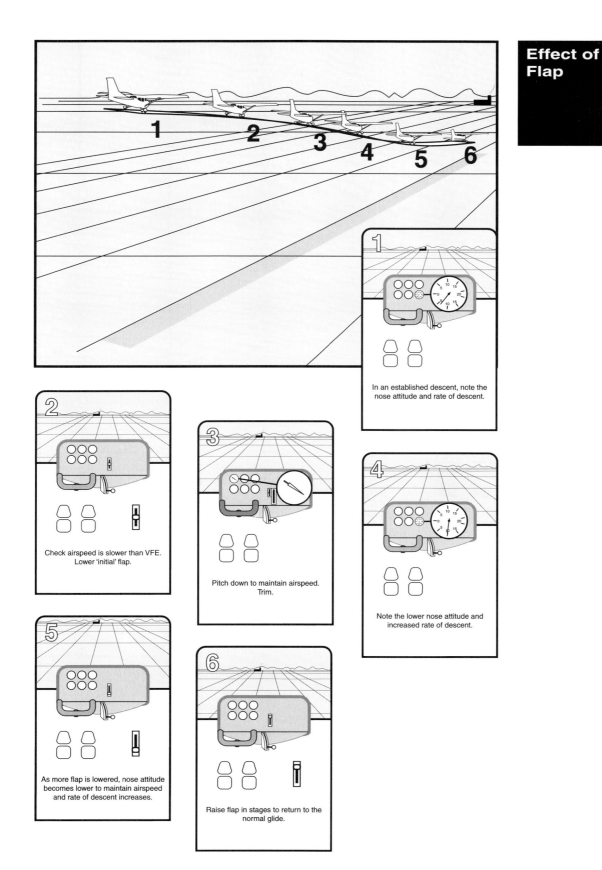

1

2

3

4

5

6

In an established descent, note the nose attitude and rate of descent.

Check airspeed is slower than VFE. Lower 'initial' flap.

Pitch down to maintain airspeed. Trim.

Note the lower nose attitude and increased rate of descent.

As more flap is lowered, nose attitude becomes lower to maintain airspeed and rate of descent increases.

Raise flap in stages to return to the normal glide.

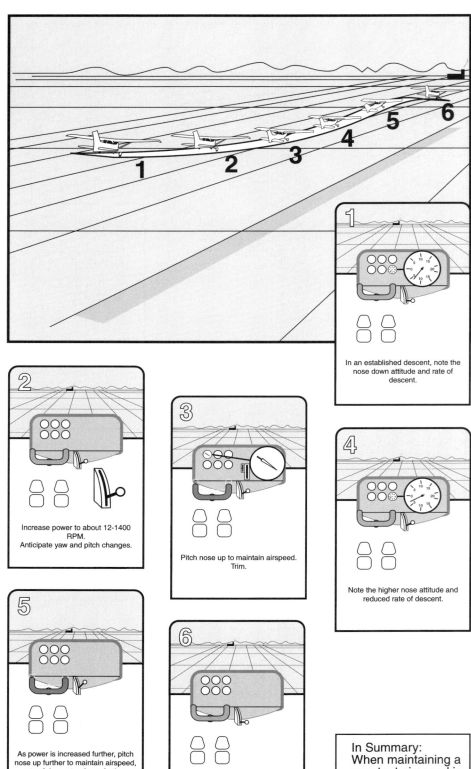

In an established descent, note the nose down attitude and rate of descent.

Increase power to about 12-1400 RPM.
Anticipate yaw and pitch changes.

Pitch nose up to maintain airspeed. Trim.

Note the higher nose attitude and reduced rate of descent.

As power is increased further, pitch nose up further to maintain airspeed, rate of descent reduces further.

Power is reduced again to return to the normal glide and attitude adjusted.

In Summary:
When maintaining a constant airspeed in the descent, power is used to control the rate-of-descent.

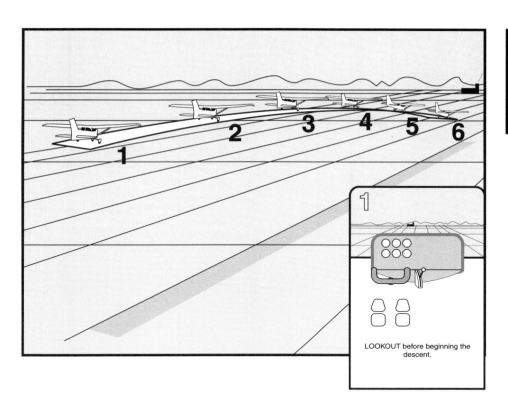

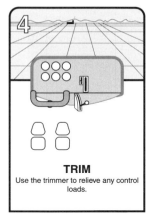

LOOKOUT before beginning the descent.

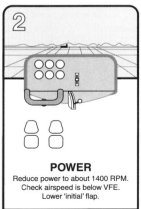

POWER
Reduce power to about 1400 RPM.
Check airspeed is below VFE.
Lower 'initial' flap.

ATTITUDE
Maintain approach airspeed.

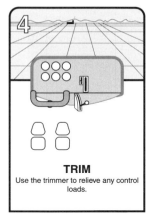

TRIM
Use the trimmer to relieve any control loads.

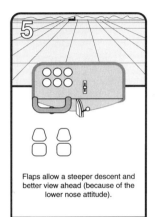

Flaps allow a steeper descent and better view ahead (because of the lower nose attitude).

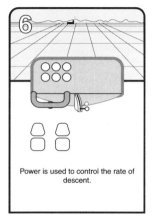

Power is used to control the rate of descent.

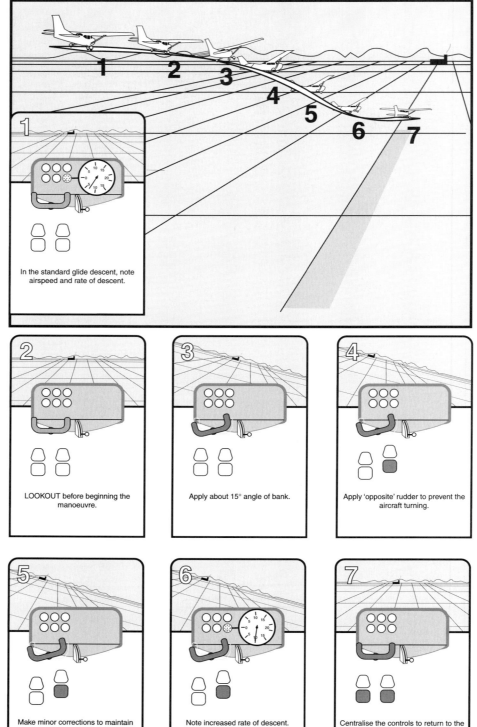

1 — In the standard glide descent, note airspeed and rate of descent.

2 — LOOKOUT before beginning the manoeuvre.

3 — Apply about 15° angle of bank.

4 — Apply 'opposite' rudder to prevent the aircraft turning.

5 — Make minor corrections to maintain airspeed, angle of bank and direction.

6 — Note increased rate of descent.

7 — Centralise the controls to return to the normal descent.
LOOKOUT

Note: Check in the aircraft's POH/FM that sideslipping is permitted.
Restrictions may apply to the aircraft you are flying.

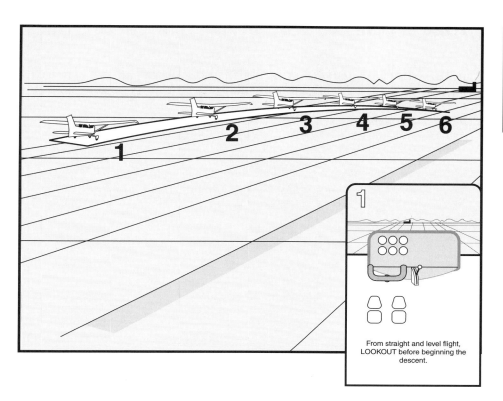

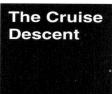

1

From straight and level flight, LOOKOUT before beginning the descent.

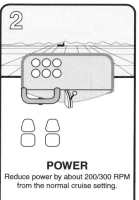

2

POWER

Reduce power by about 200/300 RPM from the normal cruise setting.

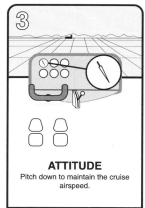

3

ATTITUDE

Pitch down to maintain the cruise airspeed.

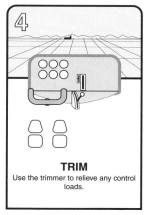

4

TRIM

Use the trimmer to relieve any control loads.

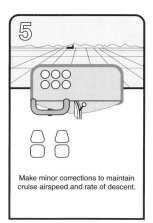

5

Make minor corrections to maintain cruise airspeed and rate of descent.

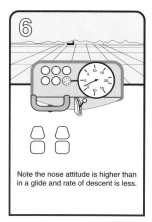

6

Note the nose attitude is higher than in a glide and rate of descent is less.

Conclusion

By the end of this exercise you will be able to descend the aircraft as appropriate to the circumstances, controlling the rate of descent and airspeed accurately enough to fly the aircraft down the final approach to land. As a result of practising differing attitudes and airspeeds, your airspeed control and particularly the use of the trimmer will be coming to you without much thought. Keep working at trimming - it will reduce your workload considerably.

You have now covered three of the four basic flight manoeuvres and it is time to brush up the fourth manoeuvre that you will already have been flying in a fashion - turning.

Carburettor Icing Supplement

It is well established that the most common cause of engine rough running and complete engine failures is *carburettor icing*. Despite this, carburettor icing remains a widely misunderstood subject, with many pilot's knowledge of it being limited to a feeling that the *carb heat* should be used regularly in flight, without really knowing the symptoms of carb icing or the conditions most likely to cause its formation.

▶ How Carburettor Icing Forms

IMPACT ICING occurs when ice forms over the external air inlet (air filter) and inside the induction system leading to the carburettor. This type of icing occurs with the temperature below 0°C whilst flying in cloud, or in precipitation (i.e. rain, sleet or snow). These conditions are also conducive to airframe icing and most light training aircraft are NOT CLEARED FOR FLIGHT INTO KNOWN ICING CONDITIONS, which clearly these are. So, assuming the aircraft is operated legally within its limitations, this form of icing should not occur and is not considered further.

Carburettor icing is caused by a temperature drop inside the carburettor, which can happen even in conditions where other forms of icing will not occur. The causes of this temperature drop are twofold:

1 *Fuel Icing* - the evaporation of fuel inside the carburettor. Liquid fuel changes to fuel vapour and mixes with the induction air. This evaporation of fuel causes a large temperature drop within the carburettor. If the temperature inside the carburettor falls below 0°C, water vapour in the atmosphere condenses into ice, usually on the walls of the carburettor passage adjacent to the fuel jet and on the throttle valve. Fuel icing is responsible for around 70% of the temperature drop in the carburettor.

2 *Throttle icing* - the temperature drop caused by the acceleration of air and consequent pressure drop around the throttle valve. This effect may again reduce the temperature below 0°C, and water vapour in the induction air will condense into ice on the throttle valve.

As fuel and throttle icing generally occur together, they are considered just as carburettor icing.

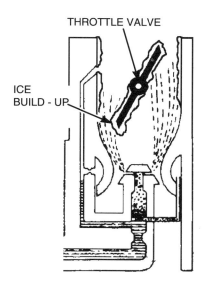

THROTTLE VALVE

ICE
BUILD - UP

▶Conditions Likely To Lead To Carburettor Icing

Two criteria govern the likelihood of carburettor icing conditions; the *AIR TEMPERATURE* and the *RELATIVE HUMIDITY*.

The ambient air temperature is important, BUT NOT BECAUSE THE TEMPERATURE NEEDS TO BE BELOW 0°C, OR EVEN CLOSE TO FREEZING. The temperature drop in the carburettor can be as much as 30°C, so carburettor icing can (and does) occur in hot ambient conditions. No wonder carburettor icing is sometimes referred to as *refrigeration icing*. Carburettor icing is considered a possibility within the temperature range of -10°C to +30°C.

The relative humidity (a measure of the water content of the atmosphere) is the major factor. The greater the water content in the atmosphere (i.e. the higher the relative humidity), the greater the risk of carburettor icing. That said, the relative humidity (RH) does not to have to be 100% (i.e. visible water droplets - cloud, rain), for carburettor icing to occur. Carburettor icing is considered a possibility at relative humidity values as low as 30%, but it is rare that the RH becomes this low in Europe. Herein lies the real danger of carburettor icing, that it can occur in such a wide range of conditions. Obviously the pilot must be alert to the possibility of carburettor icing at just about all times. Flight in or near cloud, or in other visible moisture (i.e. rain) might be an obvious cause of carburettor icing, but - VISIBLE MOISTURE DOES NOT NEED TO BE PRESENT FOR CARBURETTOR ICING TO OCCUR.

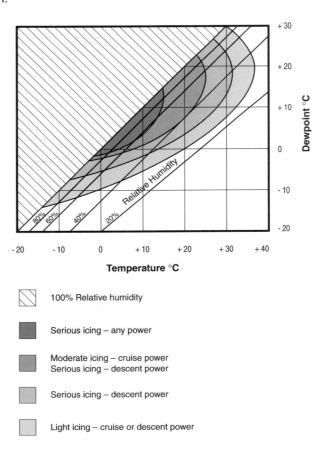

▶ Symptoms Of Carburettor Icing

In an aircraft fitted with a fixed-pitch propeller, the symptoms of carburettor icing are straightforward. A loss of RPM will be the first symptom, although this is often first noticed as a loss of altitude. As the icing becomes more serious, engine rough-running may occur.

Carburettor icing is often detected during the use of the carburettor heat control. Normally, when the carburettor heat is used a small drop in RPM occurs. When control is returned to cold (off) the RPM reverts to its value before the use of carburettor heat. If the rpm returns to a higher figure than before the carburettor heat was used, it can be reasonably supposed that some form of carburettor icing was present.

▶ Use Of Carburettor Heat

Apart from the normal check of carburettor heat during the power checks, it may be necessary to use the carburettor heat on the ground if carburettor icing is suspected. Safety considerations apart, the use of carburettor heat on the ground should be kept to a minimum because the hot air inlet is unfiltered and so sand or dust can enter the engine, increasing engine wear.

Carburettor icing is generally considered to be very unlikely with the engine operating at above 75% power, i.e. during the take-off and climb. Carburettor heat should not be used with the engine operating at above 75% power (i.e. full throttle) as detonation may occur. Detonation is the uncontrolled burning of fuel in the cylinders–literally an explosion–and will cause serious damage to the engine very quickly. Apart from the danger of detonation, the use of carburettor heat reduces the power the engine produces. In any situation where full power is required (i.e. take-off, climb, go-around) the carburettor heat must be off (cold).

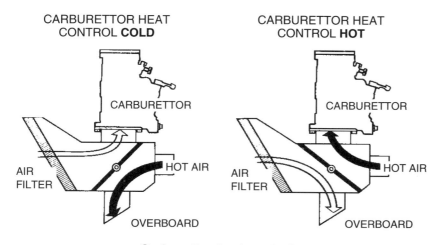

Carburettor heat control

Carburettor Icing Supplement

Very few operators recommend the use of anything other than FULL carburettor heat. A normal carburettor icing check will involve leaving the carburettor heat on (hot) for 5-10 seconds, although the pilot may wish to vary this according to conditions. The use of carburettor heat does increase the fuel consumption, and this may be a factor to consider if the aircraft is being flown towards the limit of its range/endurance in possible carburettor icing conditions.

With carburettor icing present, the use of carburettor heat may lead to a large drop in RPM and rough running. The instinctive reaction is to put the carburettor heat back to cold (off) quickly – this is, however, the wrong action. The chances are that this rough running is a good thing and the carburettor heat should be left on (hot) until it clears and the RPM rises. In this instance the use of carburettor heat has melted a large amount of accumulated icing and the melted ice is passing through the engine, causing temporary rough running.

Care should be taken when flying in very cold ambient conditions (below -10°C). In these conditions the use of carburettor heat may actually raise the temperature in the carburettor to that most conducive to carburettor icing. Generally when the temperature in the carburettor is below -8°C, moisture changes directly into ice crystals which pass through the engine.

The RPM loss normally associated with the use of carburettor heat is caused by the reduced density of the hot air entering the carburettor, leading to an over-rich fuel/air mixture entering the engine. If the carburettor heat has to be left constantly on (hot)–i.e. during flight in heavy rain and cloud–it may be advisable to lean the mixture in order to maintain RPM and smooth engine running.

It is during the descent (and particularly the glide descent) that carburettor icing is most likely to occur. The position of the throttle valve (almost closed) is a contributory factor, and even though the carburettor heat is normally applied throughout a glide descent, the low engine power will reduce the temperature of the hot air selected by the carburettor heat control. In addition, a loss of power may not be readily noticed as the propeller is likely to windmill even after a complete loss of power. So a full loss of power may only be apparent when the throttle is opened at the bottom of the descent. This is one good reason for opening the throttle to 'warm the engine' at intervals during a glide descent.

Turning

Having covered three of the basic flight manoeuvres - straight and level, climbing, and descending - turning is the one basic manoeuvre left. Initially you will fly level turns. Once proficient at them you will practise turns whilst climbing and descending. Obviously the ability to turn the aircraft smoothly and roll out accurately in a given direction will be needed in all phases of flight, especially during the circuit flying you will soon be learning.

During this exercise your control co-ordination will continue to develop, as will your ability to think and plan in three dimensions. This exercise may be referred to as *medium turns*, that is turning at 30° angle of bank - the normal angle for a level turn.

BACKGROUND BRIEFING

▶ **The Forces in the Turn**

▶ **The Use of the Controls**

▶ **Effect of Turning on Stall Speed**

▶ **The Climbing Turn**

▶ **The Descending Turn**

▶ **Effect of Offset Seating**

▶ **Turning on to Selected Headings - Using the Heading Indicator**

▶ **Turning on to Selected Headings - Using the Compass**

FLIGHT EXERCISE

▷ **Purpose**

▷ **Airmanship**

▷ **Entering the Turn**

▷ **Maintaining the Turn**

▷ **Returning to Straight Flight**

▷ **The Climbing Turn**

▷ **The Descending Turn**

CONCLUSION

BACKGROUND BRIEFING

▶Forces in the Turn

An aircraft in straight and level flight has inertia, which will act to keep it flying in the same direction unless some other force is applied. To turn the aircraft, the pilot has to create centripetal force, which acts in the direction of the turn to overcome inertia. Centripetal force is provided by banking the aircraft so that a horizontal component of lift now acts in the direction of the desired turn.

By banking the aircraft, the pilot provides the centripetal force needed for the aircraft to turn.

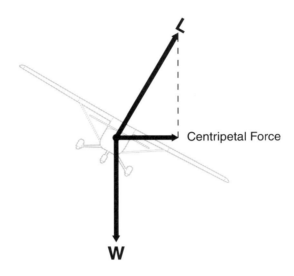

▶Use of the Controls

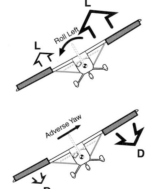

As the aircraft is rolled into the turn, aileron deflection causes adverse yaw.

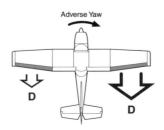

To turn, the ailerons are used to roll the aircraft and so supply the horizontal component of lift into the turn. To turn to the left, the control wheel is moved to the left. This causes the aileron on the left wing to move up, reducing the angle of attack, and so reducing the lift from the left wing. On the right wing the aileron moves down, increasing the angle of attack and so increasing lift from the right wing. This causes the aircraft to roll to the left.

You will remember from earlier exercises that increased angle of attack results in increased induced drag. This means that, as the aircraft rolls, there is more drag created from the up-going wing than from the down-going wing.

The increased drag from the upper wing causes yaw away from the direction of the turn; this is known as *adverse yaw*. Adverse yaw is at its greatest as the aircraft is rolling and the ailerons are deflected. Once the aircraft reaches the desired angle of bank and the ailerons are centralised, the roll stops and most of the adverse yaw also disappears.

Turning

To the pilot, the important point is that whilst rolling into a turn (and rolling out of the turn) rudder may well be required in the same direction as the roll to overcome adverse yaw and keep the aircraft in balance. How much rudder? Simple–just check the balance ball and use the rudder to stay in balance. Once the turn is established, and adverse yaw is no longer a major factor, little (if any) rudder pressure will be required.

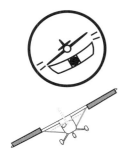

| In Balance | Slipping into the turn | Skidding out of the turn |

Viewed from behind

During the turn the pilot should check the balance ball to keep the aircraft in balance.

During the turn, the upper wing–being on the outside of the turn–is travelling faster than the inner wing and so is producing more lift, causing the aircraft to keep rolling to a steeper angle of bank. To counter this the ailerons may have to be used to 'hold off' bank to maintain a constant angle of bank.

During a turn the aircraft has to produce more lift than in wings-level flight. During a turn this is because lift is now split into horizontal and vertical components. The vertical component still has to balance weight but, because the wings are not level, greater total lift is needed to provide the necessary vertical component. The steeper the angle of bank, the more lift is needed to produce the required vertical component.

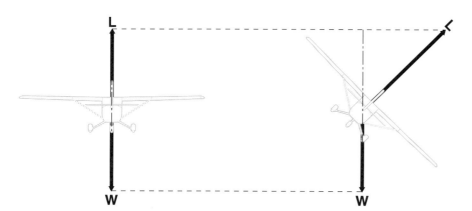

During a turn, the aircraft has to produce more lift than during wings-level flight, so that the vertical component of lift will still balance weight.

The pilot produces this extra lift by increasing the angle of attack i.e. by increasing the back pressure on the control column to attain a slightly higher nose attitude.

▶ Effect of Turning on Stall Speed

During the turn the increased angle of attack required leads to increased induced drag, this slows the aircraft if thrust is not increased to compensate. Typically, in a level 30° angle-of-bank turn, the airspeed will reduce by about 5 knots. This small reduction from normal cruise speed is not a problem and so is accepted as a temporary effect. The increased lift in a turn also increases the load factor (felt by the pilot as 'g' force); in effect the aircraft is made heavier. An increase in load factor leads to an increase in stalling speed.

In a 30° angle-of-bank turn the increase in stall speed is somewhere in the region of 7%–not yet a major factor. However, the increase in stall speed coupled with the reduction in airspeed means that there is now a reduced margin over the stall speed.

During a turn, stall speed increases and airspeed decreases. This reduces the speed margin over the stall speed.

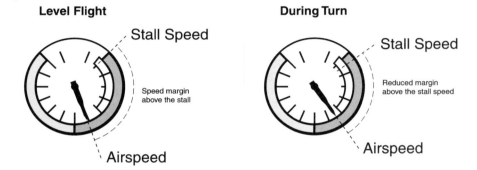

▶ The Climbing Turn

To accomplish the climbing turn you will first establish a straight climb and then enter the turn. Usually the angle of bank does not exceed 15° in a climbing turn, but even so there will be a small reduction in airspeed which is more significant at the slower airspeed used in a climb. Therefore the pilot has to pitch the nose down to a lower nose attitude to maintain the climbing airspeed, leading to a reduced rate of climb.

During a climbing turn, the outer wing has a greater angle of attack than the inner wing and so produces more lift.

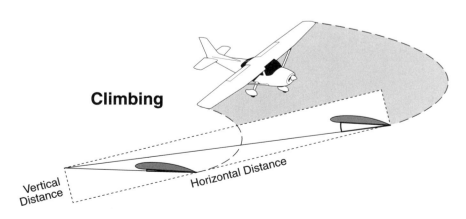

In a climbing turn, each wing follows a slightly different path up the 'spiral'. Whilst both wings travel the same vertical distance, the wing on the outside of the turn travels a greater horizontal distance than the inner wing. This means that the outer wing has a greater angle of attack and so produces more lift than the inner wing. This causes the aircraft to roll further into the turn. To prevent this happening, bank has to be 'held off' with the ailerons to prevent the aircraft rolling further into the turn so for example, in a climbing left turn, a little right aileron may be needed to maintain the angle of bank.

▶ The Descending Turn

To carry out a descending turn, the descent is established first, then the turn is entered. Up to 30° angle of bank may be used, leading to an inevitable loss of airspeed. To maintain the airspeed, the aircraft has to be pitched to a lower nose attitude and so the rate of descent will increase (unless the power setting is increased).

As in a climbing turn, the wings travel the same vertical distance, but differing horizontal distances. This spiral path followed by the wings means that the inner wing has a higher angle of attack than the outer wing. The increased lift on the inner wing tends to roll the aircraft out of the turn. This means that in a descending turn, aileron may have to be 'held on' to prevent the aircraft rolling out of the turn; i.e. in a descending left turn, a little left aileron may be needed to maintain the angle of bank.

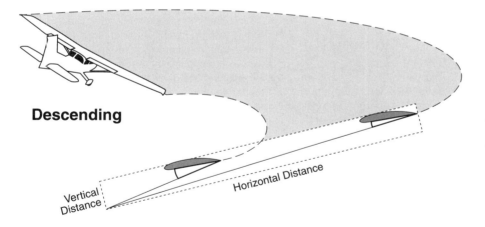

Descending

Vertical Distance

Horizontal Distance

During a descending turn, the inner wing has a greater angle of attack than the outer wing, and so produces more lift.

▶ Effect of Offset Seating

Most modern training aircraft have side-by-side seating. One practical effect of this is that, when viewed from the left-hand seat, the nose attitude appears to be higher in a left turn than in a right turn.

Seated on the left-hand side of the cockpit, the nose attitude appears to be higher in a left turn than in a right turn.

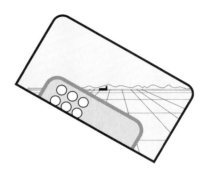

▶ Turning on to Selected Headings - Using the Heading Indicator

During a 30° angle of bank turn, start rolling out of the turn within 15° of the required heading.

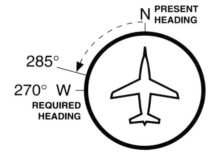

Initially you will turn on to a new heading using external references, such as a major landmark, to mark the new heading. As you become more practised at turning, you will turn on to selected headings using the heading indicator as a reference. You will need to anticipate your roll-out before reaching the desired heading. As a rule of thumb, halve your angle of bank and use that figure to anticipate your roll-out. So, in 30° bank turn, start rolling out of the turn when within 15° of the desired heading.

▶ Turning on to Selected Headings - Using the Compass

When turning with reference to the compass: Undershoot North

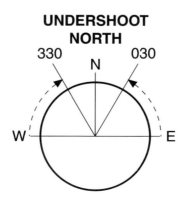

During a turn, the magnetic compass is subject to errors,–meaning that it is not displaying the actual heading. These errors are not significant on Easterly or Westerly headings - so you can just turn until the compass shows East (090) or West (270). When turning on to Southerly or Northerly headings, the errors are at a maximum. The rule of thumb to allow for these errors is summarised as UNOS:

Undershoot North Overshoot South

Turning

The amount of under/overshoot should be 30°
less or more than the heading, so for example
when turning from West (270) to North (360), you
should undershoot by rolling out of the turn when
the compass reads 330. When turning from East
(090) to South (180) you should overshoot the
heading by rolling out of the turn when the
compass reads 210.

The UNOS rule applies only in the Northern
hemisphere. In the Southern hemisphere the rule
is reversed, so that you should undershoot South
and overshoot North.

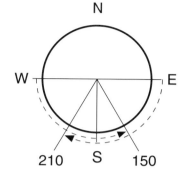

**OVERSHOOT
SOUTH**

*When turning with
reference to the compass:
Overshoot South*

Exercise

9

Turning

Flight Exercise

▷ Purpose

The purpose of this exercise is to learn to turn the aircraft on to selected headings during level, climbing or descending flight.

▷ Airmanship

Lookout

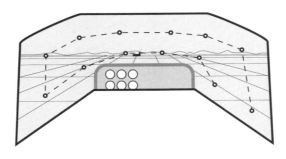

Complete a full lookout BEFORE starting a turn.

As always, lookout is the primary airmanship consideration. Always look out before turning, every time. Do this lookout in an ordered way. Start by looking over your shoulder in the direction of the turn. Then scan across, to look over your other shoulder and back across for a final check in the direction of intended turn.

Maintain the lookout scan throughout the turn and visually check the area you will be flying into as you roll out on to the new heading. If you are flying in high-wing aircraft, a lot of visibility is lost into the turn once the inner wing lowers.

When flying a high-wing aircraft it is common practice to 'lift' the wing slightly to clear the area visually before turning.

Lookout BEFORE turning is particularly important in a high-wing aircraft.

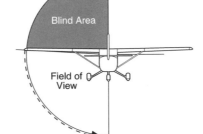
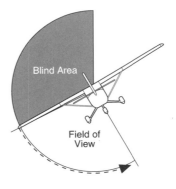

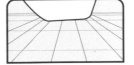

Orientation

During a series of turns, it is quite possible to get disorientated and to lose some of your sense of direction. After each turn, orientate yourself by reference to local landmarks and keep a mental check of the heading required to return to the airfield.

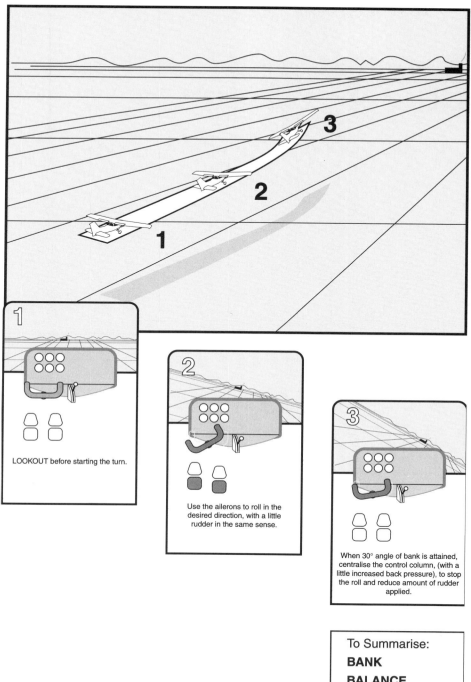

1

LOOKOUT before starting the turn.

2

Use the ailerons to roll in the desired direction, with a little rudder in the same sense.

3

When 30° angle of bank is attained, centralise the control column, (with a little increased back pressure), to stop the roll and reduce amount of rudder applied.

To Summarise:

BANK

BALANCE

BACK PRESSURE

LOOKOUT

Maintaining the Turn

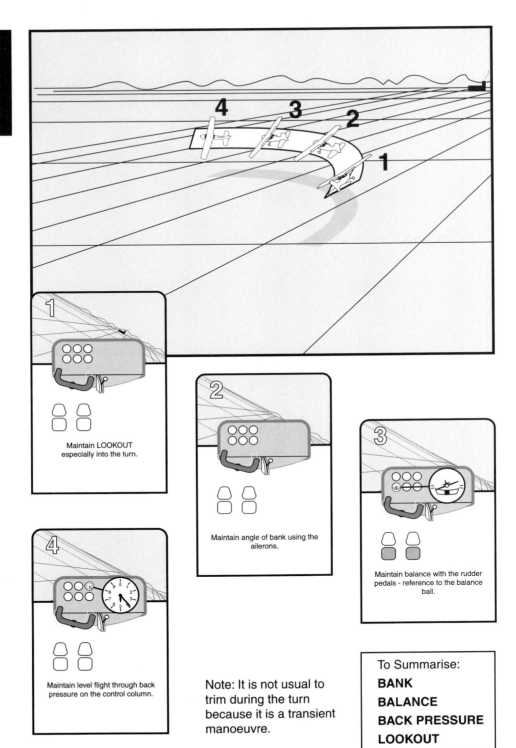

Maintain LOOKOUT especially into the turn.

Maintain angle of bank using the ailerons.

Maintain balance with the rudder pedals - reference to the balance ball.

Maintain level flight through back pressure on the control column.

Note: It is not usual to trim during the turn because it is a transient manoeuvre.

To Summarise:

BANK

BALANCE

BACK PRESSURE

LOOKOUT

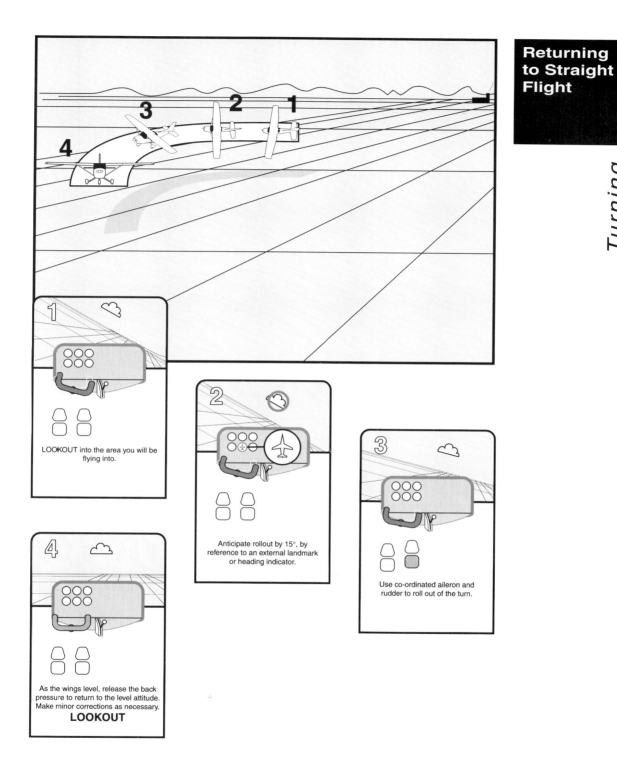

1

LOOKOUT into the area you will be flying into.

2

Anticipate rollout by 15°, by reference to an external landmark or heading indicator.

3

Use co-ordinated aileron and rudder to roll out of the turn.

4

As the wings level, release the back pressure to return to the level attitude. Make minor corrections as necessary.
LOOKOUT

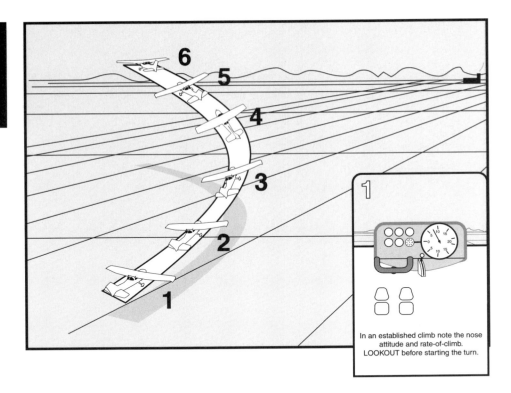

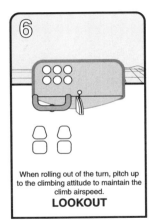

1

In an established climb note the nose attitude and rate-of-climb.
LOOKOUT before starting the turn.

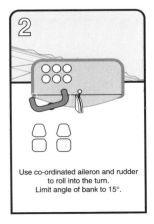

2

Use co-ordinated aileron and rudder to roll into the turn.
Limit angle of bank to 15°.

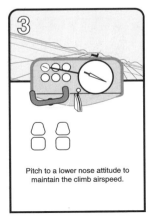

3

Pitch to a lower nose attitude to maintain the climb airspeed.

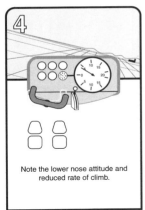

4

Note the lower nose attitude and reduced rate of climb.

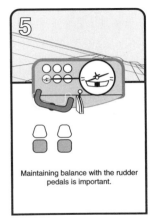

5

Maintaining balance with the rudder pedals is important.

6

When rolling out of the turn, pitch up to the climbing attitude to maintain the climb airspeed.
LOOKOUT

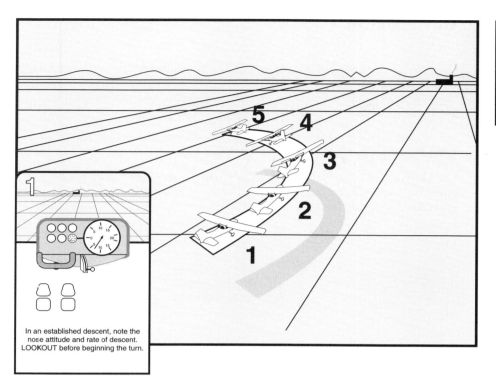

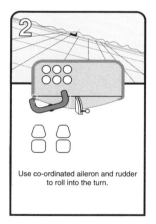

1. In an established descent, note the nose attitude and rate of descent. LOOKOUT before beginning the turn.

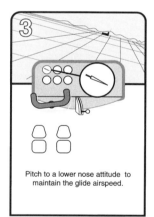

2. Use co-ordinated aileron and rudder to roll into the turn.

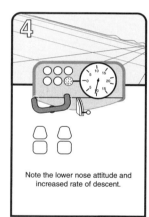

3. Pitch to a lower nose attitude to maintain the glide airspeed.

4. Note the lower nose attitude and increased rate of descent.

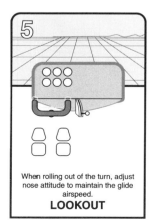

5. When rolling out of the turn, adjust nose attitude to maintain the glide airspeed.
LOOKOUT

Conclusion

During this exercise you will have learnt to turn the aircraft smoothly and accurately on to selected headings. In climbing and descending turns, the extra element of levelling out at a selected level will be introduced and so you will learn to plan ahead and co-ordinate your actions.

You should appreciate some of the aerodynamic factors affecting an aircraft when turning, particularly adverse yaw and the reduced airspeed margin over stall speed.

During the circuit flying that will soon follow, all the basic flight manoeuvres will be practised in each short circuit and you will soon be able to fly with increasing ease, confidence and accuracy.

Slow Flight

During this exercise you will learn to fly the aircraft at slow airspeeds, just 5-10 knots faster than the stall speed. The stall airspeed is that at which the angle of attack at the wing becomes so great that lift begins to decrease and the aircraft can no longer sustain level flight. This is a rather broad definition for now, but the whole subject of stalling is explained more comprehensively at the supplement to this section and in the next exercise (10b - Stalling).

To control the aircraft safely at slow airspeeds you will have to develop your co-ordination skills, particularly in keeping the aircraft in balance using the rudder and co-ordinating the use of power and attitude to maintain the specified airspeed in level, climbing, descending and turning flight. This exercise is all about awareness of slow flight. It is not intended to encourage you to regularly fly at such slow airspeed. Rather, it fulfils two purposes:

1 To become aware of the symptoms of flight at a critically slow airspeed.

2 To be able to control the aircraft safely at a slow airspeed whilst accelerating to faster airspeed i.e. when recovering from an unintentional loss of airspeed.

BACKGROUND BRIEFING

▶ **Definition of Slow Flight**

▶ **The Forces During Slow Flight**

▶ **Effect of Controls During Slow Flight**

▶ **Manoeuvring In Slow Flight**

▶ **Distractions During Slow Flight**

FLIGHT EXERCISE

▷ **Purpose**

▷ **Airmanship**

▷ **Straight and Level**

▷ **Climbing and Descending**

▷ **Turning**

CONCLUSION

BACKGROUND BRIEFING

▶ Definition of Slow Flight

For the purposes of this flight exercise, slow flight means an airspeed 5 knots faster than the stalling speed. Stalling speed is most often defined as Vs0 or Vs1, which are the stalling speeds of the aircraft under a defined set of circumstances. Vs0 relates to the stalling speed at maximum weight, with full flap, wings level and power off. Vs1 is the stalling speed at maximum weight with nil flap, wings level and power off. Vs0 and Vs1 will be stated in the aircraft's POH/FM and are also marked on the airspeed indicator (ASI). Vs1 marks the slowest end of the green arc and Vs0 marks the slowest end of the white arc.

The Vs0 and Vs1 stalling speeds as marked on the Air Speed Indicator (ASI).

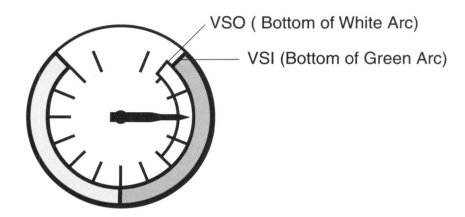

VSO (Bottom of White Arc)

VSI (Bottom of Green Arc)

▶ The Forces During Slow Flight

To fly level at a slow airspeed, an aircraft still has to produce enough lift to balance weight. As the airspeed has been reduced, the pilot has to increase some other lift-producing factor to compensate - this other factor is the angle of attack.

The slower the airspeed, the greater the angle of attack required to produce the same amount of lift.

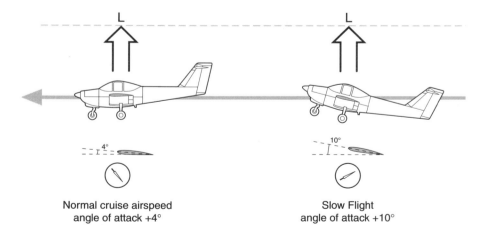

Normal cruise airspeed
angle of attack +4°

Slow Flight
angle of attack +10°

At the normal cruising airspeed, the wing will need an angle of attack of only 4° or so to produce the lift required for level flight. Once at these critically slow airspeeds, the angle of attack will need to be nearer 10° to produce the lift required for level

Slow Flight

flight. This increase in angle of attack increases the *INDUCED* drag created by the wing.

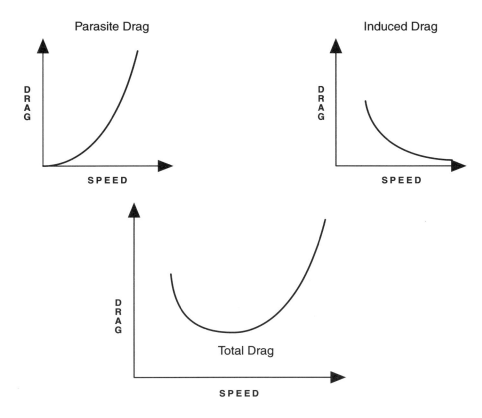

Parasite Drag

Induced Drag

LEFT> Parasite drag increases with speed

RIGHT> Induced drag is greatest at the slowest airspeed.

Total Drag

The distinct shape of the total drag curve means that once slower than the minimum drag speed, a reduction in airspeed leads to an increase in drag.

To see why this is important, we must look again at the power-required curves.

Slow flight can be regarded as flight when the airspeed is below the minimum power-required airspeed (power required = drag x airspeed).

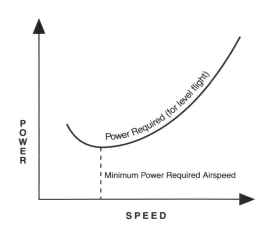

Power Required (for level flight)

Minimum Power Required Airspeed

Slow flight primarily concerns flight at less than the Minimum Power Required airspeed.

Power Required = Drag x Airspeed

When the airspeed is faster than the minimum power-required airspeed, a reduction in airspeed leads to a DECREASE in drag (and therefore a decrease in power required). Thrust is now greater than drag and so the aircraft will accelerate back to its original airspeed. In this condition the aircraft is speed-stable.

When flying faster than the Minimum Power Required airspeed, the aircraft is speed-stable.

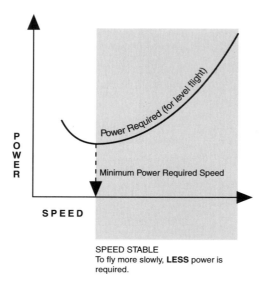

SPEED STABLE
To fly more slowly, **LESS** power is required.

When the airspeed is slower than the minimum power-required airspeed, a reduction in airspeed leads to an INCREASE in drag (and so an increase in power required). Drag is now greater than thrust and the aircraft will continue to decelerate. In this condition the aircraft is speed-unstable - to fly more slowly you actually need more power!

Slower than the Minimum Power Required airspeed, the aircraft is speed unstable.

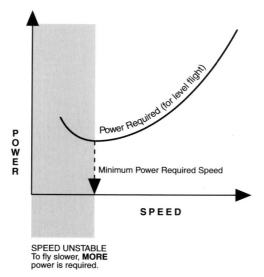

SPEED UNSTABLE
To fly slower, **MORE** power is required.

Pilots of high-performance aircraft often refer to this condition as 'flying on the back of the drag curve' - which conveys the feeling well.

▶ Effect of Controls During Slow Flight

You will remember from exercise 4 that at slow airspeeds the flying controls are less effective. They feel 'sloppy' and bigger control movements are needed.

The ailerons can be very ineffective at slow airspeeds. Furthermore, in a slow airspeed/high angle-of-attack situation, adverse yaw (described in exercise 9) is far more pronounced, especially with large aileron deflections, i.e. when rolling into or out of a turn.

The rudder is also less effective at slow airspeeds and coarser use of the rudder pedals may be necessary.

The elevator/stabilator is the most powerful of the three primary flying controls. As well as controlling the attitude, the tailplane or stabilator provides stability in pitch. The elevator or stabilator is, of course, less effective at slow airspeeds. In addition the high angle of attack of the wing can produce a considerable 'downwash' over the tail, altering its angle of attack and therefore the lift force produced by the tailplane. The effect of downwash is generally more noticeable on a high-wing aircraft than a low-wing aircraft.

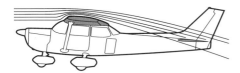 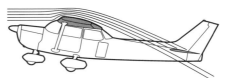

A high angle of attack increases the downwash over the tail, altering the effectiveness of the elevators. This is particularly noticeable in high wing, low-tailplane aircraft.

Slow Airspeed

The slipstream will alter the feel and effectiveness of the rudder and the elevator/stabilator (except on a 'T'-tail aircraft where the elevator is outside the slipstream). At slow airspeeds the helix of the slipstream is much tighter around the fuselage and its effect more pronounced. Changes in power setting at slow airspeeds will have a more noticeable yawing effect, which the pilot will have to anticipate and correct.

At slow airspeeds the helix of the slipstream has a greater yawing effect.

Raising and lowering of flap is another factor to consider more carefully during slow flight. The change in drag (and therefor change in airspeed) is more critical at these slower airspeeds. Do not raise the flaps if the airspeed is below Vs1 - the flaps-up stalling airspeed (ie the bottom of the green arc on the ASI).

Fast Airspeed

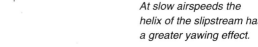 

All control movements should be smooth and co-ordinated. Harsh and excessive control movements must be avoided.

▶ Manoeuvring in Slow Flight

During flight at slow airspeed, maintaining the selected airspeed and balanced flight are all-important. Any change in power setting will have a pronounced yawing effect, which the pilot must anticipate and correct. Similarly, when turning the increased adverse yaw needs to be compensated for by the pilot.

We return to the maxim that Power + Attitude = Performance. To fly level, the required power is set and the attitude adjusted to attain the target airspeed. It may be necessary to make small adjustments to the power and attitude to stay level at the selected airspeed. An excess of power will cause the aircraft to climb, while too little power will cause the aircraft to descend. Attitude is controlling airspeed, power is controlling height/altitude.

During a turn, the small loss of airspeed normally acceptable is no longer safe so , the aircraft is pitched nose-down to maintain airspeed and power is added (during a level turn) to stop the aircraft descending. During slow flight, turns are normally made at no more than 15° angle of bank due to the increase in stalling speed as angle of bank increases.

It is worth repeating that during all these manoeuvres, keeping the aircraft in balance using the rudder and maintenance of the selected airspeed through attitude are all-important.

▶ Distractions During Slow Flight

With practice you will soon be able to control the aircraft safely at these slow airspeeds, albeit with some concentration. However, the danger of flying too slowly often manifests itself when the pilot is distracted from the primary task of flying the aircraft by some secondary factor (i.e. radio calls, talking to passengers, map reading, positioning in the circuit etc.). Your instructor will simulate a number of distractions to demonstrate to you how important it is to make the actual flying of the aircraft your Number one priority at all times.

Flight Exercise

▷ Purpose

To learn the symptoms of flight at a critically slow airspeed and to learn to control the aircraft at this slow airspeed.

▷ Airmanship

HASELL checks

All the major airmanship points relating to this flight exercise are covered by use of the HASELL check. Before beginning the flight exercise you should carry out a HASELL check. In detail the check is as below:

H **Height** sufficient height above the ground must be maintained - your instructor will decide the minimum height for flying this exercise.

Height = Safety

A **Airframe** flaps should be set as required. Brakes should be off (this may be very important on some aircraft types).

S **Security** check there are no loose articles in the cockpit, and nothing to impede the full and free movement of the controls (i.e. flightboards on the knees etc.). Hatches should be secure and harnesses reasonably tight. If possible the flight instrument gyros (the HI and AI) should be caged (i.e. locked in position). This is often not possible in modern aircraft.

E **Engine** mixture should be rich and carburettor heat will need to be set to hot at low power setting. Due to the slow airspeed, engine temperatures and pressures should be closely monitored. If the aircraft has an electric fuel pump, this should be switched on and the fuel tank with the greatest contents selected.

L **Location** **A B C C**

you should remain:

A not in the vicinity of an active Airfield

B not over Built up areas

C clear of Clouds

C outside Controlled airspace

L **Lookout** maintain a good lookout. Visually clear the area you will be manoeuvring in by looking all around. This is usually done by a complete 360° turn, or two 180° turns, checking at your level, above and below.

Flight Exercise

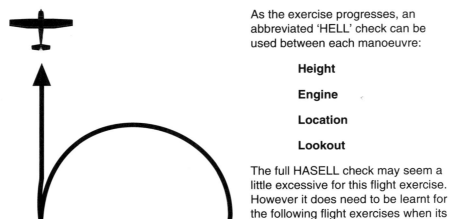

As the exercise progresses, an abbreviated 'HELL' check can be used between each manoeuvre:

Height

Engine

Location

Lookout

The full HASELL check may seem a little excessive for this flight exercise. However it does need to be learnt for the following flight exercises when its use is most important.

During the HASELL checks it will be necessary to turn the aircraft to visually clear the area all around the aircraft; checking at the aircraft's level, above and below.

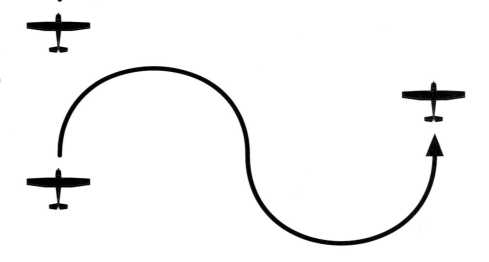

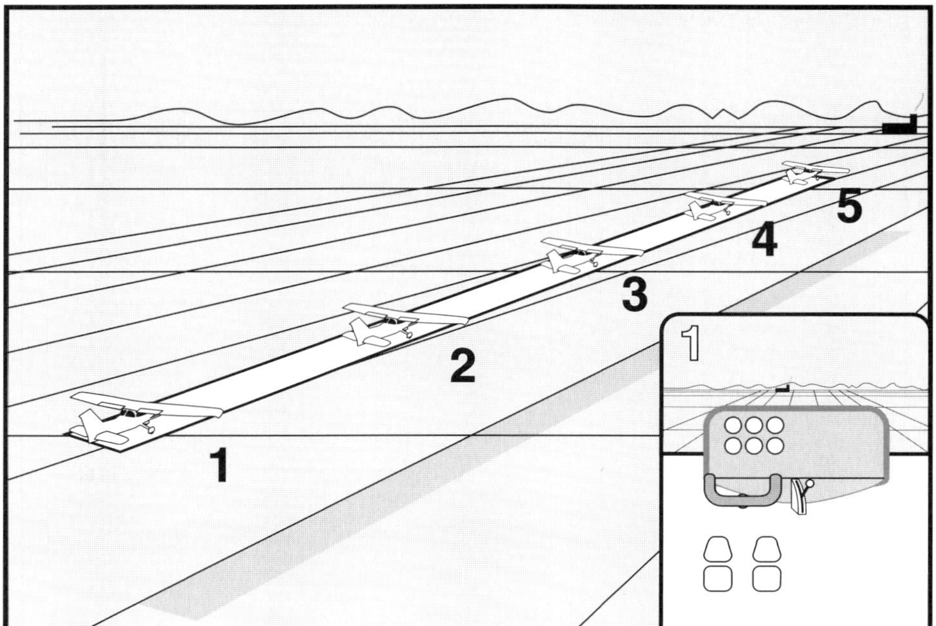

Complete HASELL checks before beginning slow flight.
Select an aiming point ahead.

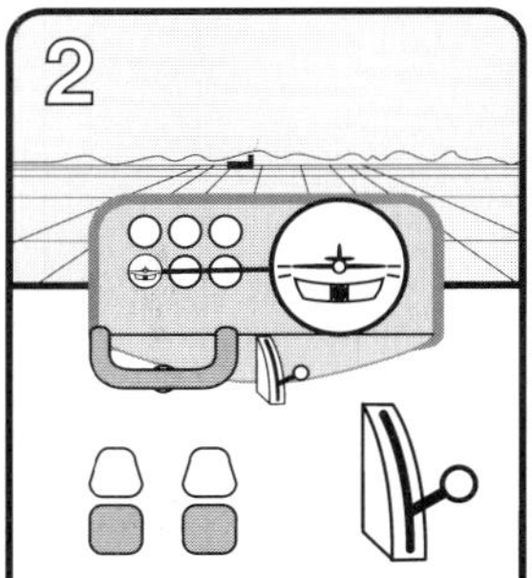

POWER
Reduce power to slow flight setting.
Maintain balanced flight.

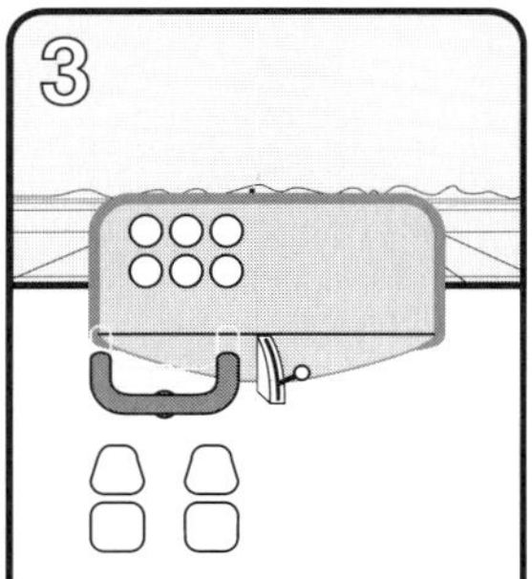

ATTITUDE
Pitch up to maintain level flight until target airspeed is reached.

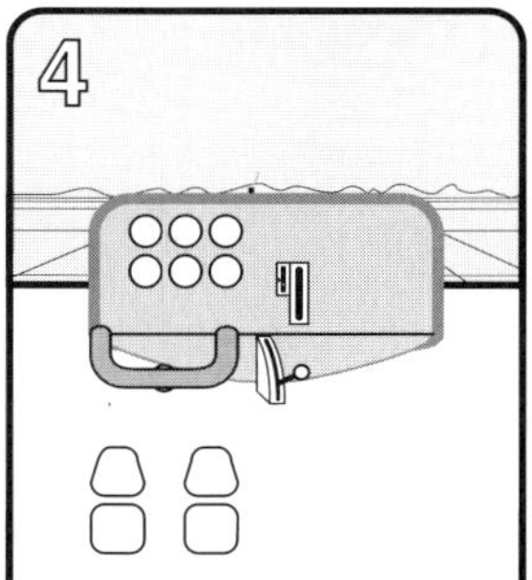

TRIM
Trim to relieve any control forces.

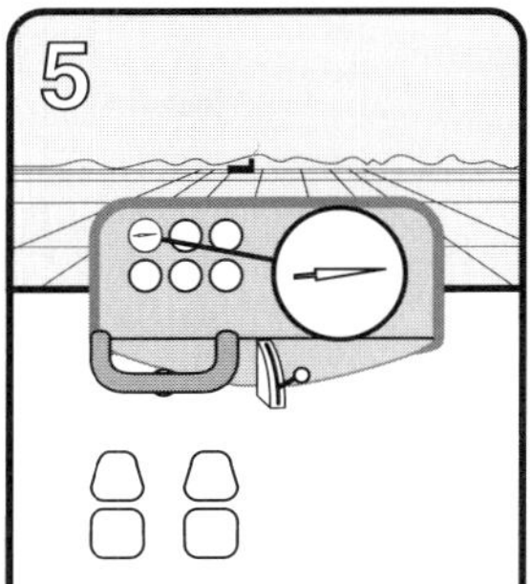

Note slower airspeed and less effective flying controls.

To summarise:
POWER
ATTITUDE
TRIM
-Cross-check altimeter and airspeed indicator.
-Make minor corrections as necessary.
LOOKOUT

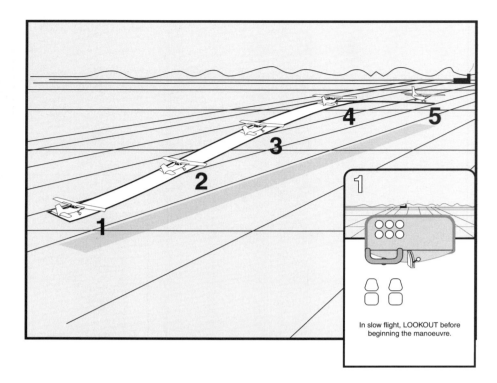

In slow flight, LOOKOUT before beginning the manoeuvre.

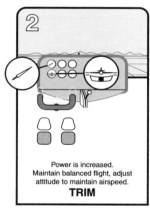

Power is increased.
Maintain balanced flight, adjust attitude to maintain airspeed.
TRIM

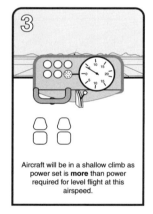

Aircraft will be in a shallow climb as power set is **more** than power required for level flight at this airspeed.

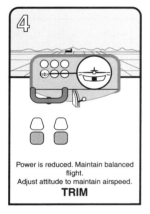

Power is reduced. Maintain balanced flight.
Adjust attitude to maintain airspeed.
TRIM

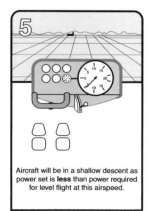

Aircraft will be in a shallow descent as power set is **less** than power required for level flight at this airspeed.

Slow Flight

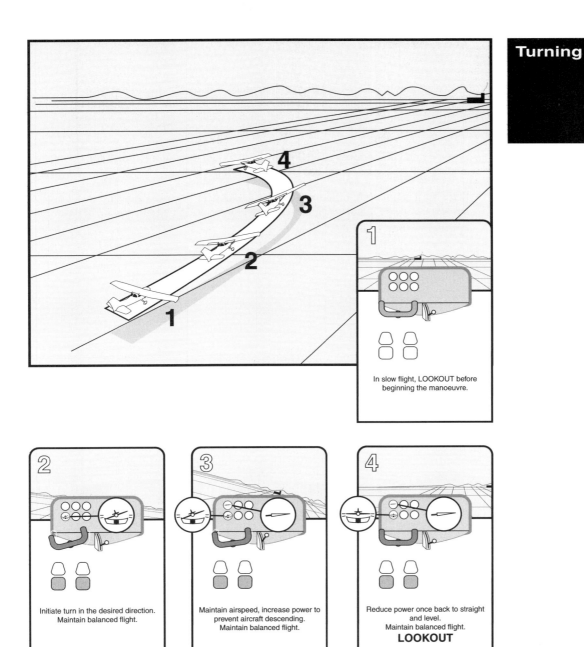

In slow flight, LOOKOUT before beginning the manoeuvre.

Initiate turn in the desired direction.
Maintain balanced flight.

Maintain airspeed, increase power to prevent aircraft descending.
Maintain balanced flight.

Reduce power once back to straight and level.
Maintain balanced flight.
LOOKOUT

Note: During slow flight, angle of bank should not exceed 15°.

Exercise

10_{*a*}

Slow Flight

Conclusion

The most immediate benefit from this exercise will be felt during the next few flights. You will recognise the symptoms of a critically slow airspeed and be able to control the aircraft safely at this speed. These skills will be needed during the approach to a stall and recovery from a stall.

Soon, when you begin circuit flying, the period just after take-off and just before landing will also require the use of your slow-flight skills.

Slow flight is not an operational exercise - except in the training syllabus you would not want to fly deliberately so close to the stalling speed for any length of time unless you had a very good reason.

Principles of Flight Supplement

Before embarking on stalling, which is all about what happens when the aircraft stops producing the lift necessary to balance weight, it makes sense to look more closely at lift.

For practical purposes, the lift force which enables an aircraft to fly, is created by the airflow around the wings. The rest of the aircraft does produce varying amounts of lift, but it is the lift from the wings that is most important.

It is simplest to visualise the airflow around the wing in terms of *streamlines* that show how the airflow is behaving. When the airflow meets the wing, it splits so that it flows above and below it. A cross-section of the wing shape is called the *aerofoil section*. A combination of the curvature of the aerofoil (known as *camber*) and the angle at which the airflow meets the wing (the angle of attack) imparts a circulation force to the airflow. This circulation force acts on the airflow so that air passing OVER the wing accelerates and air passing UNDER the wing slows. Looking at the streamlines above the front part of the wing, you can see that they have narrowed. Airflow velocity at this constriction must increase to allow the same volume of air to pass through; and at an increased velocity the pressure must decrease. The difference in airflow speeds above and below the wing means there is a difference in pressure - low pressure above the wing and high pressure below it. This pressure differential is directly related to the difference in airflow speeds and is the source of lift. The lower pressure above the wing means that the wing is 'sucked up' and something like 70% of the lift force is generated by the reduced pressure above the wing.

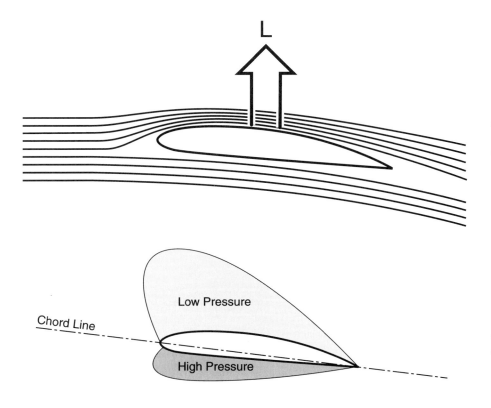

There is faster airflow and lower pressure above the wing, slower airflow and higher pressure below.

The approximate pressure distribution around a wing at normal angles of attack.

Background Briefing

The pressure differential is not evenly distributed around the aerofoil. In fact, the greatest pressure differential both above and below the wing is concentrated towards the forward part of the wing. As the angle of attack changes, so the distribution of the pressure differential changes. Lift is said to act through a point known as the *centre of pressure* (CP). As the angle of attack increases, the lift force is concentrated closer to the leading edge of the wing and the CP moves forward.

At increasing angles of attack, airflow separation starts at the rear of the wing and moves forward as the angle of attack approaches the critical angle.

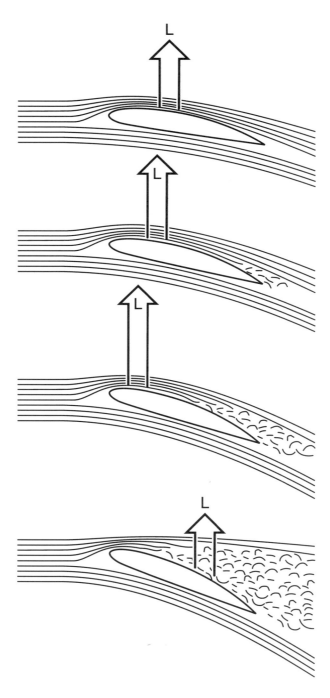

This all takes place because of the viscosity of the air. Air is not as viscous (sticky) as, say, treacle; but it is viscous enough to follow the contours of the wing and so curve the airflow. Lift is created in this fashion until the angle of attack becomes too high and the airflow stops following the contours of the wing and separates from it. Once the airflow has separated from the wing, lift is no longer being efficiently created from that part of the wing. The type of wing section used on a training aircraft is designed to have reasonably mild and predictable stalling characteristics. With this type of aerofoil, separation of the airflow starts at the rear of the wing, as the angle of attack increases. With an increasing angle of attack, the separation point moves forward and more lift is lost from the rear of the wing until the total lift produced by the wing begins to decrease. Note that lift does not completely vanish, but there is a marked reduction in lift and the aircraft is no longer producing enough to sustain level flight. The angle of attack at which this marked reduction in lift occurs is called the *critical angle of attack.*

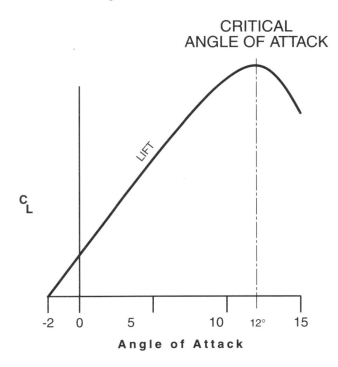

The increase in lift with increased angle of attack. Once past the critical angle of attack, lift actually decreases.

The contribution to lift attributed to the angle of attack is most commonly referred to as the *coefficient of lift* - Cl. Drawn on a graph, you can see that as the angle of attack increases, so the Cl increases. This confirms what the pilot already knows from the slow flight exercise; if one of the factors that affects lift (e.g. airspeed) is reduced, another (e.g. angle of attack) has to be increased for the same amount of lift to be produced.

Increasing the angle of attack to increase the Cl works well - up to a point. That point is the critical angle of attack. Once the critical angle of attack is reached and passed, a further increase in angle of attack actually leads to a DECREASE in Cl as the airflow separates from the wing and so total lift is reduced. The critical angle of attack marks the stall.

▶ Angle of Attack

It is obvious from the foregoing that angle of attack is a vital factor in the production of lift, so we should explore it a little more closely.

The basic definition of angle of attack used until now has been that it is the angle at which the airflow meets the wing. To be more precise, angle of attack is the angle at which the relative airflow meets the *chord line* of the aerofoil. The chord line is a straight line drawn through the aerofoil section from its leading edge to the trailing edge.

Now it can be seen that the pilot actually has two ways of altering the angle of attack. He can alter the aircraft's attitude, thus presenting the wings to the airflow at a different angle, or he can in principal alter the shape of the leading or trailing edge of the wing to move the chord line, thus altering the angle of attack even though the airflow is still coming from the same direction.

Altering the trailing edge of the wing is, of course, exactly what the pilot does when he lowers the flaps or moves the ailerons. The same is true of other flying controls not attached to the wing, such as the elevator. Even the fin/rudder is, after all, essentially a wing, but mounted vertically on the aircraft instead of horizontally. When the pilot deflects the rudder, the change in the chord line (and so the angle of attack) and the change in camber (curvature) of the fin/rudder produces lift in one direction or another.

By altering the shape of the wing (e.g. with flaps or ailerons), the pilot can alter both the camber (curvature) of the wing and the angle of attack.

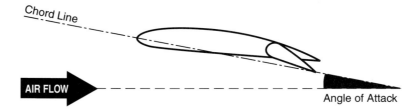

►In Summary

You should now appreciate that lift is created by airflow above and below the wing. It is the pressure differential that is the essence of lift.

Creation of lift works over a fairly limited range of angles of attack. The exact limits depend on the shape and design of the wing. Once the critical angle of attack is exceeded, there is a marked loss of lift and the wing has stalled.

►And Finally

The concept of lift is not a simple matter. A detailed exploration of the subject is well outside the scope of this book and well into gas laws, physics, advanced mathematics and serious head-scratching.

If you want to know more about lift, without leaving the ground, you will need access to either:

A A functional wind tunnel, or

B A friend with a car

Assuming that B is more likely, get your friend to drive the car at a reasonable speed, whilst you hold your hand out of an open window (maybe you did this last as a child). Keep your fingers together with your hand flat and hold it level to the airflow. As you slowly increase the angle of attack of your hand, you can FEEL the lift - your hand may even try to float up. Increase the angle of attack too far and you will feel a great resistance (drag), your hand will stop floating and instead try to pull your arm right back - your hand has exceeded its critical angle of attack. Reduce the angle of attack, the drag reduces, lift returns and your hand is floating once more.

Lift

Airflow

Learning about lift the easy way.

And this is what you really need to know about lift and stalling.

There are two important things to remember whilst you are discovering lift in this way:

1 Your arm is likely to be longer than when you last did this as a child. Lookout for hedges, lamp-posts, other cars etc.

2 If somebody asks what you are doing with your arms stuck out of a moving car, think twice before telling them that you are learning to fly.

Stalling

A well-known aviation writer was once asked what he considered the three most important factors in flight safety. He replied "Airspeed, airspeed and airspeed"; and he's got a point. Whilst the aircraft is being flown at a safe airspeed, the pilot is able to control the aircraft and remain in command of the situation. If the aircraft is allowed to stall, the rapid descent and possible control problems mean that the pilot has in fact lost control of the aircraft; until that is rectified, nothing else really matters.

The flight exercise is normally split over two flights, beginning with basic stalls and recoveries, later moving on to stalls in various configurations and manoeuvres. Once you are able to make safe recoveries from full stalls, the emphasis will be on recovering to normal flight at the first symptom of the approaching stall—recovery at the *incipient* stage.

Many students approach this exercise with some trepidation—which is basically fear of the unknown. In fact you will find that stalling is not a violent manoeuvre. Your instructor may have demonstrated a stall to you in a previous flight exercise, so you will have seen how gentle the whole process can be.

BACKGROUND BRIEFING

▶ **The Forces in a Stall**

▶ **Control Effectiveness During the Stall**

▶ **Factors Affecting Stalling Airspeed**

▶ **Wing Drop at the Stall**

▶ **Symptoms of the Approaching Stall**

▶ **Symptoms of the Stall**

▶ **The Standard Stall Recovery**

▶ **The Secondary Stall**

▶ **The Departure Stall**

▶ **The Recovery From the Incipient Stall**

▶ **The Quasi-stall**

FLIGHT EXERCISE

Exercise

10b

Flight Exercise

▷ **Purpose**

▷ **Airmanship**

▷ **The Stall and Recovery Without Power**

▷ **The Stall and Standard Stall Recovery**

▷ **The Stall With Power**

▷ **The Stall With Flap**

▷ **The Stall With Power and Flap (the Approach Configuration)**

▷ **Recovery At the Incipient (Developing) Stall**

CONCLUSION

BACKGROUND BRIEFING

▶ The Forces In a Stall

The stall occurs when there is a marked loss of lift from the wings, leading to a rapid loss of height and aircraft control problems. Although stalling is usually referred to in terms of airspeed, the stall in fact occurs whenever the critical angle of attack is exceeded. As few light aircraft carry an angle of attack indicator, the primary reference becomes airspeed. In quoting a stall airspeed we are actally referring to an airspeed at which the critical angle of attack occurs under a defined set of circumstances (e.g. wings level, power off, maximum weight etc.). You must appreciate that the stall can occur at ANY airspeed, if the critical angle of attack is exceeded.

In normal flight, as the angle of attack increases the Centre of Pressure (CP) moves forward. As the critical angle of attack is reached, the CP moves rapidly rearwards. The rearward movement of the CP and the marked loss of lift at the stall cause the aircraft to pitch nose-down - even if the control column is held fully back. This pitching nose-down (sometimes referred to as the *'g' break*) is a symptom of the full stall.

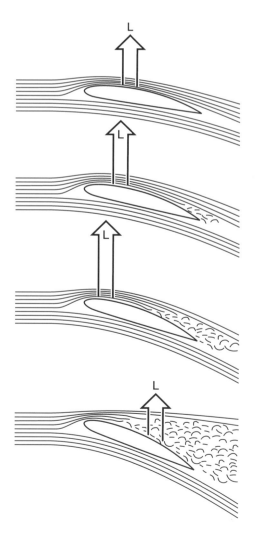

As angle of attack increases, Centre of Pressure (CP) moves forward. At the stall, the centre of pressure moves rapidly rearwards.

▶ Control Effectiveness During the Stall

At slow airspeeds the flying controls are less effective, larger control movements are needed and the controls feel 'sloppy'.

When we refer to the stall, we could more accurately refer to the *wing stall* because it is the wings that produce most lift, and the stall occurs when the lift from the wings reduces markedly. The flying controls themselves do not necessarily stall when the wing does; in fact the aircraft designer will take great care to try to ensure that they do not.

The fin and rudder are mounted vertically, so they do not stall in the same axis as the wing and should remain effective throughout the stall and recovery. However, this is not to say that it is not possible to stall the fin and rudder. In certain circumstances (such as a very steep sideslip using full rudder) it *may* be possible to stall the fin and rudder, leading to a loss of directional control.

The tailplane and elevator (or stabilator) is the primary control for recovering from the stall. The aircraft designer will ensure that even after the wings stall, the tailplane and elevator (or stabilator) remains effective so that the pilot retains the means to recover from the stall.

The situation in respect of the ailerons, being mounted on the wings, is a little more complex. Ailerons operate by altering the angle of attack of part of the wing, thereby increasing or decreasing lift of that wing. When an aileron is lowered, the angle of attack is increased. If the angle of attack of the wing was already close to the critical angle, lowering the aileron could actually cause the angle of attack to exceed the critical angle, stalling that part of the wing. As a result of this and also the effect of aileron drag (which causes adverse yaw) the ailerons tend to be ineffective throughout the stall and are not used during the stall recovery.

▶ Factors Affecting Stalling Airspeed

The stall airspeeds quoted in the flight manual and marked on the airspeed indicator as Vs0 (bottom of white arc) and Vs1 (bottom of green arc) are only valid in a very specific set of circumstances. Many factors can affect the actual stall airspeed (i.e. the speed at which the critical angle of attack is reached). Remember, the aircraft WILL stall, whatever the airspeed, if the critical angle of attack is exceeded.

- flaps/slats/slot

The use of wing trailing-edge flaps or wing leading-edge slats increases lift at a given airspeed and so the aircraft can be flown more slowly before stalling - the stalling airspeed is reduced. Fixed slots, built into the wing leading edge, have a similar effect.

- power

When power is applied, a component of thrust acts in the same direction as lift to oppose weight. In addition the propeller slipstream increases the airflow speed around the inner wing, increasing lift a little there.

As power is increased, stalling speed is decreased.

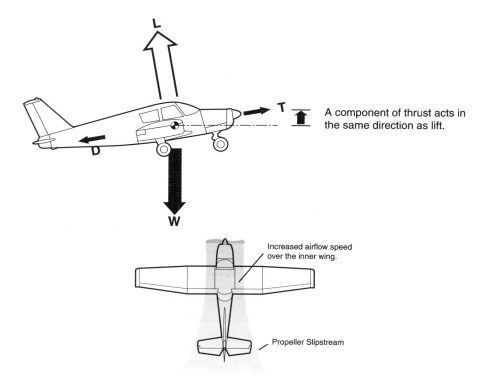

A component of thrust acts in the same direction as lift.

With power applied in the approach to the stall, a component of thrust acts with lift, so the stalling speed is reduced.

Increased airflow speed over the inner wing.

Propeller Slipstream

- altitude

Regardless of increased altitude and reduced air density, the stalling speed in terms of indicated airspeed–IAS–i.e. the airspeed reading on the airspeed indicator (ASI) remains the same.

Indicated stall airspeed at sea level

Indicated stall airspeed at 10,000 feet.

The INDICATED stalling speed remains the same regardless of altitude.

ASI

ASI

- load factor & manoeuvring

The *load factor* acting on an aircraft has a direct effect on the stalling speed. In normal level flight, Lift = Weight and the load factor is 1. The Vs0 and Vs1 speeds are calculated on the basis of a load factor of 1.

If a pilot wants the aircraft to follow a curved path–such as a turn, pulling out of a dive or some other manoeuvre–he increases lift (by increasing angle of attack) to provide the necessary centripetal force. The force is felt by the pilot as 'g'. Even in a moderate turn the total lift is greater than weight and so the load factor is greater than 1. At small angles of bank, few pilots will notice the small increase in loading ('g'). However, as load factor increases, stall airspeed increases.

Pulling out of a dive, the increase in lift increases the load factor and the stall speed increases.

Stalling an aircraft by increasing the load factor (perhaps by suddenly pulling back on the control column) is known as an *accelerated, high speed* or *dynamic stall.* This type of stall is less likely than a slow-speed stall because of the greater control forces needed to reach the critical angle of attack. Intentional stalling in this way may be prohibited in the aircraft you are flying because of the stresses imposed on the aircraft structure.

Stalling

- turning flight

When the aircraft is turning, the load factor is increased. The steeper the angle of
bank in the turn, the greater the load factor. At around 75° angle of bank in a level
turn the load factor is 4 (or 4 'g') and the stall airspeed is doubled.

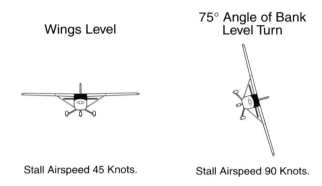

Wings Level

75° Angle of Bank
Level Turn

*As angle of bank is
increased, in a turn stall
speed increases.*

Stall Airspeed 45 Knots.

Stall Airspeed 90 Knots.

- effect of weight

Increased weight has to be opposed by increased lift to maintain level flight. At any
airspeed, more lift must therefore be produced by the aircraft. This increase in lift is
created by increasing the angle of attack. It follows that a heavier aircraft has a
higher angle of attack at a set airspeed than a lighter one and, as the aircraft slows
down, the heavier aircraft reaches the critical angle of attack at a faster airspeed
than the lighter one. The heavier the weight, the faster the stalling speed.

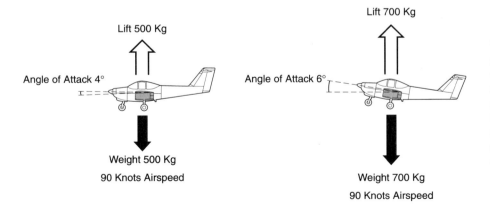

Lift 500 Kg

Lift 700 Kg

Angle of Attack 4°

Angle of Attack 6°

Weight 500 Kg

90 Knots Airspeed

Weight 700 Kg

90 Knots Airspeed

*The greater the weight,
the greater the angle of
attack at a given
airspeed. Therefore the
critical angle of attack is
reached at a faster
airspeed by a heavy
aircraft than by a lighter
one.*

- effect of centre of gravity

The position of the centre of gravity will alter the amount of downforce produced by the tailplane/stabilator. As this downforce opposes the lift produced by the wings, a greater downforce from the tailplane/stabilator reduces the total lift opposing weight; the stalling speed is faster.

At a forward centre of gravity, the stalling speed is increased.

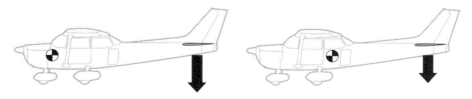

FORWARD CENTRE OF GRAVITY
Greater downforce from tailplane.

REAR CENTRE OF GRAVITY
Less downforce from tailplane.

The greatest downforce is needed at the most forward centre of gravity. So a forward centre of gravity INCREASES stall speed. Within the permitted centre of gravity range, the actual difference in stalling speeds is little more than a couple of knots.

- effect of ice/wing damage

If there is any ice or frost on the wing, or if the wing is damaged in any way (especially at the leading edge) the aerodynamic qualities of the wing will be altered. The stall speed will be increased and the stall characteristics will be altered –usually for the worse.

- gusts/turbulence

The effect of a sudden gust can be to increase the angle of attack of a part of the wing, causing it to exceed the critical angle. In practice this effect is momentary and it is highly unusual for an aircraft to enter a full stall because of a gust. However, it is common practice to increase airspeed slightly during the climb after take-off, or during the approach to land, if conditions are gusty.

A gust from a different direction than the main airflow may momentarily cause the wing to exceed the critical angle of attack.

AIR FLOW

GUST

▶ Wing Drop at The Stall

It is desirable for the wings to stay level throughout the stall and recovery. If one wing stalls before the other, the aircraft will roll and yaw towards that wing–this is referred to as a *wing drop.* A wing drop will increase the loss of height during a stall, and the recovery from the stall takes longer. Several factors make a wing drop at the stall more likely.

- the use of power

The use of power increases the yawing moment (usually to the left when the propeller is rotating clockwise). This yawing moment is mostly caused by the slipstream effect, which is more pronounced at slow airspeeds although other factors such as gyroscopic effect and torque effect are also present. In addition to these effects, the slipstream around the inner wings increases lift there and makes it more likely that an outer wing section will stall first. All these factors make a wing drop more likely during a power-on stall, usually to the left (in an aircraft with a clockwise-rotating propeller).

- the use of flaps

The lowering of flap alters the lift distribution over the wings. This change in the lift distribution across the wingspan makes a wing drop at the stall more likely.

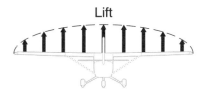
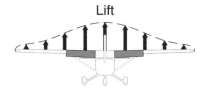

Lowering flaps alters the lift distribution across the wing span and makes a wing drop at the stall more likely.

- unbalanced flight

Unbalanced flight is possibly the prime factor leading to a wing drop at the stall. Unbalanced flight during the approach to the stall greatly increases the chance of one wing stalling before the other. The solution is quite simple. Use the rudder to keep the balance ball central and the aircraft in balance.

Unbalanced (un-coordinated) flight makes a wing drop at the stall more likely.

- turning flight

When turning there is an increased tendency for the wing to drop at the stall, but not in the way you might expect. In a balanced level turn, the higher (outer) wing has a higher angle of attack than the lower wing. Therefore the higher wing will reach the critical angle of attack first and stall, actually rolling the aircraft out of the turn. Some older aircraft types (not modern training aircraft) may literally 'flick' out of a turn at the stall.

However, the effect of power may also present in the turns. At a high power setting, with the propeller rotating clockwise, the chances of the left wing dropping are increased, whichever way the aircraft is turning. Bear in mind, however, that it is impossible to give hard and fast rules about stall characteristics. The amount of power applied, the angle of bank, fuel tank balance, flying control positions etc can all have a marked effect on stalling behaviour in terms of a possible wing drop.

With experience you will come to appreciate that different aircraft types have differing stall characteristics and even individual aircraft of the same type often have their own handling 'quirks'.

▶ Symptoms of the Approaching Stall

The pilot should become aware of the symptoms of the approach to the stall. The sense developed in this way will act as an early-warning system should you ever get into a stalling situation unintentionally. During the approach to the stall, one or more of the following symptoms should be evident:

critically slow airspeed, airspeed decreasing

stall warner operating

sloppy, ineffective controls

reduced noise

buffeting as the airflow separates from the wing

unusually high nose attitude for the manoeuvre being flown.

(Note. the aircraft's nose attitude is not directly related to the angle of attack. It is possible for the aircraft to stall with a nose-low attitude, or indeed any nose attitude, if the critical angle of attack is exceeded).

▶ Symptoms of the Stall

All of the symptoms of the approach to the stall continue right up to the stall itself. The stall is usually marked by the aircraft pitching nose-down (the 'g' break) even though the control column may be held fully back i.e. applying full up-elevator. A wing may drop and the aircraft will lose height. In addition to the symptoms present during the approach to the stall, one or more of the following symptoms will occur at the stall:

increased buffet

aircraft pitches nose-down

possible wing drop

aircraft descends

▶ The Standard Stall Recovery

By now you will appreciate that an aircraft stalls when the pilot brings the wings to the critical angle of attack. It follows that, to recover, the pilot must reduce the angle of attack to unstall the wings. This is done by moving the control column forward (although in practice you may only need to release the back pressure) even though the aircraft may already be pitching nose-down. If power is not being used in the recovery, the nose is lowered to the gliding attitude and the aircraft will accelerate back to flying airspeed. **It is the unstalling of the wings that is the critical factor in the stall recovery.**

If you also experience a wing drop at the stall, you will realise from what has gone before that the use of aileron may make the situation worse rather than better. However not using aileron is easier said than done, because all your training up until now has taught you to use aileron to control roll. To contain the wing drop at the stall you should use opposite rudder while keeping the control column centralised (i.e. the ailerons neutral). Sufficient rudder should be used to prevent further yaw, and to minimise any further roll. Do not try to level the wings using the rudder–this will lead to excessive yaw, which is precisely what should be avoided at this point. When the wings have unstalled and the aircraft begins to accelerate, the ailerons can be used in the normal way to level the wings.

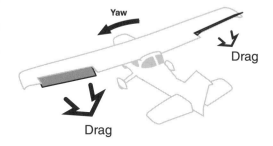

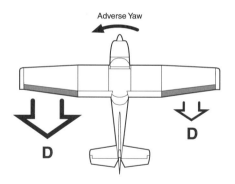

The wing with the lowered aileron produces more drag than the other wing.

L

L

Roll

Low angle of attack

High angle of attack

Use of aileron at the stall may have the reverse of the intended effect, REDUCING lift on the wing with the lowered aileron as the critical angle of attack is exceeded and causing the aircraft to roll the opposite way to the aileron applied.

c_L

c_L

-2 0   5   10   15
Angle of Attack

-2 0   5   10   15
Angle of Attack

In the first recoveries you practise, the power will be left at idle throughout the stall and recovery. Once you have practised some recoveries without power and learned to appreciate that it is the unstalling of the wings with the elevator/stabilator that is the crucial factor, power can be used to accelerate the recovery and reduce the height loss. The use of power means that the aircraft does not have to be pitched nose-down as far during the recovery and the aircraft accelerates back to a safe airspeed quicker.

Taking these elements together, a technique known as the *Standard Stall Recovery* has evolved. Learn the S.S.R. by heart, you should be able to use it instinctively:

> move the control column forward (or release back pressure)
>
> apply full power

SIMULTANEOUSLY

> use rudder to prevent further yaw and roll

When the wings have unstalled and the airspeed is increasing:

> level the wings using aileron
>
> centralise the rudder
>
> recover (gently) to the climb

▶ The Secondary Stall

If the controls are handled too harshly during the recovery from the stall, it is possible to stall again–a *secondary stall*. This can occur if the control column is moved back too quickly or too early when recovering from the descent, thus increasing the load factor and stalling the aircraft. Stalling the aircraft at a higher than normal stall airspeed is also known as an accelerated, high speed or dynamic stall. Some aircraft are prohibited from intentionally stalling in this way.

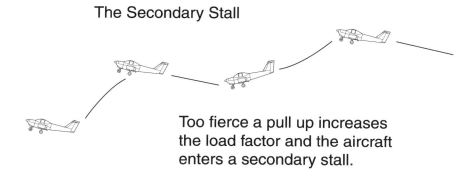

The Secondary Stall

Too fierce a pull up increases the load factor and the aircraft enters a secondary stall.

▶ The Departure Stall

Stalling in a climb with full power is sometimes referred to as the *departure stall* because it may occur just after take-off if the pilot is not controlling airspeed properly. A feature of the departure stall is the very steep nose high attitude of the aircraft at the stall, much steeper than the normal climb attitude.

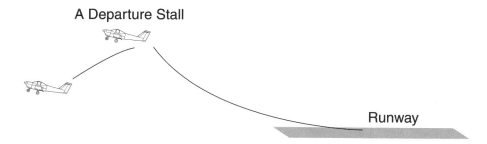

A Departure Stall

Runway

▶ The Recovery From the Incipient Stall

Once you are thoroughly familiar with various stalls and the Standard Stall Recovery (SSR), the emphasis will be placed upon recovering at the incipient (developing) stage of the stall. After all, there is no point in recognising that the aircraft is about to stall, then waiting for the full stall to develop so that you can do something about it!!

Your instructor will decide which symptom of the approaching stall should be taken as your signal to begin the recovery - normally stall-warner activation is chosen as the signal to begin the Standard Stall Recovery. The main differences in the SSR at the incipient stage are that the aircraft will not need to be pitched as far nose-down to get the aircraft accelerating and the height loss may be virtually nil.

Your instructor will want to see that you can safely recover at the incipient stage, with the minimum loss of height, before moving on from this exercise.

▶ The Quasi-Stall

During the flight exercise your instructor may demonstrate a condition known as the *quasi-stall*–a semi-stalled condition. Usually the quasi-stall is set up using initial flap and a small amount of power (i.e. the approach configuration) and then reducing the airspeed until the stall warner is just about to activate. This is the sort of flight condition that might occur during a balloon after a badly handled landing or in the late stages of an approach if the pilot is not monitoring the airspeed closely enough. The aircraft does not appear to be stalled and some of the usual symptoms of the stall (e.g stall warner operating, nose drop, stall airspeed etc) are not present. However, you will find the flying controls are very ineffective and there is an excessive rate of descent. It is obvious that if you meet the runway at this rate of descent, the aircraft could come off considerably the worse. The lessons of this demonstration will become apparent when you begin your circuit flying.

Flight Exercise

▷ Purpose

To learn the symptoms of the approach to the stall and the full stall. To learn to recover from a fully developed stall and recover at the incipient (developing) stage, in various configurations and during various manoeuvres.

▷ Airmanship

HASELL checks

Carry out the HASELL checks as detailed in the previous exercise and use HELL checks in between each stall. In terms of minimum height, the most often quoted is 'sufficient height to be able to recover by not less than 3000 feet above the ground'.

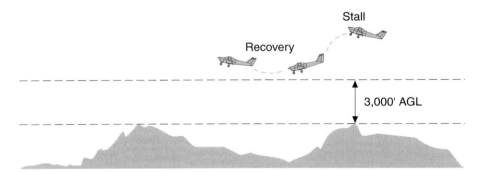

Height = safety

This will not be the same as 3000 feet QNH (i.e. above sea level) so be aware of the level of the ground you are flying over. Practising stalling with insufficient height is plain dangerous:

Height = Safety.

The more height you have, the more time you have to recover from a stall and sort out any unexpected problems.

Keep yourself orientated and stay aware of your location. It easy to drift out of your intended operating area, especially when a strong wind is blowing. Remember that the wind at, say, 4000' is likely to be much stronger than the surface wind.

Aircraft loading

The aircraft's POH/FM may place weight and CG limitations for certain manoeuvres. Ensure that the aircraft is properly loaded for the manoeuvres you intend to fly and that those manoeuvres are permitted.

Be considerate

The sound of an aircraft practising stalling may not be appreciated by those on the ground. As well as avoiding built-up areas, try to avoid using the same location for more than 10 to 15 minutes at a time.

The Stall and Recovery Without Power

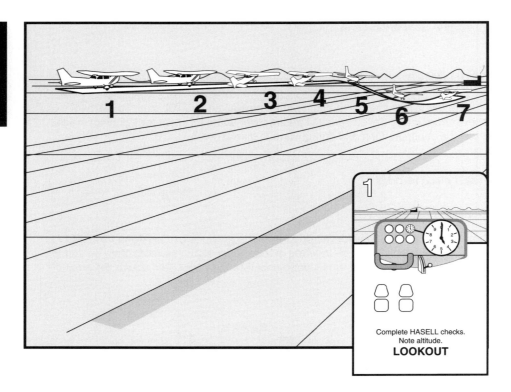

1 **2** **3** **4** **5** **6** **7**

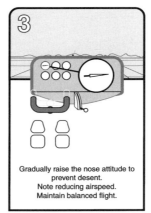

Complete HASELL checks.
Note altitude.
LOOKOUT

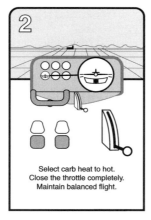

Select carb heat to hot.
Close the throttle completely.
Maintain balanced flight.

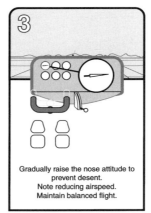

Gradually raise the nose attitude to
prevent desent.
Note reducing airspeed.
Maintain balanced flight.

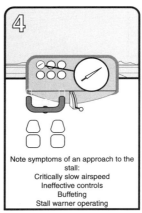

Note symptoms of an approach to the
stall:
Critically slow airspeed
Ineffective controls
Buffeting
Stall warner operating

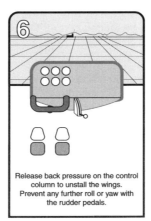

At the stall the aircraft pitches
nose-down, even with the control
column held back.

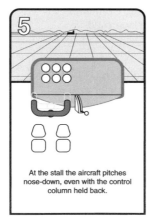

Release back pressure on the control
column to unstall the wings.
Prevent any further roll or yaw with
the rudder pedals.

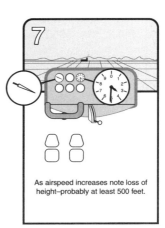

As airspeed increases note loss of
height–probably at least 500 feet.

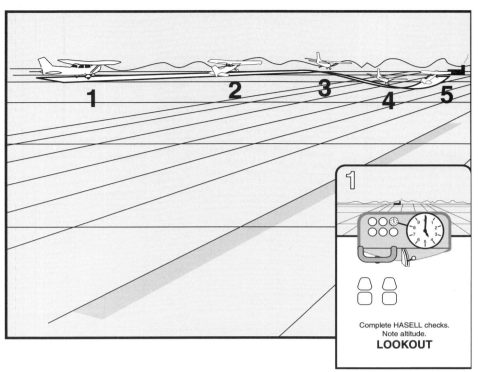

1

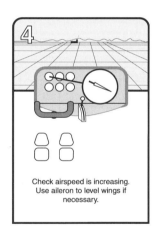

Complete HASELL checks.
Note altitude.
LOOKOUT

2

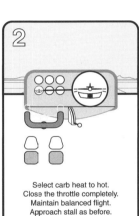

Select carb heat to hot.
Close the throttle completely.
Maintain balanced flight.
Approach stall as before.

3

S.S.R.
At the stall-**Standard Stall Recovery**.
Move control column forward.
Apply full power.
Use the rudder to prevent further yaw.

4

Check airspeed is increasing.
Use aileron to level wings if
necessary.

5

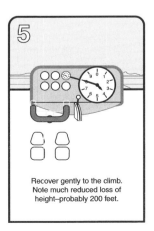

Recover gently to the climb.
Note much reduced loss of
height–probably 200 feet.

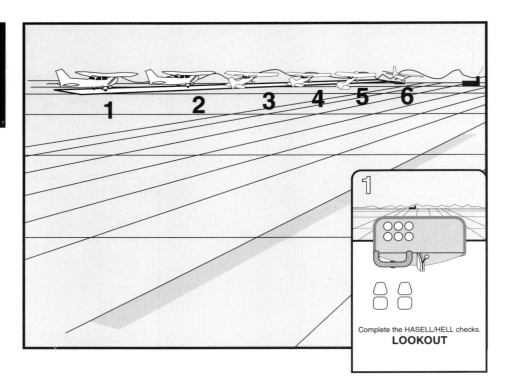

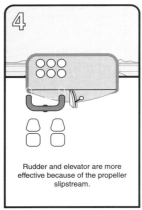

Complete the HASELL/HELL checks.
LOOKOUT

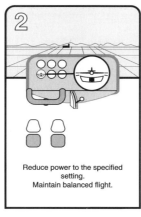

Reduce power to the specified
setting.
Maintain balanced flight.

Note airspeed slows at a much
reduced rate.

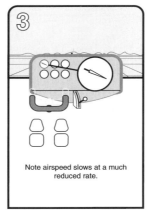

Rudder and elevator are more
effective because of the propeller
slipstream.

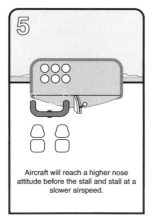

Aircraft will reach a higher nose
attitude before the stall and stall at a
slower airspeed.

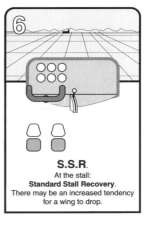

S.S.R.
At the stall:
Standard Stall Recovery.
There may be an increased tendency
for a wing to drop.

Note: In a 'T-tail'
aircraft the elevator
is unaffected by the
propeller slipstream.

The greater the
power setting, the
higher the nose
attitude prior to the
stall and the slower
the stall airspeed.

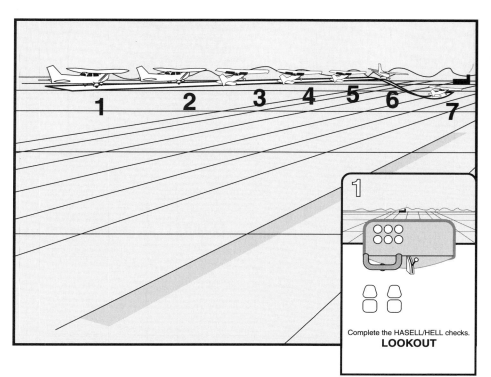

1

Complete the HASELL/HELL checks.
LOOKOUT

2

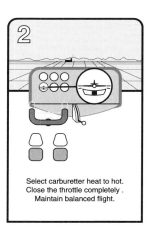

Select carburetter heat to hot.
Close the throttle completely .
Maintain balanced flight.

3

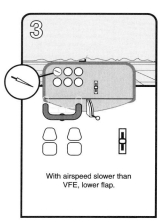

With airspeed slower than
VFE, lower flap.

4

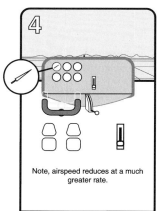

Note, airspeed reduces at a much
greater rate.

5

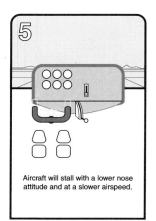

Aircraft will stall with a lower nose
attitude and at a slower airspeed.

6

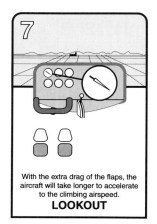

S.S.R.
At the stall:
Standard Stall Recovery.
There may be an increased tendency
for a wing to drop.

7

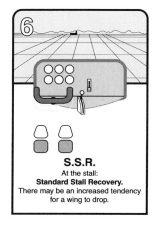

With the extra drag of the flaps, the
aircraft will take longer to accelerate
to the climbing airspeed.
LOOKOUT

The Stall With Power and Flap
(the Approach Configuration)

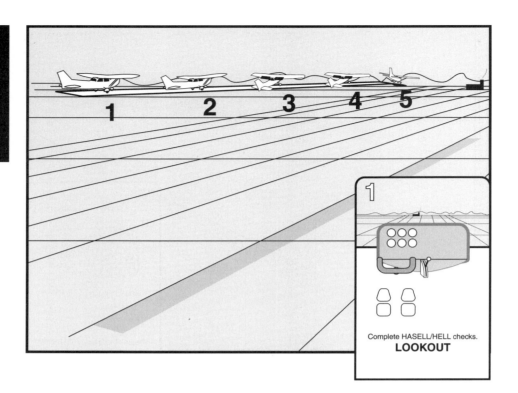

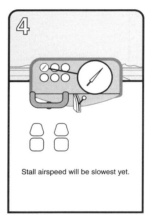

1

Complete HASELL/HELL checks.
LOOKOUT

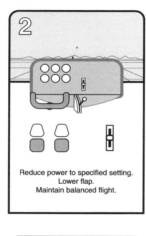

2

Reduce power to specified setting.
Lower flap.
Maintain balanced flight.

3

Note rate at which airspeed reduces.

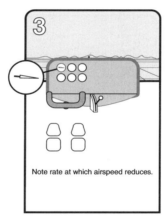

4

Stall airspeed will be slowest yet.

5

At the stall:
Standard Stall Recovery
There will be the greatest tendency
yet for a wing to drop.
LOOKOUT

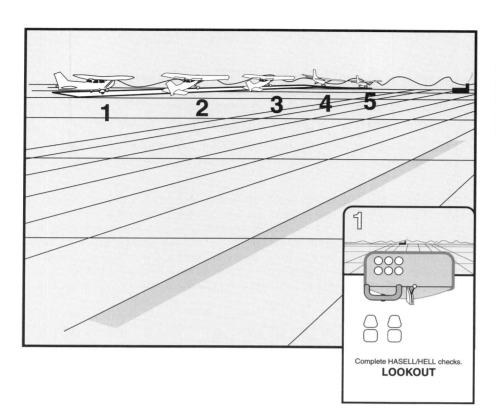

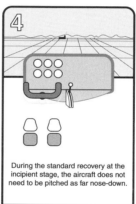

Complete HASELL/HELL checks.
LOOKOUT

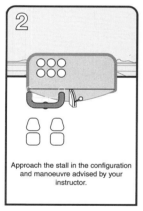

Approach the stall in the configuration and manoeuvre advised by your instructor.

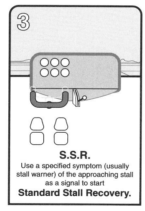

S.S.R.
Use a specified symptom (usually stall warner) of the approaching stall as a signal to start
Standard Stall Recovery.

During the standard recovery at the incipient stage, the aircraft does not need to be pitched as far nose-down.

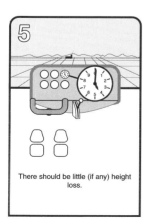

There should be little (if any) height loss.

Conclusion

In conclusion, we come back to the three most important factors in flight safety–airspeed, airspeed and airspeed. You should be able to use the SSR instinctively to recover from the stall, and–more importantly–be able to recover at the incipient stage with minimum height loss, before the full stall develops.

You should also appreciate that different aircraft types have different stalling characteristics. Even individual aircraft of the same type can behave quite differently in a stall.

The most important lesson though is to avoid an unintentional stall by ensuring that flying the aeroplane is your number one priority–always. Stalling at 3/4000 feet above the ground offers plenty of safety margin to the pilot. However, stalling at low level is extremely dangerous as the height and time available to recover are very limited. By making the flying of the aircraft your number one priority (maintaining control of the aircraft) and remembering the three most important factors in flight safety (airspeed, airspeed and airspeed) you can avoid ever having to make an unexpected stall recovery.

The emphasis of this exercise on avoidance of the stall situation is neatly summed up by an old aviation adage:

"A superior pilot is one who uses his superior judgement, to avoid situations that might require the use of his superior skills!"

The Incipient Spin

For an aircraft to spin, it has to stall. The incipient spin is, for the purposes of this exercise, the transition between the full stall with a wing drop and the point where the aircraft has rolled through more than 90° angle of bank.

All the factors that increase the likelihood of a wing drop at the stall increase the risk of a spin developing, an aircraft can spin if it stalls with a significant amount of yaw present. A fully developed spin can lead to large height loss, so being able to recover at the incipient stage is very important.

BACKGROUND BRIEFING

► **Causes Of a Spin**

► **Recovery From the Incipient Spin**

► **Accidental Spinning**

FLIGHT EXERCISE

▷ **Purpose**

▷ **Airmanship**

▷ **Entry**

▷ **Recovery**

CONCLUSION

BACKGROUND BRIEFING

▶ Causes Of a Spin

Typically, a spin will occur if an aircraft stalls during an un-coordinated manoeuvre, usually caused by misuse of the rudder leading to the aircraft flying grossly out of balance. When a spin is caused in this way, it usually occurs in the direction in which the rudder is applied. Misuse of the ailerons (i.e. trying to correct a wing drop at the stall with aileron) also increases the risk of a spin. As well as control mishandling, all the other factors that increase the risk of a wing drop at the stall increase the risk of a spin.

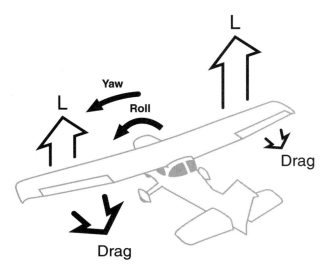

Autorotation is caused by the differing amount of lift and drag being created by the up-going and down-going wings.

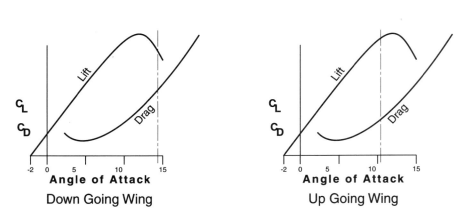

Down Going Wing   Up Going Wing

The down-going wing has a higher angle of attack than the up going wing. Thus the down-going wing creates more drag and less lift than the up-going, escalating the yaw and roll towards the down-going wing.

▶Recovery From the Incipient Spin

The recovery from the incipient spin is based around the standard stall recovery. The first action is to unstall the wings, then the rudder is used to prevent further yaw. With the wings unstalled, the flying controls are used in a co-ordinated manner to regain controlled flight. In summary:-

> move the control column forward to unstall the wings
>
> use sufficient rudder to prevent further yaw
>
> with the wings un-stalled, use the elevator, rudder and aileron in a coordinated manner to recover to the desired flight path.

Power is not usually used until the recovery is assured. Your instructor or the aircraft's flight POH/FM may have specific advice on this point.

▶Accidental Spinning

Having completed the flight exercise, it is easy to imagine that it is almost impossible to spin an aircraft accidentally except in some violent manoeuvre.

This is not the case and indeed your instructor may demonstrate to your how an accidental entry to the spin can be caused by mis-handling the aircraft. One particular manoeuvre that can go wrong is a descending turn - say a gliding turn on to final approach.

Imagine a situation where, during the turn to line up with the runway, the pilot realises that the aircraft is flying through the extended centre-line. In an attempt to increase the rate of turn the pilot (forgetting that the rudder is for balance control, NOT directional control) applies excessive rudder in the direction of the turn. The result is yaw, followed by roll (the further effect of yaw, as first seen in exercise 4) and the aircraft will probably pitch nose-down. The pilot's instinctive (and this case dangerous) reaction may be to attempt to correct the roll with aileron whilst applying back pressure on the control column.

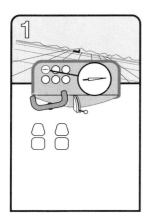 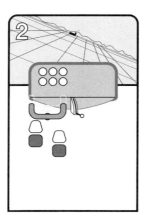 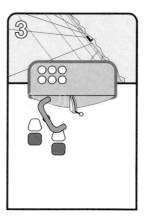

One possible scenario leading to an accidental stall/spin.

Background Briefing

This is classic case of mishandling leading to an un-coordinated manoeuvre; and if the airspeed is slow (maybe our unfortunate pilot has not been paying attention to airspeed) there is a good chance that the aircraft will stall and enter a spin. Unless there is sufficient height to make a recovery, this flight will have a swift and unpleasant termination.

Of course, prevention is better than cure. A skilful and competent pilot avoids the stall/spin situation. The flight exercise is as much as anything else an exercise in awareness–knowing the symptoms that can lead to a stall/spin and knowing how to avoid them.

Flight Exercise

▷ Purpose

To learn to recover from the incipient spin and to appreciate the symptoms and flight situations leading to an incipient spin.

▷ Airmanship

The airmanship considerations for stalling (exercise 10B) are all applicable to this exercise. Because of the possibility of a greater height loss than during stalling, you should be aware of the need for greater height to ensure a greater safety margin so as to recover to level flight by at least 3000 feet above ground level.

Height = Safety

The Incipient Spin

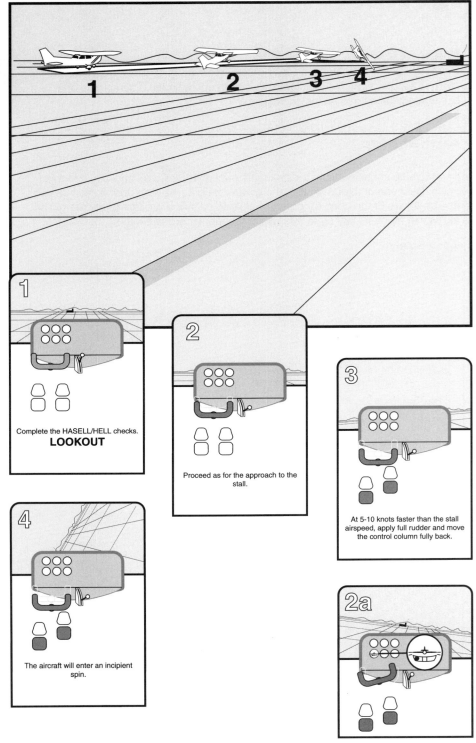

1 Complete the HASELL/HELL checks.
LOOKOUT

2 Proceed as for the approach to the stall.

3 At 5-10 knots faster than the stall airspeed, apply full rudder and move the control column fully back.

4 The aircraft will enter an incipient spin.

2a NOTE:
Your instructor may demonstrate the incipient spin through simulated *accidental* mis-handling.

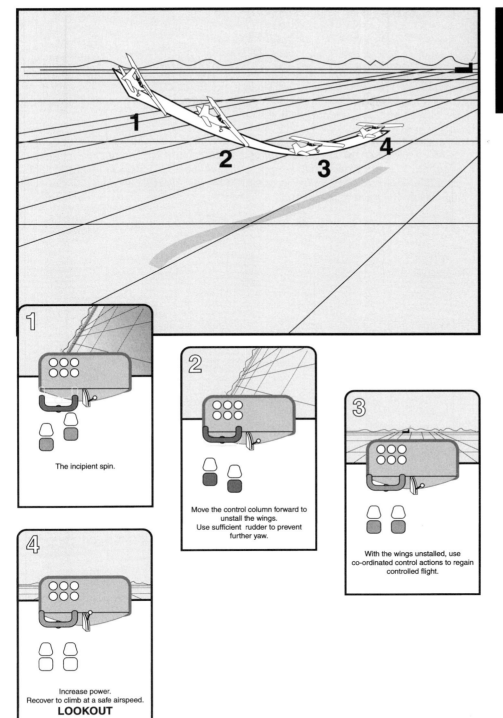

1 The incipient spin.

2 Move the control column forward to unstall the wings.
Use sufficient rudder to prevent further yaw.

3 With the wings unstalled, use co-ordinated control actions to regain controlled flight.

4 Increase power.
Recover to climb at a safe airspeed.
LOOKOUT

Conclusion

This exercise should give you the skills to recover the aircraft from an incipient spin before a full spin develops. You should develop an awareness of the factors which will cause a spin, and know how to avoid them. Being able to control the aircraft at more unusual attitudes than you are used to will also give you greater confidence in the aircraft and your ability to fly it.

It is worth reiterating that the principal objective of the slow flight, stalling and spinning exercises is to develop your awareness of how NOT to get into such a situation. It is a sad fact that a large proportion of serious accidents involving light aircraft are caused by pilots losing control of the aircraft in a stall/spin situation, with insufficient height to recover.

Such accidents **ARE** avoidable; prevention **IS** better than cure.

The Fully Developed Spin

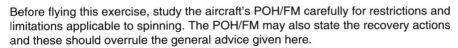

This exercise may not be a mandatory part of the training syllabus you are following. When this exercise is taught, it must be carried out in an aircraft specifically cleared for spinning which not all training aircraft are. In a developed spin the aircraft is pitching; rolling and yawing; stalled; and descending vertically at up to 5000 feet per minute. From outside an aircraft in a spin looks rather like a sycamore seed falling from a tree; the aircraft is essentially out of control. The recovery, however, is very much within the control of the pilot, provided the correct recovery actions are taken.

Before flying this exercise, study the aircraft's POH/FM carefully for restrictions and limitations applicable to spinning. The POH/FM may also state the recovery actions and these should overrule the general advice given here.

Not surprisingly, many pilots feel apprehensive about spinning. As is often the case, this is really the fear of the unknown. Sometimes this is not helped by the mystique which can surround this subject, more often than not perpetuated by those who have the least experience of spinning. Through your knowledge of the principles involved and the guidance of your flying instructor, you will become confident in your ability to recognise the full spin and recover from it.

BACKGROUND BRIEFING

▶ **The Wing Drop**

▶ **Autorotation**

▶ **Characteristics of the Fully Developed Spin**

▶ **Factors Affecting Spin Characteristics**

▶ **The Spin Recovery**

▶ **The Spiral Dive**

FLIGHT EXERCISE

▷ **Purpose**

▷ **Airmanship**

▷ **Entry to the Spin**

▷ **During the Spin**

▷ **The Spin Recovery**

CONCLUSION

BACKGROUND BRIEFING

▶ The Wing Drop

When an aircraft stalls, the wings may not stall at the same time across the whole span, (especially if the aircraft is out of balance) and the result is a tendency to roll towards the wing that stalls first. The suddenness of the stall and how far the critical angle of attack is exceeded will determine the rate of this roll. Revise exercise 10b and 11a regarding factors that increase the risk of a wing drop at the stall (and therefore the risk of a spin developing).

▶ Autorotation

When a wing has dropped, the aircraft rolls towards that lower wing and the down-going wing now has a higher angle of attack than the up-going wing. Where this higher angle of attack is beyond the critical angle, the down-going wing is producing less lift than the up-going wing and so the roll continues. This is called *autorotation*.

Additionally, the increase in drag from the down-going wing causes the aircraft to yaw towards it. This yaw further exacerbates the increased lift from the up-going wing (by moving it faster than the down-going wing) and without any further pilot input, the aircraft autorotates in to the full spin.

Entering a spin the down going wing has a higher angle of attack than the up going wing. Thus the down going wing is creating less lift and more drag than the up going wing, encouraging the aircraft to roll and yaw towards the down going wing.

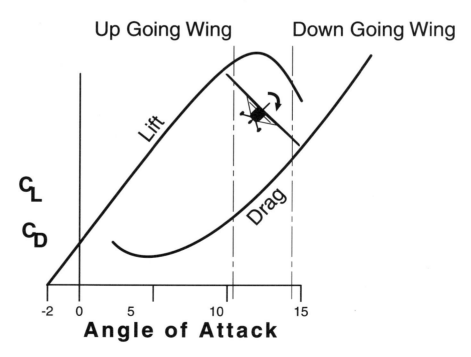

▶ Characteristics of the Fully Developed Spin

Each aircraft type has its own spinning characteristics, so you should study the aircraft's POH/FM for advice regarding the type of aircraft you are flying. The advice given here is necessarily of a general nature and may not apply to all aircraft types you will fly.

During the first two turns of the spin there are usually marked changes in the rate of roll, the rate of yaw and the pitch attitude. After these first turns the aircraft should settle into a steady spin until the recovery actions are initiated. At first you may find the view outside is little more than a blur. After a few spins you will be able to make more sense of the outside indications, particularly if you look towards the horizon rather than straight ahead over the nose of the aircraft. You may find it useful to count the turns of the spin by reference to a good landmark or the sun, which will help you stay orientated. It is also helpful to keep your head still, looking ahead to the horizon.

During the spin the AI and HI giros may well topple if they cannot be caged and so those instruments will give no useful indications. The altimeter and VSI will show a high rate of descent. The airspeed will be very slow (remember this is a stalled condition) and the turn coordinator will show the direction of the turn - ignore the indications of the balance ball.

▶ Factors Affecting Spin Characteristics

There are several factors that will have an effect on the aircraft's spin characteristics.

- CG position

A forward CG position makes the aircraft more reluctant to spin. A rearward CG makes the aircraft more likely to spin and the resulting spin will be flatter. A flatter spin (i.e. one with a higher nose attitude) is generally considered to prolong the recovery as well as making recovery more difficult. Before flight ensure that the CG position will be within the permitted range for spinning.

- weight

Heavier weights tend to make the initial spin rate slower, although the spin rate does increase as the spin continues and recovery may take longer. The distribution of weight is important. Weight at the extremes of the fuselage i.e. nose and tail, tend to flatten the spin and make recovery more difficult.

- fuel balance

It is important that the wing fuel tanks should be as closely balanced as possible. A marked imbalance between the tanks can have an adverse affect on the spin. The worst case is a full fuel tank in the wing on the outside of the spin and an empty one in the wing on the inside of the turn.

- height

The reduced air density at higher altitudes tends to lengthen the time taken to recover compared to lower altitudes (and denser air). This is not an argument to reduce the altitude for spinning, however. The difference in recovery times between the highest and lowest permitted altitudes for a light aircraft is very small compared to the safety factor of having extra height to recover from the spin.

- power

Unless the aircraft's POH/FM advises otherwise, the use of power is generally considered to be unhelpful to spin recovery. Most light training aircraft are not cleared to spin power on.

- flaps

Most aircraft are prohibited from intentional spinning with flaps down. If the flaps are lowered, spin recovery may not be possible.

- aileron position

Most often the pilot is recommended to keep the ailerons neutral throughout the spin and recovery. Again you should refer to the POH/FM for information specific to the aircraft you are flying.

▶ The Spin Recovery

There are two over-riding factors to remember when considering the recovery from the spin:

> the aircraft WILL recover from a spin that is in accordance with the POH/FM procedures and limitations, providing the correct recovery action is taken.

> the recovery actions may not be effective immediately. Quite often the spin may speed up and the aircraft pitch nose-down when the correct recovery actions are taken and before the recovery begins. The POH/FM and your instructor will advise you of the particular recovery characteristics of the aircraft you are flying.

Recovery is normally aided with the power at idle, the flaps up and the ailerons held neutral.

You will need to know the direction of the spin. If the spin is deliberate this should not be a problem. If you have entered the spin accidentally, the turn coordinator should confirm the direction of the spin - ignore the balance ball.

The turn co-ordinator will confirm the direction of the spin - in this case to the left.

The first action is to remove the yaw by applying full rudder opposite to the direction of spin. This is followed by moving the control column forward until the wings unstall and the spin stops. The rudder is then centralised, the wings levelled with aileron and the aircraft gently eased out of the dive and climbed to regain lost altitude.

TO SUMMARISE:

Confirm: direction of spin, power off, ailerons centralised

apply full rudder opposite to spin direction

PAUSE

move the control column centrally forward until the spin stops

centralise the rudder

level wings with aileron and ease gently out of the dive

Remember, the aircraft's POH/FM may list different recovery actions which will over-rule this general advice.

▶ The Spiral Dive

Some aircraft may be very reluctant to spin and may enter a spiral dive rather than a proper spin. The difference is very apparent since in the spiral dive the airspeed will be fast and increasing rapidly. Full details of the spiral dive and recovery are given in exercise 15.

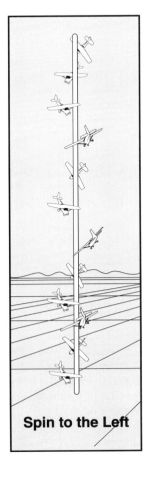

Spin to the Left

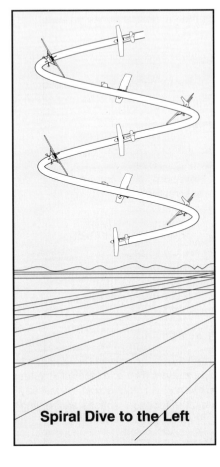

Spiral Dive to the Left

The difference between a spin and a spiral dive. The principal difference noticeable to the pilot is the rapid increase in airspeed during a spiral dive.

Flight Exercise

▷ Purpose

To learn the symptoms of the fully developed spin and the correct spin recovery procedure.

▷ Airmanship

HASELL

The full HASELL checks should be carried out before each spin, your instructor will advise on the minimum height for this exercise:

Height = Safety.

Particular reference should also be made to the look out below as a height loss of up to 1500 feet is quite possible in a multi-turn spin. Do make a positive effort to stay orientated during the exercise and avoid moving your head during the spin. To aid orientation, spinning in poor visibility, over the sea or over complete cloud cover is not recommended.

'g' tolerance

During the spin your tolerance to 'g' load may be reduced. As you recover from the spin be careful to make a gentle pull-out from the dive to avoid excessive 'g' load factor.

Airsickness

If you do feel at all unwell during this exercise do not hesitate to tell your instructor. The exercise will be discontinued and returned to another time.

Aircraft limitations

In the aircraft you are flying, spinning may only be permitted with the aircraft loaded to a narrow CG range. Weight limitations may also apply. Some aircraft have a 'Utility' category, imposing loading restrictions for certain manoeuvres.

Once again you are referred to the aircraft's POH/FM. Here any limitations and restrictions that apply to spinning will be listed. Know these limitations and abide by them; they are there for a good reason and have been researched by experienced test pilots and flight-test engineers.

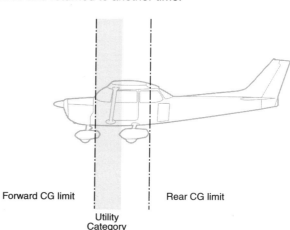

Forward CG limit   Rear CG limit

Utility
Category

Recovery instructions

It is important that there should be clear communication and understanding between the student pilot and instructor during this exercise. When the instructor wishes you to recover from a spin, he will say "recover now". You should respond by beginning the recovery actions and saying "recovering now".

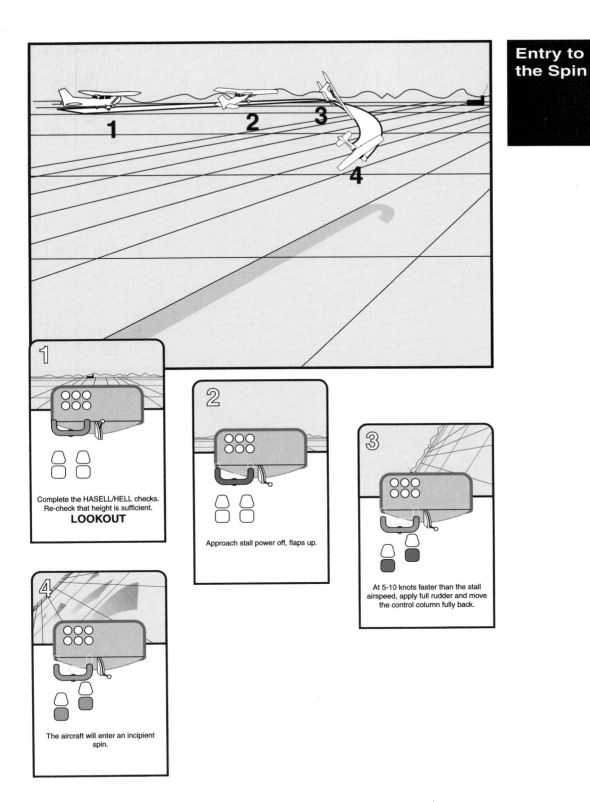

1

2

3

4

The Fully Developed Spin

1

Complete the HASELL/HELL checks.
Re-check that height is sufficient.
LOOKOUT

2

Approach stall power off, flaps up.

3

At 5-10 knots faster than the stall
airspeed, apply full rudder and move
the control column fully back.

4

The aircraft will enter an incipient
spin.

The Fully Developed Spin

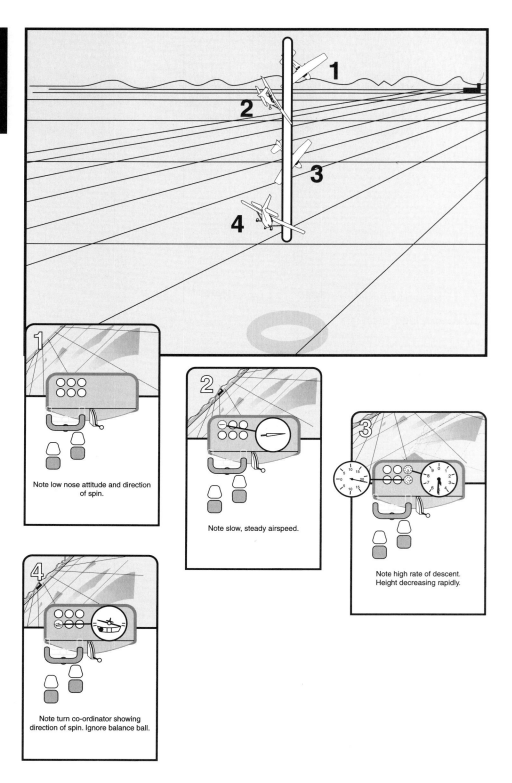

Note low nose attitude and direction of spin.

Note slow, steady airspeed.

Note high rate of descent. Height decreasing rapidly.

Note turn co-ordinator showing direction of spin. Ignore balance ball.

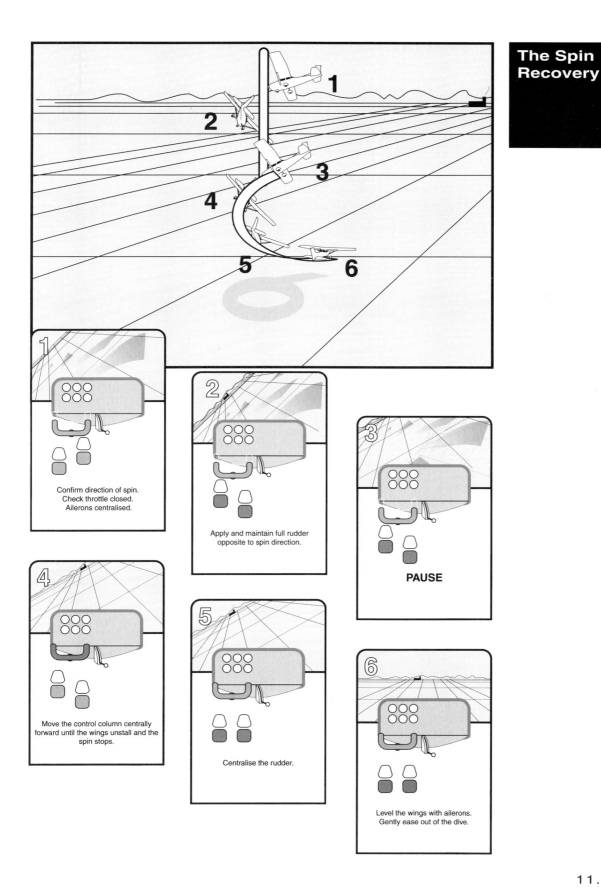

1

Confirm direction of spin.
Check throttle closed.
Ailerons centralised.

2

Apply and maintain full rudder
opposite to spin direction.

3

PAUSE

4

Move the control column centrally
forward until the wings unstall and the
spin stops.

5

Centralise the rudder.

6

Level the wings with ailerons.
Gently ease out of the dive.

Exercise

11b

The Fully Developed Spin

Conclusion

You should appreciate that accidental spinning can result from mishandling the controls when the aircraft is in—or close to—a stalled condition. Having seen the amount of height lost in a fully developed spin you will realise that it is essential to avoid the spin occurring accidentally when there may be much less height in hand. In the situation of an accidental spin, recovery at the incipient stage is of vital importance.

Hopefully enough has already been said in the preceding exercises to emphasis the important of avoiding an accidental stall/spin situation; but to summarise

1 The pilot's No 1 priority at all times - fly the aircraft

2 The three most important factors in flight safety - airspeed, airspeed and airspeed.

The take-off, standard circuit, powered approach and landing

By this stage of your training you should have had the opportunity to make a few take-offs and have assisted during a few landings. You will also have flown all the other basic manoeuvres that make up the circuit - climbing, climbing turns, level turns, straight and level flight, descending turns, powered descents. The task now is to put all of these manoeuvres together and to gain skill and experience in two manoeuvres in particular - take-off and landing.

Training in the circuit makes up a large part of your flying training course. Your first goal is the landmark event of your first solo flight. As your circuit training continues you will extend your solo flying experience and learn different take-off and landing techniques.

At first, circuit flying will seem very busy and you may feel that you are mentally lagging behind the aircraft. It is easy to get frustrated at times. However, as your skill develops, you will find that circuit flying becomes easier and even enjoyable!

The Standard Take-Off

Exercise
12

BACKGROUND BRIEFING

▶ Forces During Take-off

▶ Take-off Distance, Take-off Run

▶ Factors Affecting Take-off Distance

▶ The Pre-Take-off Checks

▶ Effect of Power During Take-off

▶ Use of Power During Take-off

▶ Use of Rudder During Take-off

▶ Use of Elevators During Take-off

▶ Checks During Take-off

▶ Air Traffic Control and Radio Procedures

FLIGHT EXERCISE

▷ Purpose

▷ Airmanship

▷ The Standard Take-off

CONCLUSION

BACKGROUND BRIEFING

▶ Forces During Take-off

At the start of the take-off run, the engine thrust overcomes the inertia of the stationary aircraft and makes it accelerate along the runway. As speed increases the thrust also has to overcome drag and the rolling friction of the tyres. At the point of rotation, the pilot increases the angle of attack of the wings by pitching the aircraft nose-up and enough lift is produced for the aircraft to leave the ground. Once established in the climb, the excess of thrust over drag governs the angle of climb as the aircraft clears obstructions and climbs to the required level.

▶ Take-off Distance, Take-off Run

The take-off run is the distance needed for the aircraft to become airborne. The take-off distance is the distance needed for the aircraft to become airborne and make its initial climb to clear an imaginary 50ft barrier.

The take-off performance can be divided into two sections:

The TAKE-OFF RUN (or Take-Off Ground Roll), the distance taken for the aircraft to become airborne, and;

The TAKE-OFF DISTANCE, that is the total distance required for the aircraft to become airborne AND clear a 50' barrier.

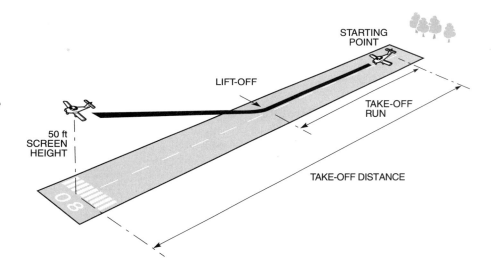

The main physical characteristics of the runway. Not all runways have a marked centre line. The runway designator is the magnetic direction of the runway to the nearest 10°, so runway 09 has a magnetic direction of 090 (i.e. East).

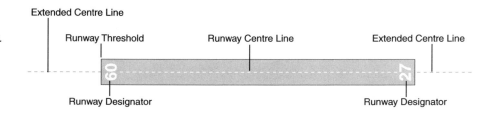

▶ Factors Affecting Take-off Distance

- weight

As weight is increased, acceleration is reduced; rotation speed is increased; and climb performance is reduced. So as weight is increased, both take-off run and take-off distance are lengthened.

- flap

A small amount of flap may increase lift without increasing drag too much. The aircraft is able to become airborne at a slower airspeed and so the take-off run is shortened. However, once airborne, flap may well reduce the climb performance.

Where flap is beneficial to take-off performance the aircraft's POH/FM will recommend a take-off flap setting and specific speeds. There is no benefit in increasing the flap setting beyond that recommended. This will only increase drag significantly for little extra lift, thus lengthening the take-off run and take-off distance.

- air density

Air density has a significant effect on take-off performance. An 'aircraft' is literally a machine of the air. The more dense the air, the better the aircraft will handle and perform. The less dense the air, the worse the aircraft's handling and performance.

An increase in temperature and/or an increase in altitude will lead to a reduction in air density. Reduced air density reduces both the lift generated by the wings and the engine power; take-off distance can be significantly lengthened and in particular the climb angle after take-off can be very shallow (i.e. a poor climb gradient). An increase in humidity also causes a reduction in air density.

- runway surface

Differing runway surfaces have a marked effect on the take-off run. Grass—in particular long grass—can lengthen the take-off distance by up to 25%. If the grass is wet, the increase in take-off distance is even greater. Soft ground (such as a grass runway after prolonged heavy rain) can lengthen the take-off run by anything up to a further 50%. An uneven or bumpy surface will have an adverse effect on the take-off, particularly if the bumps are severe enough to get the aircraft airborne before it reaches the proper rotation speed.

Runway contamination such as snow, slush and water also lengthens the take-off run and makes directional control more difficult.

- runway slope

A downsloping runway aids acceleration and so shortens the take-off run. An upsloping runway reduces acceleration and the take-off run is lengthened.

- wind velocity

The wind speed and direction (wind velocity) is probably the single most important factor in determining take-off run and take-off distance.

Background Briefing

Taking-off into wind gives a reduced groundspeed at lift-off (and therefore a shorter ground run) and steepens the climb angle after take-off (i.e. a better climb gradient). Taking-off with a tailwind will have a very adverse effect on take-off distance. A tailwind of as little as 5 knots can lengthen take-off distance by 20%.

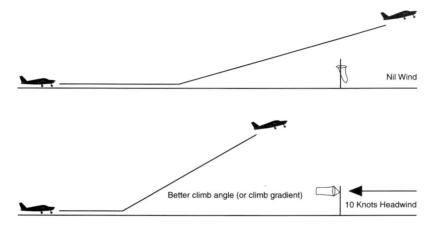

Taking-off into wind is always the best option both for take-off performance and aircraft handling.

Taking-off into wind also makes the aircraft easier to control, because the take-off run begins with an element of airspeed, provided by the wind airflow over the aircraft. When taking off into a 15 knot headwind, for example, the aircraft has 15 knots of airspeed even when it is stationary. Once it has reached 50 knots groundspeed, the aircraft has the benefit of 65 knots airspeed (i.e. 50 + 15).

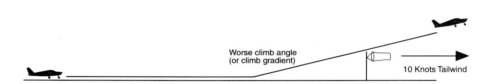

Taking off into wind enables the aircraft to get airborne at a slower groundspeed, although the airspeed is unchanged.

▶ The Pre-Take-off Checks

You will be familiar with the use of the check list to complete the power checks and the vital actions before take-off. It is worth re-emphasising that all these checks have a purpose. Do not rush these checks or carry them out automatically without properly checking each item. At this stage the pilot has unlimited time in which to make decisions. In this case the decision is whether or not to take-off. Do not allow yourself to be rushed into taking-off before you are ready, and do not hesitate to abandon the planned flight if you are unhappy with any aspect of the power checks or vital actions. Most take-off accidents occur because the pilot simply made the wrong decision in attempting a take-off in the particular circumstances.

▶ Effect of Power During Take-off

During the take-off, the use of full power will cause the aircraft to yaw. Most light aircraft have a propeller rotating clockwise, so the aircraft will tend to yaw to the left as power is increased. There are two principal reasons for this yaw:-

- slipstream effect

Again we are referring back to the lessons first learnt in exercise 4. The helix of the slipstream meets the fin and rudder at an angle, generating lift to the left or right. Where the propeller is rotating clockwise, the slipstream meets the fin and rudder on their left side, yawing the aircraft to the left. This effect is most pronounced at slow airspeeds and high power settings.

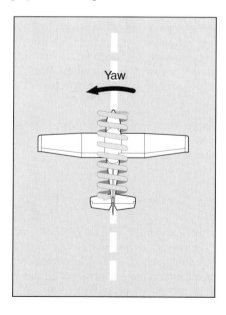

The slipstream and power effects are most pronounced at slow airspeeds and high power settings.

- torque effect

As the propeller rotates clockwise, the engine (and the aircraft attached to it) will try to rotate in the opposite direction. This creates a force pressing down on the left main undercarriage, which causes a yaw force to the left.

Torque effect causes a downward pressure on one side of the aircraft, increasing the rolling friction on the wheel on that side.

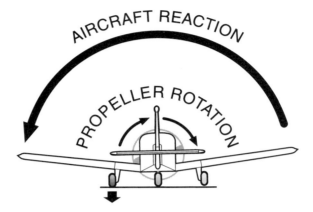

Given the relatively low power of most training aircraft, the total yaw created through these effects (and a couple of others less significant) is not excessive and direction is easily controlled through the rudder pedals.

▶ Use of Power During Take-off

Take-offs in light aircraft require the use of full power. The power should always be increased smoothly and progressively–going from idle to full power should never take place in less than two seconds. Considerate use of the throttle will aid directional control (because the yaw effect increases gradually), increases engine life and avoids the danger of a 'rich-cut'. Your instructor will explain the significance of a 'rich-cut' in relation to the aircraft you are flying.

It is normal practice to keep a hand on the throttle until above 300 feet AGL after take-off. This is partly to avoid the possibility of the throttle coming back to idle power if the throttle friction is not correctly set.

▶ Use of Rudder During Take-off

The rudder pedals are used to maintain directional control during the take-off run and to keep the aircraft in balance once airborne. The rudder pedals of most nosewheel aircraft steer the nosewheel as well as controlling the rudder. Whilst the nosewheel is on the ground, directional control through the rudder pedals is very simple. Once the aircraft is pitched nose-up, there is sufficient airspeed for the rudder to act effectively.

Many modern light aircraft are fitted with 'toe brakes' as described in exercise 5. It is important to keep your feet well clear of the toe brakes during the take-off, as inadvertently pressing the toe brakes can make directional control difficult and will lengthen the take-off run.

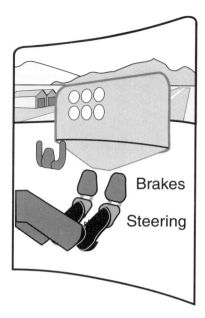

At the beginning of the take-off run, ensure that your feet are well clear of the toe brakes, with your heels on the floor.

Look well ahead of the aircraft to a distant landmark during the take-off to judge directional control. If you focus your eyes too close to the aircraft, rudder control will be erratic and you may overcontrol.

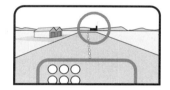

Use a landmark beyond the runway to judge directional control during the take-off.

▶Use of Elevators During Take-off

At the start of the take-off run, the pilot holds 'back pressure' on the control column to reduce the loading on the nose undercarriage. The nose undercarriage is nowhere near as strong as the main undercarriage (because of its requirement to be steerable) and the weight of the engine directly over the nosewheel makes the nose undercarriage particularly vulnerable to damage during a badly handled take-off or landing. There is no question of trying to raise the nosewheel high off the ground as early as possible; that will only increase drag, reduce controllability and ruin the view ahead. It may even be possible to scrape the tail along the ground by over-rotating. The aim is rather to reduce the weight and loading on the nose undercarriage.

At the recommended rotate speed (in the aircraft's POH/FM), the aircraft is progressively pitched nose-up to provide sufficient angle of attack for the wings to generate the lift needed to get the aircraft airborne. If the POH/FM does not have a recommended rotate speed, a speed of about 1.15 x the stalling speed (in the take-off configuration) should be used as a guideline.

TAKE-OFF RUN	**ROTATION**	**INITIAL CLIMB**
Use back pressure on the control column to reduce nosewheel loads.	Increase back-pressure so that the aircraft becomes airborne.	Establish the climb attitude.

The correct use of the elevators during the take-off.

There is no benefit in trying to get the aircraft airborne at the slowest possible airspeed. This may lead to control problems due to the slow airspeed. In addition the aircraft may settle back on to the runway and the take-off distance will be significantly lengthened. Likewise rotating at too fast an airspeed will lengthen the take-off run and increase wear and tear on the undercarriage.

▶ Checks During Take-off

During the take-off run you can make a few simple checks of the engine and the aircraft's performance. These checks act as a final decision point before the aircraft is airborne and committed to flight. The checks are:

    airspeed rising

    engine developing full power (check RPM)

    engine temperatures and pressures within limits

These checks should take no more than a couple of seconds. If you are unhappy with what you see or if something else appears to be wrong, do not hesitate to abandon the take-off–you can always fly another day.

▶ Air Traffic Control and Radio Procedures

The specific ATC procedures at your training airfield will be explained by your instructor. It is the pilot's responsibility to conform to the departure and circuit pattern in force, so do not hesitate to ask for help if you are in any doubt. As you taxy for take-off you should listen on the designated frequency to be aware of the traffic situation. Being aware of what is happening around the aircraft–situational awareness–is an important element of good airmanship.

Whilst at the holding point and having completed the pre take-off checks, you should have a good look around to check that the approach, the runway itself and the departure path are clear of aircraft; only then do you make the radio call. The correct radio procedure is to report "ready for departure" - do not use the phrase "take-off" at this stage. As you enter the runway you should again look out to the same areas - most especially to the final approach path.

Flight Exercise

▷ Purpose

To learn to make a standard take-off and initial climb.

▷ Airmanship

Lookout

The full aspects of lookout are covered in the supplement to this section. Prior to take-off, the key areas to check before calling ready for departure are the approach, runway and departure areas. You should also make a final check of the approach before lining-up on the runway.

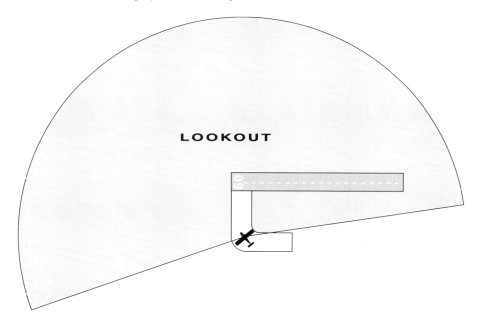

LOOKOUT

Look out along the approach path and the runway itself before requesting departure clearance; look out again before entering the runway.

Checks

The importance of the power checks and pre take-off vital actions has already been stressed. The checks during the take-off run and any after take-off checks should be completed from memory. Always ensure that you are properly checking each item and not just reciting the checklist 'parrot fashion'.

ATC liaison

It is the pilot's responsibility to integrate safely into the existing circuit pattern and the role of ATC (or the ATSU) is to assist the pilot in doing this. It is not uncommon for student pilots to feel intimidated by ATC, but remember that it is their job to assist you. Do not hesitate to query any instruction or message that you do not fully understand - request ATC to "say again".

If in doubt - 'shout'.

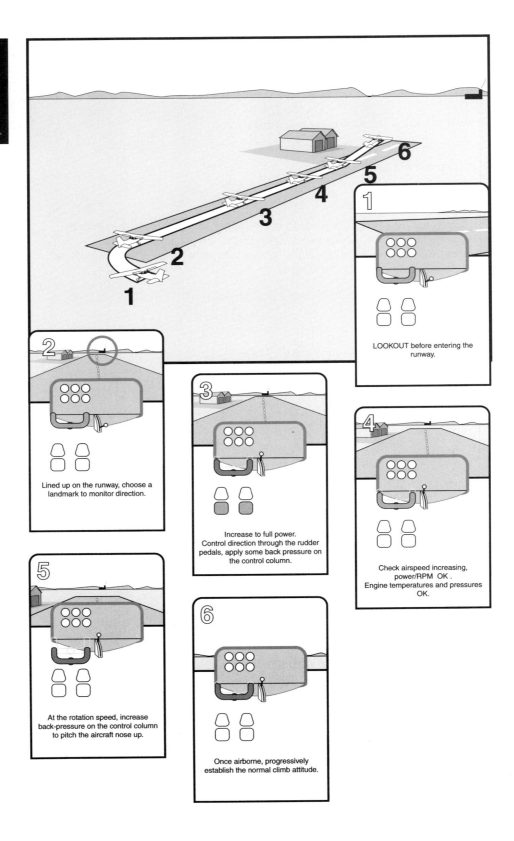

1 LOOKOUT before entering the runway.

2 Lined up on the runway, choose a landmark to monitor direction.

3 Increase to full power. Control direction through the rudder pedals, apply some back pressure on the control column.

4 Check airspeed increasing, power/RPM OK. Engine temperatures and pressures OK.

5 At the rotation speed, increase back-pressure on the control column to pitch the aircraft nose up.

6 Once airborne, progressively establish the normal climb attitude.

The Standard Circuit

BACKGROUND BRIEFING

▶ The Standard Circuit Pattern

▶ Use of Local Landmarks

▶ Effect of Wind on the Circuit Pattern

▶ Judging Distance From the Runway on the Downwind Leg

▶ The Pre-Landing Checks

▶ Spacing in the Circuit

▶ Judging the Turn onto Base Leg

▶ ATC Liaison/Radio

▶ Cockpit Workload - A.N.C.

▶ Noise Abatement

FLIGHT EXERCISE

▷ Purpose

▷ Airmanship

▷ The Standard Circuit

BACKGROUND BRIEFING

▶ The Standard Circuit Pattern

The circuit pattern consists of a rectangle, with the runway running down one side. The circuit direction is normally left-hand, that is all turns are to the left. If a right-hand pattern is in force, ATC and/or ground signals will indicate this.

The principal elements of the standard circuit; in this case runway 09, left-hand circuit.

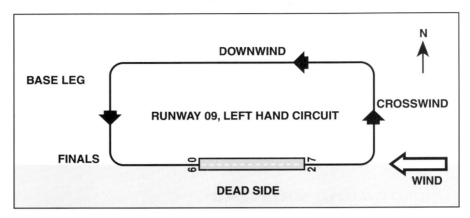

During circuit flying the QFE pressure setting is used on the altimeter, so that the altimeter indicates height above the airfield. The circuit height will vary at different airfields, but is usually 800, 1000 or 1200 feet above the airfield. For the purposes of this flight exercise we will assume a circuit height of 1000 feet.

The circuit pattern starts by climbing straight ahead after take-off to at least 500 AGL before starting a climbing turn on to the crosswind leg. When the circuit height is reached the aircraft is levelled off and turned on to the downwind leg. The downwind leg is flown parallel to the runway whilst the pre-landing checks are completed. At the end of the downwind leg a turn is made on to the base leg and the descent to land is started. From the base leg a gentle turn is made on to the final approach to align with the centreline of the runway. The aircraft should be stabilised in the landing configuration once it is established on the final approach to the runway.

The aircraft's path around a standard circuit pattern.

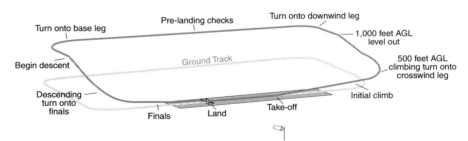

▶ Use of Local Landmarks

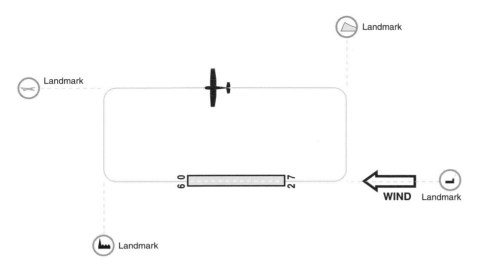

The use of a landmark to maintain direction on each leg of the circuit.

Maintaining the correct direction along each leg of the circuit is made easier by reference to a prominent landmark, rather than by constant reference to the runway or the heading indicator. As the turn on to each leg of the circuit is through 90°, it is only necessary to look for a landmark around the left wingtip (left-hand circuit) or around the right wingtip (right-hand circuit) before starting the turn. This technique is valid at any airfield of course - only the landmarks change - and it makes accurate circuit flying easier; however, it is still necessary to monitor the runway to ensure the correct ground track is being maintained during each leg of the circuit.

The use of a landmark to judge the turn from crosswind to downwind.

▶ Effect of Wind on the Circuit Pattern

Flying an accurate circuit pattern would be much easier if there was no wind. In effect the pilot could just fly a series of 90° heading changes until established on final approach.

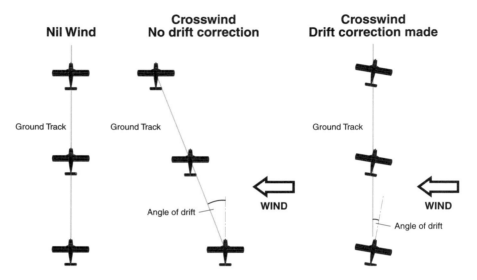

In practice, nil wind conditions are rare and not necessarily desirable. If allowance is not made for the prevailing wind velocity the aircraft will drift away from the intended ground track. By making a small adjustment of heading into wind (say 10°), the ground track should more closely resemble that required.

If allowance for the prevailing wind is not made, the aircraft will not follow the correct ground track around the circuit.

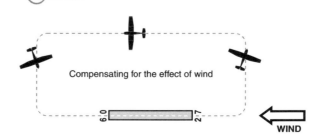

The Standard Circuit

ATC will normally state the surface wind velocity when the take-off or landing clearance is given, although the pilot can request a wind check at any time. The windsock should be visible from the air and you will learn to judge the surface wind velocity from the windsock.

▶ Judging Distance From the Runway on the Downwind Leg

During the downwind leg it is important to maintain the ground track parallel to the runway. This is best done by reference to the position of the runway relative to the wing.

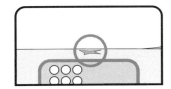

LOW WING   From pilot's seat

HIGH WING   From pilot's seat

The downwind leg ground track can be judged in relation to a landmark and the distance from the runway. The position of the runway in relation to the wing enables the pilot to maintain a ground track parallel to the runway.

▶ The Pre-Landing Checks

The pre-landing checks are carried out on the downwind leg and are set out in the aircraft's checklist; these checks will need to be memorised by the pilot. You can save yourself a lot of time and trouble if you learn the pre-landing checks before you start circuit flying.

Rather than trying to complete the checks all in one go, it is better to break up the checks with a scan outside to look out for other aircraft and to check the progress around the circuit.

Background Briefing

▶ Spacing in the Circuit

When there are other aircraft in the circuit, it is important to maintain a safe separation from aircraft ahead. Unless ATC specifically request it, orbiting (i.e. flying a 360° turn) is best avoided. It is preferable to make gentle 's' turns, or select a slower airspeed (i.e. slow, safe cruise) to increase separation from an aircraft ahead.

Avoid orbiting in the circuit to increase spacing unless specifically instructed to do so.

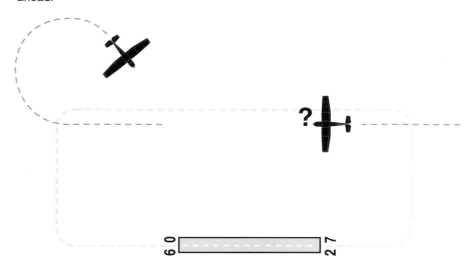

Avoid extending the downwind leg for purely spacing reasons, as you may soon be well outside the normal circuit pattern and even the Aerodrome Traffic Zone.

▶ Judging the Turn on to Base Leg

The position to commence the turn from downwind on to base leg is when the aircraft is positioned along an imaginary line drawn out at 30° from the runway threshold. When the aircraft is flying with little drift, this is when the runway threshold is at a angle of about 30° behind the wing trailing edge; in a left-hand circuit this is about the 8 o'clock position.

If there is a strong tailwind on the downwind leg, it may be necessary to start the turn on to base leg sooner than this to compensate for the effect of the tailwind.

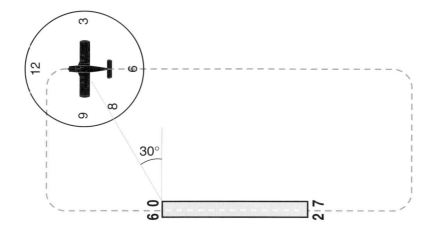

The turn on to base leg is judged in relation to the position of the aircraft relative to the runway threshold.

From pilot's seat

▶ ATC Liaison/Radio

Usually the "downwind" call is made when the aircraft is abeam the upwind end of the runway at the beginning of the downwind leg. If for any reason it is not possible to report at this point (e.g. if the radio is busy) a "late downwind" call may be more appropriate.

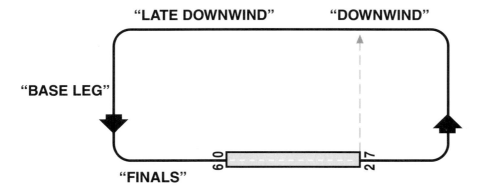

The radio position reports in the standard circuit pattern.

ATC/ATSU may allocate a priority for landing e.g. "G-BD you are number two to the Cherokee on base leg". This priority must be adhered to and the other aircraft kept in sight at all times. A further call may be requested by ATC e.g. "Report ready to turn on to base leg" or "report on base leg". The "finals" call is made once the aircraft is established on the final approach.

▶ Cockpit Workload - ANC

When you first start flying the circuit, the high workload is at once apparent. The combined tasks of manoeuvring the aircraft, performing the checks, liaising with ATC, maintaining a good lookout, judging distances and angles etc. can seem almost overwhelming at first.

Life will become more simple (and safer) if you establish a set of priorities and organise your workload in accordance with them. These priorities are, in order:

Aviate. Navigate. Communicate.

1　**Aviate**　　　　fly the aircraft. This your first priority at all times.

2　**Navigate**　　　correctly position the aircraft in the circuit.

3　**Communicate**　use of the radio comes after the first two priorities are established.

The principle of Aviate, Navigate, Communicate carries through into all flying. Stick with this principle at all times - most especially if under pressure.

▶ Noise Abatement

Increasingly airfields have specific noise abatement procedures as part of a recognised need for airfields to be good neighbours. Noise abatement procedures normally consist of avoiding certain areas (e.g. a village or town) and may slightly alter the standard circuit pattern. It is important to be aware of any particular noise abatement procedures at the airfields where you fly. Your instructor will advise of special procedures at the training airfield and other airfields you visit. Obviously, in any emergency you should over-ride these procedures if necessary.

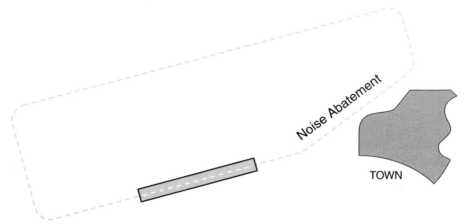

Noise abatement procedures normally involving altering the standard circuit pattern to avoid specific towns or villages.

Flight Exercise

▷ Purpose

To fly a standard circuit pattern and position the aircraft on to final approach.

▷ Airmanship

Lookout

As well as the usual requirement to visually clear the area all around the aircraft before making a turn, there are two key lookout points in the circuit to make note of:

1   Before turning from crosswind to downwind

2   Before turning from base leg on to finals

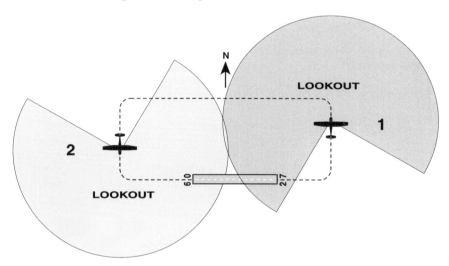

Two key lookout points in the standard circuit.

These are the points where there is the greatest risk of conflicting with other aircraft joining the circuit.

Checks

The pre-landing checks should be learnt from the checklist before you start circuit flying. The best place to learn these checks is on the ground in an available aircraft, rather than during your first circuit flight exercise. Always complete the checks thoroughly and methodically. Chanting them 'parrot fashion' is unlikely to achieve the desired result.

ATC liaison

Always make your intentions clear to ATC and be sure that you fully understand the instructions and information they pass to you. Controllers are usually sensitive to the limitations of a student pilot, but do not allow yourself to be pressured into accepting instructions which you do not fully understand or cannot safely accomplish.

If in doubt - 'shout'.

Flight Exercise

Aviate, Navigate, Communicate - A.N.C.

An example of the application of A.N.C. is a situation where you are ready to report downwind but the radio frequency is busy. Rather than waiting, finger poised over the transmit button, to get a word in - go back to your priorities. Fly the aircraft, complete the pre-landing checks, judge your progress along the downwind leg and call "late downwind" when the chance arises.

Rules of the Air

When more than one aircraft is on final approach to land, the following priorities apply unless ATC has given a different instruction:

Aircraft on final approach and landing have priority over other aircraft in the air and on the ground.

When more than one aircraft is established on final approach, the lower aircraft has priority, unless:

1   the higher aircraft has an emergency;

2   the lower aircraft has cut in front of, or overtaken, another aircraft already on final approach.

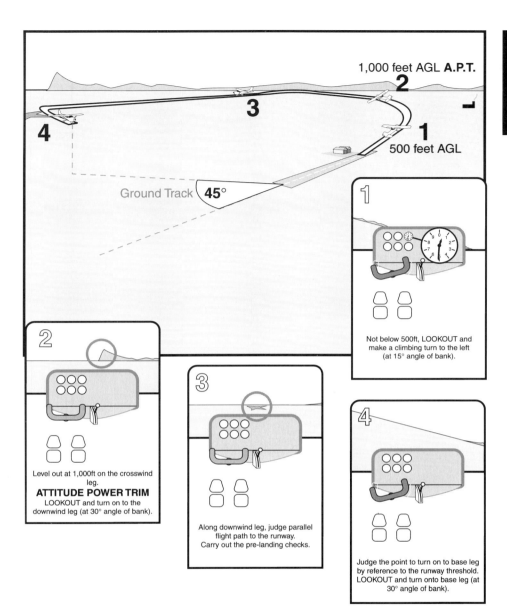

1,000 feet AGL **A.P.T.**

2

3

4

1

500 feet AGL

Ground Track **45°**

1

Not below 500ft, LOOKOUT and make a climbing turn to the left (at 15° angle of bank).

2

Level out at 1,000ft on the crosswind leg.
ATTITUDE POWER TRIM
LOOKOUT and turn on to the downwind leg (at 30° angle of bank).

3

Along downwind leg, judge parallel flight path to the runway.
Carry out the pre-landing checks.

4

Judge the point to turn on to base leg by reference to the runway threshold. LOOKOUT and turn onto base leg (at 30° angle of bank).

The Standard Circuit

The Powered Approach and Landing

Exercise

13

BACKGROUND BRIEFING

▶ Forces in the Descent and Landing

▶ Landing Distance, Ground Run

▶ The Initial Approach to Land

▶ Controlling the Descent Angle

▶ Decision Height

▶ The Landing

▶ The After-Landing Checks

▶ The Touch and Go

▶ Mislanding, the Balloon or Bounce

▶ The Go Around

▶ ATC Liaison

FLIGHT EXERCISE

▷ Purpose

▷ Airmanship

▷ The Final Approach

▷ The Landing

▷ The Go Around

BACKGROUND BRIEFING

▶ Forces in the Descent and Landing

The final approach to land is flown at a speed fast enough to give the pilot adequate control of the aircraft, but slow enough to land within a reasonable distance. The recommended approach airspeed is usually a figure in the region of 1.3 x the stalling airspeed in the approach configuration. Flying the approach at too fast an airspeed has no benefit and indeed makes the landing more difficult; while flying at too slow an airspeed (thereby reducing the margin above the stall airspeed) close to the ground is plain dangerous. Establishing the correct approach airspeed, and maintaining it to achieve a stable approach is one of the keys to making consistently safe landings. Large changes in airspeed will make the approach far more difficult and uncomfortable.

The approach is normally flown with intermediate to full flap (to allow a steeper descent, so avoiding obstructions around the airfield) and with power (to control the rate and angle of descent).

At 15-20 feet above the runway the rate of descent is reduced by pitching nose-up to the level attitude, the throttle is closed, and the aircraft is allowed to decelerate as the nose is pitched further up, to make a controlled touchdown on the main wheels. As the aircraft slows the nosewheel is lowered to the runway and the brakes are used if necessary. Once the aircraft has slowed to a safe taxying speed it is taxied clear of the runway.

▶ Landing Distance, Ground Run

The landing distance is the total distance from the point where the aircraft clears an imaginary 50ft obstacle to when it reaches a stop. The ground run (or ground roll) is the distance from where the aircraft touches down to where it comes to a stop.

The landing performance is calculated as the LANDING DISTANCE, that is the total distance from 50' over the runway to a full stop. The ground run (or ground roll) - the distance from touchdown to full stop may also be calculated.

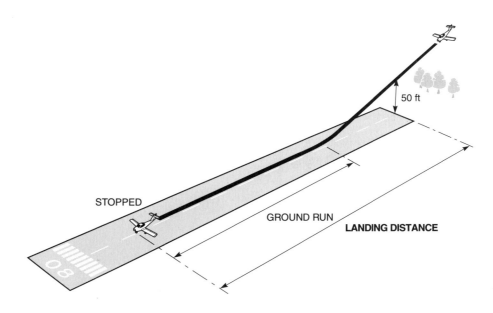

50 ft

STOPPED

GROUND RUN

LANDING DISTANCE

Several factors will affect the landing performance of the aircraft:

- weight

The heavier the aircraft, the faster the stalling speed. As a result the approach will have to be flown at a faster airspeed, the touchdown speed will be faster and the landing distance will be increased.

- flap

The use of flap permits a slower approach speed, allows a steeper approach angle, improves the view ahead of the aircraft and allows a slower touchdown speed. The shortest landing distance will be achieved with full flap extended.

- air density

With reduced air density the aircraft will have a faster true airspeed and so a faster groundspeed on the approach, even with the same indicated airspeed. The faster groundspeed will lead to a more shallow descent angle (unless the rate of descent is increased) and a faster touchdown groundspeed which will lengthen the ground run. The engine power is also reduced by a reduction in air density, although this is less important than during the take-off. High altitudes, high temperatures and high humidity all reduce air density.

- runway surface

The runway surface affects the ground run of the aircraft. A grass surface, in particular long wet grass, can lengthen landing distances by 30% or more. Runway contamination–such as standing water–snow and slush, lengthens the landing distance and makes directional control more difficult.

- runway slope

A downsloping runway significantly lengthens the ground run. An upsloping runway shortens the ground run. In addition to this direct effect on the ground run, a sloping runway can alter the pilot's perception of the approach angle. When approaching an upsloping runway, a pilot tends to believe he is too high and may approach too low in an attempt to correct this illusion. When approaching a downsloping runway, the pilot may believe he is too low and, in correcting, approach too high.

- wind velocity

The wind velocity obviously has a marked effect on landing distance. The pilot should always be aware of the wind velocity by reference to the windsock and ATC reports or incidental clues such as rising smoke, wind streaks on water etc.. Use an into-wind runway if at all possible, since doing so reduces the groundspeed during the approach, gives a slower touchdown groundspeed and shortens the landing distance.

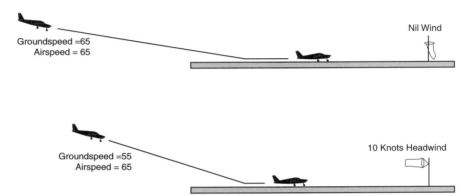

The effect of wind on the approach and landing. Landing into wind is always the preferred option.

The Powered Approach and Landing

▶ The Initial Approach to Land

Making a good landing is not a matter of extraordinary skill and luck. A safe landing is almost always the result of a stable approach and a well-executed circuit.

The descent to land is started on the base leg, when the threshold is at an angle of about 45° between the nose and the wing leading edge—i.e. about the 10 o'clock position in a left-hand circuit.

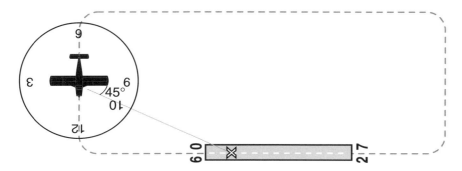

Judging the correct position to commence the descent on base leg.

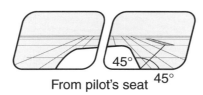

From pilot's seat

This key point may vary depending on the wind conditions and the pilot's judgement as to whether the aircraft is high or low relative to the ideal approach descent angle.

Usually initial flap is lowered at this point and the aircraft is trimmed to maintain the required approach speed. The objective is to settle the aircraft into a stabilised powered descent at the correct approach speed as early as possible in the approach.

The turn on to finals is started at a point when a 15 to 20° angle-of-bank turn will turn the aircraft on to the extended runway centre line. It is permissible to use up to 30° angle of bank, but not more. If it becomes apparent that the aircraft will drift through the extended centre line during the turn, the angle of bank should be maintained until the aircraft is on a heading to regain the extended centre line.

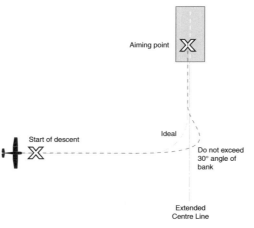

The turn on to final approach. If the aircraft drifts through the centre line, do not exceed 30° angle of bank in regaining the centre line.

Once established on the extended centre line the controls are used in the normal way to maintain this ground track.

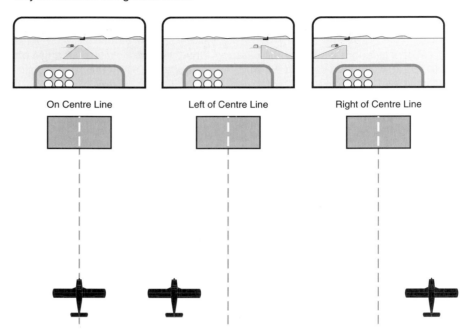

| On Centre Line | Left of Centre Line | Right of Centre Line |

The pilot should not have any difficulty visually assessing if the aircraft is on the extended centre line, or to one side.

On final approach (finals), the landing flap (intermediate to full flap) is lowered, the aircraft is pitched nose-down to maintain the approach airspeed and trimmed. Again the aim is to stabilise the aircraft at the correct approach speed, in the correct configuration, as early as possible.

▶ Controlling the Descent Angle

The pilot's task during the final approach is to maintain a constant descent angle in relation to the runway, so as to touch down at (or near) a pre-determined point on the runway. If the pilot does not control the descent angle the aircraft may *undershoot* and touchdown before reaching the runway, or *overshoot* and touchdown beyond the runway.

It is important, for the pilot to be able to judge the position of the aircraft relative to the ideal descent angle, so as to make any corrections necessary. This judgement is based on a series of visual cues that most experienced pilots take for granted. For the student pilot the visual cues need to be examined further.

Once established on the final approach, the pilot should look for the selected aiming-point (usually a spot about 150 metres beyond the runway threshold) and then establish the perspective of this aiming-point in relation to the horizontal, normally judged in relation to the horizon. If the approach is flown at a constant descent angle, the aiming-point will stay at a fixed angle relative to the horizon and the aircraft WILL reach this point. If the aiming-point moves relative to the horizon the aircraft is not going to touchdown on it - but somewhere else instead.

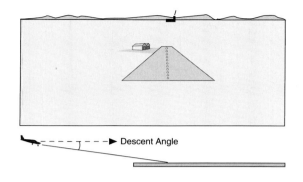

Ideal Runway Perspective

Descent angle correct

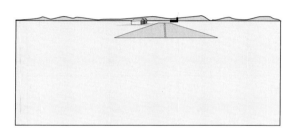

Too Low

Descent angle too shallow

Once established on finals, the pilot can make an initial judgement of the runway perspective to decide if the aircraft is high, low or on the ideal descent angle.

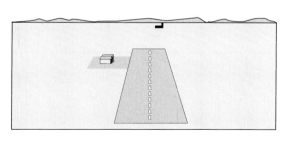

Too High

Descent angle too steep

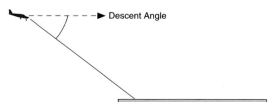

Maintaining Correct Descent Angle

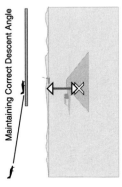
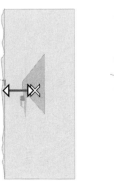

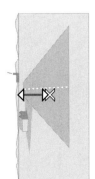
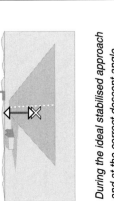
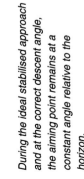
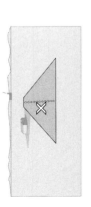

During the ideal stabilised approach and at the correct descent angle, the aiming point remains at a constant angle relative to the horizon.

Undershooting

If the aircraft is UNDERSHOOTING the runway, the aiming point moves up towards the horizon - the angle to the aiming point becomes too shallow.

Overshooting

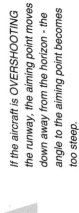
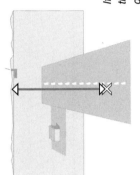

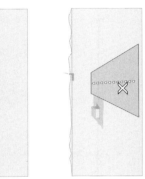

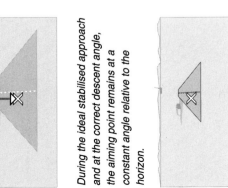

If the aircraft is OVERSHOOTING the runway, the aiming point moves down away from the horizon - the angle to the aiming point becomes too steep.

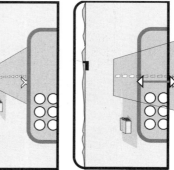

If overshooting the runway, perspective elongates.

If overshooting, aiming point moves down in relation to the aircraft, possibly even disappearing under the nose.

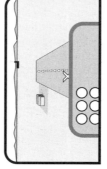
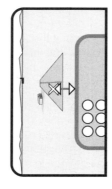
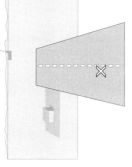
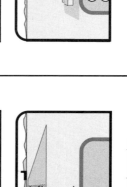

If undershooting the runway, perspective flattens out.

If undershooting, aiming point moves up in relation to the aircraft.

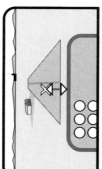
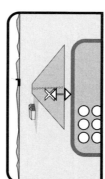
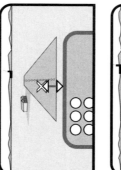
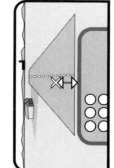
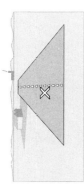

The runway perspective remains constant.

The aiming point remains fixed in relation to the aircraft.

13.9

If the aiming-point moves up towards the horizon the descent angle is becoming more shallow; the aircraft is UNDERSHOOTING and will touchdown before reaching the aiming-point. If the aiming-point moves further down below the horizon, the descent angle is becoming steeper; the aircraft is OVERSHOOTING and will touch down after passing over the aiming-point. The constant-angle approach can also be referred to as a 'constant aspect' approach.

Detecting the apparent movement of the aiming-point is only the first step in judging the descent angle. During a constant-aspect approach the runway perspective will also remain constant. If the perspective of the runway changes during the approach, the aircraft is under- or overshooting the aiming-point. An apparently shortening runway indicates that the aircraft is undershooting. An apparently lengthening runway indicates that the aircraft is overshooting. This change of perspective is the vital visual cue to the pilot that a change in power setting is probably required.

Finally, the position of the aiming-point in relation to the aircraft should also remain constant. Once established on final approach, at the correct airspeed and in the landing configuration, the nose attitude should remain virtually constant until the flare. This implies that the aiming-point should appear 'fixed' on the windscreen throughout the approach. If the nose attitude is constant, but the aiming-point is moving relative to the aircraft, the aircraft is under- or overshooting the aiming-point. An aiming-point apparently moving up the windscreen indicates that the aircraft is undershooting. An aiming-point apparently moving down the windscreen indicates that the aircraft is overshooting. The movement of the aiming-point position indicates that a change in power setting is probably required. This visual cue is, however, only valid for a fixed attitude. If the aircraft's attitude is changed significantly, the position of the aiming-point on the windscreen will also change, even if a constant aspect approach is being maintained.

All these visual cues to the aircraft's progress down the approach are valid to a height of around 50 feet. Below this height the runway and ground features will 'flatten out' around the aircraft and the pilot will be transferring attention to depth perception to judge the flare and hold-off.

Although this may all seem rather complicated, in practice it is quite simple; during a stabilised, constant aspect approach the aiming-point remains at a fixed angle relative to the horizon, the runway perspective remains constant as the runway gets closer and the aiming-point remains fixed in relation to the aircraft.

As the pilot learns to take in all these visual cues, the whole process becomes automatic and subconscious. Ask an experienced pilot how he judges the approach descent angle and chances are he will say "It just looks right". With experience you will soon come to know when an approach "just looks right".

Having now established how the pilot is going to judge progress down the approach, we can look at how this judgement is put into practice. Airspeed is controlled by the attitude of the aircraft and should remain constant at the correct approach speed. If airspeed is too slow, the aircraft is pitched nose down to accelerate. If the airspeed is too fast, the aircraft is pitched nose up to slow. After each change in attitude re-trimming may be necessary.

The Powered Approach and Landing

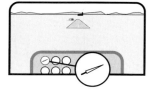

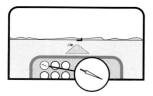

Attitude controls airspeed.

Maintain the correct airspeed through attitude.

If airspeed is too slow, pitch nose down.

If airspeed is too fast, pitch nose up.

Having stabilised at the correct airspeed, the pilot can concentrate on the approach angle, which is controlled by power. If the pilot judges that the aircraft is too low on the approach, power is increased; if too high, power is reduced. After each change of power setting it may be necessary to alter the nose attitude to maintain the correct approach speed and to retrim.

Effect of Wind on Descent Angle

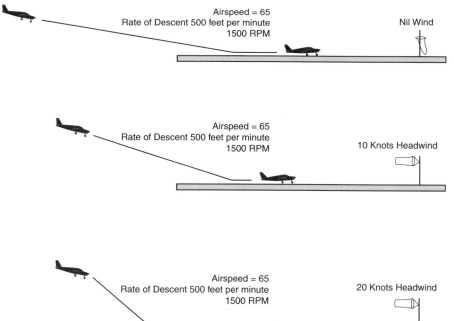

Airspeed = 65
Rate of Descent 500 feet per minute
1500 RPM

Nil Wind

Airspeed = 65
Rate of Descent 500 feet per minute
1500 RPM

10 Knots Headwind

At a given airspeed and rate of descent, the descent angle is determined by the headwind component.

Airspeed = 65
Rate of Descent 500 feet per minute
1500 RPM

20 Knots Headwind

Airspeed remains constant, so when landing into a strong headwind, more power is required to reduce the rate of descent and maintain the correct descent angle.

Airspeed = 65
Rate of Descent 400 feet per minute
1600 RPM

20 Knots Headwind

Background Briefing

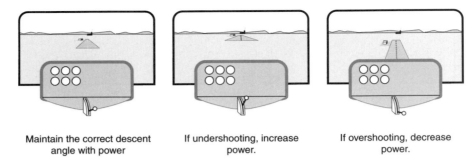

Power controls rate of descent and thus descent angle.

Maintain the correct descent angle with power

If undershooting, increase power.

If overshooting, decrease power.

The rule is 'attitude to control airspeed, power to control the rate and angle of descent', or more simply:

attitude for airspeed

power for height

The key to making a smooth, stabilised approach is to make the necessary corrections as soon as you judge that the aircraft is not on the ideal approach. A series of minor corrections is greatly preferable to a couple of major changes of power and attitude.

▶ Decision Height

At a height of 300ft on the approach, the pilot should be able to make an informed decision as to how well the approach is progressing. This decision can be made in accordance with the 'A.N.C.' principle:

Aviate: Is the aircraft properly under control, at the correct approach speed, in the landing configuration and trimmed?

Navigate: Is the aircraft properly positioned to make a safe landing?

Communicate Has any necessary landing clearance been given by ATC?

A height of 300 feet makes a good 'decision point' at which the pilot can assess the progress of the approach and the likelihood of making a safe landing.

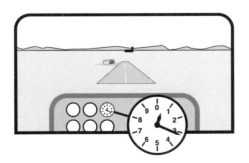

If all looks well, the approach is continued, keeping one hand on the control column and the other hand on the throttle. If for any reason there is doubt about the approach, the correct procedure is to go around, re-enter the circuit and try again. By initiating the go-around at 300ft there is plenty of time and height to make an orderly climb away. When flying dual, the instructor may allow an approach to continue if he considers that the approach can be safely completed (with his assistance if required). However, when flying solo it is not wise to press on in the hope that all will come right - it almost certainly will not. A go around can be made at any time during the approach, it is never too late. However, 300ft is a good key point at which to assess the progress of the approach.

▶ The Landing

The landing can be divided into three stages, the flare (or roundout), the hold-off and the ground run.

The flare begins at a height of 15 to 20ft when the aircraft is steadily pitched nose-up to arrest the rate of descent, and the throttle is closed fully. The aircraft should now be in a level attitude, flying a couple of feet above the runway. From the point where the flare begins, the pilot's full attention should be outside the cockpit as visual judgement during the flare and hold off is governed by depth perception. To achieve the best depth perception, the pilot should look at an intermediate point down the side of the aircraft's nose. If the pilot looks too close to the aircraft, the ground is blurred and he may level off too high. If the pilot looks too far ahead of the aircraft he may level out too late or even fly on to the runway without flaring.

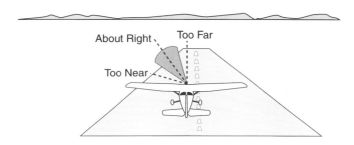

To judge height during the flare and hold-off the pilot should look in an arc to the side of the aircraft. The correct height to flare is variously described as the height of a double-decker bus, or the point at which the runway comes up around your shoulders.

Learning where to start the flare and the rate of pitching up needed to arrive in the hold-off is a matter of trial and error initially. It is the instructor's task at this stage to demonstrate the manoeuvre and correct the student's mistakes whilst the student pilot learns the correct visual cues and control movements.

The hold off is a process of slowing the aircraft while flying level a few feet above the runway. This is done by gradually pitching the aircraft nose-up as the aircraft slows, but without gaining height. In effect the pilot is increasing the angle of attack to keep the aircraft flying level whilst it decelerates and ensuring that the aircraft touches down on the main wheels in a nose-high attitude. The hold-off is often a matter of feeling the aircraft sinking and responding with a slightly higher nose attitude - sink, check; sink, check. The aim of the hold-off is to ensure that the aircraft touches down at the correct airspeed (slightly faster than the stall), on the mainwheels with the nosewheel still in the air.

The three stages of the landing.

After touchdown the control column should be held as it is (probably aft of the neutral point) and used to control the gentle arrival of the nosewheel on the runway. Once the nosewheel is on the runway, directional control is aided by nosewheel steering and the brakes can be used to bring the aircraft to a stop or slow it to a safe taxying speed. The landing is not over until the aircraft has stopped. An otherwise safe landing could be ruined if the pilot's attention was distracted by doing after-landing checks during the ground run or by trying to turn off the runway at too fast a speed.

The correct landing technique will come with practice. Landing is one manoeuvre that cannot be taught by numbers. It takes time to allow instruction and experience to build up judgement and skill.

▶ The After-Landing Checks

Once the landing is complete, the aircraft is taxyed clear of the runway, stopped and the after-landing checks are completed from the checklist. Do not attempt to do the after-landing checks during the ground run. The landing is not over until the aircraft has cleared the runway and stopped.

At some airfields it may be necessary to request taxy clearance back to the parking area once the checks have been completed.

▶ The Touch and Go

During training, it would be very inefficient if each circuit culminated in a full-stop landing, after which the aircraft cleared the runway, taxied back to the holding point and took off again. It is normal during training to make 'touch and goes'—that is, during the ground run before the aircraft has slowed too much, full power is reapplied, a take-off is made, and another circuit begins.

The 'touch and go'.

After touchdown, with aircraft under control
- raise flaps to take-off position
- full power - Carb heat to cold
- continue with normal take-off.

For a touch-and-go the landing is made as normal, but once the nosewheel has lowered on to the runway, the pilot actions are:

> raise the flaps to the take-off position
>
> apply full power (maintaining direction)
>
> continue with a normal take-off

Slightly different procedures may apply depending on the aircraft type and local procedures. When flying touch and goes, the available runway length is an important consideration as a touch and go uses more runway than either a normal take-off or a normal landing. If, during the ground run, there is any doubt that enough runway remains to take-off again, a full-stop landing should be completed instead, using brakes as necessary.

The touch and go is sometimes referred to as a 'roller'.

▶ Mislanding, the Bounce or Balloon

Having described an ideal landing, it is not surprising to know that it does not always work out that way. Problems in the landing are often caused by arriving over the runway at the wrong approach speed or over-controlling the aircraft during the landing.

Failure to flare or hold-off sufficiently, or touching down too fast, may cause the aircraft to bounce back into the air. If the bounce is only few feet high, it may be possible to complete the landing by continuing with the hold off and making a second, slower touchdown.

A bounce, controlled by the pilot, leading to a second, safe landing.

If the bounce is higher or if there is any doubt about the outcome of the landing, the pilot should go around without delay. During a bounce the major piloting error to avoid is pushing the control column forward in an attempt to force the aircraft on to the ground. In fact, the aircraft will touchdown on the nosewheel, possibly causing a further bounce, another landing on the nosewheel and so on. The nosewheel is not as strong as the main undercarriage and will not take this kind of treatment for very long. This is one reason why the aim of the landing is to touch down on the main wheels with the nosewheel still off the ground.

The danger of allowing the aircraft to touchdown on the nose wheel. After a series of touchdowns of this nature, the nose wheel may well be damaged or even collapse.

A balloon can be caused by pitching nose-up too quickly during the flare or hold-off, by approaching too fast, by failing to close the throttle or possibly by a gust of wind. During a balloon, the aircraft will climb back up to perhaps 20ft above the runway. The correct action is to go around immediately. Failure to go around will leave the aircraft decelerating rapidly with the aircraft running out of airspeed and height and the pilot running out of ideas and options. The aircraft will probably enter a semi-stalled (quasi-stall) condition, the rate of descent increases rapidly (or as the pilot sees it the runway suddenly comes up to meet the aircraft) and the end result will be a touchdown that will probably register on the Richter scale. All of this is completely avoidable if the pilot starts the go around without delay, rejoins the circuit and makes another approach. Whilst flying round that circuit, the pilot can also analyse what went wrong and resolve to correct the errors next time.

The balloon. The correct action at this stage is to GO-AROUND.

▶ The Go Around

The importance of the go-around when the pilot is uncertain of a safe approach and landing is paramount. A go-around can be made at any time during the approach, though an early decision to go-around makes life much easier and is a sign of good airmanship. When a go around is necessary, carry out the following actions:

1 Apply full power (carb heat to cold if necessary) and correct any yaw

2 Adopt a shallow climb attitude (aim for an attitude and airspeed appropriate to amount of flap extended).

3 Check airspeed, raise the flap in stages (do not raise flaps all in one go) adjusting attitude and trim and maintaining a safe airspeed. Establish the climb with take-off flap extended.

4 Retract remaining flap to 0° in stages at a safe height—normally not below 300ft AGL.

5 Integrate into the circuit pattern - climbing ahead to circuit height and then following the normal cross-wind leg path. Do not turn early on to crosswind as this may cut ahead of other circuit traffic already downwind and conflict with aircraft joining the circuit.

When full power is applied for the go-around, there is often a strong pitch-up force. The pilot may need to be firm to stop the aircraft pitching up too high, and the trim will have to be adjusted. The application of full power also causes the aircraft to yaw, so the pilot must keep in balance using the rudder. Once established in the climb it is normal to position to the *deadside* of the runway i.e if a left-hand circuit is in force, position to the right of the runway. This will give the pilot a good view of the runway and climb out path during the go around. Once established in the initial climb of the go around, the "going around" radio call can be made.

During the go-around the aircraft is positioned to the 'dead side' of the runway.

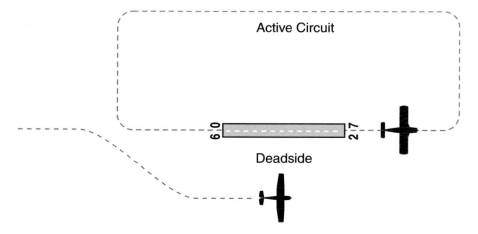

Active Circuit

Deadside

▶ ATC Liaison/Radio

During the approach and landing, a safe spacing from other circuit traffic should be maintained and the pilot must adhere to any traffic priority established by ATC. After the turn on to final approach is completed it is usual to report "finals" stating the runway and intentions e.g. touch and go, to land, to go around etc.

Most ATC controllers and radio operators are very good at not overloading the pilot with radio work or making inappropriate calls at busy moments. However, should someone choose to make a non-urgent call while you are, say, in the middle of a landing or go around, remember your priorities - A.N.C. Do not be afraid to ignore the radio and get on with the job of flying the aircraft. ATC can wait a moment or two; flying the aircraft cannot.

Exercise

13

The
Powered
Approach
and
Landing

Flight Exercise

▷ Purpose

To learn to make a safe approach and landing in the normal landing configuration, and to learn the correct go around procedure.

▷ Airmanship

Lookout

Maintain a good lookout during the final approach and landing. An aircraft lower than yours may be quite difficult to spot against the ground. However if you do spot a lower aircraft ahead of you, remember that the lower aircraft on the approach usually has right of way.

To help your lookout do not stare at the aiming-point on the runway, but take in the wider picture. This will also help your judgement of the descent angle.

ATC liaison

Maintain any traffic priority given by ATC. To do this, be sure that you have in sight at all times any aircraft you are following. Occasionally ATC may offer a 'land-after' clearance or a 'stop-go' clearance. Your instructor will explain these terms in relation to local procedures.

ANC

Flying the aircraft is always your primary task, and never more so than during the approach and landing when there is much less height available to sort out any gross piloting errors. Make airspeed control your number one priority. Once the aircraft is settled and trimmed at the correct approach speed, it is much easier to judge the descent angle. The earlier on the approach this is done, the easier the approach and landing will be.

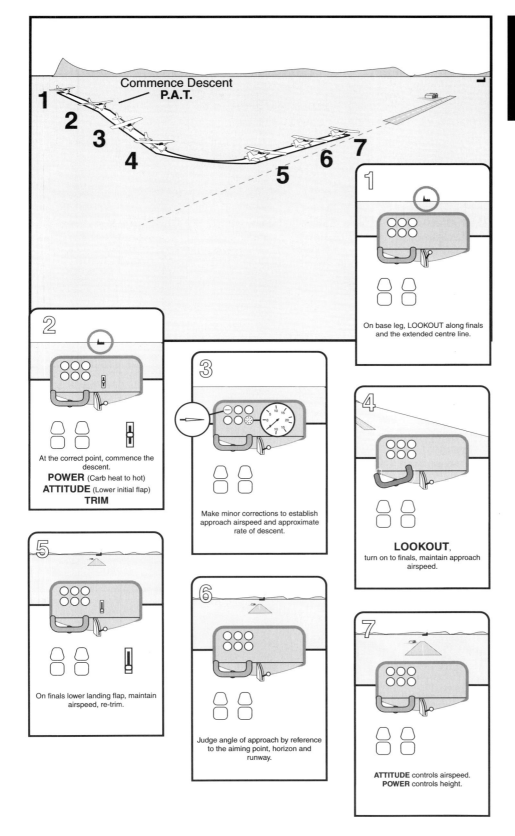

Commence Descent
P.A.T.

1
2
3
4
5
6
7

1
On base leg, LOOKOUT along finals and the extended centre line.

2
At the correct point, commence the descent.
POWER (Carb heat to hot)
ATTITUDE (Lower initial flap)
TRIM

3
Make minor corrections to establish approach airspeed and approximate rate of descent.

4
LOOKOUT,
turn on to finals, maintain approach airspeed.

5
On finals lower landing flap, maintain airspeed, re-trim.

6
Judge angle of approach by reference to the aiming point, horizon and runway.

7
ATTITUDE controls airspeed.
POWER controls height.

The Powered Approach and Landing

The Powered Approach and Landing

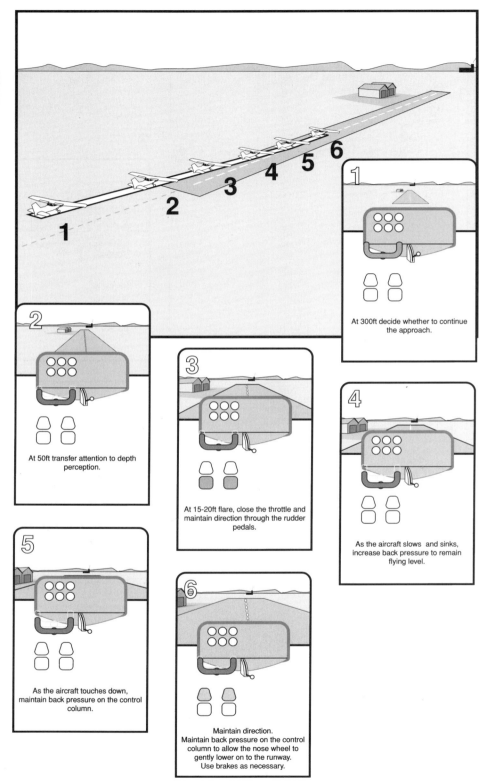

1 At 300ft decide whether to continue the approach.

2 At 50ft transfer attention to depth perception.

3 At 15-20ft flare, close the throttle and maintain direction through the rudder pedals.

4 As the aircraft slows and sinks, increase back pressure to remain flying level.

5 As the aircraft touches down, maintain back pressure on the control column.

6 Maintain direction.
Maintain back pressure on the control column to allow the nose wheel to gently lower on to the runway.
Use brakes as necessary.

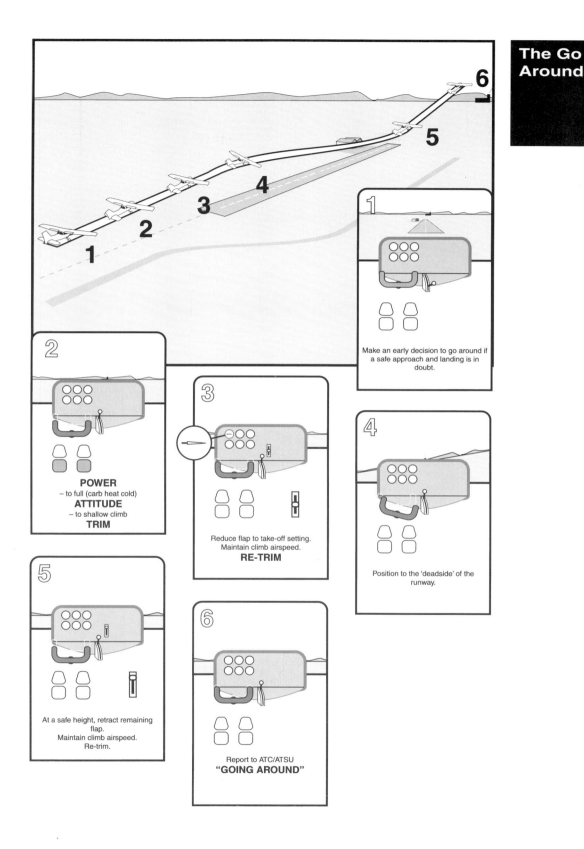

1

Make an early decision to go around if a safe approach and landing is in doubt.

2

POWER
– to full (carb heat cold)
ATTITUDE
– to shallow climb
TRIM

3

Reduce flap to take-off setting.
Maintain climb airspeed.
RE-TRIM

4

Position to the 'deadside' of the runway.

5

At a safe height, retract remaining flap.
Maintain climb airspeed.
Re-trim.

6

Report to ATC/ATSU
"GOING AROUND"

Take-Off and Climb Emergencies

BACKGROUND BRIEFING

▶ Avoiding Engine Problems

▶ Abandoned Take-off

▶ Engine Failure After Take-Off

▶ Why Not Turn Back?

FLIGHT EXERCISE

▷ Purpose

▷ Airmanship

▷ Engine Failure After Take-Off

BACKGROUND BRIEFING

▶ Avoiding Engine Problems

Possible emergency scenarios in the early part of the flight usually involve engine problems. As always, prevention is better than cure. During the power checks and pre take-off vital actions, carefully monitor the engine—do not put yourself under pressure to complete the checks. The engine is monitored again during the take-off, as detailed in the take-off checks. With experience you will be able to sense the normal acceleration and power to expect during the take-off and if something feels odd—or if the checks reveal a problem—it is likely that something, somewhere is wrong.

▶ Abandoned Take-Off

If the pilot decides that the take-off cannot be safely completed, the decision to abandon it should be taken as early as possible.

To abandon the take-off, the throttle is closed and the brakes are applied to bring the aircraft to a halt. If, for any reason, the aircraft will not be able to stop before the end of the runway, weaving the aircraft gently will increase the ground run—thereby allowing more distance to stop. In an extreme situation it may be preferable to ground-loop the aircraft rather than hit a solid obstruction head-on.

Weaving the aircraft will lengthen the distance it travels, allowing greater distance to stop. Altering direction or even ground looping is preferable to hitting a solid obstruction.

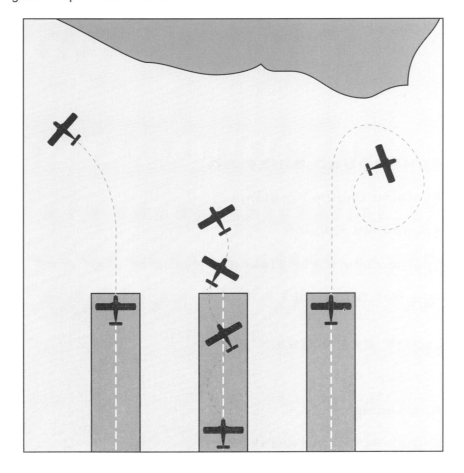

Having safely stopped, the problem can be analysed. If an engine fire is suspected, complete the 'engine fire on ground' checks.

An occasional problem during take-off is a door opening. Although the sudden wind noise and draught can be very distracting, there is rarely any serious effect on the aircraft's flying performance. If already airborne when a door opens, continue the climb to a safe height, then it should be possible to close the door or return for a landing.

▶ Engine Failure After Take-Off

This rare emergency is practised throughout training and will probably be the first airborne emergency for which you have trained. It is usually simulated when, at around 300ft AGL in the initial climb, your instructor smoothly closes the throttle and states "practice engine failure". Probably the first thing you will notice is the awful silence, then the rapidly decreasing airspeed and a certain sinking feeling. It may seem all too much to cope with, but remember the pilot's primary task - to fly the aeroplane - and the correct actions fall into place.

Given the slow airspeed in the climb out, the high nose attitude, and the element of shock leading to hesitation by the pilot, the airspeed can be lost very quickly indeed. The aircraft should be pitched nose-down immediately to the glide attitude and the glide airspeed maintained. Now you have an aircraft that is still flying and you are still in control of the situation.

With the aircraft control in hand, the next task is to select a landing area within about 45° either side of straight ahead.

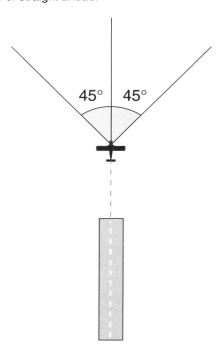

When looking for a landing site after an engine failure in the initial climb, scan the area 45° either side of straight-ahead.

Background Briefing

You are looking for an open and unobstructed area in which to land the aircraft. Time for selecting an area is limited, but take the best site you can realistically reach. Do not use flap until certain of making the landing area. It is unlikely there will be time to check for the cause of the engine failure so use the memorised emergency checklist to shut the engine systems down and minimise the fire risk:

fuel off

magnetos off

master switch off

(Note. if you are flying an aircraft with electrically operated flaps, do not turn off the master switch until you have selected all the flap needed).

Make gentle turns to line up with the landing area, preferably using not more than 15° angle of bank. The objective is to touch down wings-level with a slow groundspeed, not heading towards any really solid obstructions such as buildings or trees. By achieving this objective you should ensure that even if the aircraft does hit some obstruction during the ground run, the slow ground speed and fact that the pilot is in control of the aircraft, will minimise both any damage to the aircraft and the risk of injury to the occupants.

To summarise your actions in the event of an engine failure after take-off:

* fly the aeroplane *

pitch nose down to the gliding attitude

select a landing area ahead, use flap as necessary

complete emergency checklist and brief passengers

aim for a wings-level, slow-speed touchdown clear of obstructions

▶ Why Not Turn Back ?

Choosing a landing area ahead is all well and good, but what about the runway behind you? It may seem very close and inviting, but if you try to turn back, it is overwhelmingly probable that you will never reach the runway.

For a moment, revise some of the fundamental lessons from earlier flight exercises. In a gliding turn, more height is lost than in a wings-level glide. In addition the stalling speed during a turn is faster than that in level flight; the steeper the turn, the faster the stalling speed.

Experiments have shown that up to 1400ft of height may be needed to complete the turn back to the runway. If a pilot does attempt to turn back with insufficient height available, he will come to realise that the aircraft is going to reach the ground before completing the turn. The temptation is to pitch the aircraft nose-up in an attempt to 'stretch' the glide; or to increase the angle of bank to complete the turn more quickly. Of course these actions only increase the rate of descent, whilst the increased angle of bank and slower airspeed bring the aircraft closer to the stall. The pilot has abandoned the primary task (flying the aeroplane) and as a result is approaching the classic stall/spin situation.

Take-Off and Climb Emergencies

If the aircraft does stall during the turn, the chance of a wing drop or even an incipient spin is great; and the height needed to recover is almost certainly more than that available. Even if the pilot does complete the turn, he will be landing with a tailwind–this is a very significant factor. Landing into a 15-knot headwind at a glide airspeed of 65 knots will result in a touchdown groundspeed of about 50 knots. But landing downwind with a 15-knot tailwind means a touchdown speed of nearer 80 knots and consequently a much greater distance is needed to stop the aircraft.

Taking all these factors into account, it is clear that turning back after an engine failure in the initial climb makes no sense. Stalling or spinning into the ground, or hitting the ground in a steeply banked attitude at high speed, shows the pilot was not in control of the aircraft and almost invariably leads to a badly damaged aircraft and a high risk of injury to the occupants.

Save in exceptional circumstances, the turn back to the runway is not an option. Do not attempt it.

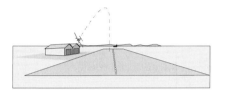 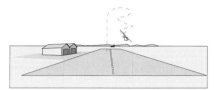

Turning back after an engine failure in the initial climb usually has an unhappy ending.

Flight Exercise

▷ Purpose

To practise the actions necessary in the event of an emergency occurring during the take-off or initial climb.

▷ Airmanship

Awareness

Emergencies during or immediately after take-off are very rare—more so if the checks have been followed properly. However, the pilot should always be prepared for the worst as emergencies, by their nature, tend to happen when least expected.

ATC Liaison

These emergencies are only practised when flying with an instructor. It will be the instructor's responsibility to liaise with ATC and make them aware of the practice emergency. A simulated engine failure after take-off is sometimes referred to as a "practice fanstop". Your instructor will make a further radio call, "climbing away", to let ATC know the practice emergency is over.

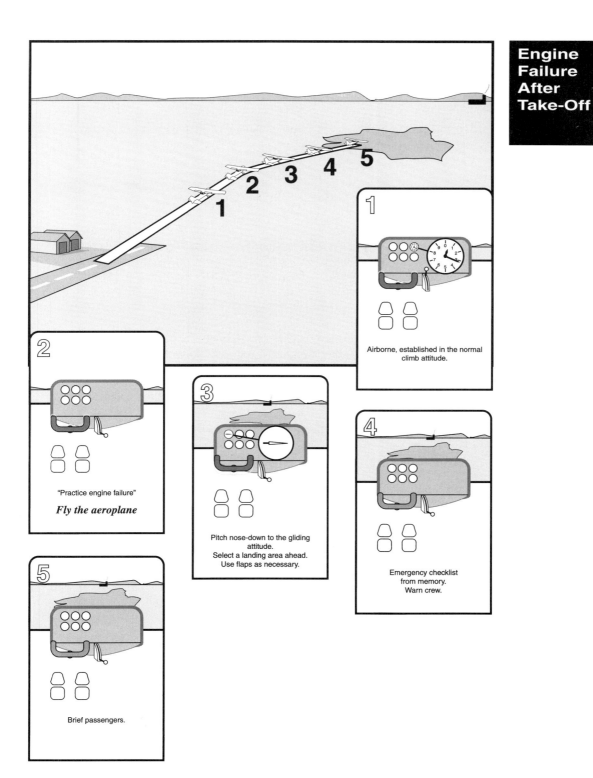

Engine Failure After Take-Off

1 2 3 4 5

1 Airborne, established in the normal climb attitude.

2 "Practice engine failure"

Fly the aeroplane

3 Pitch nose-down to the gliding attitude.
Select a landing area ahead.
Use flaps as necessary.

4 Emergency checklist from memory. Warn crew.

5 Brief passengers.

Circuit Emergencies

▶ Engine Failure in the Circuit

An engine failure in the circuit will require actions similar to those for an engine failure after take-off. The difference is that because of the greater height, the options open to the pilot are much greater.

For instance, from the crosswind leg, along the downwind leg to the base leg it should be possible to land safely back on the runway in the event of an engine failure. Even if the runway is beyond gliding range, the large, level and unobstructed areas of most airfields may well be the best landing area available if within gliding range.

▶ Radio Failure in the Circuit

If the radio fails during circuit flying, you should comply with the normal circuit pattern and make a full-stop landing. Maintain a good lookout for other traffic and look for light signals from ATC/ATSU:

Light Signal	Meaning to Aircraft in the Air
GREEN FLASHES	Clear to approach
STEADY GREEN	Cleared to land
STEADY RED	Go around, await landing clearance

The principal light signals from ATC/ATSU to an aircraft in flight

Crosswind Take-Off, Circuit and Landing

Runways take up a lot of space and it is rare for an airfield to have enough runways to permit a take-off and landing directly into wind all the time. Airfield planners are for the most part pretty good at choosing a runway direction that will be suitable for the prevailing local winds. However, when the wind direction fails to conform with the average, or if an into wind runway is not available for some reason, crosswind technique will be necessary.

BACKGROUND BRIEFING

▶ **Aircraft Crosswind Limit**

▶ **Assessing Surface Wind**

▶ **The Crosswind Take-Off**

▶ **The Crosswind Circuit**

▶ **The Crosswind Approach and Landing**

▶ **Use of Flap**

▶ **Effects of Gusts/Wind Gradient/Turbulence**

FLIGHT EXERCISE

▷ **Purpose**

▷ **Airmanship**

▷ **The Crosswind Take-off**

▷ **The Crabbed Approach**

▷ **The Wing-Down Approach**

▷ **The Combination Method**

BACKGROUND BRIEFING

▶ Aircraft Crosswind Limit

The aircraft will have a maximum demonstrated crosswind component listed in the POH/FM and this figure is given for a good reason. If a pilot attempts to take-off or land when the crosswind component exceeds this figure, there is no guarantee that proper use of the controls will allow a safe take-off or landing to be made.

This would seem to be stating the obvious, but every year a number of landing accidents are caused by pilots attempting to land when the crosswind component exceeds the figure given in the POH/FM. Furthermore, pilot experience, lack of current practice or operator procedures may dictate a lower crosswind limit than that given in the POH/FM - your instructor will advise.

Crosswind becomes significant once the crosswind component is more than 5 to 10 knots. At the end of this section is a supplement that details various rule-of-thumb methods for calculating the actual crosswind component.

▶ Assessing Surface Wind

During the pre-flight planning stage the wind velocity (Wv) -that is wind strength and direction - can be found in the actual weather reports and the forecast wind velocity in the weather forecasts.

When taxying for take-off, or in flight, the wind velocity can be noted from ATC/ATSU or can be seen from the movement of the windsock. The wind reporting point used by ATC/ATSU may be some distance from the landing runway. In these cases the windsock may give a more relevant indication of the wind velocity at the runway.

A windsock close to the runway threshold will give a more relevant indication of wind velocity than the ATC report, which might be taken from a measuring point some distance from the runway threshold.

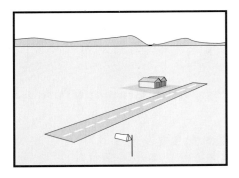

▶ The Crosswind Take-off

When taking-off in crosswind conditions, the aircraft is lined up on the runway in the normal way. However, before beginning the take-off the ailerons are moved into wind i.e. with a crosswind from the right, the control column is moved to the right.

As speed increases during the take-off run, the aileron deflection is slowly reduced to keep the wings level, so that at the point of rotation, the control column is approximately centralised.

Crosswind Take-Off, Circuit and Landing

During the take-off run, the aircraft will have a tendency to weathercock into wind and increased use of the rudder will be necessary to maintain the runway centre line.

Your instructor may recommend increasing rotate speed by 5 knots to improve control effectiveness, and it is usual to make a slightly more abrupt rotation than normal to minimise sideways drift whilst the aircraft is in transition from the wheels to wingborne flight. As nosewheel steering will aid directional control, it may help to use less back-pressure than normal on the control column during the take-off run. However, there is no question of pushing forward to keep the nosewheel on the ground. This will make the nosewheel more vulnerable to damage, and the aircraft may 'wheelbarrow'.

During take-off do not allow the aircraft to 'wheelbarrow' on the nosewheel.

Once airborne the aircraft should be gently turned to head slightly into wind so that the extended centre line is maintained during the initial climb.

▶ The Crosswind Circuit

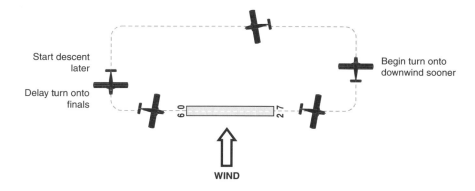

Adjustment of heading to maintain the correct circuit pattern ground track in crosswind conditions.

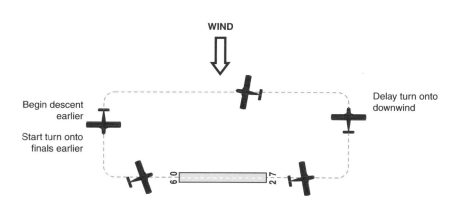

Background Briefing

The names of the various legs of the circuit are fixed in relation to the runway, not the prevailing wind, so the normal circuit pattern applies. It will, however, be necessary to adjust the heading of the aircraft and the position of certain key points to maintain the ground track of the normal circuit pattern. This is particularly important on base leg, when a significant head or tailwind will have a marked effect on the position of the key point for commencing the descent and the turn on to finals.

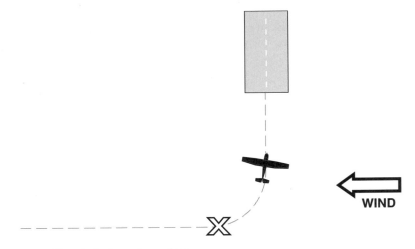

Headwind on base leg.
Descent started later, turn on to finals delayed.

The point to commence the final descent to land should be altered in accordance with the wind velocity.

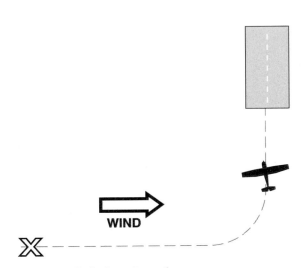

Tailwind on base leg.
Descent started earlier, turn on to finals advanced.

▶ The Crosswind Approach and Landing

The effect of the prevailing wind velocity will have to be compensated for throughout the approach and landing so that the aircraft does not drift off the runway centreline.

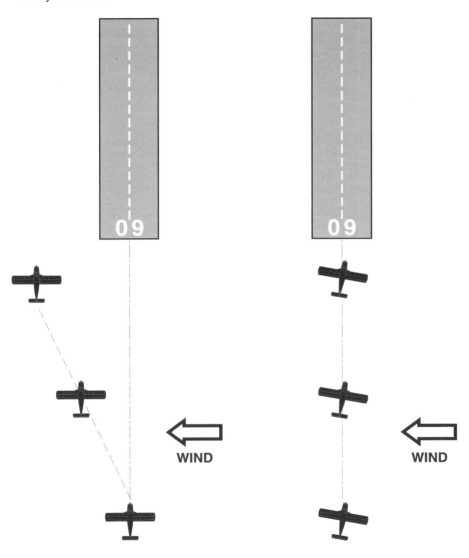

On final approach, allowance must be made for wind drift in order for the aircraft to maintain the extended centre line.

No allowance made for drift   Correct allowance made for drift

The wind velocity may change significantly as the aircraft descends and allowance for drift will have to be altered.

The allowance made for drift will alter the pilot's perspective of the runway, particularly if making a 'crabbed' approach. During the crosswind approach it is even more important not to fixate solely on the aiming point and lose the overall perspective of the approach.

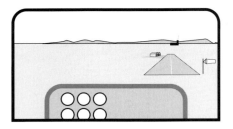

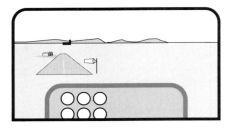

Crosswind from left   Crosswind from right

The apparent perspective of the runway in relation to the aircraft is altered by a crosswind on final approach.

The allowance for drift is particularly important during the touchdown. The wheels and undercarriage are very good at absorbing the loads of a normal touchdown, but not very good at taking the large sideways loads which will occur if the aircraft touches down with a significant amount of drift.

There are three types of crosswind approach and landing, but which one you mostly practise will be decided by your instructor, whose judgement will be based not just on personal preference but also the aircraft type you are flying.

1   The 'crabbed' approach and landing

The wings stay level but the aircraft is headed into wind during the approach, to allow for drift and maintain the centre line. Note that the aircrafts stays in balance.

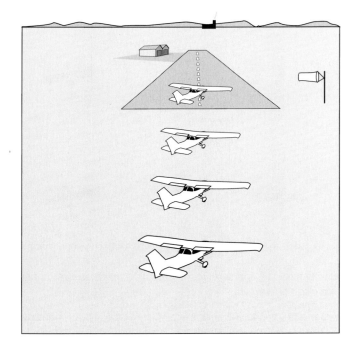

The crabbed approach

Once established on the approach, the drift correction is monitored throughout the approach, flare and hold off to stay on the centre line. When the pilot senses that the aircraft is about to touch down, the aircraft is yawed straight with rudder (using aileron to keep the wings level) and a normal touchdown is made. After touchdown direction is maintained through the rudder pedals and the ailerons are slowly moved into wind to keep the wings level.

2   The 'wing down' approach and landing

This method keeps the aircraft aligned along the runway centre line during the approach but the aircraft is banked into wind to allow for drift. The descent on base leg and the turn on to finals is judged as before, allowing for the headwind or tailwind on base leg. The turn on to finals is continued until the aircraft is lined up with the runway, then the aircraft yawed to align the fuselage along the runway centre line and opposite (into-wind) aileron is applied to leave the aircraft banked slightly into wind. The aircraft is now slightly sideslipping into wind and is slightly out of balance, hence slightly more power may be required to maintain the correct rate of descent.

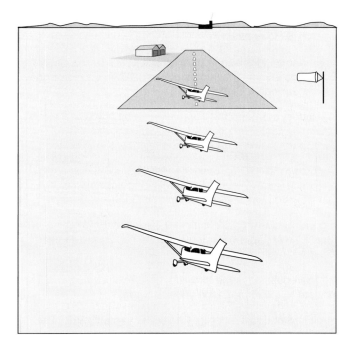

The wing-down approach

The sideslip is maintained, altering the opposite rudder and angle of bank as necessary to keep the aircraft on the centre-line. The flare and hold-off are carried out still in the sideslip and the aircraft lands on the 'up wind' wheel first. The other wheel will touchdown soon after and the ground run continues as before, with the ailerons being slowly applied into wind to keep the wings level.

3 The 'combination' method

The combination method is a technique combining the best elements of the crabbed and wing down techniques.

A crabbed approach is used because it is easier to fly and more comfortable than the wing-down, sideslipping approach. The crabbed approach is maintained to about 50 feet at which point the aircraft is lined up with the runway and banked into wind, in effect a transition to the wing-down technique. The sideslip is maintained throughout the flare, hold-off and touchdown. Because it is not necessary to judge the crucial time to yaw straight (as during the crabbed method of landing) the landing is easier.

With practice it is possible to change from the crabbed approach during the flare or even the hold-off. However, it is still important to touchdown with no sideways drift—whichever technique is used.

▶ Use of Flap

The use of full flap during the crosswind approach and landing is a contentious issue, not least because there is no definite right or wrong answer. It is a subject guaranteed to get instructors reaching for their textbooks and scribbling furiously on bits of paper. Here we will discuss the various factors at work. When you know the background you are in a better position to judge.

Use of flap reduces stalling speed, therefore the approach can be made at a slower airspeed and the landing distance is shortened. If less flap is used, the stalling speed is faster, the approach is flown faster and landing distance is lengthened.

Full flap allows a steeper approach which improves the view during the approach and shortens the landing distance. Less than full flap makes the approach more shallow, reducing the pilot's view and lengthening landing distance.

If full flap is extended, the go-around is more difficult and the initial climb rate is reduced. Statistically it is more likely that a go-around may be necessary during a crosswind approach and landing.

Full flap reduces control effectiveness on some aircraft types. Your instructor will advise if this factor is significant to the aircraft type you are flying.

The use of flap may be prohibited during a sideslip. Check the aircraft's POH/FM.

Full flap reduces the time holding-off, due to the increased drag. With reduced flap there is less drag and the aircraft may float in the hold-off for some time. This lengthens the landing distance and makes judgement and control of the landing more difficult.

As well as these points, remember that as the wind direction moves further away from straight down the runway, the headwind component is reduced. If the wind is at 90° to the runway, there is no headwind component and landing distance is lengthened accordingly.

Crosswind Take-Off, Circuit and Landing

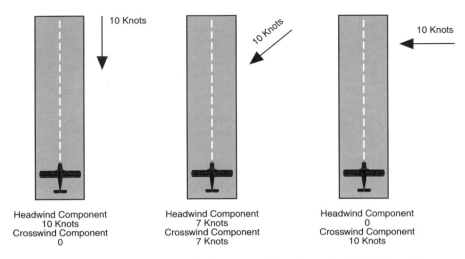

Headwind Component
10 Knots
Crosswind Component
0

Headwind Component
7 Knots
Crosswind Component
7 Knots

Headwind Component
0
Crosswind Component
10 Knots

The wind direction in relation to the runway direction dictates both headwind and crosswind component. As the headwind component reduces, the landing distance increases.

So, there is no easy answer—it really is a case of the pilot using his judgment to reach a decision in accordance with the specific circumstances. The key factors to consider to are:

1 How will the aircraft's handling be affected by the use of full flap? (e.g. will there be a loss of control effectiveness?)

2 Is the runway long enough to permit a landing with less than full flap?

Use your experience and knowledge to make the right decision for the circumstances - that is what pilot judgement is all about.

▶ Effects of Gusts/Wind Gradient/Turbulence

A gusty wind or turbulence can make an approach and landing more difficult. Wind gradient is the change of wind velocity with a change in height. A very sudden change in wind velocity through a small height change is called *windshear.* Because of the aircraft's inertia, a sudden windshear can affect the airspeed. If

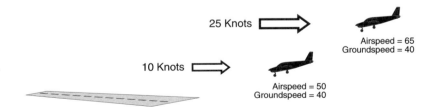

25 Knots

Airspeed = 65
Groundspeed = 40

10 Knots

Airspeed = 50
Groundspeed = 40

A sudden windshear, in this case a reduction in headwind, will have a marked effect on airspeed.

airspeed is suddenly lost due to windshear, the approach will be destabilised and it may be necessary to go around.

In a gusty wind, the arguments for and against the use of flap apply as just discussed; and commonly less than full flap is used when landing in gusty conditions. For safety it is routine to increase the approach speed when there is a gusting wind. Use a figure of half the wind gust factor, i.e. if the wind is gusting from 15 to 25 knots, the gust factor is 10 knots (25-15), therefore 5 knots is added to the approach speed for landing and to the climb speed after take-off.

Exercise
12 & 13

Crosswind
Take-Off,
Circuit and
Landing

Flight Exercise

▷ Purpose

To learn to make a safe take-off, circuit and landing, using a specified technique, when there is a significant crosswind component. To appreciate the importance of the specified maximum demonstrated crosswind component.

▷ Airmanship

Maximum Demonstrated Crosswind Component

As already stressed, the maximum demonstrated crosswind component listed in the aircraft's POH/FM is there for a good reason. Do **NOT** attempt a take-off or landing when the crosswind component is greater than this figure.

ATC Liaison

ATC/ATSU will usually specify the runway in use with regard to the surface wind. Sometimes, however, the runway in use may have a significant crosswind component, whereas another runway may be into wind. This situation may occur where one runway is much longer than another. Do not hesitate to request a landing or take-off on the into wind runway if it is available and suitable.

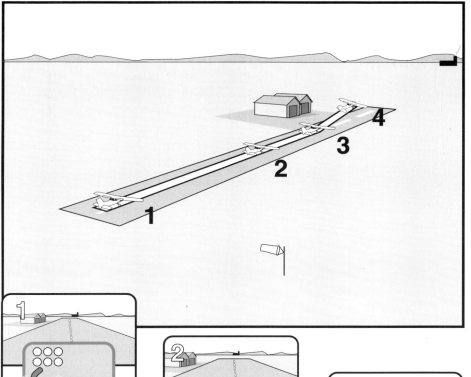

Start the take-off run with the ailerons moved into wind.

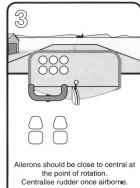

As airspeed increases, slowly reduce aileron deflection to keep the wings level.
Use less back pressure on the control column than during a standard take-off.

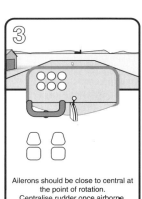

Ailerons should be close to central at the point of rotation.
Centralise rudder once airborne.

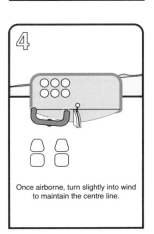

Once airborne, turn slightly into wind to maintain the centre line.

Crosswind Take-Off, Circuit and Landing

Crosswind Take-Off, Circuit and Landing

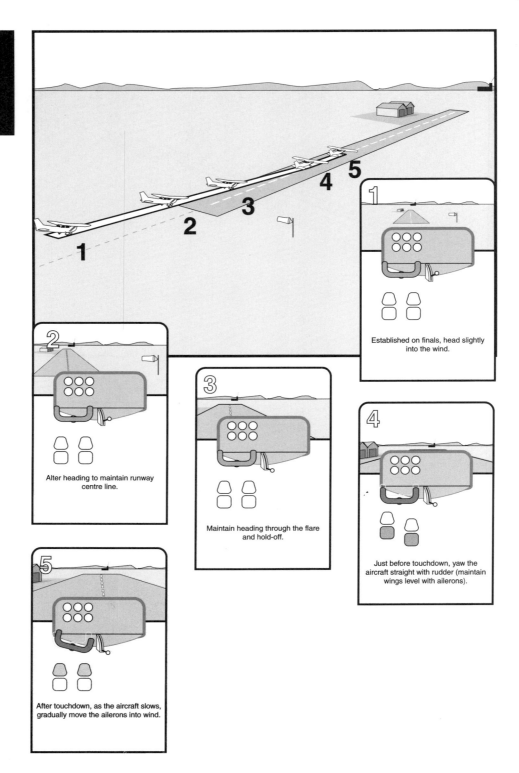

1 Established on finals, head slightly into the wind.

2 Alter heading to maintain runway centre line.

3 Maintain heading through the flare and hold-off.

4 Just before touchdown, yaw the aircraft straight with rudder (maintain wings level with ailerons).

5 After touchdown, as the aircraft slows, gradually move the ailerons into wind.

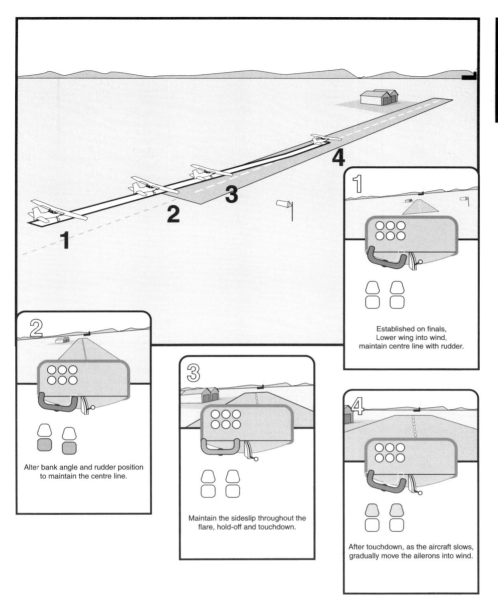

Established on finals,
Lower wing into wind,
maintain centre line with rudder.

Alter bank angle and rudder position
to maintain the centre line.

Maintain the sideslip throughout the
flare, hold-off and touchdown.

After touchdown, as the aircraft slows,
gradually move the ailerons into wind.

Crosswind Take-Off, Circuit and Landing

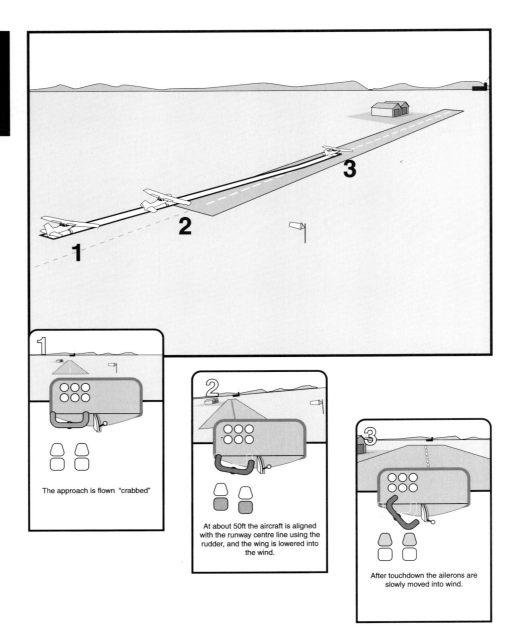

1 The approach is flown "crabbed"

2 At about 50ft the aircraft is aligned with the runway centre line using the rudder, and the wing is lowered into the wind.

3 After touchdown the ailerons are slowly moved into wind.

The Flapless Landing

On modern aircraft, flap failure is very rare. However, on some aircraft the flaps are electrically operated, so loss of electrical power will lead to loss of the use of flaps.

In certain circumstances, when flying some aircraft types, a pilot might choose to make a flapless landing in very strong wind conditions.

BACKGROUND BRIEFING

▶ **Reasons For Using Flap**

▶ **Adjustment of the Circuit**

▶ **The Flapless Approach and Landing**

FLIGHT EXERCISE

▷ **Purpose**

▷ **Airmanship**

▷ **The Flapless Landing**

BACKGROUND BRIEFING

▶ Reasons For Using Flap

The use of flap allows a steeper approach without building up airspeed, reduces the stalling speed (allowing a slower approach) reduces float during the hold off due to increased drag and shortens the landing distance. It follows that a flapless approach will be more shallow and faster, with a longer float and a longer landing distance.

▶ Adjustment of the Circuit

As the flapless approach is quite shallow, greater distance will be required to descend from circuit height. The downwind leg is extended slightly beyond the normal point so that the base leg can be started further away from the runway.

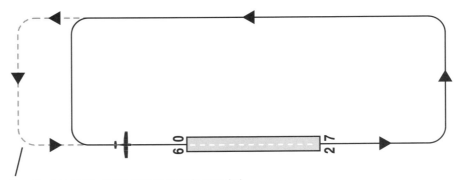

For a flapless approach the downwind leg is extended slightly to allow greater distance for the approach.

▶ The Flapless Approach and Landing

Without the use of flaps, the attitude during the approach will tend to be higher and so the view ahead is reduced. A faster approach speed is usually specified for the flapless approach (because of the faster stalling speed).

Due to the reduced drag, too fast an approach speed takes longer to correct, whereas the aircraft accelerates more quickly if you are flying too slowly. Overall, the aircraft is more sensitive to changes of power and attitude and therefore accurate airspeed control requires greater anticipation by the pilot. During the flare there is a smaller change in attitude and the aircraft will float for longer during the hold-off. Furthermore, the aircraft will land with a higher nose attitude and the touchdown speed will be faster.

Flight Exercise

▷ Purpose

To learn to make a safe approach and landing without the use of flaps, and to appreciate the longer landing distance when landing without flap extended.

▷ Airmanship

ATC Liaison

As the flapless approach alters the circuit shape slightly, it is important for other aircraft in the circuit to know your intentions. When reporting downwind, state your intention to make a flapless approach i.e. "G-CD downwind for a flapless touch and go."

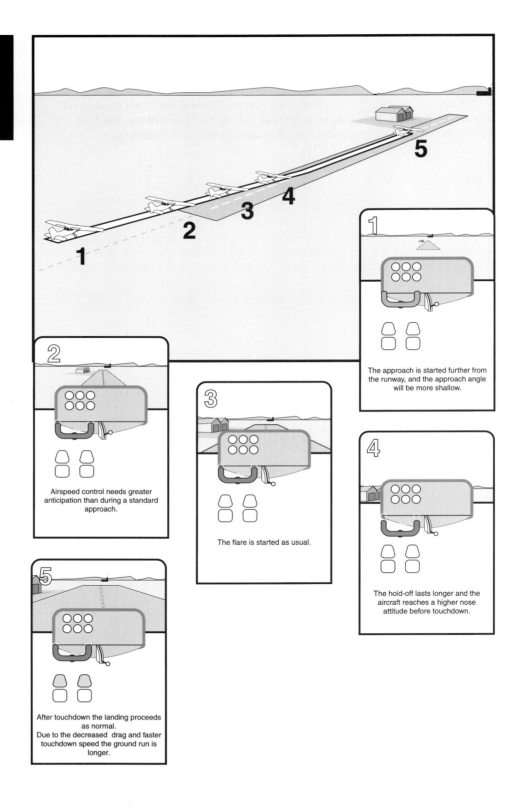

1 The approach is started further from the runway, and the approach angle will be more shallow.

2 Airspeed control needs greater anticipation than during a standard approach.

3 The flare is started as usual.

4 The hold-off lasts longer and the aircraft reaches a higher nose attitude before touchdown.

5 After touchdown the landing proceeds as normal.
Due to the decreased drag and faster touchdown speed the ground run is longer.

The Glide Approach and Landing

Practising the glide approach and landing has obvious applications for practising a landing after an engine failure. It is also a precision exercise which will improve not only your flying skills and judgement, but also your appreciation of the effect of wind on the approach path and the use of flaps to alter the descent angle.

BACKGROUND BRIEFING

▶ **Adjustment of the Circuit**

▶ **Judging the Power-Off Point**

▶ **Maintaining the Glide - the Use of Flap**

▶ **The Glide Landing**

FLIGHT EXERCISE

▷ **Purpose**

▷ **Airmanship**

▷ **The Glide Approach and Landing**

BACKGROUND BRIEFING

▶ Adjustment of the Circuit

Plan ahead whilst flying the circuit. The base leg will need to be flown closer to the runway and so the downwind leg is shorter. Start the turn on to base leg as soon as the runway threshold is visible behind the wing trailing edge.

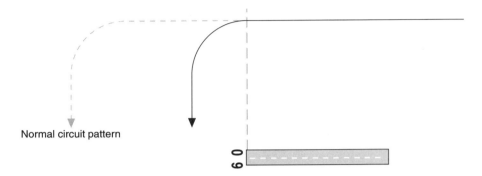

Normal circuit pattern

The turn on to base leg is started as the runway threshold appears behind the wing trailing edge.

As seen from pilot's seat

▶ Judging the Power-Off Point

Once established on base leg, the point to start the glide is judged by reference to an initial aiming point about one-third of the runway length beyond the threshold. When you are certain that you can reach this point in a glide, the descent is commenced at the best glide airspeed.

The point to commence the glide approach is when the descent angle to the aiming point is the same as the expected gliding angle of the aircraft. The gliding angle can be imagined as a cone around the aircraft. All points inside this cone are within gliding range.

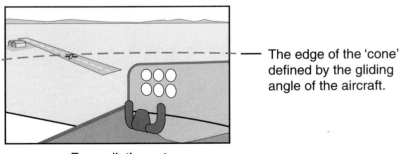

From pilot's seat

The edge of the 'cone' defined by the gliding angle of the aircraft.

With experience you will learn that the wind has a marked effect on the glide; a strong headwind on base leg or final approach steepens the glide angle and so reduces the gliding range. A glance at the windsock whilst assessing the point to start the glide descent will improve your judgement. You will appreciate that the windsock is indicating the SURFACE wind; the wind velocity at height will be different.

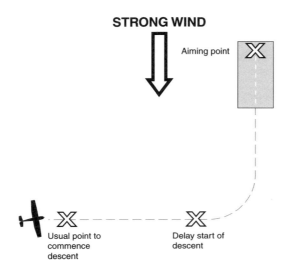

Assess the correct point to start the glide descent with regard to the wind velocity.

Once the aircraft is established in the glide, the pilot can judge whether the aiming point will be reached, using exactly the same technique as during the normal approach. If the aiming point stays fixed at a constant angle relative to the horizon, the aircraft will reach the aiming point. If the aiming point moves DOWN, further below the horizon, and the angle to it becomes steeper, the aircraft is OVERSHOOTING. This will also be obvious from both the change in runway perspective as the runway elongates and the aiming point moves down the windscreen. If the aiming point moves UP closer to the horizon and the angle to it becomes more shallow, the aircraft is UNDERSHOOTING. The runway perspective becomes more 'squat' and the aiming point moves up the windscreen.

The turn on to finals can be adjusted either to shorten or lengthen the distance to fly, depending on the pilot's judgement of whether the aircraft is under- or overshooting the aiming point.

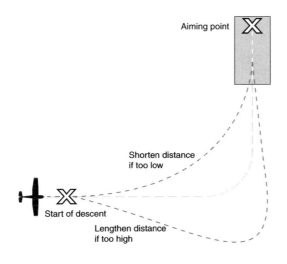

The path from base leg to finals can be altered if the aircraft is too high or too low.

▶ Maintaining the Glide - the Use of Flap

Once established on the approach the pilot continues to assess whether the glide will reach the initial aiming point. Once certain of reaching this aiming point, or if overshooting it, an initial stage of flap is lowered to steepen the approach angle. The aircraft is pitched nose-down to maintain the best glide airspeed and the aircraft is re-trimmed. Once the 'picture' has settled to the new aspect, the pilot can decide whether further flap is necessary.

After lowering each stage of flap, retrim for the new, lower nose attitude required to maintain the best glide speed. The best glide airspeed with flaps extended may be different to that with flaps up. The continual process of checking and adjusting the glide angle continues until certain of touching down at the specified aiming point. If necessary, flap can be used to steepen the glide angle sufficiently to touch down at a new aiming point closer to the runway threshold.

Flap is used to steepen the glide angle and, if necessary, move the aiming point closer to the runway threshold.

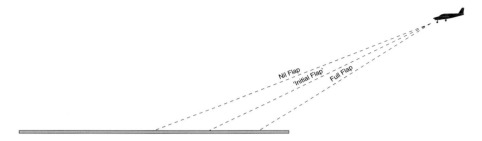

▶ The Glide Landing

Because of the steep approach angle, the lower nose attitude and the high rate of descent, the flare will have to be started slightly higher than for a normal approach. Once established in the hold-off, the landing continues as normal.

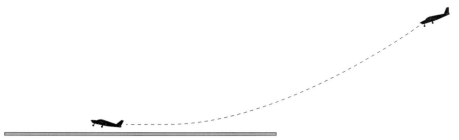

The flare is started higher due to the higher rate of descent and the larger attitude change required.

Flight Exercise

▷ Purpose

To learn to make a safe approach and landing without power, touching down close to a specified touchdown point.

▷ Airmanship

ATC liaison

During your downwind call inform ATC of your intentions i.e. "G-BD downwind for a glide approach". This will help ATC to integrate your shorter circuit with other circuit traffic.

Airspeed

As during any approach, maintenance of the correct approach airspeed is the first priority - always fly the glide approach at the best glide airspeed. If undershooting do not attempt to 'stretch' the glide by pitching-nose-up and reducing the airspeed. In fact, by flying more slowly the glide range is reduced and there is less chance of reaching the aiming point. Even more seriously, the pilot may actually stall the aircraft by losing sight of the importance of airspeed control.

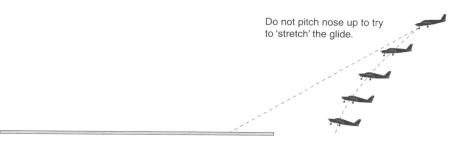

Do not pitch nose up to try to 'stretch' the glide.

Undershoot and possible stall.

Go Around

A glide approach requires practice to perfect. If you are overshooting and therefore too high to land safely on the runway, or if you are undershooting and too low to reach the runway, do not hesitate to go around without delay.

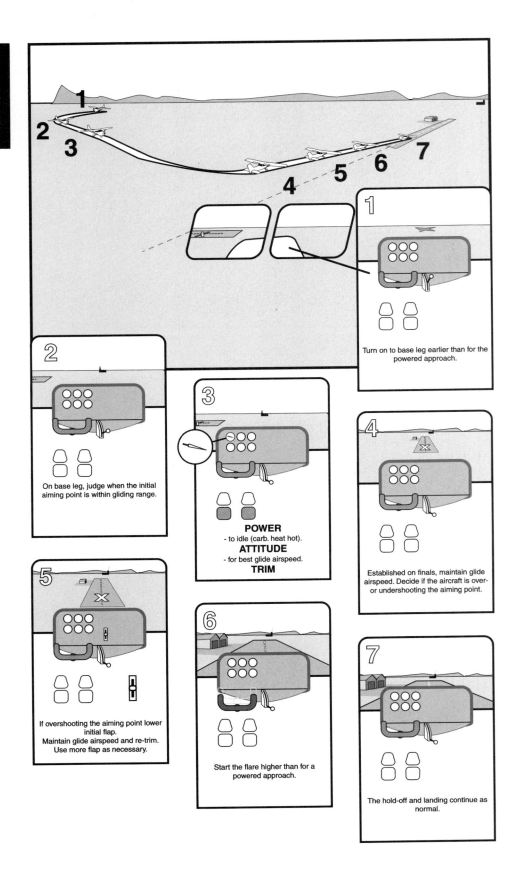

1 — Turn on to base leg earlier than for the powered approach.

2 — On base leg, judge when the initial aiming point is within gliding range.

3 —

POWER
- to idle (carb. heat hot).
ATTITUDE
- for best glide airspeed.
TRIM

4 — Established on finals, maintain glide airspeed. Decide if the aircraft is over- or undershooting the aiming point.

5 — If overshooting the aiming point lower initial flap.
Maintain glide airspeed and re-trim.
Use more flap as necessary.

6 — Start the flare higher than for a powered approach.

7 — The hold-off and landing continue as normal.

The Short-Field Take-Off and Landing

Exercise
12 &
13

The first take-offs and landings are learnt using a runway that is more than long enough to allow a wide margin of error in piloting technique. This flight exercise will teach you to operate the aircraft from runways whose length is much closer to the minimum required by the aircraft. Your handling skills and judgement will also be improved by the precision nature of the short-field approach and landing.

In a supplement to this exercise, a series of take-off and landing performance factors are listed for use when the aircraft's POH/FM does not cover all the factors the pilot needs to take account of. It is worth emphasising that whenever considering the use of a shorter than normal runway (you will come to know what is 'short' in relation to the aircraft you are flying), the few minutes needed to check the aircraft's performance in the POH/FM is time well invested. This subject is covered in detail during the technical course.

If the figures you calculate indicate the runway is too short to be used, there is little point in proceeding regardless and damaging the aircraft just to prove that your calculation was correct. All too often, when accidents do occur on short runways it is quite plain that the runway distance available was simply shorter than the take-off/landing distance required.

BACKGROUND BRIEFING

▶ **Calculation of Take-off Distance**

▶ **The Use of Flaps**

▶ **Short-Field Take-off Technique**

▶ **Climb Out - VX/VY (Best Angle of Climb/Best Rate-of-Climb)**

▶ **Calculation of Landing Distance**

▶ **The Short-Field Approach**

▶ **The Short-Field Landing**

FLIGHT EXERCISE

▷ **Purpose**

▷ **Airmanship**

▷ **The Short-Field Take-off**

▷ **The Short-Field Landing**

Exercise

12 & 13

The Short Field
Take-Off and
Landing

BACKGROUND BRIEFING

▶ Calculation of Take-off Distance

The aircraft's POH/FM will contain performance information for calculating the required take-off distance in certain conditions. All the factors affecting take-off distance have the same effect, particularly the surface wind, but are far more significant when operating from a shorter runway. Taking-off into wind is always the preferred option, although the pilot must take into account obstacles in the climb out area. This is particularly important when operating away from licensed airfields; obstructions that would not be acceptable at a licensed airfield may well be found at an unlicensed airfield or private airstrip.

▶ The Use of Flaps

The aircraft's POH/FM should state the short-field take-off technique and in particular the recommended flap setting. It is important to use not more than this specified flap setting. Increasing flap beyond that recommended for take-off may give a small increase in lift, but only with the penalty of a much greater increase in drag. The increased drag will considerably lengthen the take-off run and the take-off distance. The aircraft may fail to get airborne within the available runway length, and even if it does, the climb out will be significantly degraded.

▶ Short-Field Take-off Technique

The POH/FM technique for a short-field take-off will often state that the engine should be run up to full power whilst the aircraft is held stationary with the brakes. The engine instruments are checked and if all are within limits the brakes are released. Note that if the surface is particularly rough, or if there is loose gravel etc., it may not be advisable to run-up to full power against the brakes.

The pilot should take care to start the take-off run from the very beginning of the runway and not allow the aircraft to creep forward and waste runway.

During the take-off the pilot should be aware of the need to be airborne by the time the aircraft has travelled around two-thirds of the runway length. If the aircraft is not airborne by this time, it may not clear obstructions beyond the runway even if it does get airborne before the end of the runway. The pilot should be prepared to abandon the take-off in good time if the aircraft is not achieving the calculated performance.

The Short Field Take-Off and Landing

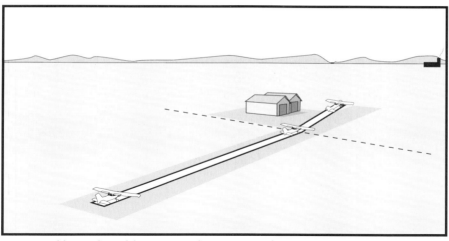

Aim to be airborne not later than 2/3 along the runway.

▶Climb-Out - VX/VY (Best Angle of Climb/Best Rate-of-Climb)

During the take-off run the aircraft is rotated at the recommended rotate speed and climbed at the VX (best angle-of-climb) airspeed if obstacle clearance is a priority, although the difference in height gained when using VX as opposed to VY (best rate-of-climb) airspeed may be fairly small. Typically, over a one mile distance, VX may give a height advantage of around 100 feet. Once the obstacles have been cleared and the aircraft has reached a safe height (above 300 feet AGL), it is accelerated to the best rate-of-climb airspeed (VY) and the flap can be retracted in stages.

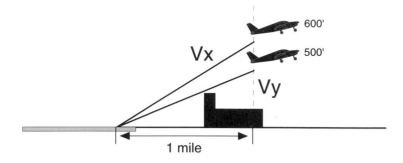

Climbing at the Vx airspeed will give the best ANGLE-of-climb after take-off.

▶Calculation of Landing Distance

All the factors affecting landing distance have the same effect as usual, particularly the surface wind, but are far more significant when operating on to a shorter runway. The aircraft's POH/FM will have a section to calculate landing distance and may state the technique to be used. Usually the technique will involve maximum braking after touchdown. On some surfaces, e.g. wet grass, gravel etc., this may not be possible and the landing distance will lengthen accordingly.

▶ The Short-Field Approach

The circuit, base leg and turn on to finals are flown as normal. Once the aircraft is established on finals, full flap is lowered and airspeed is reduced to the recommended short-field approach speed. Constant small adjustments of power and attitude will be required to maintain the airspeed and approach angle.

The aircraft is now flying on the back of the power curve. At this slow airspeed, a decreased airspeed can actually lead to an increase in power required. A high-drag, high-sink situation can quickly develop unless the pilot anticipates with throttle to control descent angle, and attitude to control airspeed.

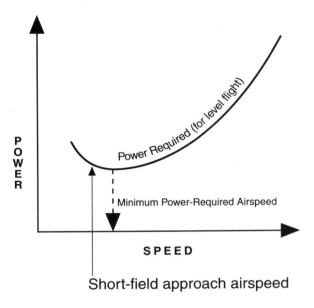

Short-field approach airspeed

Do not allow the approach angle to become too shallow, as you run the risk of hitting an obstruction before reaching the runway.

▶ The Short-Field Landing

Having cleared any obstacles in the final approach area, the aim is to touch down as early as possible into the runway. In any case the aircraft should have touched down by the time it has travelled one-third of the runway length. If the aircraft has not touched down by this point, it may not be possible to stop before the end of the runway and an immediate go-around is necessary.

The slow airspeed of the short-field approach usually requires the aircraft to have a higher nose attitude, therefore there will be less change of attitude during the flare than for a normal approach. Throughout the flare and hold-off the power is reduced, but not completely; a small measure of power is left on to prevent the aircraft touching down heavily. When the main wheels touch down (usually after very little float) the throttle is fully closed and the brakes are applied up to full braking, with the control column held back to keep weight on the main wheels and reduce stress on the nosewheel.

The Short Field Take-Off and Landing

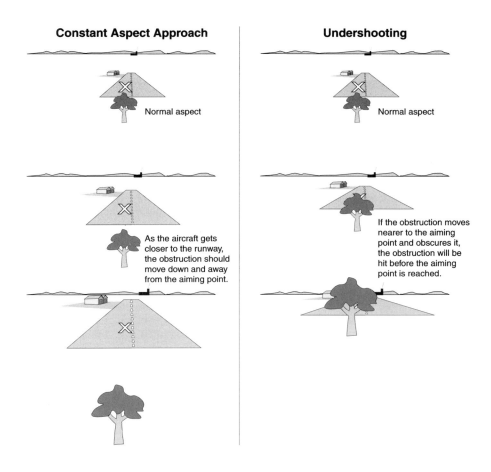

Constant Aspect Approach

Normal aspect

As the aircraft gets closer to the runway, the obstruction should move down and away from the aiming point.

Undershooting

Normal aspect

If the obstruction moves nearer to the aiming point and obscures it, the obstruction will be hit before the aiming point is reached.

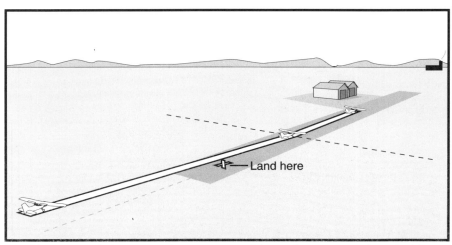

Land here

Aim to touchdown as close as possible to the runway threshold,
no later than in the first third of the runway.

Exercise

*12
&
13*

The Short
Field
Take-Off
and
Landing

Flight Exercise

▷ Purpose

To learn the correct technique for making a short-field take-off and landing, and to appreciate the factors that affect take-off and landing distance when operating on 'short' runways.

▷ Airmanship

Airspeed Control

In this flight exercise there is much emphasis on achieving a take-off and landing in the shortest distance. Do not allow this aim to override the first priority–to fly the aeroplane. During the short-field approach in particular, the airspeed must not be allowed to reduce below the recommended airspeed.

Take-off and landing performance

This exercise gives you the opportunity to compare the aircraft's POH/FM figures with real life. Your instructor will show you how to calculate take-off and landing distance from the POH/FM taking into account the conditions of the day. During the flight exercise you can see how these figures compare with the actual distances being used for take-off and landing. This should give you some appreciation of the need for an extra safety margin when calculating take-off and landing performance.

As already stressed, if the calculations show that the runway is too short to be used safely, there is little point disregarding the figures in the hope that "it will be all right". It won't, and it'll be expensive to prove the point.

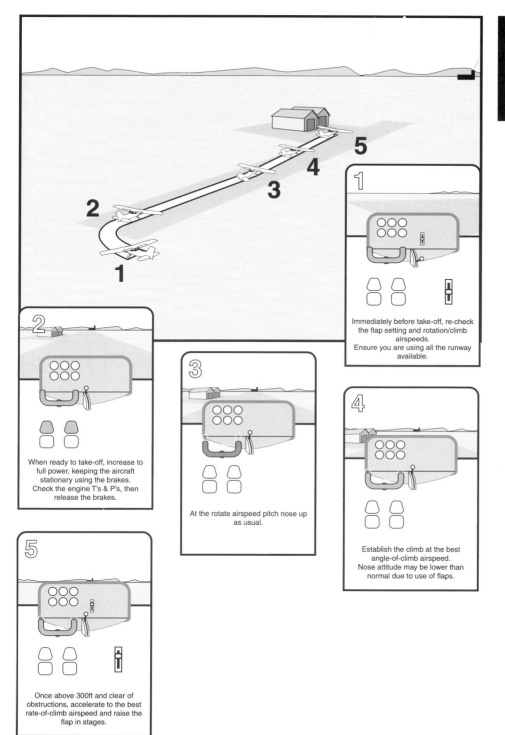

1
Immediately before take-off, re-check the flap setting and rotation/climb airspeeds.
Ensure you are using all the runway available.

2
When ready to take-off, increase to full power, keeping the aircraft stationary using the brakes.
Check the engine T's & P's, then release the brakes.

3
At the rotate airspeed pitch nose up as usual.

4
Establish the climb at the best angle-of-climb airspeed.
Nose attitude may be lower than normal due to use of flaps.

5
Once above 300ft and clear of obstructions, accelerate to the best rate-of-climb airspeed and raise the flap in stages.

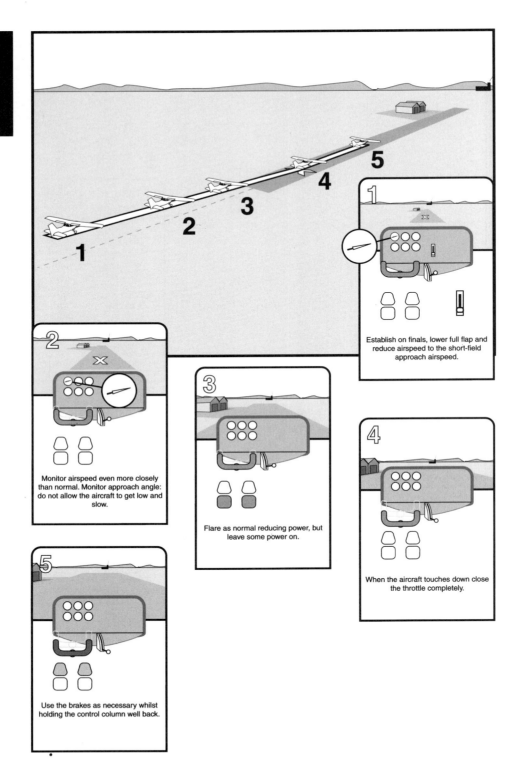

1 Establish on finals, lower full flap and reduce airspeed to the short-field approach airspeed.

2 Monitor airspeed even more closely than normal. Monitor approach angle: do not allow the aircraft to get low and slow.

3 Flare as normal reducing power, but leave some power on.

4 When the aircraft touches down close the throttle completely.

5 Use the brakes as necessary whilst holding the control column well back.

The Soft-Field Take-Off and Landing

BACKGROUND BRIEFING

▶ Operation From a Soft Field Runway

▶ Definition of Soft Field

▶ Soft-Field Take-off

▶ Soft-Field Landing

▶ Operation From a Soft-Field Runway

The runway surface has a marked effect on take-off and landing distances and the best technique to use. If you are used to flying from a tarmac runway, you may be surprised at how different it is to operate from a grass runway. Likewise, the runway surface can be affected by factors which make it a 'soft-field'. Sometimes the runway state may simply be too soft or rough to allow safe operation of the type of aircraft you are flying. Some aircraft have specific design features to handle rough and semi-prepared surfaces. Most training aircraft do not.

▶ Definition of Soft Field

When defining a 'soft' field, the emphasis is on the surface state. Rough ground, long grass, mud, sand or a covering of light snow can all be described as soft field. For this exercise we assume that the runway length and obstacles are not a problem as soft-field technique increases both take-off and landing distance. The principal aims of the soft-field take-off technique are to protect the nosewheel and get the wing producing lift (thereby reducing the rolling friction from the main wheels) as quickly as possible.

Remember, the technique described for a 'soft' field is also applied to operation from a rough surface.

▶ Soft-Field Take-off

The soft-field take-off is normally started from the turn on to the runway. Avoid a tight, high speed turn because this may unbalance the fuel in the fuel tanks (possibly uncovering the fuel ports) and place undue stress on the undercarriage. At the start of the take-off the control column is held well back to lift the nosewheel clear of the ground as early as possible. Once the nosewheel has lifted, the back pressure is reduced to keep the aircraft in a shallow nose up attitude. In this attitude the aircraft will fly itself off the ground at the minimum flying airspeed. As soon as the aircraft is airborne, the aircraft should be pitched nose-down slightly to keep the aircraft flying just above the runway in 'ground effect'.

During the take-off run the nose wheel is lifted clear of the ground as early as possible. The aircraft is held in a shallow nose up attitude until it flies off the runway. The aircraft is then pitched nose down to fly level in ground effect until it accelerates to the climb airspeed.

Ground effect is an aerodynamic phenomenon that occurs up to a height of around half the wingspan of the aircraft (i.e. if its wingspan is 30 feet, the aircraft can fly in ground effect up to 15 feet). Ground effect alters the airflow behind the wing and in effect reduces the induced drag generated by the wing, allowing the aircraft to fly more slowly than is possible when it is above ground effect.

After a soft-field take-off the aircraft is flown level in ground effect until it has accelerated to the required climb airspeed. Once this airspeed is reached, the aircraft climbs away as normal.

The aircraft's POH/FM will specify the flap setting and airspeeds to be used, and may specify a different soft-field technique, which would overrule this general advice.

▶ Soft-Field Landing

The approach to the soft-field landing is flown as normal, preferably with full flap extended. During the flare and hold-off a small measure of power is left on and the hold-off is continued for as long as possible so that the aircraft touches down at the slowest possible airspeed with a nose-high attitude. After touchdown the throttle is closed completely and increasing back pressure on the control column is used to keep the nosewheel off the ground for as long as possible.

The aircraft's POH/FM may specify a different soft-field technique, which would overrule this general advice.

During the soft-field landing the touchdown is made with a small measure of power, in a nose-high attitude, at the slowest possible airspeed. After touchdown the nosewheel is kept off the ground for as long as possible. Do not use the brakes unless necessary.

The Bad-Weather (Low Level) Circuit

BACKGROUND BRIEFING

▶ Circumstances Necessitating a Low-Level Circuit

▶ The Bad-Weather Circuit

▶ Low-Level Illusions

▶ Circumstances Necessitating a Low-Level Circuit

The low-level circuit has numerous applications. This flight exercise assumes conditions of low cloud and poor visibility on arriving at the airfield to land. In later flight exercises the low-level circuit is used to inspect an unprepared landing area - the precautionary landing.

▶ The Bad-Weather Circuit

This circuit starts by flying overhead the runway in the landing direction in the slow safe cruise configuration at a height of 600ft AGL. This simulates the aircraft arriving over the airfield in low cloud and poor-visibility conditions. Once over the upwind end of the runway, a continuous level turn (not more than 15° angle of bank) is flown until the aircraft is positioned downwind, still in sight of the runway and closer than during a standard circuit. The pre-landing checks are completed and the downwind path is maintained parallel to the runway. As the aircraft passes abeam the runway threshold, the time is checked to measure 20-30 seconds (depending on wind velocity). At the 20-30 second point, a 15° angle of bank turn is started to position the aircraft on to finals. The final descent is not started until the pilot has a good view of the landing runway in order to judge the approach descent angle. Once established on the final approach, the approach and landing are carried out as normal.

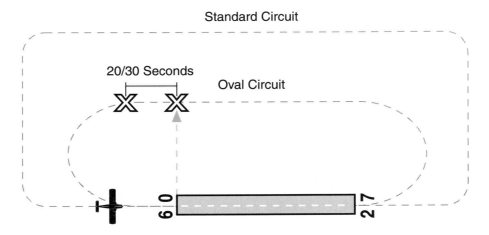

The bad weather (low level) circuit compared to the normal circuit pattern.

This oval circuit may also be used by high-performance aircraft and is favoured by the military.

▶ Low-Level Illusions

When flying at low level, the visual cues and perspectives that the pilot has come to take for granted can alter significantly. The topography may look quite different. Hills and valleys are far more pronounced, obstructions are far more predominant and of course must be avoided. The effect of wind on the aircraft's ground track will also be more apparent. The sensation of speed is greater when flying downwind and the pilot may try to slow the aircraft. Remember that airspeed is the important factor, not groundspeed.

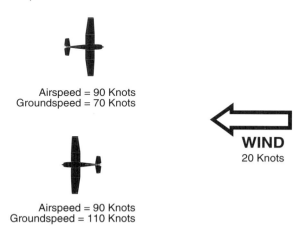

Airspeed = 90 Knots
Groundspeed = 70 Knots

WIND
20 Knots

Airspeed = 90 Knots
Groundspeed = 110 Knots

Maintain the airspeed by reference to the Air Speed Indicator (ASI), NOT the apparent speed over the ground.

When turning, the wind effect may make it appear that the aircraft is slipping into, or skidding out of the turn, and there is a temptation to overbank or use large amounts of rudder. Concentrate on maintaining the safe airspeed and keeping the aircraft in balance. The priority is the aircraft's flight path through the air, not its ground track.

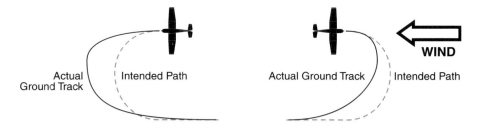

Actual Ground Track   Intended Path   Actual Ground Track   Intended Path

WIND

A strong wind distorts the ground track of the aircraft during a turn. Maintain a safe airspeed by reference to the ASI and balance by reference to the balance ball.

Supplement 1 Lookout

Before starting this supplement, revise the first lookout supplement at exercise 6. By this stage you should have developed a scanning technique that suits you and you will be aware of the need to clear an area visually before moving into it e.g. before starting a climb or descent. The key lookout points around the circuit are:

(1) Before take-off check final approach path and runway.

(2) Look out before turning

(3) Look out before turning, especially for aircraft joining the downwind leg.

(4) Look out before turning.

(5) Before turning on to finals look out, especially along the extended centre line.

(6) On finals look out for lower aircraft on finals and aircraft on the runway.

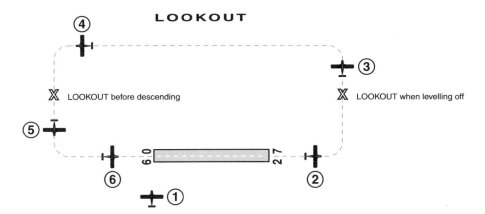

The key lookout points in the circuit.

If ATC is in operation, they will indicate the landing order. Comply with this order and keep the other traffic in sight at all times. If you cannot see the other reported traffic, ask for their position (if in doubt - shout). Aircraft tend to congregate at airfields so it is not surprising that the greatest risk of collision is when flying within 5nm of an airfield. Be alert at all times—near misses and mid-air collisions do not always happen to other people. Take specific steps to improve and maintain your lookout in the circuit.

1 Follow established procedures

Adhere to the prevailing runway pattern. Do not stray outside the pattern and do not cut corners or try to cut in ahead of other traffic.

2 Talk and listen

Use the radio as an aid to your lookout. Report your position accurately to alert other aircraft and listen to radio reports to know where other aircraft are and what they are doing.

3   Beware the blind spots

Every aircraft has blind spots from the pilot's seat. During the turn, the wing of a high-wing aircraft blanks the area on the inside of a turn. In a low-wing aircraft the area outside the turn is blanked during a turn. Door posts, windscreen braces, even the compass–all can obstruct your view. Know the aircraft's blind spots and adjust your lookout to compensate.

LEFT> In a high wing aircraft. the wing will block lookout into the turn. Always lookout before turning, whether in a high, mid, or low wing aircraft.

RIGHT> Be aware of the blind spots created by the aircraft's structure.

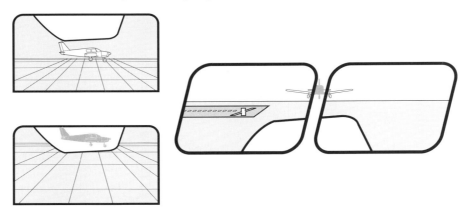

4   Divide your scanning

Obviously it is necessary to check the instruments to fly accurately - you cannot look out of the windows all the time. The proportion of eyes inside/eyes outside time should be no more than 5 seconds scanning the instruments for each 15 seconds scanning outside.

5   Keep scanning

Keep practising and refining your lookout scan. Using a proper lookout scan will increase your chances of spotting traffic fourfold.

Supplement 2 Take-off and Landing Distance Factors Supplement

The figures given below are those recommended by the Civil Aviation Authority to be used when the aircraft's POH/FM does not have the appropriate factor. They do not overrule factors already included in the aircraft's POH/FM.

VARIATION	INCREASE IN TAKE-OFF DISTANCE (to 50')	FACTOR
10% increase in aircraft weight	20%	1.2
Increase of 1000' in runway altitude	10%	1.1
Increase in temperature of 10°C	10%	1.1
Dry Grass		
- Short (under 5 inches)	20%	1.2
- Long (5 - 10 inches)	25%	1.25
Wet Grass		
- Short	25%	1.25
- Long	30%	1.3
2% uphill slope	10%	1.1
Tailwind component of 10% of lift off speed	20%	1.2
Soft ground or snow *	at least 25%	at least 1.25

VARIATION	INCREASE IN LANDING DISTANCE (from 50')	FACTOR
10% increase in aircraft weight	10%	1.1
Increase of 1000' in runway altitude	5%	1.05
Increase in temperature of 10°C	5%	1.05
Dry Grass		
- Short (under 5 inches)	20%	1.2
- Long (5 - 10 inches)	30%	1.3
Wet Grass		
- Short	30%	1.30
- Long	40%	1.40
2% downhill slope	10%	1.1
Tailwind component of 10% of landing speed	20%	1.2
snow *	at least 25%	at least 1.25

Once the take-off/landing distance has been calculated, a further safety factor should be included. This safety factor is:

TAKE-OFF: 1.33 x Calculated take-off distance

LANDING: 1.43 x Calculated landing distance

Supplement 3 Take-off and Landing Crosswind Calculation

The crosswind component can be estimated by using a mental rule-of-thumb calculation. There are several different rules of thumb, three of which are listed below. They all give pretty much the same answer, so choose one that you find easiest to calculate. Each method starts by gauging the angle between the runway direction and the wind direction. A factor is then applied to the wind direction.

The One-Two-Three rule of thumb

Angle between runway and wind direction

30° one over two i.e. 1/2 wind strength

40° two over three i.e 2/3 wind strength

50° three over four i.e. 3/4 wind strength

60° and beyond, full wind strength

For example, runway 09, w/v 120/12 knots.

The angle between runway direction and wind direction is 30° (120 - 090). Therefore crosswind component is 1/2 wind strength = 6 knots.

The sixths rule of thumb

Angle between runway and wind direction

10° = 1/6 wind strength

20° = 2/6 (1/3) wind strength

30° = 3/6 (1/2) wind strength

40° = 4/6 (2/3) wind strength

50° = 5/6 wind strength

60° and beyond = 6/6 i.e. full wind strength

For example runway 32, w/v 000/18 knots. The angle between runway and wind direction is 40°. Therefore crosswind component is 2/3 of 18 knots = 12 knots.

The clock rule of thumb

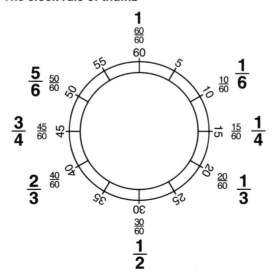

The minutes around a clock or watch face represent the difference in degrees between the runway and wind direction, from 0° to 60°.

For example; runway 24, w/v 250/20. The angle between runway and wind direction is 10°. Therefore crosswind component is 1/6 of 20 knots = 4 knots (rounded up to the nearest knot).

Supplement 4 Wake Turbulence

▶ What is wake turbulence?

For practical purposes, wake turbulence is caused by the vortices which every aircraft creates at the wingtips as a consequence of the generation of lift. A vortex is a cylinder of rotating air; the air inside a vortex can have a velocity of up to 150 knots. The strength of a vortex is directly proportional to the size, weight and speed of the generating aircraft. The heavier and slower the aircraft, the stronger the vortex it creates. The size of the vortices is related to the wingspan of the aircraft. A Boeing 747 with a wingspan of 65 metres generates a vortex at the wingtip 65 metres in diameter. Vortices descend at a rate of about 500 feet per minute and move out from the wingtips at around 5 knots. Therefore, in a light crosswind a vortex may stay stationary; a stronger crosswind may move the vortices opposite to the expected path.

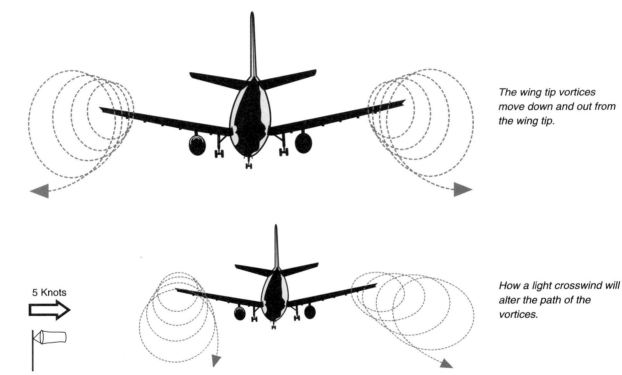

The wing tip vortices move down and out from the wing tip.

5 Knots

How a light crosswind will alter the path of the vortices.

An aircraft encountering such a vortex can suffer severe control difficulties. It may roll even with full opposite aileron and rudder applied. Such a loss of control close to the ground would obviously be potentially catastrophic.

Vortices normally have a life of around 1½ minutes (i.e. 90 seconds) although they tend to persist in calm or light wind conditions and can have a life of up to 2½ minutes. They usually end suddenly rather than slowly dying out.

A small training aircraft generates insignificant vortices which will not be a problem to following aircraft. However, once the aircraft size is that of a commuter or executive jet type or larger, vortices become a significant hazard. The lighter the following aircraft, the more at risk it is from the wake turbulence from an aircraft ahead.

Exercise 12&13

Each aircraft is allocated a wake-turbulence category by ICAO (International Civil Aviation Organisation) and this category is used to establish a minimum separation between aircraft to avoid the following aircraft encountering wake turbulence.

ATC will advise the recommended separation from the leading aircraft, which will be dictated by its wake turbulence category. As an example, ICAO Medium category aircraft include Boeing 737, 727, Shorts 360, Gulfstream II, HS125, Citation III. ICAO Heavy category aircraft include Boeing 747, 767, DC-10, Airbus 310.

Note: At the time of writing the Boeing 757 is being considered for re-classification into the Heavy category.

LEFT> Examples of some aircraft in the Medium category. Top to bottom: Dash-7, Canadian Challenger, B737.

RIGHT> Examples of some aircraft in the Heavy category. Top to bottom: B767, DC10, B747.

▶How to avoid wake turbulence

Wake turbulence is in itself invisible. The only precautions you can take are to avoid the areas where wake turbulence may exist and to allow sufficient separation behind the leading aircraft to ensure that its vortices have ceased.

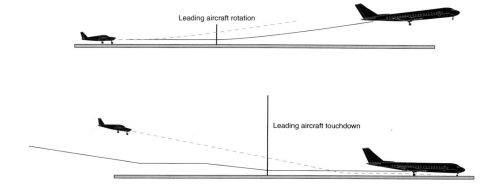

Leading aircraft rotation

Leading aircraft touchdown

Arrange the flight path to avoid areas where wake turbulence may exist.

▶Departure

Wake turbulence starts at the point where the aircraft rotates on take-off.

When taking-off behind larger aircraft, aim to be airborne before the rotation point of the leading aircraft and climb out above its flight path.

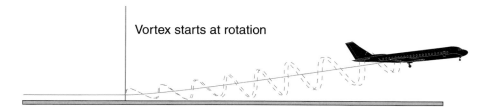

Vortex starts at rotation

The table below assumes the following aircraft is in the light category - which covers most single-engine aircraft.

Leading aircraft	Following light aircraft
Heavy and Medium	2 minutes

Leading aircraft	Departing from intersection
Heavy and Medium	3 minutes
(full-length take-off)	

Time separation is from the time that the leading aircraft rotated for take off.

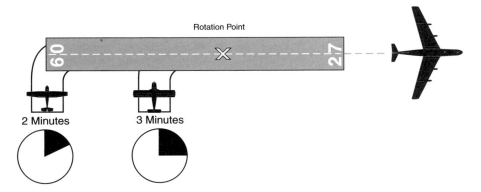

Recommended time separation for a light aircraft departing behind a larger aircraft.

▶ En-route

Wake turbulence when flying en-route is not generally a serious problem, mostly because aircraft tend to be further apart and there is more height to sort out any control problems. The general advice is to avoid flying below or close behind the flight path of a significantly larger aircraft.

▶ Approach and landing

Wake turbulence may be a significant problem when following an aircraft on approach. Vortices are generated until the aircraft's nosewheel contacts the runway during the ground run. A following aircraft should aim to approach above the leading aircraft's flight path and touchdown well beyond its touchdown point if possible.

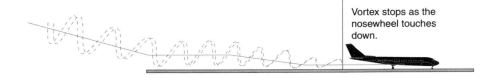

Vortex stops as the nosewheel touches down.

Medium Aircraft Leading

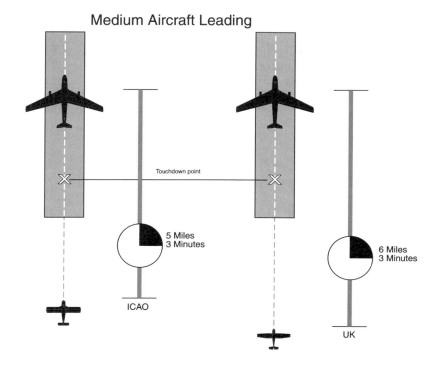

Recommended spacing for a light aircraft when landing behind a Medium category aircraft.

Heavy Aircraft Leading

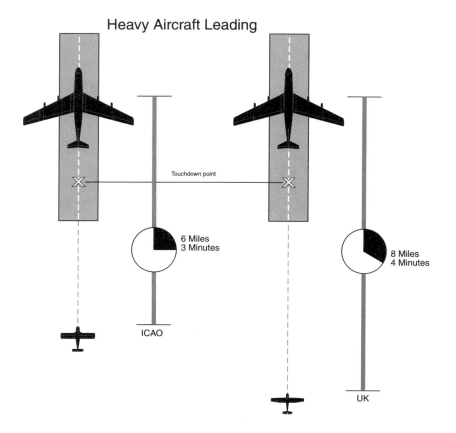

Recommended spacing for a light aircraft when landing behind a Heavy category aircraft.

The recommended separation differs slightly between ICAO and UK procedures. This table assumes the following aircraft is in the Light category. In summary:

Leading Aircraft	ICAO		UK	
	Miles	**Minutes**	**Miles**	**Minutes**
Heavy	6	3	8	4
Medium	5	3	6	3

Note - aircraft in the heavy category should use the prefix "heavy" during their initial contact on a radio frequency. To gauge distance, refer to the runway length. An 1800m runway equals one mile, so five miles is five runway lengths of an 1800m runway.

▶ Helicopters

Helicopters create stronger vortices than a fixed-wing aircraft of similar weight. A helicopter creates the greatest downwash and vortices when hovering or hover-taxying. Avoid passing under or close behind the flight path of a helicopter.

▶ In Summary

Wake turbulence is invisible. Know where to expect wake turbulence, and how long it may persist.

Heavy, slow aircraft create the strongest vortices. Light aircraft are the most vulnerable to wake turbulence.

Know the wake turbulence minima. Spacing is at the pilot's discretion, so increase spacing beyond minimum if you wish.

Alter your flight path to avoid areas where there is a risk of wake turbulence.

Wake turbulence persists longer in calm or light-wind conditions.

Solo Flights and Local Flying

The first time exercise 14 appears in a pilot's logbook will signify the never-to-be-forgotten experience of the first solo flight. In the space of one circuit you have truly started your flying career with the 'P1' logbook time to prove it. Although there is still much to learn, the first solo is a milestone of your progress. In later flights you will increase your solo time in the circuit, followed by short solo flights away from the airfield.

BACKGROUND BRIEFING

▶ **First solo**

▶ **Solo Consolidation**

▶ **Local Procedures**

▶ **Cruise Checks**

▶ **Use of the Compass**

▶ **Use of the QDM Procedure**

▶ **Rejoining the Circuit**

BACKGROUND BRIEFING

▶First Solo

Many pilots view the prospect of their first solo with some trepidation. Reaching the first solo flight is not a matter of flying a set number of hours nor performing a set number of perfect landings. Your instructor will send you solo based on his judgement of the safety and consistency of your flying and judgement. Before flying solo you will have practised some emergencies, such as the engine failure after take-off; and manoeuvres such as the go-around.

Before sending you solo, your instructor will brief you on a few specific points and remind you to go around if you are not satisfied with the approach.

Then it's over to you. Relax as much as possible and let your training take over. Enjoy every moment of this flight–there is only ever one first solo!

▶Solo Consolidation

Following the first solo flight you will continue dual flying with your instructor, interspersed with longer periods of solo flying. Do not expect to fly solo every lesson; weather conditions, circuit traffic or other considerations make that unlikely.

Be wary of becoming overconfident as your solo time increases. It is not unknown for students with a few hours solo time to let their new-found confidence get the better of them and lead them into fraught situations. Always fly as if your instructor was with you and do not accept inaccuracies in your flying which he would not. At an ATC airfield do not accept instructions you do not fully understand or that you are not certain you can safely accomplish, (e.g. a request to do an orbit on finals). If you do not properly hear a message, ask for it to be repeated–"say again". Should weather deteriorate while you are flying, exercise your judgement and land early. This says far more about your judgement and ability as a pilot than if you struggle on in worsening conditions.

Referring back to exercise 2 you might remember the adage:

"Better to be down here, wishing you were up there;

than up there wishing you were down here !"

▶ Local Procedures

After several solo flights in the circuit, you will make flights away from the airfield. Your instructor will revise any specific local procedures, routings, reporting points etc. and before flying solo away from the airfield, you will practise basic map reading and refresh your memory of the local landmarks in the training area.

▶ Cruise Checks

During cruising flight you should make a series of regular checks to monitor the aircraft and the progress of the flight. Cruise checks are normally carried out at 10-minute intervals. The most commonly used mnemonic for the cruise check is FREDA, which can also be used as the 'approaching airfield' check.

F	**Fuel**	Is there sufficient fuel to complete the flight and leave a good safety margin? Are the fuel tanks in balance?
R	**Radio**	Is the correct frequency set? Are any radio reports required? Will it be necessary to change frequency in the next 5-10 minutes?
E	**Engine**	Check engine temperatures and pressures. Check the suction gauge and the ammeter. Apply carb heat and check for carb icing. Check mixture.
D	**Direction**	Is the correct heading being flown? Is the heading indicator synchronised with the compass?
A	**Altitude**	Is the correct QNH/QFE set on the altimeter subscale? Is the present level sufficient for terrain clearance and will it allow you to keep clear of controlled airspace? Will the altimeter pressure setting need to change in the next 5-10 minutes (e.g. when approaching an airfield)?

Always complete the FREDA check methodically and remember to look out between each item.

▶ Use of the Compass

The compass is normally used solely as a reference to synchronise the Heading Indicator (HI). Should the HI become inoperative, headings will have to be flown with direct reference to the compass. Always allow time for the compass to settle before taking a reading, and remember that the presentation of the compass may tempt you to turn the wrong way when changing headings.

Revise the compass turning errors outlined in exercise 9. The 30° error applies for turns on to North and South. At intermediate headings e.g. NE (045°) or SW (225°), the error is about 15°. On Easterly or Westerly headings there is no error. The compass may also be affected by acceleration or deceleration. These effects are most pronounced on Easterly or Westerly headings.

When reading the compass, always check that the wings are level; the aircraft is in balance, and that the airspeed is steady.

▶ Use of the QDM Procedure

Most airfields with ATC will be equipped with direction finding equipment (DF). When a radio transmission is made from an aircraft, the DF indicates to the controller the direction of the transmission. The controller can then pass on the direction to fly to reach the airfield. The most commonly given direction is a 'QDM'; which is the magnetic track from the aircraft to the airfield, in other words a magnetic heading to fly assuming nil wind.

Of course, normally there is a wind velocity to consider, so having obtained a QDM, make allowance for drift. If using QDMs to fly to an airfield, recheck the QDM every five minutes or so to make sure a steady ground track to the airfield is being maintained. If the QDM changes, the aircraft is not following a direct ground track to the airfield and a heading alteration is needed. The rule is 'QDM more, steer more (alter heading right); QDM less, steer less (alter heading left)'. For example, if the QDM changes from 320° to 330°, it is more, so the heading needs to be 'more' by increasing it, say from 325° to 335°.

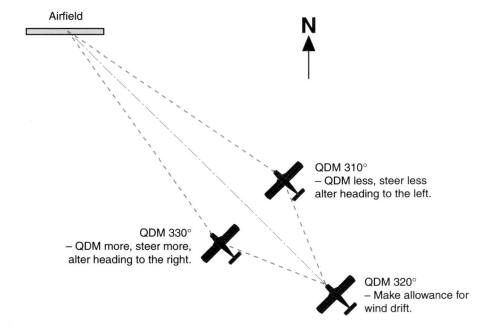

The use of QDMs to navigate to an airfield.

▶ Rejoining the Circuit

On returning to the airfield it is the responsibility of the joining aircraft to integrate safely into the existing circuit pattern. The ATC/ATSU unit may indicate a circuit joining point (e.g. join downwind, join long finals etc) in which case that instruction can be followed.

Local Flying

If an overhead join is indicated e.g "report overhead", or if landing at a non-radio airfield, the overhead joining procedure is used.

The aircraft is flown to overhead the airfield at the height (i.e. with QFE set on the altimeter) instructed by the ATC/ATSU - usually 2000 feet AGL i.e. 2000 feet above the airfield. If no height is advised, the aircraft is flown at a height 1000 feet above the circuit height.

If a left-hand circuit is in force, keep the airfield on the left of the aircraft. If it is a right-hand circuit, keep the airfield on the right. Once overhead check the signals square to confirm the runway in use and circuit direction. The aircraft is positioned to the 'dead side' of the runway, and a descending turn is commenced - all turns must be made in the circuit direction. The aim of the descent on the dead side is to join the crosswind leg over the upwind end of the runway level at circuit height. At the end of the crosswind leg the aircraft turns on to the downwind leg and the circuit continues as normal.

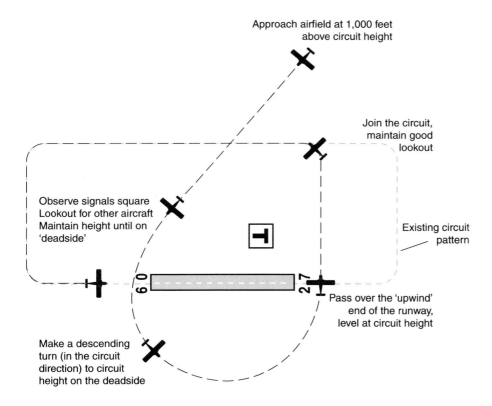

Approach airfield at 1,000 feet above circuit height

Join the circuit, maintain good lookout

Observe signals square
Lookout for other aircraft
Maintain height until on 'deadside'

Existing circuit pattern

The standard overhead join.

Pass over the 'upwind' end of the runway, level at circuit height

Make a descending turn (in the circuit direction) to circuit height on the deadside

Background Briefing

Do not turn on to downwind too early. As a general rule on the crosswind leg, the tailplane of the aircraft should cross the runway before turning downwind.

It should go without saying that maintaining a good lookout is of paramount importance. The onus is on the joining aircraft to spot other aircraft already in the circuit and to integrate safely into the existing circuit pattern.

When flying crosswind, do not turn on to the downwind leg until the tailplane is clear of the runway as viewed from the pilot's seat

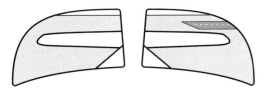

The overhead join is often standard procedure at smaller airfields and should be considered mandatory when arriving at a non-radio airfield. In this case the overhead join is the only safe way for the pilot to view the signals square and so confirm the runway in use, circuit direction and any other procedures or warnings.

Non-standard joining procedures may apply at some airfields. Always check if there are special procedures for the airfield into which you are flying.

Advanced Turning

Advanced turning involves turning at steeper than normal angles of bank. Steep turns are normally defined as those with an angle of bank of 45° or more. In this exercise you will practise steep turns at up to 60° angle of bank and also steep descending turns. These steep angles of bank are not normally used in everyday flying, except possibly as a collision avoidance manoeuvre. However, advanced turning improves co-ordination and flying skills and will increase your appreciation of some key aerodynamic principles - such as load factor and manoeuvring speed (Va).

BACKGROUND BRIEFING

▶ **Forces in the Turn**

▶ **Use of Power**

▶ **Offset Seating**

▶ **Load Factor and Va**

▶ **Stalling in the Turn**

▶ **The Spiral Descent**

▶ **The Steep Gliding Turn**

▶ **The Collision Avoidance Turn**

▶ **Physiological Effects**

FLIGHT EXERCISE

▷ **Purpose**

▷ **Airmanship**

▷ **Entering the Turn**

▷ **Maintaining the Turn**

▷ **Returning to Straight and Level Flight**

▷ **The Descending Turn**

▷ **Recovery From the Spiral Descent**

▷ **The Approach to the Stall in the Turn**

CONCLUSION

BACKGROUND BRIEFING

► Forces in the Turn

To turn an aircraft, it is banked so that the wings provide a horizontal component of lift in the desired direction of turn. The horizontal component of lift acting in the direction of the turn is called *centripetal force* and it opposes the force acting against the turn - *centrifugal force*.

For an aircraft to turn, it is banked so that the wings provide the horizontal component of lift (centripetal force) necessary to balance the opposing centrifugal force.

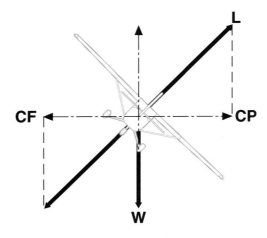

As the angle of bank becomes steeper in a turn, the wings have to create greater lift, to provide both a horizontal component of lift in the direction of the turn and a vertical component of lift to oppose weight and so maintain level flight.

The steeper the angle of bank, the greater the total lift required, to generate sufficient vertical component of lift to oppose weight and maintain level flight.

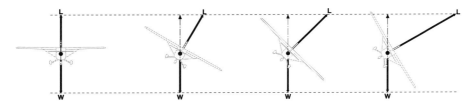

The extra lift required in the steep turn is supplied primarily by increasing the angle of attack. This means that, for a given airspeed, the angle of attack in the turn is greater than that during level flight; therefore, both stalling speed and induced drag are greater during the turn. The steeper the angle of bank, the greater the angle of attack and the closer the aircraft is to the stall.

► Use of Power

During the medium level turn (up to 30° angle of bank) the small loss of airspeed caused by increased drag is quite acceptable. During a steep turn, the much greater increase in drag causes a far more significant loss of airspeed. Pitching nose-down to maintain airspeed will lead to a loss of height, so power must be increased to maintain height and counter drag. In a light aircraft full power may be required to sustain a 60° angle of bank turn without descending. For practical purposes the maximum angle of bank a light aircraft can sustain in level flight is determined by the maximum engine power available.

The increased power and slipstream effect alters the pitch and yaw forces acting on the aircraft and the effectiveness of the rudder and elevator (refer back to exercise 4). The effect on yaw may be evident from the differing rudder pressure needed to keep the aircraft in balance during a left-hand turn as opposed to that required during a right-hand turn.

▶ Offset Seating

During a normal turn, the effect of offset seating is apparent - though not very significant. As seen from the left seat the nose attitude is higher in a left-hand turn than in a right-hand turn. As experience grows, the mind adapts to this illusion and you probably do not notice it.

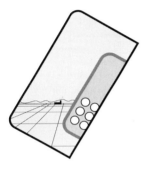

The effect of offset seating is far more apparent when turning at a steep angle of bank.

When turning at steep angles of bank, the effect of offset seating is very apparent and you will have to allow for the different nose attitudes in a left-hand or right-hand turn.

▶ Load Factor and Va

During unaccelerated level flight, the wings create sufficient lift to support the weight of the aircraft. Lift is equal to weight and the load factor is 1. As this is the normal force that acts on people and objects, it goes unnoticed.

During a turn, centrifugal force acting in the same direction as weight increases the load factor, because the wings have to support both the weight of the aircraft and the centrifugal force. As angle of bank in a level turn is increased, centrifugal force and load factor increase.

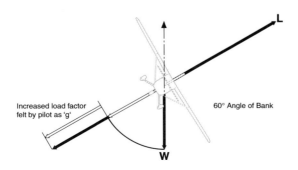

Increased load factor felt by pilot as 'g'

60° Angle of Bank

W

In a level 60° angle-of-bank turn, sufficient lift must be generated to oppose weight, and the same amount again in centrifugal force. The load factor is two.

In a turn at 60° angle of bank, lift is opposing equal amounts of weight and centrifugal force. In this instance the load factor is +2 and the pilot is said to be "pulling" +2g. The aircraft structure is designed and certified to withstand certain maximum load factors. A training aircraft will typically be certified to a maximum load factor of +3.8g; the aircraft's POH/FM will list the load-factor limitations.

To guard against the danger of overstressing the aircraft, a design speed known as Va (manoeuvring speed) is calculated. Va is the maximum airspeed at which full and abrupt control movements can be made without the risk of overstressing the aircraft. The quickest way to increase the load factor is to make an abrupt and large movement of the elevators, thereby increasing or decreasing the angle of attack and centrifugal force and so abruptly changing the load the wings have to support.

At an airspeed faster than Va, a sudden pull back on the control column is quite capable of increasing the load factor far enough to exceed the load-factor limits. For this reason the Va airspeed should not be exceeded during the steep turn. Conversely, when the aircraft is flying slower than the Va airspeed, a similar sudden pull back on the control column will stall the wings (by exceeding the critical angle of attack) before the limiting load factor is reached.

Va is also the maximum speed for flight in turbulence and is the limiting speed for stalling the aircraft. Va is not marked on the airspeed indicator, however it will be found in the POH/FM and may be placarded in the cockpit.

▶ Stalling in the Turn

The steeper the angle of bank in a turn, the faster the stalling speed—because of the increased angle of attack. This increase in stalling speed (and possible slower airspeed due to the increased drag), reduces the safety margin of airspeed above stall speed. In essence, the aircraft is flying closer to the stall and care must be taken to maintain a safe flying speed.

Stall speed increases by the square root of the load factor. For example, in a 60° angle of bank turn, the load factor is 2 and the stall speed is 1.41 x the wings level stalling speed; ie 41% faster than during level flight.

In a level turn, load factor increases as angle of bank becomes steeper. Stalling speed increases as load factor increases.

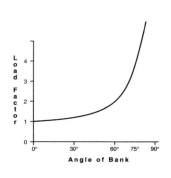

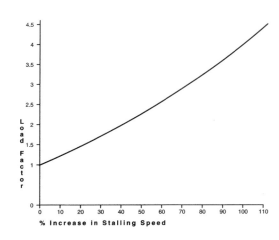

The approaching stall will probably first be announced by the stall warner and a pronounced buffet as the airflow separates from the wing. Recovery is simple–relax the back pressure on the control column, thereby reducing the angle of attack and wing loading. The stall warning and buffet will stop almost immediately. The aircraft can now be rolled wings level-with aileron, and straight and level flight is re-established.

A full stall in a steep turn is an accelerated stall (refer to exercise 10B) and as such may not be permitted in the aircraft type you are flying. The aircraft's POH/FM and your instructor will advise.

As an aircraft reaches the stall in a steep turn, the rate of turn will reduce to zero as lift is lost from the wings. If the aircraft does stall fully, factors such as the high power, turning flight and possibly an out-of-balance aircraft, make a wing drop–even a spin–far more likely.

Level Flight

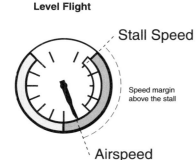

Stall Speed

Speed margin above the stall

Airspeed

During Steep Turn

Stall Speed

Reduced margin above the stall speed

Airspeed

In a steep turn the airspeed margin above the stall is considerably reduced.

▶ The Spiral Descent

During the steep turn, considerable back pressure on the control column is required to reach the attitude and angle of attack necessary to maintain level flight. For each angle of bank there is a certain attitude (maintained with a certain amount of back pressure on the control column) that will maintain level flight at a given power setting. If too little back pressure is applied (i.e. the attitude is too nose-low), or if the aircraft is overbanked, it will descend and possibly enter a spiral descent (also known as a spiral dive). The spiral descent is a condition recognisable by the rapidly increasing airspeed, steep angle of bank and increasing rate of descent. In this situation the natural tendency is to increase the back pressure on the control column - trying to pitch the aircraft nose-up. However, if the spiral descent is established and the aircraft is at a steep angle of bank, this action may only serve to increase the airspeed and possibly overstress the aircraft (due to the excessive load factor when flying faster than the Va speed).

The correct recovery action is to close the throttle, roll the aircraft wings-level and then progressively pitch up to a shallow climb attitude. As the airspeed slows, power is reapplied and the aircraft is stabilised in a normal climb.

▶ The Steep Gliding Turn

This manoeuvre is entered from a normal glide and usually involves an angle of bank of 45°. A lower nose attitude than in a wings-level glide is required to maintain a safe airspeed, increasing the rate of descent.

During the steep gliding turn, airspeed is usually increased above the normal gliding speed to maintain a safe margin above the stalling speed. As a general rule, increase airspeed by 5 knots for each 10° angle of bank beyond 30°; i.e. at 50° angle of bank, increase airspeed by 10 knots. Since this faster airspeed and increased angle of bank leads to a high rate of descent, you should appreciate the dangers of entering a steep gliding turn close to the ground.

▶ The Collision Avoidance Turn

Your instructor may include this manoeuvre in the flight exercise; it is one of the practical applications of advanced turning.

The exercise simulates the late sighting of an approaching aircraft on a collision course straight ahead. You then immediately make a steep turn to the right, through about 90° of heading - any more and you may turn back into the path of the other aircraft. Then the aircraft is rolled wings-level and normal flight resumed. There is no emphasis on accurate flying in the collision avoidance manoeuvre - the emphasis is to avoid the other aircraft.

If you wonder why the collision avoidance turn is normally to the right, now is a good time to revise the rules of the air (see exercise 6).

▶ Physiological Effects

This exercise is possibly the first time in the flying training course that you have experienced significantly increased load factor—felt by the pilot as increased 'g'.

Tolerance of 'g' will be affected by your health, fitness, hunger or fatigue. If you do experience any problems with 'g', tensing the stomach muscles (as if expecting a punch to the stomach) before the 'g' builds up will help. Exceptionally, as 'g' builds up you may experience a partial loss of vision, known as *grey-out.* Reducing the load factor (by releasing back pressure on the control column) will reverse this.

Despite the foregoing, it is worth stressing that it is unlikely you will have any adverse physiological effects from the 'g' levels involved in steep turns - just the sensation of being pressed down in your seat.

Flight Exercise

▷ Purpose

To learn to turn the aircraft at steeper than normal angles of bank, both during level flight and in a descent.

To appreciate the increased stall airspeed associated with steep turns; the effect of increased load factor; and the significance of the Va airspeed.

▷ Airmanship

Lookout

As always, look out before turning. In this instance it is particularly important to look all round the aircraft as you will be changing direction at a faster rate than normal. During the first few turns you may need to scan the instruments to get the angle of bank and nose attitude correct. Once you know the outside picture to aim for, you should be able to scan outside at least 80% of the time during the turn.

Stalling speed

Check the aircraft's POH/FM for the expected stalling speed in the turn. If no figure is listed, multiply the wings-level stalling speed (flaps up) by 1.4 to give an idea of the stalling speed during a 60° angle-of-bank turn.

Orientation

After a few turns you may become disorientated, especially if the HI 'topples' and no longer shows the actual heading. Between turns use a prominent landmark to reorientate yourself and do not allow the aircraft to drift downwind out of your chosen area.

Va

Know the Va and limiting load factors of the aircraft and avoid exceeding these (thus overstressing the aircraft) at all costs.

If you suspect you may have overstressed the aircraft–perhaps during solo practice–return to the airfield right away and report the situation.

HASELL

It is usual to carry out HASELL or HELL checks before starting a steep turn. Your instructor will advise on this and the minimum height for carrying out steep turns.

**Entering
the Turn**

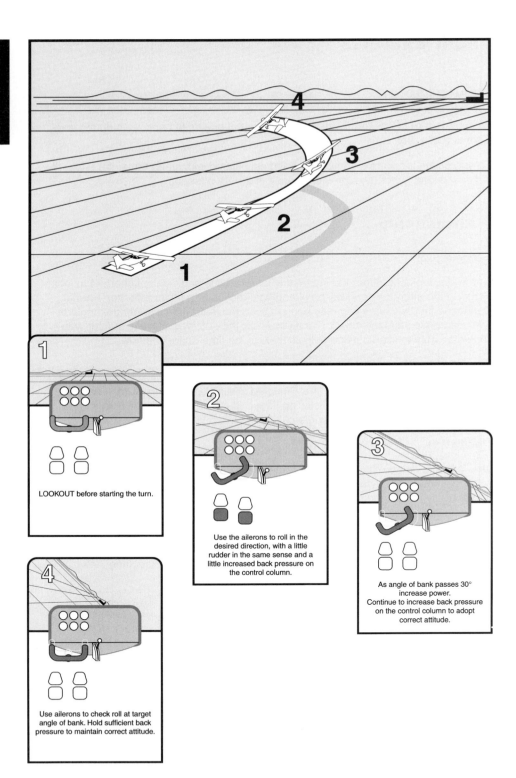

1

LOOKOUT before starting the turn.

2

Use the ailerons to roll in the desired direction, with a little rudder in the same sense and a little increased back pressure on the control column.

3

As angle of bank passes 30° increase power.
Continue to increase back pressure on the control column to adopt correct attitude.

4

Use ailerons to check roll at target angle of bank. Hold sufficient back pressure to maintain correct attitude.

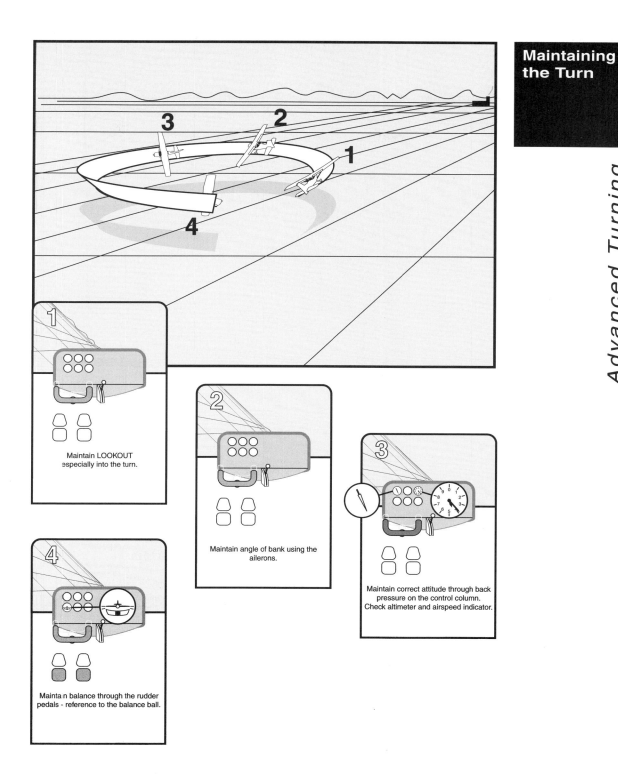

Maintain LOOKOUT especially into the turn.

Maintain angle of bank using the ailerons.

Maintain correct attitude through back pressure on the control column.
Check altimeter and airspeed indicator.

Maintain balance through the rudder pedals - reference to the balance ball.

Advanced Turning

15.9

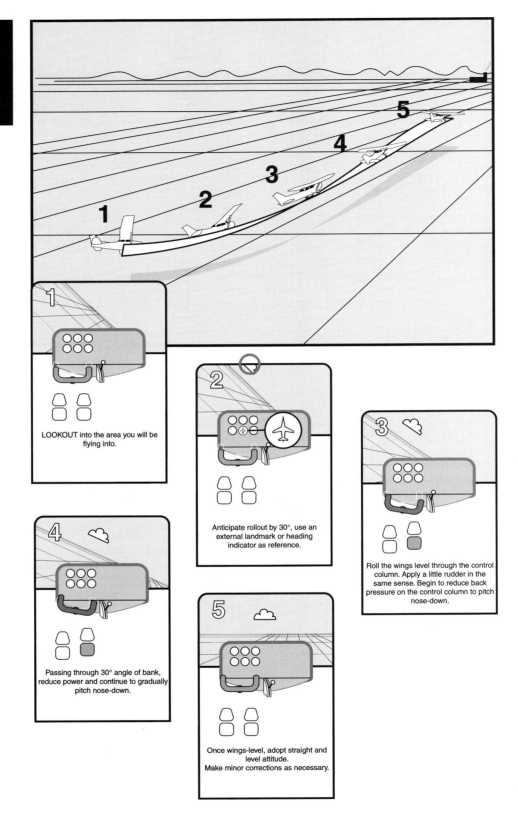

1 LOOKOUT into the area you will be flying into.

2 Anticipate rollout by 30°, use an external landmark or heading indicator as reference.

3 Roll the wings level through the control column. Apply a little rudder in the same sense. Begin to reduce back pressure on the control column to pitch nose-down.

4 Passing through 30° angle of bank, reduce power and continue to gradually pitch nose-down.

5 Once wings-level, adopt straight and level attitude.
Make minor corrections as necessary.

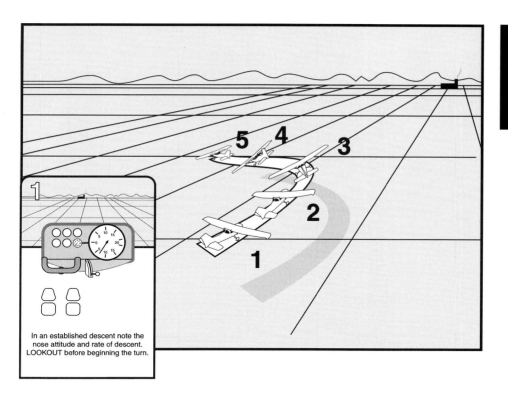

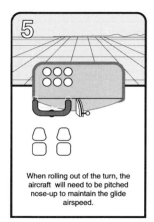

In an established descent note the nose attitude and rate of descent. LOOKOUT before beginning the turn.

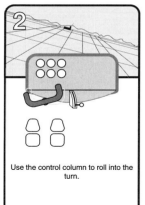

Use the control column to roll into the turn.

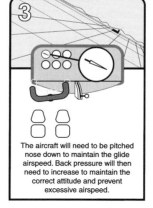

The aircraft will need to be pitched nose down to maintain the glide airspeed. Back pressure will then need to increase to maintain the correct attitude and prevent excessive airspeed.

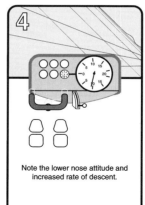

Note the lower nose attitude and increased rate of descent.

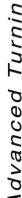

When rolling out of the turn, the aircraft will need to be pitched nose-up to maintain the glide airspeed.

Recovery from the Spiral Descent

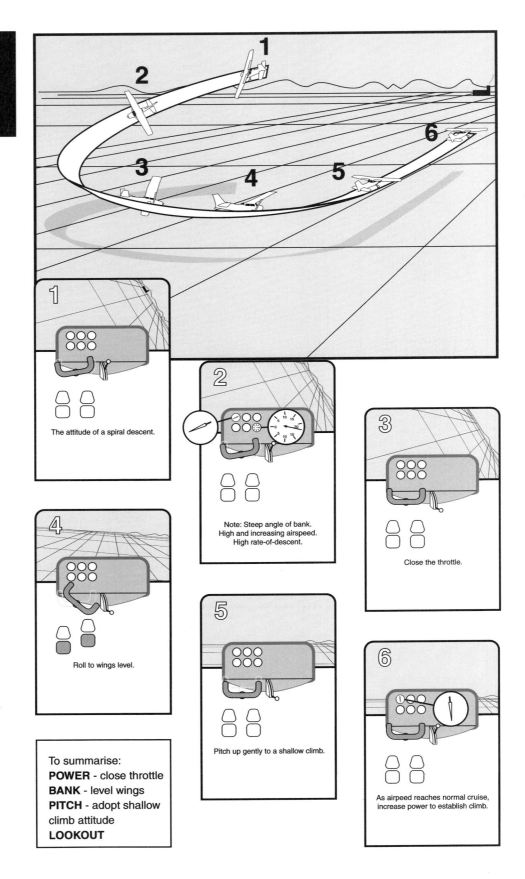

1 The attitude of a spiral descent.

2 Note: Steep angle of bank. High and increasing airspeed. High rate-of-descent.

3 Close the throttle.

4 Roll to wings level.

5 Pitch up gently to a shallow climb.

6 As airspeed reaches normal cruise, increase power to establish climb.

To summarise:
POWER - close throttle
BANK - level wings
PITCH - adopt shallow climb attitude
LOOKOUT

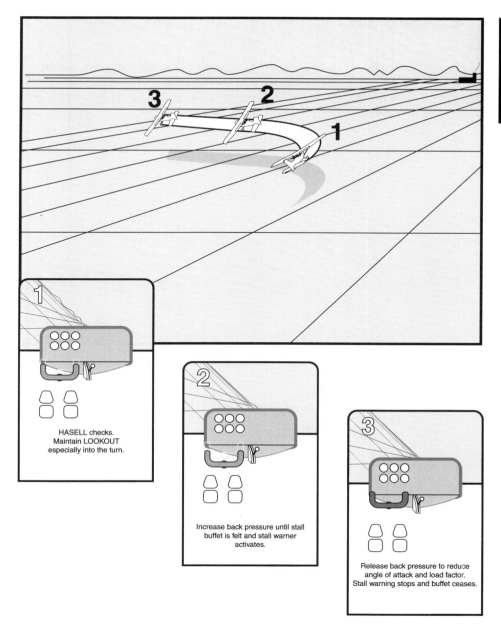

1 HASELL checks.
Maintain LOOKOUT
especially into the turn.

2 Increase back pressure until stall
buffet is felt and stall warner
activates.

3 Release back pressure to reduce
angle of attack and load factor.
Stall warning stops and buffet ceases.

Conclusion

This flight exercise is one of those that is not designed to teach an everyday flying manoeuvre. Rather, it should improve your handling and co-ordination skills, whilst giving you an appreciation of the factors involved when turning at steep angles of bank and the effect of increased load factor.

Operation at Minimum Level

Minimum level for civilian flying is normally defined as flight below 1000 feet AGL. Operation at minimum level may be necessary when using entry or exit lanes in controlled airspace, during a precautionary landing or during a bad weather circuit.

Flight at minimum level might also be necessary to remain in visual flying conditions when the cloud base is unusually low. Good airmanship would dictate a diversion or turn back rather than being forced down to minimum level. However, the fact remains that as a non-instrument-rated pilot, it is vital to remain CLEAR OF CLOUD and in visual contact with the ground. Should a non-instrument pilot enter cloud, the chance of losing control of the aircraft is very high indeed. By staying in visual conditions you will be able to control the aircraft, navigate, and keep your options open.

BACKGROUND BRIEFING

▶ **The Low-Flying Rules**

▶ **Precautions Prior to Descending**

▶ **Visual Impressions of Flight at Minimum Level**

▶ **Effect of Wind**

▶ **Turbulence and Windshear**

▶ **Lookout**

▶ **Weather Considerations**

BACKGROUND BRIEFING

▶ The Low-Flying Rules

Revise the low-flying rules before flying this exercise. In summary an aircraft 'en-route' must remain:

500'	from any person, vessel, vehicle or structure
1500'	above the highest point of a built-up area within 2000' of the aircraft, or high enough to glide clear; whichever is higher
3000'	from an open-air assembly of 1000 people or more

A summary of the low flying rules in the UK.

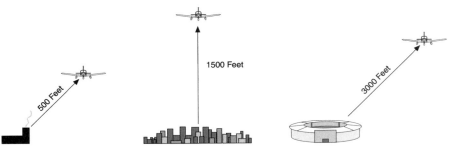

500 Feet

1500 Feet

3000 Feet

Minimum Separation

There are few exceptions to these rules and the aviation authorities are generally quick to prosecute cases involving low flying without a valid reason.

This exercise is normally practised at between 600 and 1000 feet AGL to observe the low-flying rules, in an area where operation at minimum level will cause the least disturbance to those on the ground.

▶ Precautions Prior to Descending

By now you will appreciate the adage that 'height is safety'. As you reduce your height, you reduce your safety margin in the event of any problem or distraction.

Before descending to minimum level, carry out a FREDA check and ensure that the harnesses are tight, due to the increased possibility of turbulence at low level. It may be appropriate to fly in the slow safe cruise configuration as you would do in conditions of poor visibility.

Review your chart for terrain or obstacles that may affect your flight. Aeronautical charts have a minimum terrain and obstacle level for portrayal on a chart. In the case of UK 1:500 000 charts, ground less than 500 feet above sea level and obstacles less than 300 feet above local ground level do not appear on the chart. In theory, it is possible to find a mast 299 feet above the ground, on top of a hill 499 feet above sea level, which is not shown on the chart. Such an obstruction, at 798 feet above sea level, could ruin your day if you are flying at 800 feet QNH. Remember, height is safety.

Avoid areas where other air traffic may pose a particular hazard - e.g. gliding fields, microlight, hang glider and parascending sites, parachuting drop zones, military low-level routes etc. At minimum level, the range of the radio–being line of sight–will be reduced and contact with a more distant ATC unit may be interrupted.

▶ Visual Impressions of Flight at Minimum Level

At minimum level the topography of the ground is far more apparent. Hills and obstacles that may not even show on the chart take on a much greater importance at minimum level and can pose a danger to the aircraft.

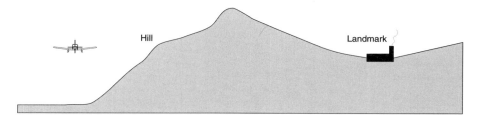

When flying at minimum level, hills or mountains may obscure landmarks.

Flying at minimum level produces a far greater impression of speed. This is only because reference points are now much closer, so that speed over the ground is more apparent. At lower levels the visible horizon is closer to the aircraft and landmarks will be in view for a much shorter time; some landmarks may even be hidden to the pilot behind a small hill, trees or buildings. Height keeping is accomplished as much visually as by reference to the altimeter. Remember the altimeter, when set to QNH, is reading altitude above mean sea level - NOT height above the ground. Even when the altimeter is set to QFE, it is only reading height above a specific piece of ground such as an airfield–NOT the height above the ground directly under the aircraft. Unless the aircraft is fitted with a radar altimeter (highly unlikely in a light aircraft), you must rely on visual cues just as much as the altimeter to gauge the aircraft's height above the ground. Always keep a hand on the throttle in order to make any power corrections as quickly as possible.

▶Effect of Wind

The effect of wind on the ground track of the aircraft is far more apparent when flying at minimum level. This can cause dangerously misleading impressions to the unwary pilot.

The aircraft's groundspeed slows, during a turn into wind, giving the impression of a change in airspeed - which is almost certainly not the case. The effect of wind distorting the ground track means that the aircraft also appears to skid out of the turn, even if it is in balance. During a turn downwind, the increased groundspeed gives the illusion that the airspeed is accelerating and distortion of the ground track will make it appear that the aircraft is slipping into the turn.

The distortion of ground track when turning downwind or into wind.

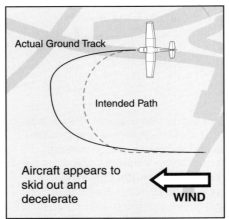

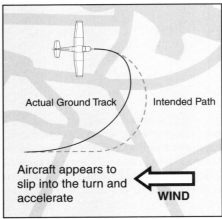

Check the ASI and balance ball before believing an external indication that the aircraft is accelerating or decelerating, or out of balance.

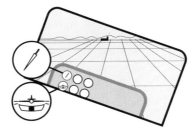

In each case always check the airspeed indicator (ASI) and balance ball before assuming that the aircraft is flying too fast or too slow, or out of balance.

The best advice is to always use small angles of bank when flying close to the ground in strong winds. If attempting to circle a point, the angle of bank will have to be varied during the turn to maintain a constant turn radius.

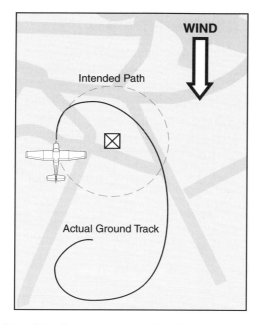

If the angle of bank is not varied when circling a point, the ground track will be distorted by the wind.

When flying straight and level a strong crosswind will make the drift angle far more apparent. Remember that the direction the aircraft is heading is not necessarily the same as the ground track. This is particularly important when manoeuvring to avoid obstructions. The slower the airspeed, the more noticeable the effect of wind drift.

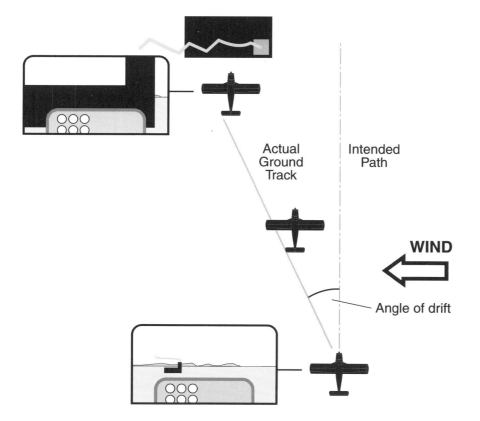

Even when making allowance for a crosswind, estimate the aircraft's ground track in order to avoid ground based obstructions. Remember in strong wind conditions there may be a large angle of drift and thus some difference between the aircraft's heading and track. Be particularly wary when flying 'up-wind' of an obstruction.

▶ Turbulence and Windshear

Turbulence and windshear are far more common at low level, and more dangerous because of the reduced height of the aircraft. Turbulence may make it difficult to maintain an exact height, heading and airspeed. The aircraft may need to be flown at the Va airspeed. If the flaps are extended the limiting load factors are reduced.

Windshear occurs when the wind velocity (i.e. direction and speed) suddenly changes. This can have a marked effect on airspeed as windshear affects the air through which the aircraft is flying. Always be ready to act quickly to maintain a safe airspeed.

Sudden windshear in the air that the aircraft is flying through will have a marked effect on the airspeed.

10 Knots ⇨   Groundspeed = 60
               Airspeed =70

25 Knots ⇨   Groundspeed = 60
               Airspeed = 85

When flying in hilly areas, the effects of up and down draughts and valley winds must also be anticipated. Avoid flying downwind of hills at low level, particularly in strong-wind conditions. In fact, flying at low level in or near a hilly area in such conditions is not at all advisable.

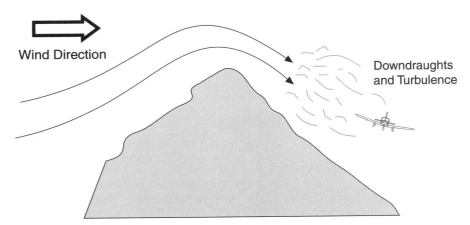

Wind Direction

Downdraughts and Turbulence

The dangers of flying downwind of high ground, especially when at low level, in strong wind conditions.

▶ Lookout

As always, lookout is important. At minimum level you are looking out not just for other aircraft, but also for terrain or obstacles that may be a threat to the aircraft.

The airspace band below 1000' AGL has the greatest concentration of air traffic (especially high-speed camouflaged jet fighters) and so the greatest danger of a near-miss or even a collision. Military aircraft, helicopters, agricultural aircraft, microlights, gliders, hang- gliders etc., may all be mixing at low level, together with other hazards such as flocks of birds or even model aircraft and kites! Keep your eyes scanning outside the cockpit as much as possible. Do not look inside for more than 4 - 5 seconds at a time.

▶Weather Considerations

Haze, smoke, mist or fog can all reduce visibility and the appearance of terrain. Rain showers may reduce visibility in one area, whilst snow or sleet can obliterate all visual references. If rain is falling on to the windscreen, there may be a visual illusion, caused by refraction of light, that makes terrain and obstacles appear lower than they really are - the dangers are obvious.

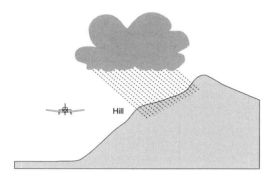

Landmarks, terrain etc may be obscured by weather, such as rain, sleet or snow and low cloud.

Be especially aware of the dangerous combination of rising ground and lowering cloud base. If you are already at minimum level, you must change heading to maintain visual flying conditions. Do not try to scrape through in the hope that conditions will improve - they almost certainly will not. If unable to divert around and away from bad weather, consider a precautionary landing.

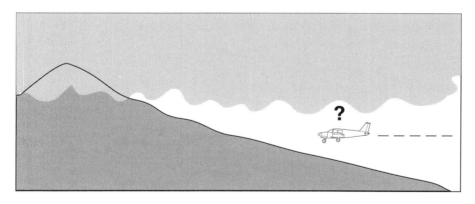

At all costs avoid the lethal combination of lowering cloud base and rising ground level.

Forced Landing Without Power

Nowadays, a total engine failure in a modern aircraft is rare; an engine failure caused by mechanical failure even more so. However, such an emergency remains a possibility. When flying a single-engine aircraft, the pilot should always have a contingency plan in the event that the engine breaks the habit of thousands of hours of trouble-free use and decides to fail.

The forced landing procedure involves little that has not already been learnt by now, but the time pressure involved and the need to carry out the proper checks and drills does make this exercise a challenging one.

Once proficient in the forced landing technique and in current practice, there is no reason why any pilot should not be able to make a safe forced landing. An oft-quoted example is that of a 1930s flying school taking delivery of a new aircraft type that turned out to be prone to engine stoppage during aerobatics. In a short space of time this one school suffered no less than 91 engine failures followed by forced landings, all without injury to the pilots or damage to the aircraft. Perhaps the key point is that the pilots had learnt to prepare for an engine failure and were in current practice for forced landings. That, in itself, is the first lesson of this exercise.

BACKGROUND BRIEFING

▶ **Common Causes of Engine Failure**

▶ **Gliding Angle**

▶ **The Basic Sequence**

▶ **Attain and Maintain the Best Glide Airspeed**

▶ **Assess the Surface Wind**

▶ **Select a Suitable Landing Area**

▶ **Plan the Approach Path**

▶ **Check For Cause of Failure**

▶ **Secure the Aircraft For Landing**

▶ **RT Distress Call**

▶ **Engine Fire**

▶ **Ditching**

FLIGHT EXERCISE

FLIGHT EXERCISE

▷ **Purpose**

▷ **Airmanship**

▷ **The Standard Pattern Forced Landing**

▷ **The Constant-Aspect Forced Landing**

CONCLUSION

BACKGROUND BRIEFING

▶ Common Causes of Engine Failure

The shameful fact is that the vast majority of engine failures in single-engine aircraft are due to pilot error. Prevention is always better than cure, so follow some simple guidelines to avoid becoming an unwilling member of the 'Pilot Error' club of engine failures.

Fuel
It stands to reason that you have a better chance of completing your flight safely if you have enough fuel to reach the destination and enough in reserve to reach any reasonable diversion. It also helps if the fuel is reaching the engine.

It is essential to visually check the fuel and oil levels during the preflight checks.

DO carry out proper fuel planning before flight. If you are relying on the fuel consumption figures in the POH/FM, be sure you are using the mixture-leaning techniques recommended in that publication.

DO allow plenty of safety margin for the unexpected such as winds different from those forecast, changed routings, diversions, higher than expected fuel consumption, errors in visually assessing the fuel contents etc.

DO always visually check the fuel contents during the preflight check.

DO know the working and arrangement of the aircraft's fuel system. Not all fuel systems are as simple as, say, that of the Cessna 150!

DO NOT rely entirely on the fuel gauges - they are never completely accurate.

DO NOT rely on word-of-mouth testimony about the aircraft's fuel consumption; e.g. "Our Cessna is good for 7 hours on full tanks"–their Cessna may have long-range fuel tanks!

Carb heat
Revise the carburettor icing supplement at exercise 8, then recheck the operating procedures for the aircraft you are flying. Carburettor icing is the chief suspect in a large number of otherwise unexplained engine failures.

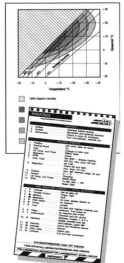

Revise the carb icing supplement in Exercise 8.

Checks
Perform your preflight, power and pre take-off vital actions and in flight (FREDA) checks carefully. The engine may give notice of its intention to quit which the checks will pick up. Even in the case of an impending mechanical failure, rising oil temperature and falling oil pressure–for example–may give the pilot some advance warning and the chance to divert to the nearest airfield.

Carry out all checks thoroughly and methodically.

▶ Gliding Angle

You will by now appreciate that a light training aircraft glides quite well without power. The key to a successful forced landing is the pilot's knowledge and judgement of the glide performance of the aircraft - he must be able to select a landing site that is within gliding range and position the aircraft onto a final glide approach into this site. Obviously the subject of gliding performance needs to be revised.

A typical training aircraft has a best Lift/Drag (L/D) ratio of 10:1. Thus, in a glide at best glide-range airspeed, the aircraft travels 10 feet forward for every 1 foot lost in height. However, this information is of mostly academic interest to the pilot, even when converted into a glide range - e.g. from 1000 feet the aircraft can glide 10,000 feet (or 1.6 nm) in still air. Unless the pilot has a way of accurately measuring the precise height above the ground and exact distances from the aircraft, the problem of estimating glide range still remains.

It is far simpler for the pilot to have a technique that allows glide performance to be easily assessed visually, without the need for mental arithmetic and distance measuring. This technique is based on the glide ANGLE of the aircraft.

Given the previous example of a L/D ratio of 10:1, the glide angle in still air works out at 7°. For the sake of simplicity, we will round this off to 10°.

The average light aircraft has a still-air glide angle of about 10°, viewed by the pilot as 10° down from the horizontal (e.g. the horizon).

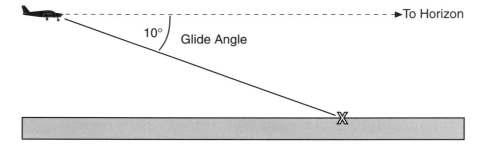

Now the pilot has a straightforward method of estimating glide range, no matter what the height. The pilot simply looks down from the aircraft at an estimated angle of 10° from the horizontal (this is normally gauged by reference to the horizon which will be at the pilot's eye level) and anything within the resulting cone is within the gliding range of the aircraft.

Forced Landing Without Power

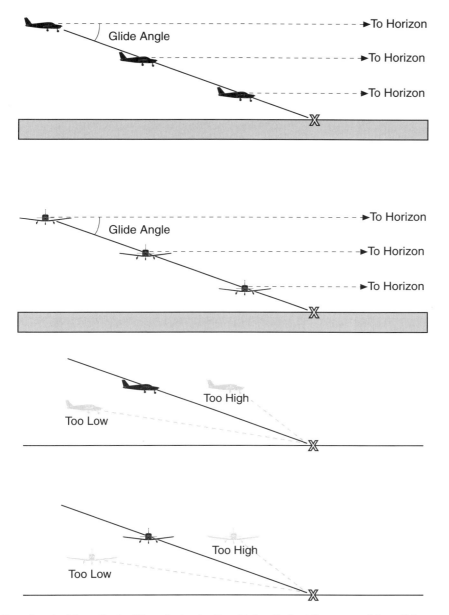

The glide angle is a constant, assuming still air. Whatever the height, a point within the gliding angle of the aircraft is within gliding range.

The pilot can judge gliding angle in just the same way as the descent angle is judged during an approach. Too steep an angle to the aiming point means the aircraft is too high. Too shallow an angle means the aircraft is too low.

Bear in mind the effect of the wind velocity which will slant the cone of the gliding angle downwind. The glide angle is steeper into a headwind and more shallow with a tailwind.

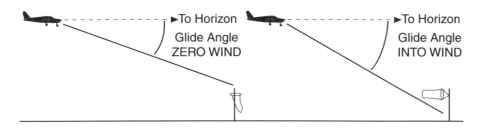

Gliding angle is steeper when flying into a headwind.

Knowledge of the glide angle also allows the pilot to assess the progress of the glide. Just as during a normal descent to land, if the descent angle to the aiming point remains constant, the aiming point will be reached. If the angle to the aiming point becomes steeper, the aircraft is overshooting the aiming point. If the angle to the aiming point becomes more shallow, the aircraft is undershooting the aiming point.

Judgement of gliding angle during the final glide to land.

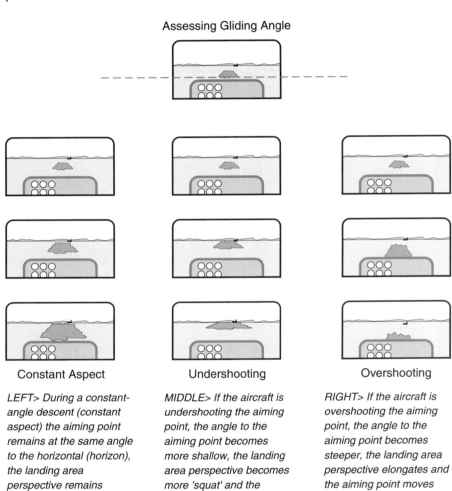

Assessing Gliding Angle

| Constant Aspect | Undershooting | Overshooting |

LEFT> During a constant-angle descent (constant aspect) the aiming point remains at the same angle to the horizontal (horizon), the landing area perspective remains constant and the aiming point stays at the same angle relative to the aircraft (usually judged by its position in the windscreen).

MIDDLE> If the aircraft is undershooting the aiming point, the angle to the aiming point becomes more shallow, the landing area perspective becomes more 'squat' and the aiming point moves up in relation to the aircraft.

RIGHT> If the aircraft is overshooting the aiming point, the angle to the aiming point becomes steeper, the landing area perspective elongates and the aiming point moves down in relation to the aircraft.

Different aircraft have different L/D ratios and so different glide angles. Generally, a high-performance aircraft will have a worse L/D ratio and so a steeper glide angle than a slower, lighter aircraft which usually has a better L/D ratio and so a more shallow glide angle.

▶The Basic Sequence

In the event of an engine failure, the No 1 priority is:

* fly the aeroplane *

With that essential under control you can consider your sequence of actions. As a general guide the usual sequence is:

Attain and maintain the best glide airspeed (and trim)

Assess the surface wind

Select a suitable landing area

Plan an approach pattern

Check for the cause of the engine failure

Secure the aircraft for landing

RT distress call

For convenience we will consider each of these points in this order. Bear in mind that in an emergency the pilot should use his judgement to decide the best course of action. This sequence can only act as a guide to the appropriate actions.

▶Attain and Maintain the Best Glide Airspeed

An unexpected engine failure will come as quite a shock to any pilot and there is bound to be an element of hesitation and confusion whilst the pilot assesses the situation. Remember the pilot's first priority–to fly the aeroplane–and the first action is obvious. The usual technique is to maintain level flight as the airspeed decelerates to the best glide airspeed. The aircraft is then pitched nose-down to the glide attitude and trimmed to maintain the glide airspeed.

Sometimes pilots talk about converting excess speed into height in the event of an engine failure. This can have some merit if flying a high-performance aircraft which may be able to zoom-climb several hundred feet before the airspeed reduces to the best glide airspeed. However, an average light aircraft with a cruising speed of 90 knots and a best-glide speed of 65 knots does not have the speed margin to allow for the ideal of trading speed for height.

In any case, the important point is to attain the best glide-range airspeed and then trim so that the aircraft will maintain this airspeed without constant adjustment by the pilot. This is important since flying at the best glide-range airspeed will give the pilot both the greatest number of options for a landing area and the time to carry out the appropriate actions. If the aircraft is not accurately trimmed, the pilot will be constantly having to adjust the airspeed back to that required and less height (and so less time) will be available. The reduced glide-range reduces the options open to the pilot, and flying the aircraft is much harder.

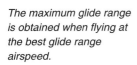

The maximum glide range is obtained when flying at the best glide range airspeed.

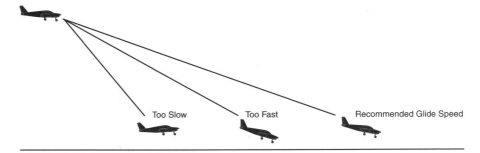

Too Slow   Too Fast   Recommended Glide Speed

Only one airspeed will give the best glide range (which may be quoted in the manual for flaps up or flaps down). Trying to 'stretch' the glide, by pitching nose-up and reducing airspeed, is a recipe for disaster–reducing the glide range and increasing the risk of a stall and possibly even a spin. It is better to make a controlled touchdown short of your chosen field than to spin in from 300 feet.

▶ Assess the Surface Wind

It is good airmanship to have an idea of the wind velocity in the area you are flying over. The best indicator of surface wind velocity is smoke. In the absence of smoke, wind streaks on water or cloud shadows over the ground give a guide to wind direction remembering that cloud shadows indicate the wind velocity at altitude, not the surface wind velocity. As a last resort, the wind velocity reported when you took off, or even the runway direction used, will give some guidance.

Continue to assess the wind throughout the approach. The amount of drift when flying crosswind or base leg and the groundspeed when flying into wind or downwind will indicate the wind strength.

▶ Select a Suitable Landing Area

Having assessed the wind velocity, you can select a landing area within glide range, the aim being to land into wind in an open, level area clear of obstructions.

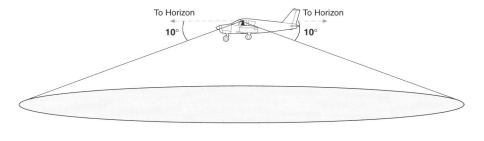

During a flight, the pilot should have an appreciation of the cone formed by the gliding angle of the aircraft. In the event of an engine failure, a landing area will have to be selected within this cone.

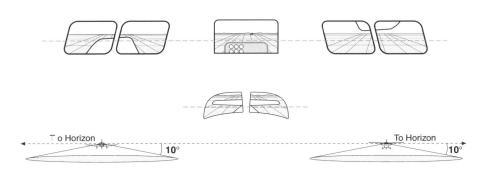

The gliding 'cone' can be assessed by looking around the aircraft and assessing a line at about 10° below the horizontal (usually judged in relation to the horizon).

Obviously the pilot must first decide what is within gliding range, as discussed. In selecting a landing site, it is better to choose a field close by which you can see in some detail rather than a field at the very edge of the glide range, which may turn out to be unsuitable when you get closer. If flying towards particularly hostile terrain (e.g. a built-up area, mountains or the sea) it makes sense to turn away early. If you are having trouble finding a suitable landing site, flying downwind will give a more shallow glide angle and thus increase the glide range, opening up more options to the pilot.

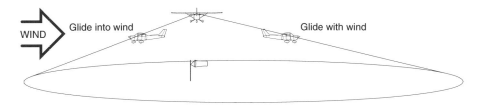

The gliding 'cone' is slanted downwind.

Remember to look all round to find a suitable site. In practice you can be sure that your instructor will sometimes position the aircraft so that all the best sites are on the other side of the aircraft; real-life situations have a habit of pulling this trick as well.

Background Briefing

Obviously the best landing site will be an airfield, with an into-wind runway at least 2000 metres long and a good pub within walking distance! Sadly, such ideal landing sites have a habit of being out of reach when the engine does fail and the pilot will have to select the best of the landing sites within glide range - pub or no pub! To select a suitable landing area check the five S's:

> ### Size and Shape
>
> ### Surface and Slope
>
> ### Surrounds

- Size and Shape

The chosen site should be big enough to land the aircraft and stop safely, allowing a reasonable margin for error. Judging the length of a field can be very difficult from altitude, especially if there is nothing of a known size close by to act as a reference. To help your judgement, compare the size of fields around your home airfield with the known runway length. In practice, few fields are more than a few hundred metres in length, but that is adequate to land most light aircraft safely. Obviously the bigger the field, the greater the allowable margin for error in piloting skill.

The field shape is an important factor. A long thin field will only offer one choice of approach path and landing run. A wider field gives a wider choice of approach paths and landing runs and is a better choice if all other factors are equal.

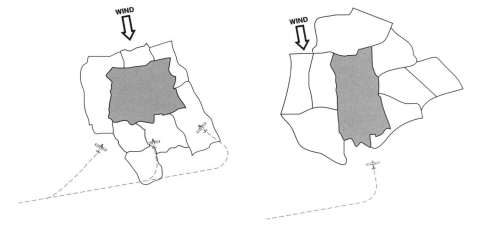

A large, wide field offers more options to the pilot than a long, thin field.

- Surface and Slope

The best surface to land on is something similar to that found at an airfield–i.e. a level, unobstructed area of short, dry grass. You may have a choice of different surface types; some are acceptable and some need to be avoided if at all possible, such as tall standing crops, where there is the distinct danger that the aircraft will turn over on landing. If it is necessary to land in a ploughed field, aim to land along the furrows–not across them. A short crop or one recently cut (i.e. short stubble) should be acceptable. Wet ground and water-logged ground, (often indicated by darker shades of the surface) or standing water should be avoided: soft ground increases the danger of the aircraft turning over on landing. Where possible avoid built-up areas, woodland and sites containing livestock or solid obstructions such as buildings, trees, walls etc.

Forced Landing Without Power

Beaches generally do not make good landing sites. If a beach is your chosen option, aim to land on the strip of firm sand a few metres from the water's edge.

The slope of the surface is difficult to judge from altitude. If a slope is apparent from 2000 feet, the chances are that it is likely to be a severe gradient, which should be avoided. Where the site has a river or some water in or close to it, the ground usually slopes down to the water. Wherever possible, avoid sloping ground and select a level landing site. If sloping ground cannot be avoided, aim to land uphill.

- Surrounds

Ideally the approach area should be clear of obstructions that may endanger the aircraft e.g. tall structures, power lines, high ground, etc.

The undershoot and overshoot areas should offer alternative landing sites in the event that the chosen site cannot be reached or turns out to be unsuitable for some reason. A reasonable site with a couple of similar areas nearby offers more options to the pilot than one ideal site surrounded by hostile terrain, obstructions or power lines.

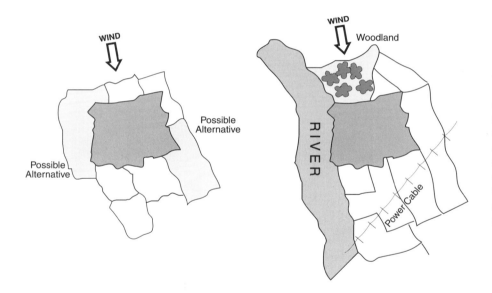

Choose a landing area with reasonable surrounds, preferably a couple of alternative landing sites. This is better than an ideal landing site surrounded by hostile terrain (water, woodland, power lines, high ground etc.) and no alternative landing site.

▶ Plan the Approach Path

Having selected a suitable landing site, you need to plan a descent pattern to place the aircraft on finals for an initial aiming point about one-third of the distance into the landing site. There are many variables in planning the pattern, such as starting height, wind velocity, position in relation to landing site etc.. There are also two different basic forced landing patterns - the standard circuit pattern which is the one traditionally taught in civilian FTO's; and the constant aspect pattern, favoured by the military and beginning to gain support in civilian flying.

The 'Standard Circuit' Forced Landing Pattern

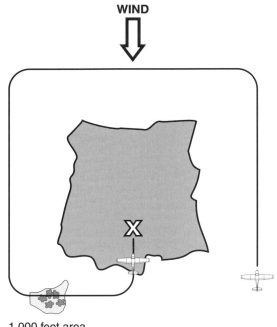

1,000 feet area

- The standard circuit pattern forced landing

The key point in this pattern is the *1000ft area*. This area should ideally be marked by a prominent landmark and is the area in relation to the landing site at which you would normally begin a glide approach during circuit flying. The aim is to be established on base leg once over this area, at a height (AGL) of not less than 1000ft. From your preflight planning you should know the approximate elevation of the ground above sea level. Assuming you are flying with QNH set on the altimeter, add the ground level to 1000ft to get the minimum altitude at the 1000ft area. For example, if the terrain is 600ft above sea level, you should aim to be at the 1000ft area not lower than 1600ft QNH.

The standard circuit forced landing pattern.

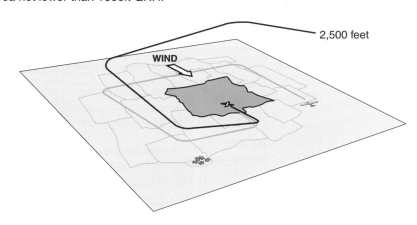

Forced Landing Without Power

The initial pattern is flown with the aim of arriving over the 1000ft area a little above 1000' AGL. It is still important to keep the landing site in view and not get too far away from it, a well chosen and prominent landmark in the 1000ft area will make it easier to keep the landing site in view and judge the progress of the pattern. Do not make the mistake of flying too close to the field, especially when downwind. The field should be no closer than a wing length away during the downwind leg. The pattern should allow for a slightly longer base leg than normal and a shorter final approach. All turns in the pattern should be made towards the landing site and it should be in view at all times.

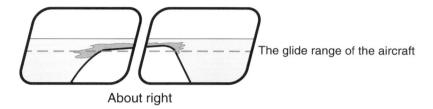

The glide range of the aircraft

About right

The glide range of the aircraft

Too close, angle too steep.

Assessing the gliding angle to the landing site when downwind.

The glide range of the aircraft

Too far away, angle too shallow.

Background Briefing

The initial touchdown aiming point is about one-third of the way into the site. Over the 1000ft area the pilot can judge if the aircraft will reach this aiming point and adjust the circuit if necessary.

From the 1000ft area, adjust the circuit as necessary to final approach.

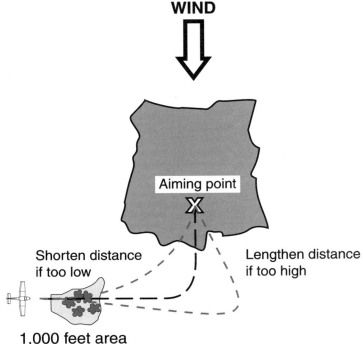

WIND

Aiming point

Shorten distance if too low

Lengthen distance if too high

1,000 feet area

The view of the landing area when turning on to finals.

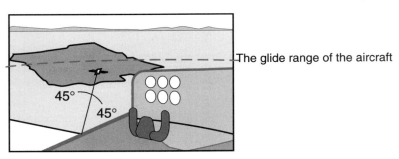

The glide range of the aircraft

45°

45°

From pilot's seat

As the aircraft nears final approach, the use of flap can be considered. Bear in mind that it is better to adjust the circuit pattern before considering the use of flap; this leaves more options open to the pilot. As each stage of flap is lowered, the nose attitude is readjusted to maintain airspeed. Remember to allow the aircraft to settle after each stage of flap. Do not be tempted to lower all the flap in one go if you are high. There is always a way to get rid of height, but there is no way of getting it back if you get too low on the final approach. When certain of making the aiming point (probably in the last 500ft of the approach) increased flap can be used to bring the expected touchdown point closer to the landing site threshold.

Forced Landing Without Power

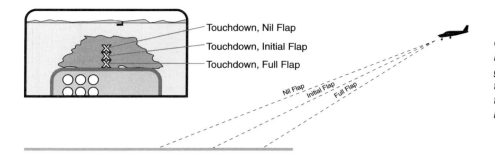

Touchdown, Nil Flap
Touchdown, Initial Flap
Touchdown, Full Flap

Nil Flap
Initial Flap
Full Flap

On the final approach, flap is used to steepen the glide angle and move the touchdown point closer to the beginning of the landing site.

Ways to lose height in the glide on final approach

- Sideslipping
- 'S' Turns
- Lower more flap
- Increase airspeed

Ways to gain height in the glide on final approach

Intentionally Left Blank

There is always some way of losing height in the glide. It is better to reach the far end of the landing site at taxying speed, than the near end of the site at flying speed.

Avoid extreme manoeuvres near the ground, especially steep angles of bank. Plan to touchdown wings-level at the slowest safe airspeed, use as much braking as necessary and steer to avoid obstructions.

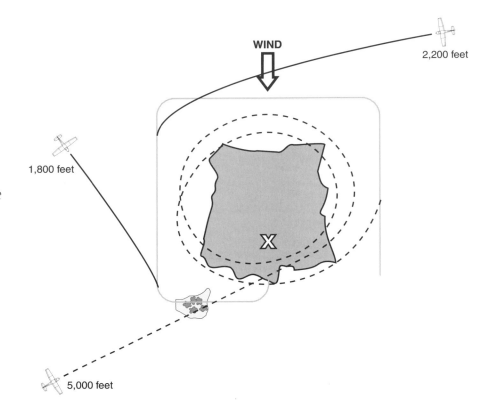

You can enter the standard pattern at a point decided by the aircraft's height and position relative to the landing site.

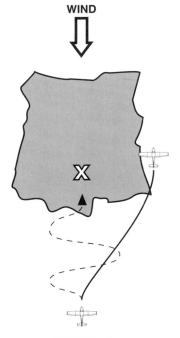

Even if there is an ideal landing site dead ahead, it is better to enter the standard pattern (height permitting) rather than make a rushed steep descent straight into the site.

Forced Landing Without Power

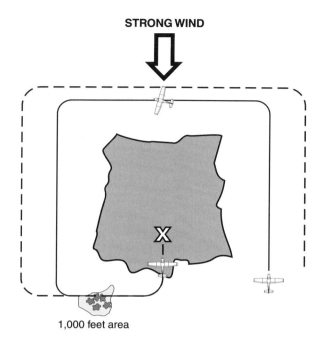

STRONG WIND

1,000 feet area

Adjust the pattern to allow for the prevailing wind.

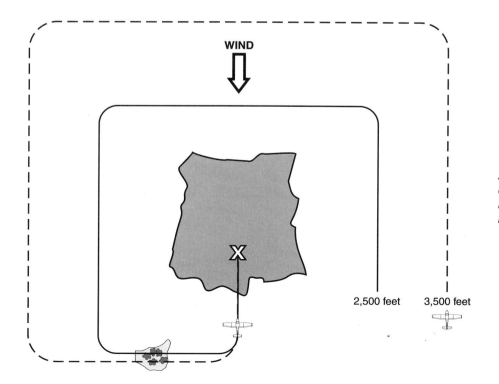

WIND

2,500 feet   3,500 feet

Adjust the pattern depending on the starting height in relation to the landing site.

The 'Constant Aspect' Forced Landing

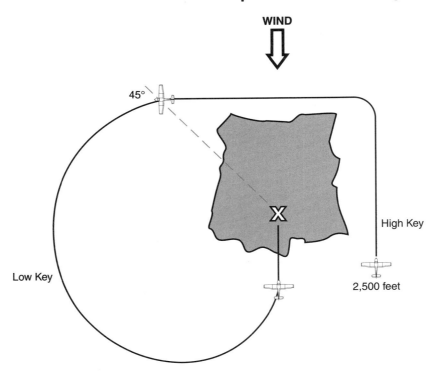

- The constant aspect forced landing

This pattern has two defined points; the 'High Key' point, usually an area abeam the landing site where the aiming point is visible just ahead of the wing leading edge; and the 'Low Key' point, a position abeam the aiming point when flying downwind.

From the high-key point, the aircraft is flown parallel to the expected landing direction until the aiming point is visible behind the wing. The aircraft is then turned on to the crosswind leg and flown on this track until the aircraft is at a 45° angle to the aiming point - to the pilot the aiming point will be behind the wing, (the 8 o'clock position in a left-hand pattern).

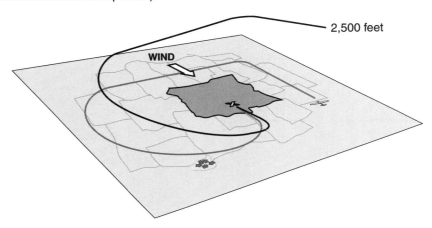

The constant aspect forced landing pattern.

Forced Landing Without Power

From this point a continuous turn is flown with reference to the aiming point, the objective being to maintain a constant descent angle to the aiming point.

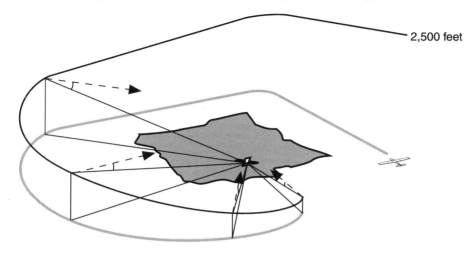

2,500 feet

The descending turn is adjusted to maintain a constant glide angle to the aiming point. If the angle becomes too shallow, the aircraft must be moved closer to the aiming point - the turn is tightened. If the angle to the aiming point becomes too steep, the aircraft must be moved away from the aiming point - the turn is widened out.

If the angle of the aiming point in relation to the horizontal (i.e. the horizon) remains constant at the correct glide angle, the rate of turn is correct. If the aiming point moves up towards the horizon, the angle to the aiming point is becoming too shallow and the aircraft is undershooting the aiming point. The angle of bank should be increased to move the aircraft closer to the aiming point and so steepen the angle to it. If the aiming point moves down, further below the horizon, the angle to it is becoming too steep - the aircraft is overshooting the aiming point. The angle of bank should be reduced to move the aircraft away from the aiming point and so make the angle to it more shallow.

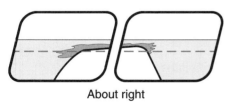

About right

The glide range of the aircraft

Too close, angle too steep.

The glide range of the aircraft

Assessing the gliding angle to the landing site when downwind.

Too far away, angle too shallow.

The glide range of the aircraft

Background Briefing

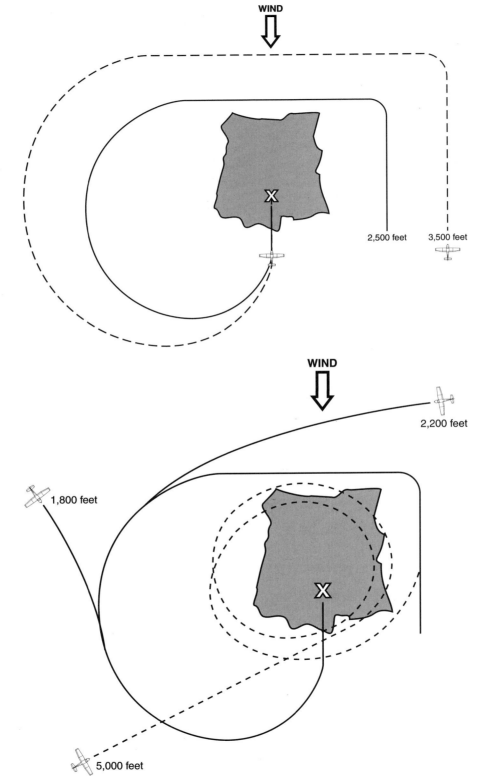

WIND

As glide angle is not affected by height, the pattern will automatically be further from the landing site if started higher, although the aiming point remains within glide range.

2,500 feet

3,500 feet

WIND

2,200 feet

1,800 feet

The pattern can be entered at any point, as dictated by the height and position of the aircraft relative to the landing site.

5,000 feet

Forced Landing Without Power

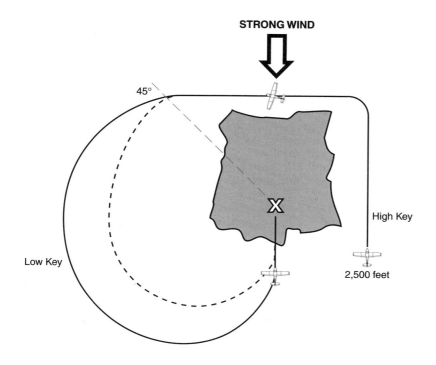

STRONG WIND

45°

Low Key

High Key

X

2,500 feet

In strong wind conditions, the judgement of the gliding angle should automatically keep the aircraft closer to the aiming point and thus within glide range.

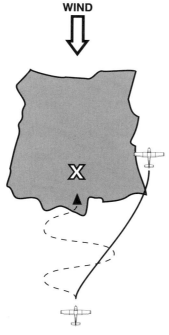

WIND

X

2,500 feet
Engine Failure

Even if the ideal landing site is right ahead, it is better (height permitting) to route to the overhead and enter the pattern rather than make a steep dive straight into the field.

Background Briefing

At the low-key point the turn is tightened slightly to steepen the angle to the aiming point. As the aircraft nears the final approach and the aiming point is closer, the glide angle is easier to judge and the pilot can consider the use of flap.

The view of the landing area whilst turning on to finals.

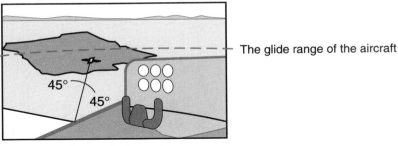

The glide range of the aircraft

45°

45°

From pilot's seat

Bear in mind that it is better to adjust the circuit pattern before considering the use of flap; this leaves more options open to the pilot. As each stage of flap is lowered, the nose attitude is readjusted to maintain airspeed. Remember to allow the aircraft to settle after lowering each stage of flap. Do not be tempted to lower all the flap in one go if you are high. There is always a way to get rid of height, but there is no way of getting it back if you get too low on the final approach. When certain of making the aiming point, (probably in the last 500ft of the approach) increased flap can be used to bring the expected touchdown point closer to the landing site threshold.

On final approach, flap can be used to steepen the glide angle and so move the touchdown point closer to the landing site threshold.

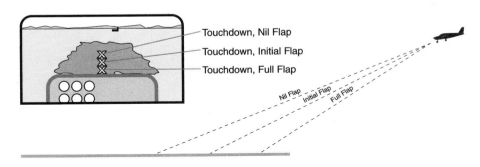

Touchdown, Nil Flap

Touchdown, Initial Flap

Touchdown, Full Flap

Nil Flap
Initial Flap
Full Flap

Ways to lose height in the glide on final approach	**Ways to gain height in the glide on final approach**
- Sideslipping	
-'S' Turns	
- Lower more flap	Intentionally Left Blank
- Increase airspeed	

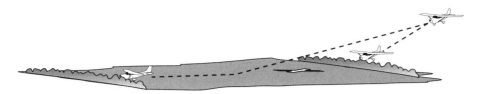

It is better to touchdown late and reach the far end of the landing site at taxying speed, than undershoot and reach the near hedge at flying speed.

Avoid extreme manoeuvres near the ground, especially steep angles of bank. Plan to touchdown wings-level at the slowest safe airspeed, use as much braking as necessary and steer to avoid obstructions.

► Check for Cause of Failure

As already discussed, most engine failures are caused by pilot error. The sequence of 'cause of engine failure' checks will be covered in the aircraft's POH/FM or checklist and usually concentrate on the common causes of engine failure. They will normally advise to:

- change fuel tanks (if possible), turn the fuel pump on (if applicable), check the fuel contents and check the mixture control;

- check carburettor heat is selected to hot (this is normally done immediately the engine fails) and exercise the throttle;

- check that the magnetos are on both and operate each individual magneto in turn, check the primer is locked;

- check the engine temperatures and pressures.

If there is no obvious problem, attempt to restart the engine. If the engine failure is clearly due to some mechanical failure, or if you suspect an engine fire, carry out the engine fire checks and do not attempt to restart the engine.

► Secure the Aircraft for Landing

Assuming the engine will not restart, or cannot be restarted, the aircraft and occupants should be prepared for landing. The checks should be carried out in accordance with the POH/FM procedure or aircraft checklist and are similar to the actions in the event of an Engine Failure After Take-Off (EFATO). Remember that if the aircraft has electrically operated flaps, do not turn off the master switch until all necessary flap selections have been made and any radio calls you intend to transmit have been completed.

Passengers should be briefed to fasten their harnesses tight; shoulder straps are particularly important in reducing the risk of injury. The doors should normally be unlocked but not opened fully. Again, check the aircraft's POH/FM or checklist for specific advice about the aircraft you are flying.

▶RT Distress Call

You will have noticed that this action has come a long way down the sequence. This is a prime case of using your judgement to decide the best course of action given your actual situation. In the case of a forced landing into reasonably friendly terrain, not too far from civilization, there is very little that ATC can do to help you. Even the local emergency services contacted by ATC will only arrive long after you have landed. It is the pilot's skill and judgement that will determine the outcome of the forced landing and the distress call will only alert interested observers. Remember the correct order of priorities:

Aviate, Navigate, Communicate.

One time an early distress call is very important is when flying over the sea, over very hostile terrain or a remote area. In this case, making the distress call while still at a reasonable height will increase the chances of it being received and so alerting search and rescue services. Give as accurate a position as possible. If time permits using the distress code on the transponder (7700) may also help your position to be recorded.

In any case, after transmitting the Mayday call do not get involved in irrelevant detailed discussions with ATC - your No 1 priority is to fly the aeroplane. A long exchange with ATC regarding relatively unimportant information (i.e. pilot qualifications, height and heading etc.) could distract you from the more important task of flying the aeroplane and carrying out the correct procedures.

▶Actions After Landing

So you have safely landed the aircraft in the site of your choice. What do you do now ? If your immediate thoughts centre around relaxing in your seat and maybe having a cigarette—think again!

When the aircraft stops, your first action must be to evacuate. Get yourself and your passengers well away from—and upwind of—the aircraft; remember to take the fire extinguisher and first-aid kit with you. Do not return to the aircraft until you are certain that there is no further danger.

If no-one comes to your aid, you should walk towards the nearest sign of civilization and locate a telephone to contact the local police. After this, your actions will depend on whether or not the forced landing is a notifiable accident. The FTO will detail specific procedures in the event of a forced landing in one of their aircraft - i.e. they want to be contacted as soon as possible!

▶ Engine Fire

If you experience an engine fire in flight, you should immediately close down the engine in accordance with the aircraft's POH/FM or checklist. If the fire goes out, continue with the forced-landing procedure, but do not attempt to restart the engine.

If the fire does not go out, you are faced with a very serious emergency indeed–for which there are few hard and fast rules. The priority is to get the aircraft on to the ground as quickly as possible, before the fire reaches the cabin or causes some type of structural failure. Using full flap at the VFE speed should give an impressive rate of descent. Increasing the airspeed, turning or sideslipping will all further increase the rate of descent; sideslipping also has the advantage of directing any flames away from the cockpit.

It is stressed that an engine failure is a very rare occurrence. An engine fire is even more rare and very few pilots are ever faced with such a situation.

▶ Ditching

This is one emergency for which there is no practice. There are factors to consider, however, and precautions to take to avoid the possibility of a ditching.

In the event of an engine failure over water, head towards any land that is within glide range. If dry land is out of glide range, look for any shipping in the area. If possible, descend over a ship and land ahead and to one side, to increase your chances of being seen and picked up. Bear in mind that ships cannot just stand on the brakes and stop. Even a medium-sized ship may need half a mile to stop, while a supertanker can take up to five miles to come to a halt. If glide range is not a consideration, aim to descend at the best glide-endurance speed–about 25% slower than the best glide-range speed–to give the longest time airborne.

Make an early distress call with as accurate a position report as possible and squawk 7700 on the transponder. Your potential survival chances after the ditching are directly related to how quickly search and rescue services can locate and rescue you.

Open the door and if possible wedge it with a shoe or similar to avoid it being jammed shut if the fuselage structure deforms during the ditching. Make sure your passengers are well strapped-in and briefed to expect the sudden deceleration of a ditching. A cushion, rolled-up clothing or an arm should be used to protect the face and head during the actual ditching.

Background Briefing

From 2000ft the swell of the sea should be apparent. The swell of the sea is the undulation of the surface caused by some distant force. If you throw a stone into a pond, the ripples that spread out are the swell on a smaller scale. In most conditions your aim would be to land parallel to the swell, touching down on a crest if possible. Wind streaks across the surface will help confirm the wind direction, and it should be possible to land with an element of headwind to give a slower touchdown speed. In very strong wind conditions (more than 35 knots) it is best to land directly into wind to give a very slow touchdown speed. In this case, take care not to land directly into a rising swell or large wave. The massive deceleration could be disastrous.

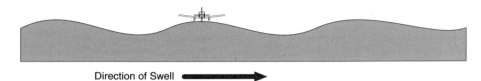

Direction of Swell ➡

In a strong swell and light wind ditch along the swell. Only land into the swell if ditching into a very strong headwind.

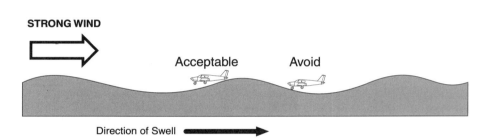

STRONG WIND

Acceptable   Avoid

Direction of Swell ➡

A fixed-undercarriage nosewheel aircraft has a good chance of 'nosing in' on touchdown. To reduce this danger, land in a shallow tail-down attitude at the slowest controllable airspeed–but at all costs do not stall into the sea. With good technique–and a little luck–the tail should touchdown first, causing a gentle deceleration, followed by stronger deceleration as the nosewheel digs into the water.

If you ditch in a high-wing aircraft, the cabin may well have to fill with water to allow the doors to be fully opened. A light aircraft will usually float for a few minutes, so there should be time for an orderly evacuation.

Forced Landing Without Power

There are some standard precautions to take to avoid having to ditch or to increase your chances of survival after ditching.

- Always fly the shortest sea crossing available.

- Fly as high as possible to reduce the time you are out of gliding range of dry land.

- File a flight plan whenever you are flying outside gliding range of land. Always maintain contact with an ATC unit.

- Carry basic survival equipment–the absolute minimum should be life jackets and a dinghy. Life jackets should be worn at all times but must not be inflated inside the aircraft. Regard the dinghy as essential. In the late winter/early spring, the sea temperature around North-West Europe is cold enough to kill a person in less than thirty minutes. Even in late summer, survival time in the water may be no more than a couple of hours. Additionally, a single life-jacket in the water is far more difficult to spot than a dinghy. Always have the dinghy to hand; a dinghy out of reach in the luggage compartment may as well be left behind at the airfield.

- Consider the use of ancillary survival equipment, such as flares, smoke canisters or an ELT (Emergency Locator Transmitter). Survival equipment does not come cheap, but neither does human life.

Proper survival equipment saves lives.

(Photo courtesy: Beaufort Air Sea Equipment)

Flight Exercise

▷ Purpose

To learn to make a safe forced landing in the event of an engine failure. Additionally, to learn the correct procedures in the event of an engine fire or ditching.

▷ Airmanship

Lookout

During forced-landing practice maintain a good lookout, particularly at lower levels which are often inhabited by helicopters, agricultural aircraft and military fast jets.

Low flying

Revise the low-flying rules. Forced landing practice does not absolve the pilot from any of the low flying regulations, so be particularly careful not to infringe the 500 or 1500ft rules. Vary the practice area so as not to annoy those on the ground.

Engine handling

Always warm the engine at regular intervals throughout the descent, usually every 500 feet or so. In general terms, make all the throttle movements smooth and monitor the engine temperatures and pressures. You would not want to turn a practice forced landing into the real thing - especially if the practice was not going too well!

Checks

Learn the forced-landing checks so that you can accomplish them from memory. There may not be time to consult the checklist in a real emergency.

Forced Landing Without Power

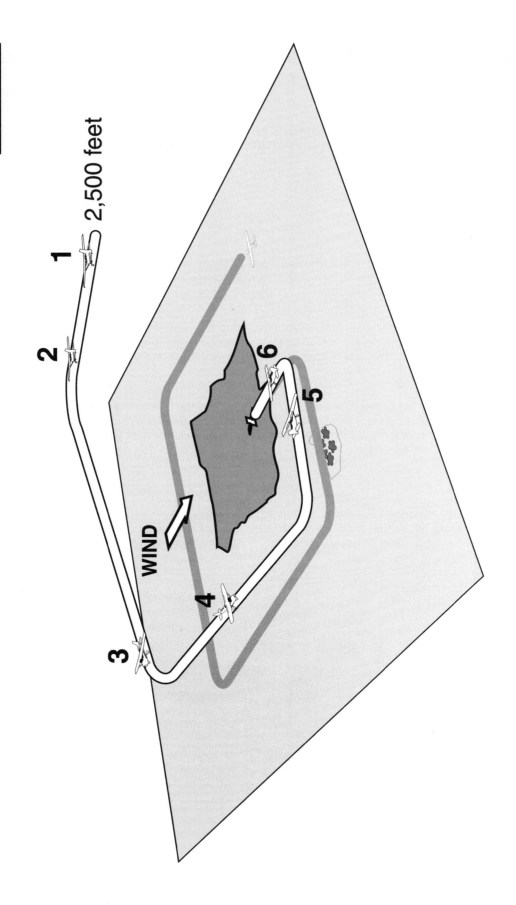

The
Standard
Pattern
Forced
Landing

2,500 feet

1

2

3

4

WIND

5

6

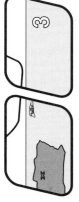

Initial actions:
Attain best glide airspeed, trim
Assess surface wind.
Select a suitable landing area.

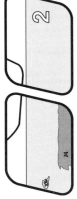

Plan the approach pattern.

Check for cause of engine failure.

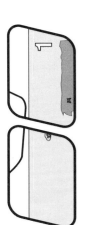

Secure aircraft for landing.

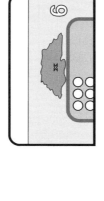

RT DISTRESS CALL

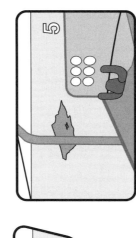

As seen from a high wing aircraft

At all times *fly the aeroplane*

Forced Landing Without Power

17.31

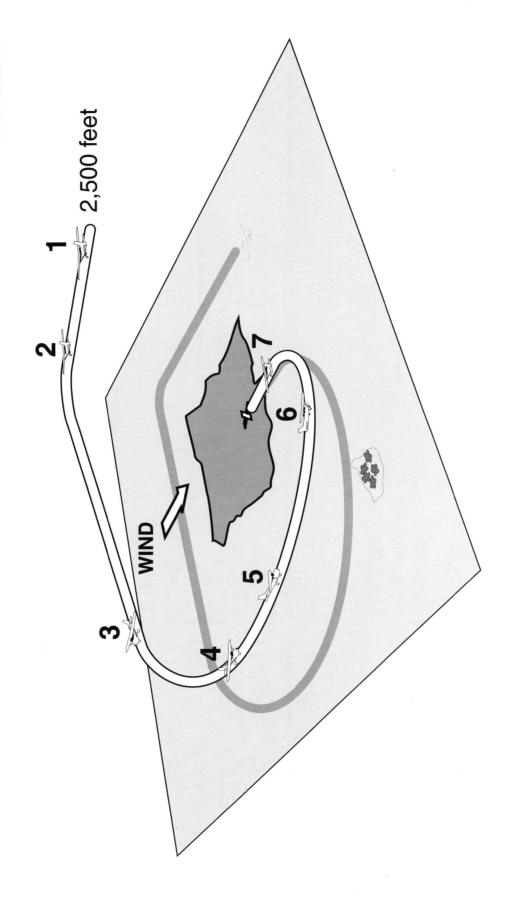

Forced Landing Without Power

The
Constant
Aspect
Forced
Landing

2,500 feet

1

2

WIND

3

4

5

6

7

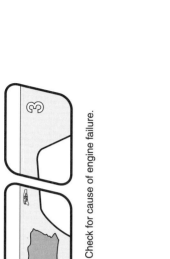

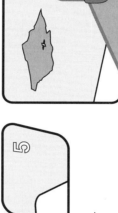

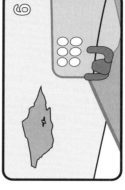

Check for cause of engine failure.

Plan the approach pattern.

RT DISTRESS CALL

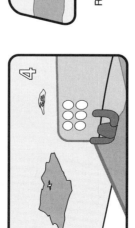

Initial actions:
Attain best glide airspeed, trim
Assess surface wind.
Select a suitable landing area.

Secure aircraft for landing.

As seen from a low wing aircraft

At all times *fly the aeroplane*

Forced Landing Without Power

Conclusion

By the completion of this exercise, which will take more than one flight lesson, you should be confident of making a safe forced landing from a variety of altitudes and situations. From now on your instructor will regularly simulate an engine failure, probably when you least expect it.

Being proficient in the forced-landing procedure to pass your flying test is one matter. Remaining current and staying alert to the possibility of an engine failure is just as important, requiring good airmanship and self-discipline. Near-perfect practice forced landings during your training will count for little if you are faced with a real emergency after years of not even considering the possibility of an engine failure, let alone practising the correct procedure.

The basic forced landing procedure that you practise during training can only act as a guide to the correct actions in the event of an engine failure. In a real emergency there are two golden rules:

1   *Fly the aeroplane*

2   **Pilot judgement should dictate pilot actions.**

The Forced Landing With Power
- the Precautionary Landing

To make a precautionary landing at an unprepared landing site is a rare occurrence–not least because a situation requiring such a procedure is usually quite avoidable. There are some situations, however, such as a fuel-system problem or impending pilot incapacitation, which might compel the pilot to land away from an airfield. This procedure also has applications when landing at an unfamiliar private airstrip-type runway.

BACKGROUND BRIEFING

▶ **Conditions Necessitating a Precautionary Landing**

▶ **Selection of a Landing Area**

▶ **The Surrounding Area Inspection**

▶ **The Landing Site Inspection**

▶ **The Landing**

▶ **After Landing**

FLIGHT EXERCISE

▷ **Purpose**

▷ **Airmanship**

▷ **The Precautionary Landing**

CONCLUSION

BACKGROUND BRIEFING

▶Conditions Necessitating a Precautionary Landing

There are some possible scenarios where an unusual failure or problem could cause the pilot to consider landing away from an active airfield. Possibly a fault has developed in the fuel system and there is not enough fuel available to reach an airfield. In this case landing whilst power is still available is obviously a better option than waiting for the fuel to run out. Alternatively the pilot may have some health problem (for instance gastro-enteritis) and again may want to land as soon as possible, but with no suitable diversion airfield available.

Unfortunately, the most common scenario preceding a precautionary landing is one of worsening weather (lowering cloud base and reducing visibility), lack of fuel, little daylight remaining and the pilot being totally lost. It is this worst-case scenario which will be simulated during the flight exercise. The outstanding feature of such a set of circumstances is that the situation could have been completely avoided if the pilot had been applying good airmanship. Despite this, it should be emphasised that having got into such a situation, a precautionary landing is far more preferable than the other option which might tempt the pilot–flight into instrument flying conditions (i.e. entering cloud). Flight into cloud by a non-instrument rated pilot has an exceptionally high mortality rate compared to a precautionary landing, which the pilot is certain to walk away from.

▶Selection of a Landing Area

All the factors relating to field selection during a forced landing without power (i.e. the five S's) are relevant to the precautionary landing. The main difference is that the pilot can be more selective in searching for a suitable landing site; during the flight exercise it may be assumed that you have found a disused airfield or private airstrip. The first factor to consider is the surface wind velocity. Landing into wind is always the preferred option–consider possible landing sites with this in mind.

It must be emphasised that the procedure is just as relevant to a disused runway thousands of metres in length as to a totally unprepared site. A disused runway may be marked with a white cross to show that landing may be dangerous; a white cross with a white bar indicates that the runway has been inspected in the last six months and at that time was considered fit for emergency use. These signals are found at ex-military airfields.

Markings found on disused runways. A white cross indicates that the runway is unfit to be used by aircraft. A white cross underlined with a white bar indicates that the runway has been inspected within the last 6 months and at that time was fit for emergency use.

▶ The Surrounding Area Inspection

The flight exercise assumes that the aircraft is flying in the deteriorating weather conditions previously outlined. Therefore, we can expect the pilot to have set up the 'slow safe cruise' configuration. The exercise is normally started from 600ft AGL from the point at which the pilot has located what appears to be a suitable landing area, (with regard to the size and shape of the site). The first task is to decide if there are any local obstructions that will endanger the aircraft during the approach, go-around or circuit (i.e. checking the site surroundings). The aircraft is descended to approximately 300ft AGL, approaching in the expected landing direction. Whilst being flown level at 300ft AGL, slightly to the right of the landing area, the pilot visually searches all around for obstructions that might endanger the aircraft. At the end of the landing area the pilot makes a go-around back to circuit height (600ft AGL) and enters a bad-weather circuit. During the circuit the pilot should note any particular landmarks and verify the landing direction on the heading indicator.

▶ The Landing Site Inspection

Once satisfied that it is safe to descend lower, the second approach is flown down to 100ft AGL over the landing area to examine the surface and slope. While flying level at this height, to the right of the landing area, the pilot should now inspect the landing surface itself, looking particularly for any solid obstructions that could damage the aircraft. At the end of the landing area the pilot again makes a go-around and re-enters the bad-weather circuit, making use of the landmarks noted during the previous circuit.

▶ The Landing

When at the beginning of the downwind leg, the normal pre-landing checks are carried out. With the experience of the two previous approaches, the pilot should know if the circuit position needs to be altered for a safe approach to be made. The pilot should also have had a chance to gauge the surface wind and be able to fly the approach to land accordingly. The aim is to make a short or soft-field landing, as appropriate. If at any stage the approach looks unsafe, or the landing area unsuitable, do not hesitate to go around, conditions permitting.

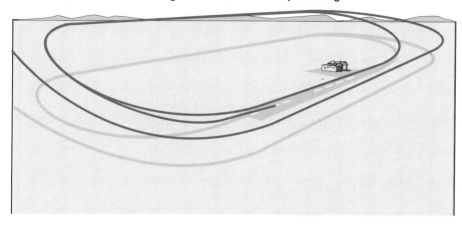

The circuits around the landing site are flown as oval 'bad weather' circuits. The first inspection pass is flown at 300' AGL, the second at 100' AGL. If the site is suitable, a landing is made from the third approach.

▶ After Landing

After landing, the engine should be shut down as soon as the aircraft has stopped. Do not attempt to taxi; there may be hidden obstructions that could seriously damage the aircraft. The pilot will need to contact the local police, the land owner and the FTO. If a flight plan has been filed for the flight, it is particularly important that an ATC unit is contacted so that unnecessary search and rescue action is not started.

Above all, even if the situation that caused the forced landing is resolved, do not attempt a take-off until the site has been thoroughly inspected and the relevant performance calculations carried out. In the case of an FTO aircraft, the FTO will undoubtedly want to send its staff to the site before authorising a take-off.

Flight Exercise

▷ Purpose

To learn to make a safe precautionary landing, to understand the application of the various elements of the precautionary landing procedure if landing at an unprepared site and to appreciate how to avoid a situation that might necessitate a precautionary landing.

▷ Airmanship

Low flying

The FTO will only permit this exercise to be practised out at a carefully chosen site, usually an active airfield. The various implications of the low flying involved in this procedure are covered in detail in exercise 16, which should be revised in full before flying this exercise.

Avoiding conditions leading to a forced landing with power

It is obvious that the conditions simulated during this exercise are not conducive to safe visual flying.

Accidents are rarely the result of a single error or fault, but more usually a combination of circumstances. The overwhelming desire to reach your destination, (also known as "get-home-itis") can cloud your judgement if you allow the perceived pressures to overcome commonsense and good flying practice. Flying into continuing worsening weather, becoming totally lost without seeking assistance, allowing fuel to run short or not allowing a safe margin of daylight at the planned landing time, are all avoidable errors. Having said all that, if you get into this sort of situation, make an early decision to find a landing site. If you leave the decision as late as possible, (maybe hoping the situation will somehow improve), you run the risk of adding one more adverse factor against yourself and turning an incident into an accident.

Exercise

17
b

The Forced Landing With Power

The Precautionary Landing

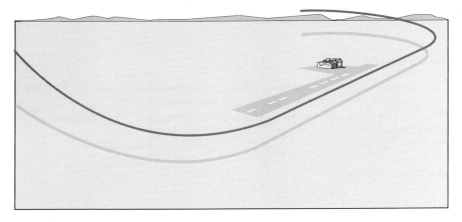

The first inspection pass is flown at 300' AGL to check the landing site surroundings.

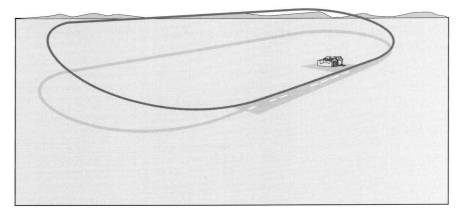

The second inspection pass is flown at 100' AGL to examine the surface of the landing site.

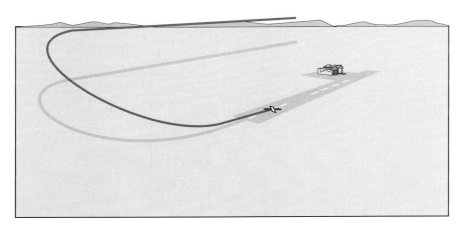

If the first two inspections and circuits are satisfactory, a short/soft-field landing is made from the third approach.

Conclusion

The forced landing with power exercise can be applied in full, or in part, to several different situations. The area inspection or landing-site inspection might well be advisable when using a private airstrip type runway. Usually the land owner or operator will advise. Occasionally such an inspection may be advisable when landing at an airfield 'out of hours'. Some airfields have a variety of non-aviation uses (e.g. vehicle testing, agricultural uses etc.) and outside published hours the runway may well be obstructed in some way. In this case it is advisable to overfly the airfield above the normal circuit height if possible to assess the runway and then make as near as possible a standard overhead join.

Flight Planning

Exercise

18
a

Trainee salesmen or saleswomen are often taught about the five P's:

Proper Planning Prevents Poor Performance.

The same applies to flying, except that the possible consequences of poor performance can be much worse than a lost sale. In this day and age it is simply not safe to jump into your aeroplane, point it in the general direction of the destination and hope for the best. Many accidents that occur during cross-country flights can be traced back to a lack of proper flight planning. The time spent flight planning is time (and trouble) saved in the air - proper planning DOES prevent poor performance.

BACKGROUND BRIEFING

▶ **Route Selection**

▶ **Chart Selection**

▶ **Safety Altitude/Minimum Safety Altitude (MSA)**

▶ **Chart Preparation**

▶ **Weather Considerations**

▶ **Daylight**

▶ **Completion of the Flight Log**

▶ **Fuel Planning**

▶ **Weight and Balance**

▶ **Take-off and Landing Performance**

▶ **Alternate Airfields**

▶ **Radio Frequencies**

▶ **NOTAMS and Pre-Flight Bulletins**

▶ **Aircraft Documentation**

▶ **Flight Notification**

▶ **And Finally**

BACKGROUND BRIEFING

▶ Route Selection

During your early navigation exercises, your instructor will select the route for you. In later flights, you may just be given the destination and expected to select a suitable route. Choose a route with regard to the following factors:

Terrain — avoid high ground or hostile terrain if practicable. Hostile terrain includes mountains, uninhabited areas, moorland and the sea or large lakes. Check that maintaining a safe height above terrain will not put you into controlled airspace. Check also for significant obstructions.

Restricted airspace — danger areas, prohibited areas and restricted areas should be avoided, unless you plan to use a specific 'crossing' service.

Controlled airspace — remember you may not enter controlled airspace without a specific clearance from the controlling ATC unit - and they may not be able to give such a clearance. Be realistic—you are unlikely to be given a clearance directly over a busy international airport.

Active airfields — an airfield can make a very good turning point or en-route point. Remember that you will need clearance to cross through an active ATZ, which may not be forthcoming at a very busy airfield. Where possible avoid a VRP for an airfield that is not your destination. Do not plan to pass over an active gliding site, hang-glider site, microlight site or parachute area. Military airfields usually have a MATZ and possibly an associated AIAA. Although it is not mandatory to get clearance to enter these areas, it would be very poor airmanship not to make radio contact.

Miscellaneous restrictions — be aware of other airspace restrictions, such as those around nuclear installations, bird sanctuaries, HIRTAs, gas venting areas etc..

▶ Chart selection

The chart key will state the vertical limits of the chart and markings used.

Make sure you know the scale of the chart(s) you plan to use and the limit of its coverage, including vertical limits. Most charts have a defined level above which no airspace information is depicted - check the chart key for this information. Also check the key to be sure that you understand the symbols used and the portrayal of terrain.

Check the chart edition and date; 1:500 000 charts are usually reissued on an annual basis. Do not fly with an out-of-date chart. Charts are reissued for a reason and there are always significant changes between editions–using a current chart is a legal requirement.

THIS CHART WILL BECOME OBSOLETE AFTER APPROXIMATELY 12 MONTHS. INFORMATION CIRCULARS SHOULD BE CHECKED FOR THE PUBLICATION OF THE NEXT EDITION.

USERS ARE REQUESTED TO REFER CORRECTIONS AND ANY COMMENTS ON THE PORTRAYAL OF TOPOGRAPHICAL AND AERONAUTICAL INFORMATION TO:- NATIONAL AIR TRAFFIC SERVICES, AERONAUTICAL CHART SECTION, AP7, ROOM T1120, CAA HOUSE, KINGSWAY, LONDON. WC2B 6TE.

Ensure that you are using a current chart.

►Safety Altitude/Minimum Safety Altitude (MSA)

It stands to reason that your flight will pass much easier if you plan to fly higher than the terrain between the departure and destination points. This would seem to be stating the obvious, yet countless accidents can be directly attributable to pilots quite simply flying a perfectly serviceable aircraft into the ground - usually in poor weather conditions. This most basic of piloting errors is also known as CFIT (Controlled Flight Into Terrain) by the airline industry and referred to in several unprintable terms by other pilots.

To avoid this most basic of pilot-error accidents, the pilot must have a clear idea of the MINIMUM safe altitude for each part of the route, which will ensure a safe vertical distance above the ground or obstructions. As long as the pilot flies above this safety altitude, CFIT is not a threat. Calculation of safety altitude (also known as MSA - *Minimum Safety Altitude*) takes only a few minutes before flight, but could add many years to your life - if you know what I mean.

Calculation of safety altitude/MSA is done after the intended route has been drawn on the chart. Check an area of at least 5 nm each side of track, and around the destination for the highest point - either the ground itself or an obstruction.

If the highest point is terrain, add 300ft (to allow for obstructions not marked on the map) and then add a further 1000ft safety margin. Round up the figure to the next 100ft and you have the safety altitude; i.e. highest ground 745ft, add 300ft (745 + 300 = 1045), add 1000ft (1045 + 1000 = 2045) and round up to the nearest 100ft = **2100ft.** If the highest point is an obstruction, there is obviously no need to add the 300ft margin; but otherwise the process is the same i.e. the highest obstruction = 810ft; add 1000ft (810 + 1000 = 1810) and round up to the nearest 100ft; **1900ft.**

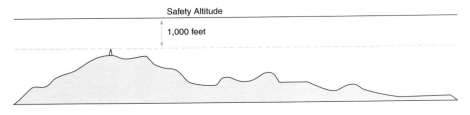

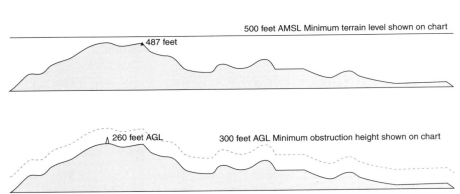

Safety Altitude or MSA is usually no lower than 1000ft above terrain or obstructions.

In the case of UK 1:500,000 charts, terrain is shaded once it is higher than 500ft AMSL and obstructions are portrayed once they are higher than 300ft AGL. The importance of this is that, in theory, it is possible to find a hill reaching 499ft, topped by an obstruction of 299ft (making a point 798ft above sea level), which will not show on the chart. Therefore the safety altitude should never be lower than 1800ft in the UK.

The chart may also show a safety altitude figure or maximum elevation figure. Check the chart key to be sure you understand how this figure has been calculated and what it represents.

In flight, always be aware of the safety altitude/MSA for the part of the route you are flying. Remember that , if you fly below the safety altitude, you are eroding your safety margin if the weather conditions are such that you have difficulty visually assessing terrain and obstructions. Do be especially aware if you are forced to descend below safety altitude by lowering cloud and worsening weather. This would be a good time to turn back or divert.

Quite simply, CFIT occurs when pilots descend below the safety altitude/MSA without good sight of the ground. To avoid ending your flight in this way, do not descend below the safety altitude/MSA unless you have clear sight of the ground ahead.

►Chart Preparation

The routing for your flight is drawn on your chart and then measured for distance and direction. Your instructor may recommend ancillary markings on your chart to aid your en-route flying.

Flight Planning

Drift lines may be drawn at 5° and 10° angles from each turning point and into each turning point. These will help you estimate any off-track error in flight.

Distance or time marks may also be used to aid en-route navigation. Typically marks may be made at one-quarter, half and three-quarter distance; or at set time intervals (say every six minutes). To calculate the time marks you will already have worked out your ground speed so that you can convert the time interval into a distance.

When folding the chart before flight, ensure that it will open up easily along the route of the flight. This avoids the difficult and unprofessional chore of trying to open up and refold your chart, whilst trying to fly the aeroplane, when you realise that the next bit of your route is folded away!

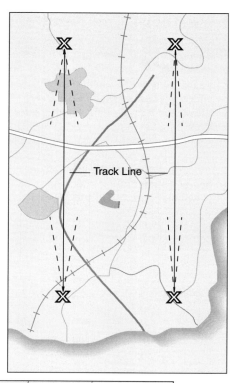

Drift lines may be drawn from the departure and destination points at 5° or 10°.

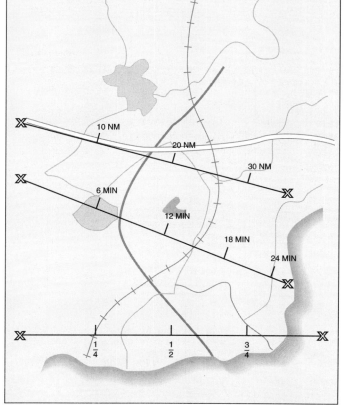

The track line may be marked at set distance intervals, set time intervals or set fractions of the track distance.

Background Briefing

▶ Weather Considerations

The actual and forecast weather will be one of the principal factors deciding if the planned flight will be possible. Weather information may be available in a variety of forms i.e. general meteorological situation charts, area weather reports, TAFs (weather *forecast* for an airfield) and METARs (*ACTUAL* weather at an airfield). Whatever the format of the weather information you are using, remember that the weather forecast must be treated with caution. A weather forecast is an educated guess at the conditions most likely to occur within a specified time period; even professional weather forecasters are the first to admit that forecasts cannot be 100% correct 100% of the time. Never rely completely on a forecast. Always obtain an actual weather report - such as a METAR - in addition to the forecast to confirm what weather **actually** is and if it is in accordance with the forecast.

Ensure that you are using the most recent weather information available and that it covers the whole route you will be flying and possible diversion airfields.

```
22/05/1994   07:19
(C) Forecasts for E1 UK MAIN
=================================================================================

FCIE31 EIDB 220600
EIDW 0716 01007KT 9999 SCT020 BKN040 TEMPO 0716 7000 BKN010 OVC020=
EINN 0716 VRB05KT 9999 SCT025 BKN050=
EICK 0716  01007KT 9999 SCT025 BKN040=

FCUK31 EGGY 220600
EGLL 0716 24006KT 7000 SCT007 BKN012 TEMPO 0710 5000 -RA BKN007
          PROB30 TEMPO 0708 BKN005 BECMG 0811 9999 BKN020 PROB30
          TEMPO 1416 8000 SHRA BKN015=
EGKK 0716 24008KT 6000 BKN007 TEMPO 0709 4000 -RA BKN005 BECMG
          0811 9999 BKN020 PROB30 TEMPO 1416 8000 SHRA BKN014=
EGSS 0716 25010KT 4000 -RA SCT002 OVC004 TEMPO 0709 6000 BKN007
          PROB30 TEMPO 0709 BKN002 BECMG 0912 9999 BKN018 PROB30
          TEMPO 1416 8000 SHRA BKN012=
EGHH 0716 23010KT 9999 SCT007 BKN025 TEMPO 0712 7000 BKN007 PROB40
          TEMPO 1216 8000 SHRA BKN014=
EGPK 0716 05018G30KT 9999 SCT020 SCT035 TEMPO 0709 04012KT=
EGPF 0716 06010KT 9999 SCT015 PROB30 TEMPO 0708 BKN014 BECMG 0709
          06018G28KT=
EGCC 0716 04008KT 9999 SCT015 BKN025 TEMPO 0716 7000 -RA SCT010
          BKN014 PROB30 TEMPO 0716 4000 RA BKN008=
```

Always check ACTUAL as well as FORECAST weather conditions.

```
22/05/1994   07:19
(C) Actuals for E1 UK MAIN
=================================================================================

SAIE31 EIDB 220700
EIDW 01010KT 9999 SCT017 OVC035 09/07 Q1008 TEMPO
     7000  BKN010=
EINN 03005KT 9999 SCT014 09/06 Q1009 NOSIG=
EICK 35005KT CAVOK 09/07 Q1008 NOSIG=

SAUK31 EGGY 220650
EGLL 23006KT 3400 -RA -DZ BKN007 OVC010 12/11 Q1005 TEMPO
     7000 BKN012=
EGKK NIL=
EGSS 25010KT 7000 -RA SCT006 OVC008 10/09 Q1004=
EGHH NIL=
EGPK 04014KT 9999 SCT016 SCT042 BKN100 09/03 Q1011=
EGPF 05007KT 9999 SCT032 BKN045 BKN120 10/00 Q1011 NOSIG=
EGCC 02003KT 9999 -RA OVC010 10/08 Q1004 NOSIG=
EGBB 30005KT 3400 OVC004 10/09 Q1004 BECMG 6000 BKN007=
EGAA 07013KT 9999 -RA SCT028 BKN040 08/04 Q1011=
EGPH 08011KT 040V120 9999 SCT016 BKN100 BKN250 09/03 Q1012 NOSIG=
```

▶ Daylight

The flight will have to be safely completed before nightfall because night flying requires specific training, experience and ratings. During your training you should always plan to complete the flight at least one hour before the end of daylight. Even once you are qualified, your licence does not permit flight after nightfall unless you have successfully completed a course of night flying. Sunset (and sunrise) tables are available from a variety of sources. Night is generally taken to start half an hour after sunset, although in poor weather conditions darkness may fall well before that. You should also be aware that nightfall occurs at the surface before it occurs at altitude. At high altitude, an aircraft may remain in daylight for sometime after dusk at the surface.

	JAN		FEB		MAR		APR		MAY		JUN		JUL		AUG		SEP	
	1	15	1	15	1	15	1	15	1	15	1	15	1	15	1	15	1	15
15																		
ABERDEEN																		
SR	0847	0837	0808	0737	0703	0626	0539	0501	0420	0350	0323	0312	0318	0335	0406	0434	0509	0538	06⁻
SS	1536	1553	1635	1708	1740	1810	1846	1917	1951	2020	2041	2104	2105	2052	2022	1949	1905	1827	17⁴
BELFAST																		
SR	0848	0840	0817	0749	0715	0640	0557	0523	0446	0419	0356	0348	0353	0408	0435	0501	0532	0557	06ʑ
SS	1608	1629	1701	1730	1801	1829	1902	1929	1959	2024	2051	2103	2104	2053	2026	1957	1917	1842	18(

Check the sunset times at your planned destination.

▶ Completion of the Flight Log

Using a flight computer, complete the relevant sections of the flight log. Always make a mental check of the information you are putting into the flight log, i.e. does the direction look about right, is the planned heading into wind compared to the track (drift is seldom more than 15°)? Does the time for each leg seem sensible given the distance and groundspeed? As a rule of thumb, 60 knots ground speed means covering 1 nautical mile a minute; 90 knots, 1½ nautical miles a minute; and 120 knots, 2 nautical miles a minute.

▶ Fuel Planning

Always complete a fuel plan.

Check the source of the fuel consumption figure you are using. If the figure comes from the aircraft's POH/FM it will be based on a specific mixture leaning procedure. If you are not following this procedure, fuel consumption could be up to 25% more than the figure shown in the POH/FM. Multiply the fuel consumption by the expected flight time to give the

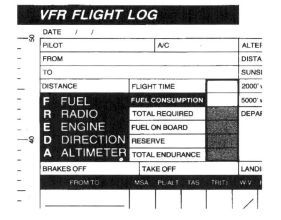

fuel required for the route. The difference between this figure and the usable fuel in the aircraft is your safety margin to allow for increased flight time, diversion, increased fuel consumption etc. You should always plan to complete your flight with at least one hours worth of fuel endurance still in the tanks.

▶Weight and Balance

Now that you know the fuel load and any passengers and/or baggage you will be taking, the weight and balance check can be carried out, you must use the documents for the specific aircraft you will be flying.

The weight and the centre-of-gravity position must be within the specified limitations before continuing your planning. If it is not, you will have to decide which items of disposable load (i.e. passengers, baggage, excess fuel) to leave behind.

▶Take-off and Landing Performance

Knowing the planned take-off and landing weight and the weather at your departure and destination airfields, you should consider whether it is necessary to calculate the take-off distance required or landing distance required. If in any doubt, do the calculation; five minutes spent now could save much trouble later.

The graphs/tables for the performance calculations will be found in the POH/FM for the specific aircraft you will be flying. The official source of information for airfield data (e.g. runway lengths, runway surface etc) is the AIP (Aeronautical Information Publication).

▶Alternate Airfields

Your intended destination airfield may become unavailable for any number of reasons (bad weather, runway blockage, unexpected change in operating hours etc.) and in the event of this happening you should have an alternative airfield already considered.

The alternate airfield should be one that you could reasonably use. There is no point planning to divert to an airfield that may not be available or whose runway, for instance, is shorter than the take-off or landing distance you require.

▶Radio Frequencies

The official source of information for radio frequencies is the AIP, although some radio frequencies are also noted on charts and in commercially produced flight guides. Make sure the station you are planning to call will be open. Military airfields are often closed at weekends; conversely, some smaller civilian airfields are closed during the week.

▶NOTAMS and Pre-Flight Bulletins

Aeronautical information can (and does) often change at short notice, with serious implications for the safety of your flight. Check the latest NOTAMS and pre-flight bulletins for information that may be relevant to the airfield and route that you will be using. Don't forget to check the alternate!

```
A2            Prepared at AFTN Date/Time: 20 MAY 0001 1994 by AIS    PAGE   1
--------------------------------------------------------------------------
|BRITISH ISLES:        SELECTED AERODROMES LONDON FIR.      |   BULLETIN A2  |
|---------------------------------------------------------------|            |
| Read in conjunction with Bulletin A1.                    |            |
|---------------------------------------------------------------------------|
| EGBB CC GW HH KK LC LL MC MH/UM SS                               |
--------------------------------------------------------------------------
EGBB (BHX)          BIRMINGHAM               N5227 W0145           FIR-EGTT

PROCS        Wef 26 MAY. Control area & zone. Various procs changed. Amdt
             8/94 refers. (P14JUN)

PROCS        Wef 26 MAY. STARs OLV 1C & 1D introduced. Amdt 8/94 refers
             (P14JUN)

PROCS        Wef 26 MAY. Holding and apch to land procs amended. Amdt 8/94
             refers. (P14JUN)

PROCS        Wef 26 MAY. SID Daventry 1F introduced. Amdt 8/94 refers.
             (P14JUN)

PROCS        Wef 26 MAY. Lichfield/Whitegate SIDs, Level acceleration
             requirement withdrawn. Amdt 8/94 refers. (P14JUN)

PROCS        Wef 26 MAY. Trent SIDs, 1G added, Level acceleration requirement
             withdrawn. Amdt 8/94 refers. (P14JUN)

PROCS        Wef 26 MAY. Visual Circuits for RWY 33. Amdt 8/94 refers.
             (P14JUN)

PROCS        Wef 26 MAY 0001 Ref AIRAC AIP Amd 8/94 (Cycle 6) RAC 3-5-5-5
             (26 MAY 94) STAR via CHASE. Amend Honiley definition rdl against
             CHASE hold to read HON R334 instead of 344 (C388/94)

'TST' NDB    operating posn 285deg/300m ARP freq 433khz. (C448/94)

RADAR        Watchman 10cm primary radar u/s (C451/94)

RWY 15/33    RWY 15 stop end, RWY 33 touchdown u/s (C442/94)

'BIR' LOC    WEF 26 MAY. Introduced freq 433 khz. Locs 'GM'  & 'GX' withdrawn
             Amdt 8/94 refers (P14JUN)
```

Check NOTAMS and pre-flight bulletins for anything that may affect your flight.

▶ Aircraft Documentation

Certain documentation relating to the aircraft must exist and be valid for the flight to be legal. Although you can go to the extreme of checking all the aircraft documentation before each flight, the two most important documents are probably the C of A and the C of M R. The Certificate of Airworthiness (C of A) must be valid to cover the period of your flight. There must also be a valid Certificate of Maintenance Review (C of M R); check the hours flown since the last maintenance check and the certificate expiry date.

▶ Flight Notification

Complete the aircraft's technical log giving details of the intended flight and obtain an instructor's authorisation for the flight.

'Booking out' for the flight is normally done at this stage directly onto the airfield movement record, or by telephone to ATC/ATSU. Unless you know otherwise, do not assume you can book out over the radio, many ATC/ATSU will not accept flight details over the radio.

Consider whether it will be necessary to file a flight plan for your flight. If so, remember that the flight plan must be filed at least one hour before taxiing.

▶ And Finally...

Before you get into the aircraft run through a brief mental check:

Think through the 'I'm Safe' checklist (exercise 2)

Have you checked the performance and C of G ?

Are you happy with the flight planning - particularly with regard to weather, fuel and daylight remaining?

Was the pre-flight check satisfactory? Did you visually check the fuel and oil contents?

NEVER allow yourself to be pressurised into skipping checks or rushing flight planning in the interests of saving time - you can always fly another day.

In Flight Navigation

If the flight has been properly planned and prepared for, the flying should be easier and all the more enjoyable. The key is to organise your workload and avoid surprises, always thinking one step ahead.

BACKGROUND BRIEFING

▶ **Departure Procedures**

▶ **Principles of Map Reading**

▶ **Maintaining Airspeed, Altitude and Heading**

▶ **Heading Correction**

▶ **ETA Correction**

▶ **Turning-Point Procedure**

▶ **Organising Cockpit Workload**

▶ **Assessing Weather En Route**

▶ **Divert Procedure**

▶ **Lost Procedure**

▶ **Arrival Procedures**

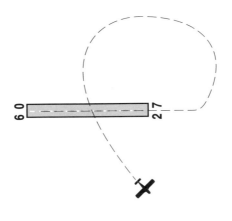

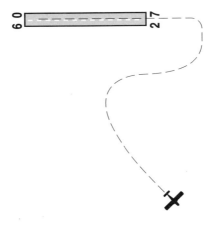

The ideal departure is to set course from overhead the departure airfield. If this is not possible, you may have to set course on leaving the circuit, or at a larger airfield route via a 'Visual Reporting Point' (VRP).

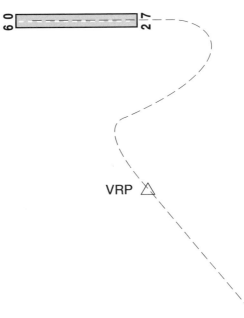

▶ Departure Procedures

Before take-off ensure that your own watch and the aircraft's clock are showing the correct time. If in doubt, ask ATC/ATSU for a time check. When lining up on the runway, check the compass and heading indicator against the runway direction and make a mental note of the required heading after take-off.

The actual departure procedures will vary at different airfields. It may not be possible to climb to the overhead to set heading and you may have to route via a VRP which is not directly on track, although you should have allowed for that during your flight planning.

When you level out at your assigned altitude, run through a 'FREDA' check and note the ETA for the first turning point or destination. Check within the first five minutes or so that you are following the planned track.

▶ Principles of Map Reading

A flight always starts at a known point; when this point is your home airfield, the local landmarks are no doubt well known to you. As the flight progresses, the aim is to be constantly aware of your position by relating the actual landmarks and ground features to their position on the chart. Map reading is not a difficult or complicated procedure. Once practised in the main principles, you will find cross-country flying easier and more enjoyable.

Having started from a known point, review the chart to determine what will be visible outside, assuming the aircraft is following the correct track. Picturing what will be visible and relating the actual view to what is shown on the chart can be broken down into three levels:

- general location

Major topographical features, such as a coastline, a mountain range, or a large city will be visible for quite some time and indicate the general location, e.g. high ground to the West, large city to the West at the base of the hills

- local area

Within the general location, smaller features will define the local area the aircraft is over. Towns, line features (i.e. rivers, canals, railway lines, motorways) woodlands, lakes etc. will all be visible for several minutes at a time and will enable the pilot to confirm the local area he is flying over - e.g. a north/south-orientated motorway, a large woodland area to the south east.

- specific landmark

A specific landmark is used to establish the aircraft's EXACT location. The landmark could be almost any feature, although it makes sense to select one that is both distinct and likely to be visible from some distance away. Possible landmarks include a small town, an airfield, a unique ground feature (castle, stately home), motorway service area etc.

Background Briefing

The critical point to appreciate is that each landmark should have several UNIQUE features so that the pilot can be sure of having identified it correctly. Usually any landmark should have at least THREE unique features, for instance:

Landmark   Netherthorpe Airfield

Feature 1   North/south motorway (with service station) 3 miles to the west

Feature 2   Small town (Worksop) 2 miles to the east

Feature 3   East/west railway line & canal 1/2 mile to north

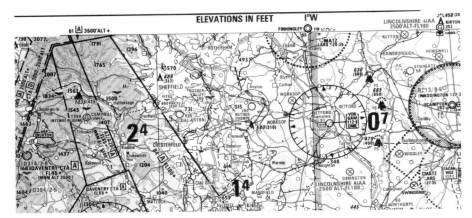

map detail (Netherthorpe).

Map reading is only one task facing you during a cross country flight, and within your priorities (Aviate, Navigate, Communicate) it is secondary to the primary task of flying the aeroplane. To integrate map reading with your other tasks, the best technique is to establish the present position and then look along the track line on the chart to choose a landmark 5-6 minutes flying time ahead. You can then concentrate on flying the aeroplane, maintaining the correct airspeed, altitude and heading whilst looking ahead for the features defining the next chosen landmark. The aircraft is unlikely to stray far from track in the space of 5-6 minutes and this selective approach is preferable to constantly looking at the chart and trying to identify every landmark the aircraft passes.

To establish the correct map reading technique, think 'Time; Map; Ground':

Time   Check the time, where should you be along track?

Map   Select distinctive features on the map to look for.

Ground   Look out for these features.

▶ Maintaining Airspeed, Altitude and Heading

You will soon realise that when flying cross-country that it is very unusual for the track and groundspeed achieved to be grossly different from those calculated during the flight planning. Even if the actual track is 5° different from that required, over a 30-mile leg the aircraft will be no more than 2.5 miles off-course and you should still be able to see enough landmarks to establish position. Likewise, at an average light training-aircraft cruising speed, a difference in ground speed of 10 knots will only make the actual time of arrival at the end of a 30-mile leg about two minutes different from that planned. Gross navigational errors usually occur only if the flight log is incorrectly calculated, if the pilot is not flying the calculated heading or if the heading indicator is not reading correctly. So always stick to the flight log plan unless you have definite proof that a change of heading or ETA is required.

Maintain the desired heading primarily with reference to a distant landmark. This avoids the need to monitor the HI constantly, improves lookout and makes visual navigation easier.

▶ Heading Correction

If, having flown the planned heading, you establish that you are definitely off-track, an alteration of heading is necessary. There are a number of ways of calculating the change in heading required. All of these methods are based on the *1 in 60 rule.* The 1 in 60 rule states that each 1° off-track = 1 nm off track at 60 nm. So, if an aircraft is 3° off track at 60 nm from departure point, it is 3 nm off track; or 1.5 nm off-track at 30 nm from departure point.

1 in 60 Rule

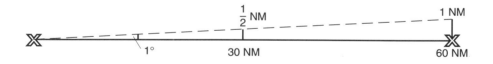

The 1 in 60 rule states that each 1° angle off-track equals 1nm after 60nm.

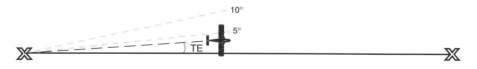

TE = Track Error, about 3° in this case

Track Error (TE) is the angle off-track, measured from the departure point. Drift lines assist in estimating track error.

The number of degrees off-track is known as the *track error* (TE). Once the TE is established, the number of degrees of heading alteration required can be established.

1 Double track error

If you double the track error, and alter your heading by that figure, you should regain track in the same distance as has been travelled so far.

Double Track Error

If the TE is calculated and then the heading altered by double the TE, the aircraft will (theoretically) regain track in the same distance as flown so far

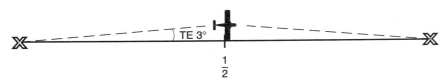

Alter heading by 6°

2 Track error and closing angle

Using fan lines you can estimate the track error (TE) and the closing angle (CA) to the destination. Adding the two figures together will give the total heading correction to fly directly to the destination.

By estimating Track Error (from the departure point) and Closing Angle (to the destination); and adding them together, the required change in heading to reach the destination can be calculated.

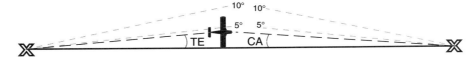

TE = Track Error — in this case about 3°
CA = Closing Angle — in this case about 2°

TE + CA = Heading Correction (3° + 2° = 5°)

3 Using distance markers

If your track is marked with distance marks, you can use these to calculate the heading change to fly directly to the destination. Estimate the track error (TE), and multiply it by the factor to give the total heading change required.

one-quarter distance   TE x 1.5

one- half distance,   TE x 2

three-quarters distance TE x 3

e.g. 5° off at three-quarters distance, TE x 3 = 15° heading change.

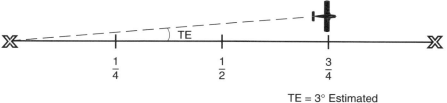

TE = 3° Estimated
3° x 3° = 9° Heading Correction

Using distance markers, TE can be factored to give the heading alteration necessary to reach the destination.

On your flight log, make a note of the position and time of your heading change and the new heading to be flown.

▶ ETA Correction

If you are using distance markers, the halfway point is a good place to check time elapsed so far, because it should take as long again to reach the destination. If you are using time markers, it should be evident whether you are going to be significantly early or late on the ETA as you pass each point.

12 minutes to here (elapsed time)
therefore total leg time (Estimated) 24 minutes.

By checking the time elapsed at a known point, the ETA can be checked and revised.

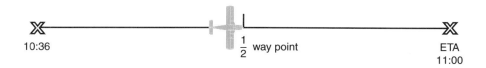

10:36

$\frac{1}{2}$ way point

ETA
11:00

Time is the forgotten element of cross-country flying and VFR navigation. All too often pilots make the mistake of incorrectly identifying a landmark they could not possibly have reached yet, or one almost certain to have been passed some time ago. This is a principal reason for using the Time; Map; Ground technique. This maintains your awareness of where you should expect to be. Avoid the temptation to refer continually to the features on the ground and trying to fit them into a position on the chart. It is easy to convince yourself that you are well off-course when, in fact, the flight is proceeding according to plan.

As already discussed, even a significant difference between calculated and actual groundspeed will only alter the time the aircraft passes a landmark by a minute or two. If it is necessary to alter the ETA, note the change of ETA in the flight log.

▶ Turning Point Procedure

As you arrive at an en-route turning point, execute the four Ts:

Time make a note of the actual time of arrival (ATA) in the flight log

Turn turn onto your new heading. Look for a significant landmark to confirm the direction is correct

Talk if applicable, report your position

Task from your ATA, calculate your ETA for the next point

▶ Organising Cockpit Workload

The key to good VFR navigation, and for that matter good flying in general, is time management–time IS elastic !

Sometimes during a flight the pilot may make mistakes because he feels there is not enough time to carry out all the necessary tasks. Workload suddenly seems to pile up and the pilot is all too aware that he is mentally behind the aeroplane - not a satisfactory state of affairs.

The answer is simple. Manage your time - in effect, stretch time by thinking ahead. This is precisely what professional pilots do and why they always appear to be in control. Knowing where they are and what is happening at that moment, they look ahead five or ten minutes to where they will be then and what will be happening ahead. This means they can plan actions and anticipate problems well before these actions are needed or the problem arises. The calm atmosphere of a professional flight crew is due to the crew using their judgement and experience to think ahead. In another context this awareness, preparation and anticipation is known as 'Situational Awareness'.

There are some simple pointers to put you in this frame of mind.

1	**Organise your priorities**	they remain, as ever, Aviate; Navigate; Communicate; in that order
2	**Navigate ahead**	so, you know your exact location now. Look along the track on your map and decide what will be the next significant landmark, when do you expect to see it, what will it look like ?
3	**Carry out checks**	the FREDA check, in particular, will save a lot of time and trouble. In checking each item, think ahead:

ITEM	CHECK	THINK AHEAD
FUEL	Sufficient and in balance	What is my endurance from now? Will the safety margin be sufficient? Is there enough to divert or hold?
RADIO	Frequency in use	What will be the next station I call? Have I noted the frequency? When do I expect to change? What is the next report required?
ENGINE	T's and P's mixture, carb heat, suction and ammeter	If changing power, will the mixture need to be altered? If there is evidence of carb icing, when will I next check?
DIRECTION	Is the correct heading being flown? Is the HI aligned with the compass?	If approaching a turning point, what will be the next heading? What landmark am I using to maintain heading?
ALTITUDE	Is the correct level being flown? Is the correct pressure setting being used?	Will a new setting be needed soon? Will I be climbing or descending soon? If flying in accordance with the quadrantal rule, will a change of level be necessary after the next turning point? If using a regional pressure setting, will it change on the hour? What is the safety altitude?

4   **What if?...**   A good question for quiet moments when everything else has been checked. What if the weather gets worse; will I need to divert? What if the radio fails? What if I have an engine problem? What would I do?

You do not need to be clairvoyant to think ahead, and you should not allow the 'what if ?…' process to get you unnecessarily worried. Instead you should start feeling more relaxed and confident, and you may be surprised at how much more time you seem to have to enjoy your flying.

▶ Assessing Weather En Route

Although you would not have started the flight if the actual and forecast weather were not suitable, the en-route weather can deteriorate and there is no point complaining that it was not in the forecast. The destination airfield may have an ATIS (Automatic Terminal Information Service) frequency or be on the VOLMET service (a spoken list of airfield METARs), so that you can make an early check of weather conditions there. Never attempt to 'press on' in conditions that you are not happy with, such as a lowering cloud base forcing you below safety altitude; reduced visibility making visual navigation difficult, or rain or snow obscuring the way ahead. Make an early decision to turn back to the departure airfield or to divert to another airfield. If turning back on a reciprocal track, remember that the wind will be coming from the other side of heading, while a tail wind will turn into a head wind and vice versa.

▶ Divert Procedure

Should a diversion become necessary, an early decision will reduce your workload and–in the case of deteriorating weather–enable you to divert in weather conditions which are still reasonable.

1   Aim to divert from a known point, i.e. a positively identified landmark.

2   Draw a track line to the diversion. Estimate the direction and heading required (remember to allow for magnetic variation and wind).

3   Note the time as you turn on to the diversion heading. Map-read to confirm you are following track.

4   Calculate ETA at the diversion destination.

5   Inform ATC/ATSU of your intentions.

6   Continue navigation as usual. Expect to have to alter heading or ETA.

▶ Lost Procedure

It is said that there are two kinds of pilots; those who have been lost and those who will be! There is quite a difference between being lost and being temporarily uncertain of position. Being uncertain of position may happen, for instance, when flying over featureless terrain where good landmarks may be 10 - 20 minutes apart. In between such landmarks you can estimate your probable location, but this is just an educated guess until the next landmark is identified. If you have been uncertain of your position for more than 20 - 30 minutes, you should consider yourself lost.

Sometimes you can ascertain from the general topography the probable general location and then identify local-area ground features to pinpoint the exact position. Beware though, of making the ground features fit into the picture you are looking for. It is easy to persuade yourself that an ordinary road is actually a motorway, or that a small lake is really a large reservoir.

Most pilots will know when they are really lost, and in this case action must be taken to identify position. Above all - stay calm and act logically. Being lost is not an emergency in itself and there is usually no reason why you should not be able to locate your actual position before too long. Take heart; military pilots have a saying, "You've never been really lost until you're lost at Mach 2!"

In-flight Navigation

1 Assess your situation. What is your remaining fuel endurance? How much daylight is left? Are you flying at a safe height - what is the safety altitude? Would slow safe cruise be appropriate? Make a note of the time.

2 Why are you lost? Did you incorrectly fix your position earlier? Check the heading indicator against the compass. Could a metallic object near the compass be affecting the reading? Has the planned heading been flown (it is possible to confuse 300°, 330° and 030° especially)? Does the planned heading and ETA look sensible? Have you been flying the correct heading for this part of the route?

3 Use the radio. There is no reason to remain lost for long if you are able to contact an ATC/ATSU station. Transmit on the frequency you have been using and tell them you are lost. Use a PAN call if necessary. The use of a transponder will speed up the location process. It may be necessary to change frequency to contact a radar unit. If all else fails, transmit on the emergency frequency - 121.5MHz Follow the instructions you receive, but remain in visual flying conditions.

4 If, for some reason, you are unable to make radio contact, climb if possible to increase radio range. If still not successful, transmit blind and consider using the radio-failure transponder code (7600).

5 If you have to establish your position without outside help, draw a circle of uncertainty. This is done by estimating your position (based on time since last positive position fix, the distance that will have been flown in that time and the direction flown) and then drawing a circle around it, whose radius is 10% of the distance since the last known position fix.

Last known position

Radius of circle
10% of
line length

A circle of uncertainty is drawn by calculating the direction and distance flown since the last positive fix, and drawing a circle at the end of this line whose radius is 10% of the line length.

Now read from ground to map, looking for prominent landmarks and features that can be related to a position inside the circle of uncertainty. If you are still unable to locate your position, consider following a line feature. For example railway lines normally run into towns.

Periodically re-assess your situation, especially with regard to fuel and daylight remaining. If you do not see an airfield during your search, consider making a precautionary landing in a suitable field before the situation becomes critical.

▶ Arrival Procedures

When arriving at a destination airfield, be sure to identify it positively before finally putting away your chart. An airfield guide will help in identifying the airfield.

You should know whether to expect an overhead join or some other specific arrival procedure, so position the aircraft accordingly as you complete a final FREDA check. Integrate with the existing circuit traffic, and after landing follow any specific taxi instructions. Here, again, an airfield guide will help you navigate on the ground - but if in doubt ask for assistance.

If you are landing at your home base, you will already know the booking-in and technical-log completion procedure. At a strange airfield, look for the 'C'; a black C inside a yellow box. This is the point for visiting pilots to book in, check weather etc. If you filed a flight plan for your flight, ensure that the flight plan has been closed. If you have had to divert, your specified destination must be informed within 30 minutes of your ETA there. This action, ensuring that your flight plan has been closed, is most important because otherwise expensive and unnecessary search and rescue action could be started.

Book in where the black 'C' is displayed.

Decide whether it is necessary to refuel; do not neglect to refuel just because of time pressure. When the aircraft is being refuelled, be present to supervise. Make sure you get the correct amount of fuel in the correct tanks, and know the location of the nearest fire extinguisher. Above all, be sure you are actually getting the correct fuel. It is not unknown for piston-engine aircraft requiring AVGAS to be refuelled with JET-A1 or AVTUR. It may sound excessive to say "don't trust anybody else when it comes to fuel"; but remember this. Putting in the wrong fuel or not enough of it might be someone else's mistake, but it will be you–the pilot–who is faced with the consequences.

Refuelling points on the aircraft and the fuel pumps should display a distinctive sticker showing the fuel type and grade.

▶ VDF - VHF Direction Finding

Availability

The COM section of the AIP lists communication frequencies for the stations you will need to contact and indicates those which have a VDF facility. VDF frequencies may also be noted on the chart. Controllers sometimes refer to VDF by the shorthand of 'DF'. The specified VDF frequency may not be the same as the usual approach frequency, and you may have to make initial contact on the usual contact frequency to request a frequency change to use the VDF service.

ATC liaison

The most common use of the VDF service is to request a QDM - the magnetic track to an airfield. It is important to request your QDM in plenty of time because it may be necessary for the controller to set-up the VDF equipment. When ready, the controller will ask you to transmit for VDF. The normal procedure is to transmit with your callsign, request for a QDM and a count to five, to give the controller plenty of time to obtain a reading. The VDF reading will be passed to you together with its classification which indicates the maximum possible error in the bearing:

Class A	± 2°
Class B	± 5°
Class C	± 10°
Class D	more than 10°

Homing

Once a QDM has been obtained, that heading can be flown (allowing for wind drift) and the aircraft should track towards the airfield. The pilot should recheck the QDM every five minutes. If the QDM changes, the aircraft has drifted from the direct track. When flying towards a station: QDM more, steer more (increase heading); QDM less, steer less (reduce heading).

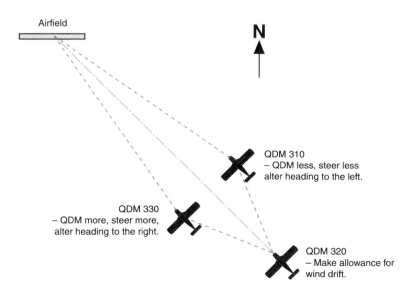

Airfield

N

QDM 310
– QDM less, steer less
alter heading to the left.

QDM 330
– QDM more, steer more,
alter heading to the right.

QDM 320
– Make allowance for
wind drift.

The use of VHF direction-finding to track towards an airfield.

▶ Radar Services

Availability

The COM section in the AIP will specify a station offering a radar service using the callsign 'Radar' or' Approach'. In addition, the RAC section contains details of other stations offering a radar service, such as the UK Lower Airspace Radar Service (LARS).

▶ Primary Radar

Principles and Limitations

Radar works by emitting a radio pulse from an antenna and measuring its return. The time taken for the pulse to travel out to an object and be reflected back to the antenna allows the distance of the object to be calculated, as radio waves travel at a known speed - the speed of light. The direction of the antenna when the pulse is received gives the direction of the object.

This information is displayed on a screen, and is known as 'primary' radar. Primary radar operates at high radio frequencies and so, like VHF, it follows the 'line of sight' principle. If an object is over the horizon, or very close to the ground, it may not be visible to primary radar.

To the uninitiated the primary radar screen does look very cluttered. As well as aircraft, the radar screen may be showing ground reflections, weather clutter (e.g. heavy showers) atmospheric blips etc.. The controller will offer a radar service if satisfied that he will have no problem in tracking the primary return that represents your aircraft. Occasionally, radar contact may be lost for a short period; for example if there is a heavy shower between the radar and the aircraft, or if the aircraft passes directly overhead the radar station.

ATC liaison

To use a radar service, make a specific request for a specific service. Never assume you are receiving a radar service until the controller has confirmed that to you. The two principal radar services are:

Radar Information Service (RIS) - the controller passes details of any other traffic and the pilot decides on avoiding action.

Radar Advisory Service (RAS) - the controller passes details of other traffic and gives avoidance advice. If you choose not to take this advice, you must inform the controller.

When using these services the pilot remains responsible for terrain clearance, remaining in VMC and navigation. Occasionally a radar controller may advise a number of heading changes for traffic avoidance. The pilot should maintain visual navigation during these heading changes. If the controller uses the phrase "Resume your own navigation" make sure you are confident that you know your present location. If in doubt, ask the controller to confirm your position:

If in doubt - Shout

▶The Transponder

Availability

The ground-based system needed to pick up transponder signals is known as *Secondary Surveillance Radar (SSR)* and is not available at all radar units. However, most of the larger civil and military airports have SSR equipment.

Principles and Limitations

The ground-based SSR transmits a radio pulse which interrogates the transponder in the aircraft. The transponder then transmits a series of radio pulses back to the SSR, whose sequence is the function of the four figure code set on the transponder.

On the controller's radar screen the four figure code appears next to the aircraft's primary return enabling the controller to identify the aircraft easily.

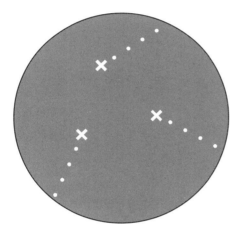

Primary radar returns as they appear on a controller's radar screen.

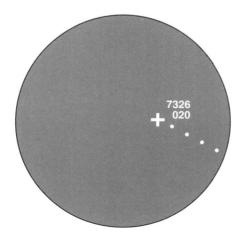

SSR as it appears on a controller's radar screen. The code is displayed next to the primary return, with the flight level read out underneath - in this case FL020.

For various reasons, controllers can often see an SSR return on their screen even if primary radar is unable to detect the aircraft.

The aircraft transponder may be equipped with Mode C–flight level readout–which is marked as 'ALT' on the selector switch. When Mode C is selected, the aircraft's flight level is displayed on the controller's SSR readout. It is usual for the pilot to select Mode C at all times if the transponder is so equipped.

When selecting a code or changing between codes, the transponder should be set to 'standby'. This is because it is possible to dial through an emergency code and if the transponder is 'on' ATC alarms will be activated.

A typical transponder unit. The four-figure code is selected using the dial under each window. The "Ident" button is usually under the ident light - which illuminates when the transponder is interrogated by ground based SSR. The selector switch usually has five positions:

OFF - self explanatory

SBY - Standby. The unit is not transmitting a signal. This mode should always be selected when changing a code

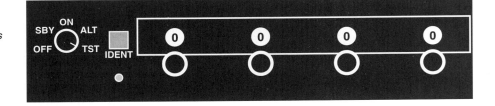

ON - The transponder is transmitting to any SSR which interrogates it.

ALT - Mode C. The transponder transmits the aircraft's Flight Level

TST - Test mode. Usually selected with '0000' code set. The ident light should illuminate.

The code '7326' set on the transponder, in this case with Mode C selected.

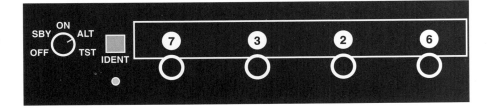

Some of the standard phraseology used in reference to transponder operation is listed below.

Controller request	Pilot action
Squawk standby	Set the transponder to the 'standby' position.
Recycle squawk	Set the transponder to 'standby', check that the correct code is selected set the transponder to 'on' again.
Squawk ident	Press the transponder 'ident' button. This causes the code displayed on the controller's radar screen to highlight and flash, remaining highlighted for several seconds.

The transponder is a particularly useful piece of equipment if you become lost or if you have some other emergency. If ATC know that your aircraft is transponder-equipped, you can usually be located in less than a minute.

▶ Standard and Emergency Codes

The most frequently used transponder code is the *conspicuity code* - 7000. This code can be used when outside controlled airspace and if no other code has been allocated to you. Select Mode C ('Alt') if this is available on the transponder. Remember to set the transponder to 'standby' before entering controlled airspace, if no other code has been allocated to you.

There are three possible emergency codes. When these are used, alarms will go off at all receiving stations and you are guaranteed instant attention. Only set an emergency code if you require assistance, but do not hesitate to use an emergency code in a real emergency.

> 7700 - Emergency (i.e. Mayday situation)
>
> 7600 - Communications failure
>
> 7500 - Unlawful interference (i.e. hijack)

Supplement 2 - Lookout

Before starting this supplement, revise the lookout supplements at exercise 6 and exercise 12/13.

By now you are well advanced towards gaining your Private Pilot's Licence and you should have developed the good lookout habits that will serve you well in all your future flying.

Make sure you are applying the specific steps outlined in the previous lookout supplements. With regard to cross-country navigation, there are a few additional steps you can take to improve your lookout and avoid a near miss or collision.

1 Follow standard procedures

In most near misses, at least one aircraft was not where it was meant to be. In cruising flight select a sensible cruising level - why fly at 2500ft QNH if there is a flight level available above the transition level? If flying at a flight level use, the quadrantal rule.

2 Avoid crowds

Aircraft tend to congregate around certain points - radio beacons, Visual Reporting Points etc. Review your route to see whether flying over such a point is really necessary. Aircraft also congregate over airfields so be especially vigilant there. Below 1000ft AGL the mix of military fast jets, helicopters, microlights etc can make for a dangerous cocktail. Check NOTAMs and pre-flight bulletins for details of air displays, rallies, military exercises and other events you will want to avoid if not participating.

3 Use the radio

Talk to any station that may be able to provide traffic information. Even if they do not want to talk to you for some reason, listening out on the frequency will provide you with local traffic information. Use the transponder if your aircraft is so equipped.

4 Organise yourself

Through proper preflight planning and organising your cockpit workload, you allow yourself more time to lookout. Isn't that what you would rather be doing anyway?

5 Keep scanning!

A good lookout is your best aid to spotting traffic and avoiding a near miss or collision. A proper, disciplined lookout scan gives you a four-times better chance of spotting conflicting traffic.

Instrument Flying

The licence for which you are training - the PPL - enables you to fly an aircraft in visual weather conditions. The skills needed to fly without visual reference (i.e. in cloud, in poor visibility or at night) are learnt in separate courses and the pilot must attain further licences and ratings before being allowed to fly in such conditions.

Nevertheless, the PPL course does touch upon instrument flying so that you can appreciate the techniques and skills involved and also so that should you inadvertently fly into cloud or an area of poor visibility, you will be able to control the aircraft whilst turning out of the area. It is of course much better airmanship to avoid such situations altogether, because there are many factors or skills related to instrument flight not covered in this brief introduction to instrument flying. Instrument flying requires constant practice to stay proficient, more so than almost any other flying skill. Should you deliberately enter cloud, perhaps years after last practising instrument flying, there is a very good chance that you will lose control of the aircraft. ***Don't do it.*** A study made a few years ago showed that upon entering cloud, a pilot without instrument training lost control of the aircraft on average in less than three minutes.

Having said all that, the basics of instrument flying are not difficult to master and there may be times when—even in quite good visibility—the lack of a clear horizon makes increased use of the instruments necessary.

BACKGROUND BRIEFING

▶ **Physiological Considerations**

▶ **Instrument Interpretation - the Attitude Indicator**

▶ **Power + Attitude = Performance**

▶ **Selective Radial Scan**

▶ **Unusual Attitudes**

▶ **Deliberate Flight Into Instrument-Flying Conditions**

FLIGHT EXERCISE

Exercise

19

Instrument Flying

FLIGHT EXERCISE

▷ **Purpose**

▷ **Airmanship**

▷ **Maintaining Level Flight**

▷ **The Climb**

▷ **The Cruise Descent**

▷ **The Turn**

▷ **Unusual Attitudes - the approach to the stall**

▷ **Unusual Attitudes - the spiral dive**

CONCLUSION

Instrument Flying

Background Briefing

▶ Physiological Considerations

Instrument flying is merely an extension of visual flying. The basic flying techniques are the same and the aircraft reacts in the same way to the same control movements. However, without outside reference the pilot has to work harder to interpret the information from the instruments in front of him and form a mental picture of the aircraft's position and attitude.

The balance mechanism of the inner ear (the *vestibular apparatus*) sends a constant stream of information to the brain. Even with your eyes closed, you know if you are standing, lying down, at an angle etc. When moving in three axes (e.g. when flying) signals from the inner ear can conflict with what is actually seen to be happening–for instance, in a properly balanced turn there is usually no sensation of turning. During visual flight this is not a problem; since the information from the eyes is obviously correct, the brain overrules the balance sensation.

During instrument flying, with no external reference, the situation is not so clear-cut. The instruments have to be interpreted to build the mental picture of the aircraft's attitude. When this information conflicts with the balance information from the inner ear, a million years of evolution are pitted against a few hours of training. When flying with your instructor he may ask you to close your eyes and then state what the aircraft is doing. Alternatively, he may ask you to try to fly the aircraft without external reference and without reference to the instruments. The end result of either experiment is a sobering reminder of the fallibility of the inner-ear mechanism when flying. When the brain is unable to resolve the conflict between the balance sense and instrument readings, spatial disorientation can occur and it is quite possible to lose control of a perfectly serviceable aircraft–usually in a spiral dive.

During the instrument flying exercise, you will first learn how to interpret the instruments and then how to trust the instruments so that the mental picture you build up from their indications overrules your balance sense. In practice, once you can quickly interpret the instruments, the rest follows naturally. If you do feel disorientation beginning remember–***BELIEVE YOUR EYES, TRUST THE INSTRUMENTS.***

Although instrument flying needs the same basic flying skills as visual flight, you may find yourself having to go back to some of the basics of flying that you now take for granted; e.g. "Power Attitude Trim" to establish level flight; 'holding off' aileron in a turn; minor corrections and trimming accurately to maintain the desired performance; etc. The level of concentration needed is quite high and it is easy to become tense and tire quickly. In the early stages of this exercise your instructor will get you to take a short break every fifteen minutes or so. While instrument flying, consciously try to relax as much as possible whilst maintaining your concentration–remember that concentration is a mental, not physical act.

All the human factors that might affect your performance when flying visually; namely tiredness, illness, or hunger, will have a greater detrimental effect during instrument flying.

▶Instrument Interpretation - the Attitude Indicator

During your visual flying, you will have become used to the various instrument indications and how they relate to what the aircraft is doing. The one instrument you may not be so familiar with is the Attitude Indicator (A.I.) which is also sometimes known as the 'Artificial Horizon'.

The model aircraft in the A.I. represents the aircraft as seen from behind with the centre dot representing the nose. The horizontal line across the display represents the horizon, and markings around the display relate to angles of bank and pitch. Instrument markings vary slightly between the different types and models. Your instructor will explain the roll markings on the A.I. in the aircraft you are flying. During instrument flying the A.I. is the master instrument (the primary reference) because it is the only instrument displaying both pitch and roll.

Roll is displayed in general terms by the angle of the model aircraft wings to the horizon line and more precisely by the position of the pointer at the outer edge of the instrument. The angle of roll shown on the A.I. relates exactly to the actual angle of bank of the aircraft.

The A.I. also displays pitch above or below an imaginary horizon line. Usually the area above the horizon line is coloured blue to represent sky; the area below the horizon line is coloured brown or black to represent the ground. There may be marks to indicate degrees of pitch-up or pitch-down. In the display of pitch the A.I. is scaled; you will see that even a small change of pitch on the A.I. involves a large pitch change to the aircraft.

This scale effect takes a little getting used to-and it is easy to over-control in pitch at first. The wings of the model aircraft can be referred to as the 'bar' and your instructor may talk of the *bar width* above or below the horizon.

The Attitude Indicator

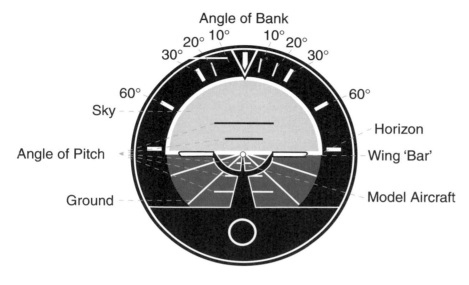

Straight and level flight

The attitude indicator displays the aircraft's pitch and roll attitude.

The Attitude Indicator

Nose-low attitude, 15° angle of bank to the left

Background Briefing

The model aircraft can usually be adjusted up or down and your instructor may adjust the model aircraft for you in visual conditions, but as a general rule, you should never try to adjust the model aircraft when instrument flying.

A level, 15° angle of bank to the right attitude

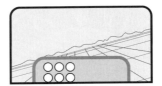

Outside View

The Attitude Indicator

The Cruise-Climb Attitude

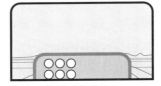

Outside View

The Attitude Indicator

Note that on the attitude indicator, the model aircraft is one 'bar width' above the horizon.

The Cruise Descent Attitude

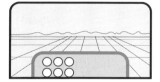

Outside View

The Attitude Indicator

Note that on the attitude indicator, the model
aircraft is one 'bar width' below the horizon.

A nose-low, 15° angle of bank to the left attitude

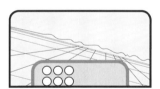

Outside View

The Attitude Indicator

▶ Power + Attitude = Performance

The basic technique of controlling an aircraft still applies when instrument flying. Setting a certain power and selecting the appropriate attitude will dictate performance in terms of climb, descent, level flight and airspeed. Therefore, the A.I. and the RPM gauge are the 'control instruments', you select and maintain the performance required by reference to these two instruments. Additionally the A.I. allows you to control the turning performance of the aircraft.

POWER

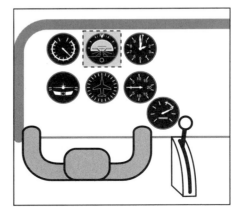

+

ATTITUDE

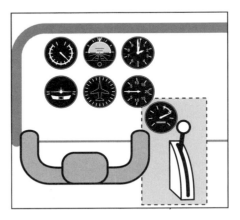

Power + Attitude = Performance.

=

PERFORMANCE

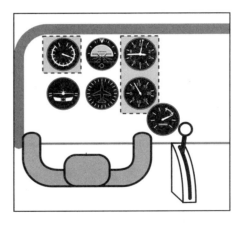

The other flight instruments are the 'performance instruments' which are used to make adjustments and maintain the required aircraft performance. So, whenever changing the aircraft's performance (e.g. from level flight to a climb), the initial change is made with reference to the control instruments, then the performance instruments are checked to make any minor corrections.

▶ Selective Radial Scan

To fly accurately on instruments alone, it is necessary to develop an instrument scan so that you can quickly build up and update a mental picture of what the aircraft is doing. The instrument scan is *radial*–it radiates out from the A.I. and returns back to the A.I. Because the A.I. is the master instrument, always look at it before looking at any other instrument–and after looking at another instrument, look back to the A.I. In other words your scan is always routed through the A.I.

The Attitude Indicator is the master instrument.

The Attitude Indicator is the master instrument.
The instrument scan always routes through the
Attitude Indicator.

The instrument scan is also *selective* –you select which instruments have information relevant to the manoeuvre being flown. For instance, in level flight the A.I., H.I. and ALT. give the pilot the basic information he needs. These three instruments form the 'Primary Scan'. The other flight instruments can be scanned less regularly, say once for every three primary scans. These instruments form the 'Secondary Scan'. Remember that at all times, the scan routes through the A.I. Never look from one instrument to another without checking the A.I.

The Selective Radial Scan
Straight and Level Flight

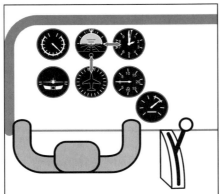

The Primary Scan

The Selective Radial Scan
Straight and Level Flight

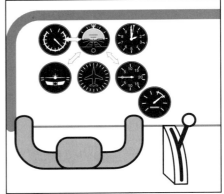

The Secondary Scan

You will find that any distraction away from your scan (i.e. a FREDA check, changing radio frequency, writing down a clearance etc.), distracts from the task of flying the aircraft and it is possible to lose part of the mental picture. Break up your tasks so that you can maintain the instrument scan and remember to keep checking the A.I. - the master instrument.

There is little point in trying to memorise a SRS (Selective Radial Scan) for each manoeuvre or flight phase. Once you understand the principle of the SRS, you should be able to decide on a suitable scan yourself. Practice and experience will enable you to gather all the information you need from the scan, and anticipate how an indicated change in one instrument will affect another instrument. For example a banked attitude should cause a change of heading.

Turns are normally limited to Rate 1, when instrument flying, which is 15° angle of bank at 90 knots airspeed. Descents are normally made as a cruise descent, while the climb can be cruise climb or best rate-of-climb. Small changes of altitude (i.e. less than 100ft) can be corrected by adjusting the attitude only. Larger changes of altitude (i.e. more than 100ft) will require a power adjustment as well.

The Basic 'T'

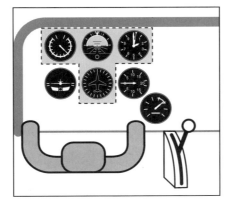

The standard pattern of the flight instruments.

The standard arrangement of the flight instruments is known as the *basic 'T'*. This is used on all modern light aircraft and means that even when flying a different aircraft type, the instrument scan should remain the same.

▶ Unusual Attitudes

As well as practising basic flight manoeuvres on instruments, you must be able to recover from an unusual attitude back to controlled flight solely by reference to the instruments. There are two principal unusual attitudes which may occur; the approach to the stall and the spiral dive.

When you realise that an unusual attitude has developed, you should first check the ASI, to ascertain the airspeed is fast and accelerating, or slow and decelerating. If the airspeed is fast and accelerating, the throttle should be closed. If the airspeed is slow and decelerating, full power should be applied. The aircraft should then be rolled wings-level with the ailerons.Once the wings are level, the elevator is used to pitch the aircraft nose-up or down to the level attitude. As the airspeed returns to normal cruise, power can be returned to the normal cruise setting and normal level flight can be resumed.

In summary:

Check airspeed, then

Power

Bank

Pitch

It is essential to follow this sequence correctly, most especially in the case of the most common unusual attitude–the spiral dive.

In a well–developed spiral dive, the instinctive reaction is to pull back on the control column. However, due to the steep angle of bank, this action will only tighten the turn–increasing the airspeed and the load factor. By continuing this course of action the pilot will probably overstress the aircraft, always provided the aircraft does not hit the ground at high speed first. The correct actions, (Power, Bank, Pitch), properly applied will recover the aircraft to level, controlled flight smoothly and quickly.

▶ Deliberate Flight Into Instrument Flying Conditions

Instrument flying by a pilot without an instrument flying qualification is both *illegal* and *highly dangerous.* Accidents occuring in instrument flying conditions very often involve pilots without instrument flying qualifications, or a pilot not in current instrument-flying practice.

Even if you are qualified to fly in instrument flying conditions, do not consider doing so if you are not in current practice or if some other factor (pilot fatigue, aircraft system failure, lack of pre-flight preparation etc.) is likely to make instrument flying more difficult or less safe.

Flight Exercise

▷ Purpose

To learn to fly basic manoeuvres solely by reference to the instruments and to be able to recover from unusual attitudes solely by reference to the instruments.

▷ Airmanship

Lookout

For once, lookout is not a consideration for you! Your instructor will be responsible for lookout and navigating the aircraft.

Simulated instrument flight

Your instructor may simulate instrument flight using a 'hood' or screens. Alternatively, he may fly the aircraft into actual instrument flying conditions. Remember that as a non-instrument rated pilot you may not practise this exercise, or enter actual instrument flying conditions, when flying solo.

Instrument checks

Before flight, it is all the more important to check the flight instruments—particularly the A.I.—which you may not have checked closely before.

In flight, check that the systems supplying the flight instruments are working properly. In most light aircraft the flight instruments are connected as follows:

Electrical System	**Turn Co-ordinator**
Suction System	**A.I. and H.I.,**
Static System	**Altimeter, V.S.I.**
Pitot and Static System	**A.S.I.**

None of the instruments has a direct failure warning, except the turn co-ordinator which may display a red flag if electrical power is lost. The electrical and suction systems are monitored by their own gauges and warning systems, and the in-flight FREDA checks should cover these items.

There is no warning of a pitot or static failure. However, the pitot heat can be used to prevent the pitot head freezing over and the aircraft may have an alternate static source to use if the primary source ices over or is blocked in some other way.

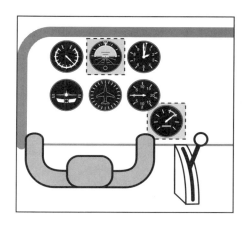

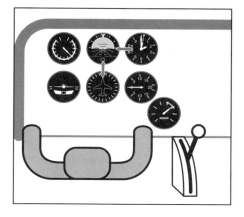

POWER ATTITUDE TRIM
Apply cruising power setting and
select the straight and level attitude
on the attitude indicator.

The primary scan.

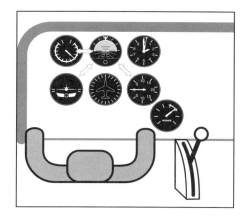

The secondary scan.

The Climb

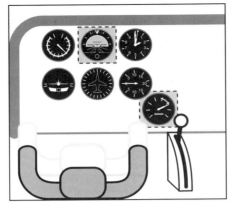

POWER ATTITUDE TRIM
Apply full power, pitch nose-up to the climbing
attitude on the Attitude Indicator.

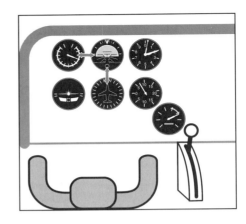

The primary scan.

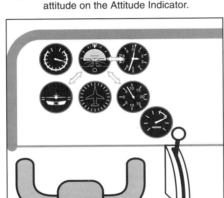

The secondary scan.

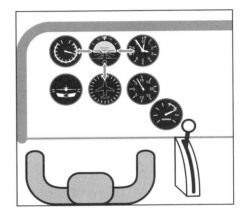

As the aircraft approaches the required level,
include the altimeter in the primary scan.

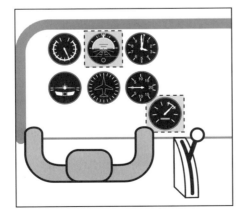

Level off
ATTITUDE
POWER
TRIM

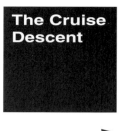

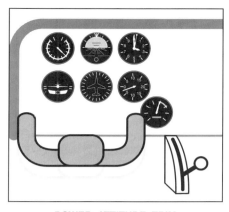

POWER ATTITUDE TRIM
Reduce power, select a shallow nose-down
attitude—about one 'bar width' below the
horizon.

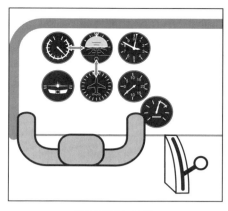

The primary scan.

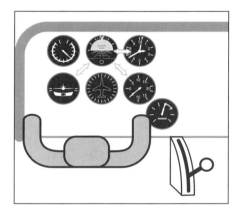

The secondary scan.

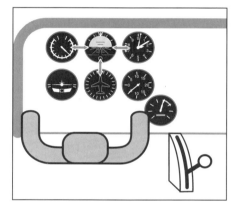

As the aircraft approaches the required level,
include the altimeter in the primary scan.

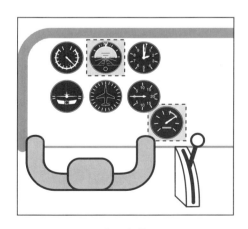

Level off
POWER ATTITUDE TRIM

The Turn

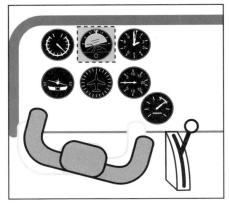

Select the 15° angle-of-bank attitude on the
Attitude Indicator. Increase back-pressure
on the control column slightly.

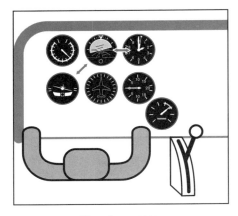

The primary scan.
Note the rate of turn indicated on the turn
co-ordinator.

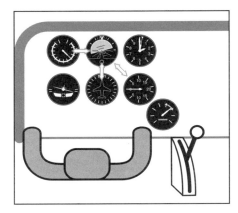

The secondary scan.

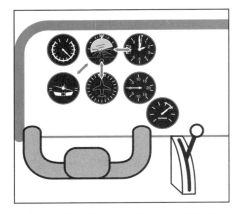

Approaching the required heading, include
the heading indicator in the primary scan.

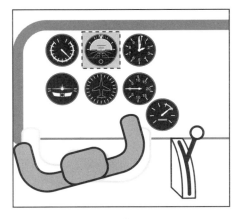

Return to wings-level flight by reference to
the Attitude Indicator.

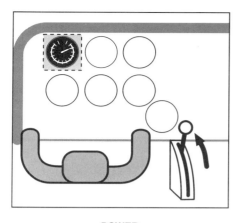

POWER
Check airspeed
Apply full power

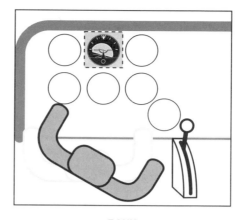

BANK
Check Attitude Indicator
Roll wings level

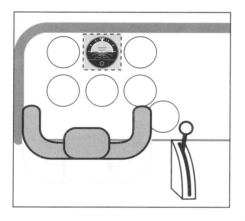

PITCH
Check Attitude Indicator
Pitch to level flight

In summary:
Check Airspeed
POWER
BANK
PITCH

Unusual Attitudes -the spiral dive

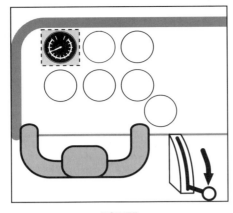

POWER
Check airspeed
Close the throttle

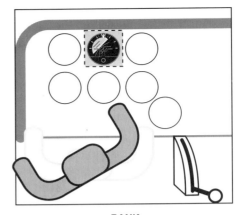

BANK
Check Attitude Indicator
Roll wings-level

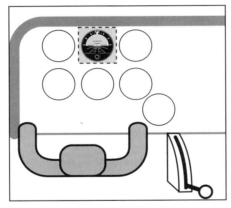

PITCH
Check Attitude Indicator
Pitch to level flight

In summary:
Check Airspeed
POWER
BANK
PITCH

Conclusion

Enough has already been said about the dangers of a non-instrument pilot attempting to fly in instrument conditions. If you still consider illegal instrument flying as a realistic option, perhaps you should seek psychiatric help!

This exercise is taught with two aims:

1 To enable you to control the aircraft whilst returning to visual conditions, should you inadvertently enter cloud or an area of poor visibility.

2 To enable you to use the instruments as an aid to visual flying when the horizon is obscured, i.e. when flying over the sea on a hazy day.

If you do enjoy instrument flying, as many pilots do, your instructor will advise you of courses and ratings available once you have qualified for your PPL.

index

A

B

C

index

D

E

F

index

index

J

K

L

M

N

O

P

Q

R

index

S

index

T

U

V

W

X

Y

Z

notes

notes

notes

notes

notes

notes

notes